Learning Technologies for Transforming Large-Scale Teaching, Learning, and Assessment

Demetrios Sampson • J. Michael Spector
Dirk Ifenthaler • Pedro Isaías • Stylianos Sergis
Editors

Learning Technologies for Transforming Large-Scale Teaching, Learning, and Assessment

Editors
Demetrios Sampson
Department of Digital Systems
University of Piraeus
Piraeus, Greece

School of Education
Curtin University
Perth, WA, Australia

Dirk Ifenthaler
Curtin University
Perth, WA, Australia

Economic and Business Education
Learning, Design and Technology
University of Mannheim
Mannheim, Germany

Stylianos Sergis
Department of Digital Systems
University of Piraeus
Piraeus, Greece

J. Michael Spector
Department of Learning Technologies
University of North Texas
Denton, TX, USA

Pedro Isaías
Institute for Teaching & Learning
Innovation (ITaLI)
The University of Queensland
St. Lucia, QLD, Australia

ISBN 978-3-030-15132-4 ISBN 978-3-030-15130-0 (eBook)
https://doi.org/10.1007/978-3-030-15130-0

This Springer imprint is published by the registered company Springer Nature Switzerland AG
The registered company address is: Gewerbestrasse 11, 6330 Cham, Switzerland

Foreword

Digital learning is recognized as a key innovation for achieving effective market-driven, on-demand, and competence-based on-the-job professional training at the workplace and beyond. Indeed, the digital learning industry has experienced a global explosive growth during the last decade, with a high worldwide demand for providing (among others) learning programs that efficiently address emerging competence needs of the academic and industry workforce at large scale.

In this context, the expanding affordances of digital technologies, supported by innovative pedagogies, have been exploited to scale up the reach of learning and training providers to potentially thousands of learners across the globe, simultaneously. It is clear, however, that this unprecedented opportunity is closely associated with challenges that did not exist before, but need to be overcome nonetheless. When the reach of learning increases to such ranges, so do the number, the diversity of characteristics, and the needs of learners exposed to it. Therefore, it is now evident that addressing these novel issues is a core priority if we are to effectively reap the undeniable benefits of digital technologies for large-scale teaching, learning, and assessment.

These issues that have emerged from the affordances of new technologies can also be overcome by them. Groundbreaking advancements in fields such as Massive Open Online Courses can foster learning environments that not only host thousands of learners but can also keep an individual track of each one in terms of progress, challenges, and learning. State-of-the-art educational data analytics can collect and process such data and offer personalized support to both educators and learners for improving the teaching and learning experiences. Innovations such as these are exploited every day, and it is essential that we can benefit and learn from them to fully explore and utilize the potential of designing and delivering learning at large scale.

The rationale for this edited volume emerged from the desire to understand how this vastly expanding field is growing in the contemporary research and practice. This book compiles papers presented at the CELDA (Cognition and Exploratory Learning in the Digital Age) conference, which has as its goal continuing to address these challenges and promote the effective use of new tools and technologies to support teaching, learning, and assessment. Given the emerging global trend to exploit the potential of existing digital technologies to improve the teaching, learning, and assessment experiences for all learners in real-life contexts, this topic has been selected for the unifying theme for this volume.

The edited volume showcases how emerging educational technologies and innovative practices have been used to address core global educational challenges, providing state-of-the-art insights and case studies of exploiting innovative learning technologies, including Massive Open Online Courses and educational data analytics, to address key global challenges, spanning from online teacher education to large-scale coding competence development.

Piraeus, Greece Demetrios Sampson
Perth, WA, Australia
Denton, TX, USA J. Michael Spector
Perth, WA, Australia Dirk Ifenthaler
Mannheim, Germany
St. Lucia, QLD, Australia Pedro Isaías
Piraeus, Greece Stylianos Sergis

Preface

The aim of this volume entitled *Learning Technologies for Transforming Large-Scale Teaching, Learning, and Assessment* is to provide a contemporary glance at the drastically expanding field of delivering large-scale education to unprecedented numbers of learners.

It provides state-of-the-art insights and case studies of exploiting innovative learning technologies, including Massive Open Online Courses and educational data analytics, to address key global challenges, spanning from online teacher education to large-scale coding competence development.

Potential readership includes academics and professional practitioners working in the field of digital technologies for online and blended teaching, learning, and assessment at large scale.

Piraeus, Greece — Demetrios Sampson
Perth, WA, Australia
Denton, TX, USA — J. Michael Spector
Perth, WA, Australia — Dirk Ifenthaler
Mannheim, Germany
St. Lucia, QLD, Australia — Pedro Isaías
Piraeus, Greece — Stylianos Sergis

Contents

Part I
Teaching, Learning and Assessment at Large-Scale: Trends and Challenges

Chapter 1
Releasing Personal Information Within Learning Analytics Systems

Dirk Ifenthaler and Clara Schumacher

Abstract Besides the well-documented benefits of learning analytics, serious concerns and challenges are associated with the application of these data-driven systems. Most notably, empirical evidence regarding privacy issues such as for learning analytics is next to nothing. The purpose of this study was to investigate if students are prepared to release any personal data in order to inform learning analytics systems. A total of 330 university students participated in an exploratory study confronting them with learning analytics systems and associated issues of control of data and sharing of information. Findings indicate that sharing of data for educational purposes is correlated to study-related constructs, usage of Internet, awareness of control over data, and expected benefits from a learning analytics system. Based on the relationship between the willingness to release personal data for learning analytics systems and various constructs closely related to individual characteristics of students, it is concluded that students need to be equally involved when implementing learning analytics systems at higher education institutions.

1 Introduction

At a time of growing interest in learning analytics systems of higher education institutions, it is important to understand the implications of privacy principles to ensure that implemented systems are able to facilitate learning, instruction, and academic decision-making and do not impair students' perceptions of privacy.

D. Ifenthaler (✉)
Curtin University, Perth, WA, Australia

Economic and Business Education, Learning, Design and Technology,
University of Mannheim, Mannheim, Germany
e-mail: dirk@ifenthaler.info

C. Schumacher
University of Mannheim, Mannheim, Germany
e-mail: clara.schumacher@bwl.uni-mannheim.de

D. Sampson et al. (eds.), *Learning Technologies for Transforming Large-Scale Teaching, Learning, and Assessment*, https://doi.org/10.1007/978-3-030-15130-0_1

Students may benefit from learning analytics through optimised learning pathways, personalised interventions, and real-time scaffolds (Gašević, Dawson, & Siemens, 2015). Learning analytics provides instructors detailed analysis and monitoring on the individual student level, allowing to identify particularly instable factors, like motivation or attention losses, before they occur (Gašević, Dawson, Rogers, & Gašević, 2016). Instructional designers use learning analytics information to evaluate learning materials, adjust difficulty levels, and measure the impact of interventions (Lockyer, Heathcote, & Dawson, 2013). Learning analytics further facilitates decision-making on institution level and help to analyse churn and identify gaps in curricular planning (Ifenthaler & Widanapathirana, 2014).

However, serious concerns and challenges are associated with the application of learning analytics (Pardo & Siemens, 2014). For instance, not all educational data is relevant and equivalent. Therefore, the validity of data and its analyses are critical for generating useful summative, real-time, and predictive insights (Macfadyen & Dawson, 2012). Furthermore, limited access to educational data may generate disadvantages for involved stakeholders. For example, invalid forecasts may lead to inefficient decisions and unforeseen problems (Ifenthaler & Widanapathirana, 2014). Moreover, ethical and privacy issues are associated with the use of educational data for learning analytics (Ifenthaler & Tracey, 2016). That implies how personal data are collected and stored as well as how they are analysed and presented to different stakeholders (Slade & Prinsloo, 2013).

Currently, privacy is gaining increasing attention and first attempts of frameworks for privacy in learning analytics are established (Drachsler & Greller, 2016; Ferguson, Hoel, Scheffel, & Drachsler, 2016; Sclater & Bailey, 2015). However, most research towards privacy issues in learning analytics refer to guidelines from other disciplines such as Internet security or medical environments (Pardo & Siemens, 2014). Due to the contextual characteristics of privacy, an adoption from other contexts to questions of learning analytics seems not to be recommendable (Nissenbaum, 2004). More importantly, empirical evidence regarding privacy issues for learning analytics is scarce. Therefore, the purpose of this exploratory study was to investigate if students are willing to release any personal data for informing learning analytics systems.

2 Theoretical Framework

2.1 Privacy in the Digital Age

The most general definition of privacy is freedom from interference or intrusion (Warren & Brandeis, 1890). A legal definition of the concept of privacy is a person's right to control access to his or her personal information (Gonzalez, 2015). More precisely, privacy is a combination of control and limitations, which implies the possibility of individuals to influence the flow of their personal information and to hamper others to access their information (Heath, 2014).

Within the digital world, this view on privacy seems to be no longer valid. Many individuals are willing to share personal information without being aware of who has access to the provided data and how the data will be used as well as how to control ownership of the provided data (Solove, 2004). Accordingly, data are generated and provided automatically through online systems, which limits the control and ownership of personal information in the digital world (Slade & Prinsloo, 2013). Only recently, this phenomenon has been adopted by higher education institutions through the implementation of learning analytics.

2.2 *Learning Data and Privacy Issues*

Socio-demographic information, higher education entrance qualification grades, or pass and fail rates, i.e. educational data, have been used by higher education institutions for a long time. Such data provide useful insights for academic decision-making as well as resource allocation (Long & Siemens, 2011; Prinsloo & Slade, 2014). The advancement of digital technologies enables higher education institutions to collect even more data, for example real-time data from all student activity within the higher education institutions' systems. Hence, the application of learning analytics offers huge potential for personalised and adaptive learning experiences and real-time support (Berland, Baker, & Bilkstein, 2014).

However, before utilising educational data, higher education institutions are required to address privacy issues linked to learning analytics: They need to define who gets access to which data, where and how long will the data be stored, and which procedures and algorithms are implemented to further use the available data (Ifenthaler & Schumacher, 2016).

Slade and Prinsloo (2013) as well as Pardo and Siemens (2014) established several principles for privacy and ethics in learning analytics. They highlight the active role of students in their learning process, the temporary character of data, the incompleteness of data on which learning analytics are executed, transparency regarding data use, as well as purpose, analyses, access, control, and ownership of data.

Drachsler and Greller (2016) established the DELICATE checklist to implement 'trusted' learning analytics considering ethical and privacy aspects, suggestions of current legal frameworks, and privacy fears associated with learning analytics. The checklist includes aspects such as determining the institution's goals for implementing learning analytics, explaining intentions, involving all relevant stakeholders and the data subjects and seeking their consent but also technical aspects, and how to involve external providers. However, empirical evidence towards student perceptions of privacy principles related to learning analytics is lacking (Ifenthaler & Tracey, 2016).

Ifenthaler and Schumacher (2016) propose a privacy calculus model to inform stakeholders about the complex decisions required for LA systems. Figure 1.1 shows the deliberation process for releasing information for LA systems. Students assess their concern over privacy on the basis of the specific information required

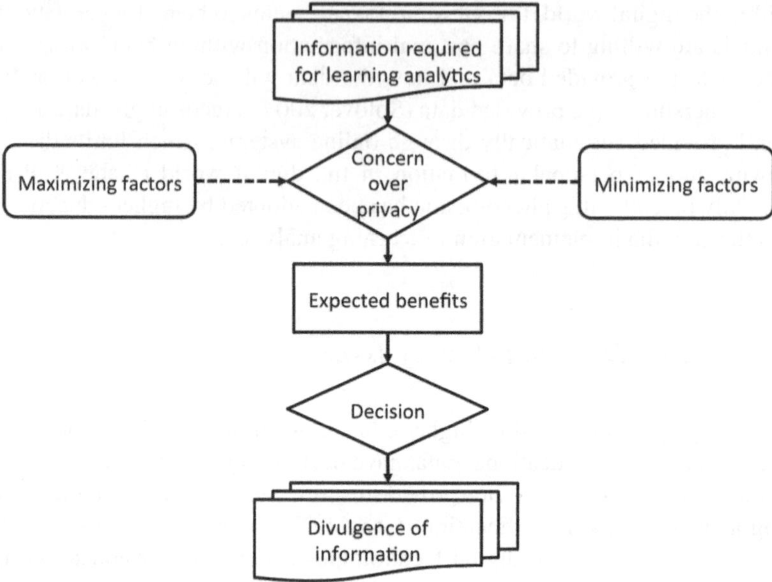

Fig. 1.1 Privacy calculus (Ifenthaler & Schumacher, 2016)

for the LA system (e.g., name, learning history, learning path, assessment results). This decision can be influenced by risk-minimizing factors (e.g., trust in the learning analytics systems and/or institution, control over data through self-administration) and risk-maximizing factors (e.g., non-transparency, negative reputation of the learning analytics system and/or institution). Concerns over privacy are then weighed against the expected benefits of the LA system. The probability that the students will disclose required information is higher if they expect the benefits to be greater than the risk. Hence, the decision to reveal information on LA systems is a cost–benefit analysis based on available information to the student (Ifenthaler & Schumacher, 2016).

2.3 Purpose of the Study

The purpose of this study was to investigate the expected benefits of learning analytics and if students are willing to release any personal data for informing learning analytics systems as well as if other constructs such as study interest and use of Internet are related. Three overarching research questions and associated hypotheses were addressed as follows:

1. LA systems require rich data to provide the expected benefits. Large amounts of data are produced by students. However, students are often passive recipients of analytics information provided in dashboards (Prinsloo & Slade, 2014).

It is therefore important to understand students' expectations towards transparency of data used by LA systems (Ennen, Stark, & Lassiter, 2015; Nam, 2014). We assume that students have high expectations towards transparency of data in LA systems (Hypothesis 1a) and expect sensitive and responsible processing of available data (Hypothesis 1b). Further, we assume that student's willingness to provide personal data is related to their anticipated control over data (Hypothesis 1c).

2. Students have to adjust to different learning and teaching requirements, manage workloads and course loads, as well as matching the universities' expectations and personal interest (Bowles, Fisher, McPhail, Rosenstreich, & Dobson, 2014). LA systems may provide scaffolds to overcome the before mentioned hurdles (Mah, 2016). Specifically, we assume that disclosing personal information within LA systems is related to study-related constructs such as year of study (Hypothesis 2a), course load (Hypothesis 2b), and study interest (Hypothesis 2c). Further, it is increasingly recognised that a majority of students possess a core set of technology-based competencies, however, no empirical evidence exists how these competencies influence the use and acceptance of LA systems. For example, Trepte, Dienlin, and Reinecke (2013) report that students who frequently use social media tools are more open to disclose personal information in online environments. Therefore, we assume that releasing any personal data for LA systems is related to the students' percentage of use of the Internet for learning (Hypothesis 2d) and social media (Hypothesis 2e).
3. Students may disclose personal data for learning analytics systems if the overall benefits for learning are greater than the assessed risk of releasing personal data (Culnan & Bies, 2003). We assume that releasing personal data for LA systems is related to the anticipated benefits from a specific LA system (Hypothesis 3).

3 Method

3.1 Participants and Design

The study was designed as an online laboratory study implemented on the university's server and conducted in June 2015. Participants received one credit hour for participating in the study.

The initial dataset consisted of 333 responses. After removing incomplete responses, the final dataset included N = 330 valid responses (223 female, 107 male). The average age of the participants was 22.75 years (SD = 3.77). The majority of the participants studied in the Bachelor's program (80%), with 20% of the participants studying in the Master's program. The average course load in the current semester was five courses (SD = 1.70). Participants reported that 33% of their Internet use was for learning, 33% was for social networking, 26% for entertainment, and 8% for work.

3.2 *Instruments and Materials*

3.2.1 Study Interest Questionnaire

The study interest questionnaire (FSI; Schiefele, Krapp, Wild, & Winteler, 1993) includes 18 items (Schiefele et al., 1993) which focus on study-related interest such as feeling- and value-related valences as well as intrinsic orientation (Cronbach's $\alpha = 0.90$). All items were answered on a five-point Likert scale (1 = not at all important; 2 = not important; 3 = neither important nor unimportant; 4 = important; 5 = very important).

3.2.2 Control Over Data Scale

The control over data scale (COD) focuses on access, control, and use of data in learning analytics systems, including four subscales: (1) Privacy of data (PLA; 5 items; Cronbach's $\alpha = 0.78$), (2) Transparency of data (TAD; 8 items; Cronbach's $\alpha = 0.72$), (3) Access of data (AOD; 11 items; Cronbach's $\alpha = 0.83$), and (4) Terms of agreement (TOA; 6 items; Cronbach's $\alpha = 0.73$). All items were answered on a five-point Likert scale (1 = not at all important; 2 = not important; 3 = neither important nor unimportant; 4 = important; 5 = very important).

3.2.3 Sharing of Data Questionnaire

The sharing of data questionnaire (SOD) focuses on specific personal information participants are willing to share in learning analytics systems, such as date of birth, educational history (self and parents), online behaviour, academic performance, library usage, etc. The 28 items are answered on a Thurstone scale (1 = agree, 0 = do not agree; Cronbach's $\alpha = 0.74$).

3.2.4 Demographic Information

Demographic information included age, gender, Internet usage for learning and social media, years of study, study major, course load, etc.

3.2.5 Learning Analytics System Comparison

Three different examples of learning analytics systems were presented to the participants (see Fig. 1.2).

The first example was based on the Course Signals project including simple visual aids such as completion of assignments, participation in discussion comple-

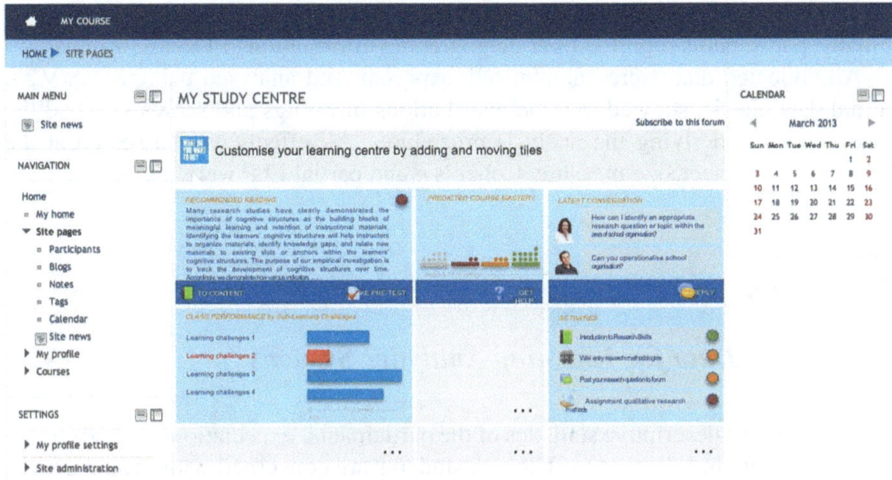

Fig. 1.2 Example of a learning analytics system providing detailed insights into learning and performance

mented by the possibility to contact students at-risk (Pistilli & Arnold, 2010). The second example included a dashboard showing general information about the student, average activities over time (e.g., submissions, learning time, logins, interactivity), and average performance comparison across study major and university. The third example provided detailed insights into learning and performance including personalised content and activity recommendation (e.g., reading materials), self-assessments, predictive course mastery, suggestions for social interaction, and performance comparisons. Participants rated each of the examples regarding acceptance of the learning analytics system and expected benefits for learning (ALA; 10 items; 1 = strongly disagree; 2 = disagree; 3 = neither agree nor disagree; 4 = agree; 5 = strongly agree; Cronbach's $\alpha = 0.89$).

3.3 *Procedure and Analysis*

Over a period of 2 weeks in June 2015, students were invited to participate in the laboratory study which included three parts. In the first part, participants received a general introduction regarding learning analytics and use of personal data in digital university systems. Then they completed the study interest questionnaire (FSI; 18 items; 8 min). In the second part, participants were confronted with three different learning analytics systems. After a short time to familiarise with each of the learning analytics system, they were asked to rate acceptance and expected use for learning of the learning analytics systems as well as to compare the three different systems (30 min). In the third part, participants completed the control over data scale (COD;

30 items; 20 min) and the sharing of data questionnaire (SOD; 28 items; 20 min). Finally, participants reported their demographic information (14 items; 7 min).

All collected data were anonymised, exported, and analysed using SPSS V.23. Initial data checks showed that the distributions of ratings and scores satisfied the assumptions underlying the analysis procedures. All effects were assessed at the 0.05 level. As effect size measure, Cohen's *d* and partial Eta^2 were used.

4 Results

4.1 Using Data for Learning Analytics Systems

Table 1.1 shows descriptive statistics of the participants' expectations towards transparency of data in LA systems. Clearly, students are concerned with the collection, storage, and frequency of use of their produced data as well as which benchmarks the LA system uses. Less concern seems to exist with regard to analytics calculations and scientific findings of the LA systems.

Table 1.2 shows descriptive statistics of participants' perceptions of terms of use of LA systems. Evidently, students expect sensitive and responsible processing of data in LA systems which shall be reflected in the institutions' terms of use. Acceptance towards the use of data seems to increase if data is anonymised and used for research. In contrast, students do not agree to disclose personal data to lecturers.

Clearly, students report high expectations towards transparency of data in LA systems. They further expect sensitive and responsible processing of available data. To sum up, Hypothesis 1a and 1b are accepted.

Table 1.1 Expectations towards transparency

Item (shortened and translated from German)	*M*	SD	Min	Max
Transparency which data are collected.	4.36	0.90	1	5
Transparency which data are analysed.	3.98	1.12	1	5
Transparency which calculations are performed.	3.61	1.16	1	5
Transparency which benchmarks are applied.	4.24	0.92	1	5
Transparency on scientific findings of the LA system.	3.69	1.16	1	5
Transparency of benchmark data in comparison of personal data	3.79	1.14	1	5
Transparency where data are stored.	4.43	1.00	1	5
Transparency on the frequency of access of data.	4.41	1.00	1	5

Note. Items were answered on a 5-point Likert scale (1 = strongly disagree; 2 = disagree; 3 = neither agree nor disagree; 4 = agree; 5 = strongly agree)

Table 1.2 Expectations towards terms of use of LA systems

Item (shortened and translated from German)	*M*	SD	Min	Max
The institution uses personal student data for purposes of direct communication between the university and the student.	2.84	1.34	1	5
The institution tracks student behaviour for internal purposes and for third-party applications.	2.61	1.28	1	5
The institution uses Google Analytics data of students for internal purposes.	2.98	1.33	1	5
The institution uses anonymised student data for research conducted within the university.	3.69	1.22	1	5
The institution shares anonymised student data with external research collaborators.	2.82	1.36	1	5
Lecturers can access personal student data for optimising individual learning processes.	2.38	1.25	1	5

Note. Items were answered on a 5-point Likert scale (1 = strongly disagree; 2 = disagree; 3 = neither agree nor disagree; 4 = agree; 5 = strongly agree)

Table 1.3 Descriptives and zero-order correlations for study-related variables, Internet usage variables, and data as well as learning analytics-related variables ($N = 330$)

Variable	1	2	3	4	5	6	7
1. Study year (SY)	–						
2. Course load (CL)	−0.378***	–					
3. Study interest (FSI)	−0.008	0.071	–				
4. Internet use for learning (IUL)	0.123*	−0.076	0.014	–			
5. Internet use for social media (IUS)	−0.156**	0.023	−0.066	−0.032	–		
6. Control over data (COD)	0.141**	−0.038	0.111*	0.290***	0.007	–	
7. Benefits of learning analytics system (BLA)	0.076	−0.017	−0.009	0.630***	−0.006	0.362***	–
M	3.58	5.36	2.99	35.00	32.95	2.71	3.13
SD	2.30	1.70	0.28	21.21	20.43	0.39	0.97

Note. $^{*}p < 0.05$, $^{**}p < 0.01$, $^{***}p < 0.001$

4.2 Disclosing Personal Information, Study-Related Constructs, and Benefits of LA Systems

Table 1.3 shows the zero-order correlations among the variables with regard to hypotheses 1c, 2a, 2b, 2c, 2d, 2e, and 3. Students' *study year* was negatively related to their *course load*, as was their percentage of *Internet use for social media.* Students' *study year* was positively related to their percentage of *Internet use for learning*, as was their anticipated *control over data.* Their *study interest* was related to their anticipated *control over data.* Additionally, their percentage of *Internet use for learning* was positively related to their anticipated *control over data* as well as their expected *benefits of the learning analytics system.* Finally, students' anticipated *control over data* was positively related to their expected *benefits of the learning analytics system*.

A hierarchical regression analysis was used to determine whether study-related variables (SY, CL, FSI), Internet usage (IUL, IUS), control over data (COD), and expected benefits of learning analytics systems (BLA) were significant predictors of *sharing of data for a specific learning analytics system* (SOD; dependent variable). Table 1.4 shows the four steps of entering data into the equation. The final regression model explained a statistically significant amount of variance in *sharing of data* (SOD), $\Delta R^2 = 0.370$, $F(7, 329) = 28.58$, $p < 0.001$.

Specifically, students' study year (SY) positively predicted their willingness to share personal data for a specific learning analytics system (SOD), indicating that the higher the study year (SY), the higher the students' liberality to provide personal data for educational purposes. Accordingly, Hypothesis 2a is accepted.

The percentage of Internet usage for learning (IUL) and social media (IUS) positively predicted the students' release of personal data for learning analytics

Table 1.4 Regression analysis predicting sharing of data on study-related variables, Internet usage, control over data, and expected benefits of learning analytics systems ($N = 330$)

	R2	Δ*R2*	*B*	SE *B*	*β*
Step 1	0.038	0.029			
Study year (SY)			0.538	0.170	0.186**
Course load (CL)			−0.081	0.231	0.726
Study interest (FSI)			−0.094	1.295	0.942
Step 2	0.322	0.311			
Study year (SY)			0.432	0.145	0.149**
Course load (CL)			0.010	0.195	0.002
Study interest (FSI)			−0.127	1.093	−0.005
Internet use for learning (IUL)			0.165	0.014	0.525***
Internet use for social media (IUS)			0.040	0.015	0.122**
Step 3	0.352	0.340			
Study year (SY)			0.366	0.143	0.127*
Course load (CL)			−0.005	0.191	−0.001
Study interest (FSI)			−0.609	1.077	−0.026
Internet use for learning (IUL)			0.149	0.015	0.474***
Internet use for social media (IUS)			0.037	0.015	0.114*
Control over data (COD)			3.144	0.806	0.185***
Step 4	0.383	0.370			
Study year (SY)			0.373	0.140	0.129**
Course load (CL)			−0.035	0.186	−0.009
Study interest (FSI)			−0.376	1.054	−0.016
Internet use for learning (IUL)			0.106	0.018	0.339***
Internet use for social media (IUS)			0.037	0.014	0.113*
Control over data (COD)			2.339	0.813	0.138**
Benefits of learning analytics system (BLA)			1.606	0.400	0.234***

Note. *$p < 0.05$, **$p < 0.01$, ***$p < 0.001$

purposes (SOD), indicating the higher the usage of the Internet for learning and social media, the higher their disposition to share personal data for learning analytics systems. Hence, Hypotheses 2d and 2e are accepted.

The students' awareness about control of data (COD) positively predicted their preparedness to share personal data for a specific learning analytics system (SOD), indicating that the higher the awareness about the control of personal data, the higher their disposition to share personal data for learning analytics systems. Thus, Hypothesis 1c is accepted.

The expected benefits of a learning analytics system (BLA) positively predicted the students' release of personal data for learning analytics purposes (SOD), indicating the higher the expected benefit of the learning analytics system, the higher the readiness to provide personal data for learning analytics purposes. Consequently, Hypothesis 3 is accepted. As shown in Table 1.2, no significant correlations were found for course load (CL) and study interest (FSI). So, Hypotheses 2b and 2c are rejected.

5 Discussion

Many open questions remain in the advancing field of learning analytics. Especially with regard to producing, processing and sharing data, critical issues need to be addressed (Ifenthaler & Tracey, 2016). For example, who should get access to which data, where and how long will the data be stored, which algorithms are applied, which analysis procedures are in place and which deductions are conducted. Further, are students aware of the data they produce and which of the produced data is collected?

The findings of this exploratory study highlight an overall interest of students in LA systems. However, findings clearly document concerns of students towards releasing personal data. Students expect transparency with regard to (1) the type of data being collected, (2) the access and analysis of available data, as well as (3) the storage of data. Further, students expect sensitive and responsible management and processing of data.

Findings emphasise the relationship between the intended use of LA systems and privacy principles, that is, control over data and sharing of data. Accordingly, students, teachers, and administrators need to be actively involved when implementing learning analytics at higher education institutions (Ifenthaler & Schumacher, 2016). Strategies for obtaining consent need to be implemented, for example (1) students may opt in at the start of a course with further opt-in consent while changes occur, (2) students may opt in at the start of a course with further opt-out consent while changes occur, or (3) students may opt out at the start of a course with further opt-out consent while changes occur (Kay, Korn, & Oppennheim, 2012). Ifenthaler and Schumacher (2016) further argue that questions such as who should receive access to which data, where and how long the data will be stored, which analyses and deductions are conducted, and whether the students are aware of the data being collected from them need to be discussed in future research. The European Commission recommends informing the learners in an understandable way about data protection and privacy issues of the online platform (European Commission, 2014). LA system may therefore include options to see which data is collected while interacting with the system, or which algorithms are applied to produce the information displayed in dashboard.

Not surprisingly, additional findings show that spending time on the Internet is associated with the openness of sharing data for LA systems. This effect may be explained by the trust students generate with regard to online systems in general and LA systems in particular (Ennen et al., 2015). Hence, the relationship between perceived control over personal data and expected benefits as well as sharing personal data is closely related to the phenomenon of trust (Nam, 2014).

5.1 Implications

From a holistic point of view, learning analytics may provide multiple benefits for higher education institutions and for involved stakeholders. As such, different data analytics strategies can be applied to produce summative, real-time, and predictive insights (Ifenthaler, 2015). For example, students may use summative learning analytics implemented as an interactive dashboard to analyse learning outcomes of individual courses after completing a semester of study or track their progress towards self-defined goals (e.g., credit points). Students may also be able to compare their own learning paths and outcomes between individual units or courses. This may enable students to understand their learning habits and to adjust their learning strategies as well as private habits in order to be successful in their studies. On the same dashboard or within a learning management system, students may receive *real-time learning analytics information* based on their currently available data. Automated interventions may point them to learning materials and tips for progressing in a particular study unit. Students may take self-assessment on a specific topic and receive just-in-time feedback or get recommendations to participate in online discussions or connect to peers using preferred social media. *Predictive learning analytics* for students may help to optimise the learning path in a specific study unit by providing them probabilities of success when choosing a particular pathway. Such predictions are expected to increase the overall engagement and success rates of students (Ifenthaler, 2015).

However, reliable and valid LA systems require rich and current information of students including personal characteristics and preferences, academic performance, educational pathways, and log files of various online learning systems. If the underlying learning analytics algorithms do not have access to the required information, the above-described benefits cannot be produced. While higher education institutions implement learning analytics systems (Ifenthaler, 2017a), students may find themselves in a dilemma situation concerning the release of personal information for LA systems. In order to overcome such a dilemma situation, it is necessary to provide students transparency of the implemented LA system and its underlying algorithms, as well as clear guidelines towards access, analysis, control, ownership, and use of relevant data (West, Huijser, & Heath, 2016).

From a learning design point of view, research and practice may focus on usability, personalisation, and adaptivity of LA systems. Understanding these factors may be crucial for implementing LA systems at higher education institutions (Ifenthaler, 2017a). Integrating real-time educational data and analysis into the design of learning environments, i.e., learning analytics design, seems to be a promising approach (Ifenthaler, 2017b). Valid pedagogical recommendations may be suggested on the fly as learning analytics methodologies and visualisations evolve and as reliable tools become available and ready for classroom practice (Ifenthaler et al., 2014; Kevan & Ryan, 2016). Learning analytics design will generate valuable insights for planning and optimizing learning environments. Educators may specify benchmarks which help to identify alignment or misalignment towards learning outcomes. In addition, detailed insights into learning processes may facilitate micro-interventions whenever the learner needs it.

Closely related to issues of learning design is the question of adequate features implemented in LA systems (Park & Jo, 2015; Schumacher & Ifenthaler, 2018) and the availability of required data. While learners directly interact with the dashboard of the LA system, they retrieve information of the LA system and, at the same time, produce additional data (which can be used for further analysis).

5.2 Limitations and Outlook

There are obvious limitations of the presented study which need to be addressed in future research. First, the results rely on self-report data and thus possibly include a response bias, meaning that participants tend to respond in a certain way regardless of the phenomenon in question. Second, the sample was from a single institution. Third, the participants had no prior experience in using learning analytics systems at their institution and their prior knowledge about learning analytics was very limited. Moreover, they were only exposed to the three examples of learning analytics systems for a very limited time and in a linear order. Therefore, the findings of the presented research are limited towards external validity.

While higher education institutions adopt learning analytics and start to implement LA systems, on-going research is needed focusing on (1) the effectiveness of the implemented LA systems, (2) strategies of change management while implementing LA systems, and (3) building multi-institutional perspectives and international comparisons. Additional studies might focus on (4) students with experience in using LA systems as well as experimentally varying the order of presentation of different LA systems.

Future studies should also expand the (5) perspective of ethics and privacy to include different stakeholders, such as teachers, tutors, learning designers, departmental chairs and deans of schools, university management, and governing authorities. Also, learning analytics research needs to address (6) issues where students do not want to share data; however, systems would require these data to produce reliable and valid results.

In conclusion, students are more than shattered bits of information given and produced while interacting with learning analytics systems (Solove, 2004). Learning analytics may reveal personal information and insights into an individual learning history; however, they are not accredited and far from being unbiased, comprehensive, and valid.

References

Berland, M., Baker, R. S., & Bilkstein, P. (2014). Educational data mining and learning analytics: Applications to constructionist research. *Technology, Knowledge and Learning, 19*(1–2), 205–220. https://doi.org/10.1007/s10758-014-9223-7

Bowles, A., Fisher, R., McPhail, R., Rosenstreich, D., & Dobson, A. (2014). Staying the distance: Students' perception of enablers of transition to higher education. *Higher Education Research & Development, 33*(2), 212–225.

Culnan, M. J., & Bies, R. J. (2003). Consumer privacy: Balancing economic and justice considerations. *Journal of Social Issues, 59*(2), 323–342. https://doi.org/10.1111/1540-4560.00067

Drachsler, H., & Greller, W. (2016). *Privacy and analytics—It's a DELICATE issue. A checklist for trusted learning analytics.* Paper presented at the Sixth International Conference on Learning Analytics & Knowledge, Edinburgh, UK.

Ennen, N. L., Stark, E., & Lassiter, A. (2015). The importance of trust for satisfaction, motivation, and academic performance in student learning groups. *Social Psychology of Education.* https://doi.org/10.1007/s11218-015-9306-x

European Commission. (2014). *New modes of learning and teaching in higher education.* Luxembourg: Publications Office of the European Union.

Ferguson, R., Hoel, T., Scheffel, M., & Drachsler, H. (2016). Guest editorial: Ethics and privacy in learning analytics. *Journal of Learning Analytics, 3*(1), 5–15.

Gašević, D., Dawson, S., Rogers, T., & Gašević, D. (2016). Learning analytics should not promote one size fits all: The effects of instructional conditions in predicting academic success. *Internet and Higher Education, 28*, 68–84.

Gašević, D., Dawson, S., & Siemens, G. (2015). Let's not forget: Learning analytics are about learning. *TechTrends, 59*(1), 64–71. https://doi.org/10.1007/s11528-014-0822-x

Gonzalez, D. (2015). *Managing online risk.* Oxford, UK: Elsevier.

Heath, J. (2014). Contemporary privacy theory contributions to learning analytics. *Journal of Learning Analytics, 1*(1), 140–149.

Ifenthaler, D. (2015). Learning analytics. In J. M. Spector (Ed.), *The SAGE encyclopedia of educational technology* (Vol. 2, pp. 447–451). Thousand Oaks, CA: Sage.

Ifenthaler, D. (2017a). Are higher education institutions prepared for learning analytics? *TechTrends, 61*(4), 366–371. https://doi.org/10.1007/s11528-016-0154-0

Ifenthaler, D. (2017b). Learning analytics design. In L. Lin & J. M. Spector (Eds.), *The sciences of learning and instructional design. Constructive articulation between communities* (pp. 202–211). New York, NY: Routledge.

Ifenthaler, D., Adcock, A. B., Erlandson, B. E., Gosper, M., Greiff, S., & Pirnay-Dummer, P. (2014). Challenges for education in a connected world: Digital learning, data rich environments, and computer-based assessment—Introduction to the inaugural special issue of technology, knowledge and learning. *Technology, Knowledge and Learning, 19*(1–2), 121–126. https://doi.org/10.1007/s10758-014-9228-2

Ifenthaler, D., & Schumacher, C. (2016). Student perceptions of privacy principles for learning analytics. *Educational Technology Research and Development, 64*(5), 923–938. https://doi.org/10.1007/s11423-016-9477-y

Ifenthaler, D., & Tracey, M. W. (2016). Exploring the relationship of ethics and privacy in learning analytics and design: Implications for the field of educational technology. *Educational Technology Research and Development, 64*(5), 877–880. https://doi.org/10.1007/s11423-016-9480-3

Ifenthaler, D., & Widanapathirana, C. (2014). Development and validation of a learning analytics framework: Two case studies using support vector machines. *Technology, Knowledge and Learning, 19*(1–2), 221–240. https://doi.org/10.1007/s10758-014-9226-4

Kay, D., Korn, N., & Oppennheim, C. (2012). Legal, risk and ethical aspects of analytics. *Cetis Analytics Series, 1*(6), 1–30.

Kevan, J. M., & Ryan, P. R. (2016). Experience API: Flexible, decentralized and activity-centric data collection. *Technology, Knowledge and Learning, 21*(1), 143–149. https://doi.org/10.1007/s10758-015-9260-x

Lockyer, L., Heathcote, E., & Dawson, S. (2013). Informing pedagogical action: Aligning learning analytics with learning design. *American Behavioral Scientist, 57*(10), 1439–1459. https://doi.org/10.1177/0002764213479367

Long, P. D., & Siemens, G. (2011). Penetrating the fog: Analytics in learning and education. *Educause Review, 46*(5), 31–40.

Macfadyen, L., & Dawson, S. (2012). Numbers are not enough. Why e-Learning analytics failed to inform an institutional strategic plan. *Educational Technology & Society, 15*(3), 149–163.

Mah, D.-K. (2016). Learning analytics and digital badges: Potential impact on student retention in higher education. *Technology, Knowledge and Learning, 21*(3), 285–305.

Nam, C. W. (2014). The effects of trust and constructive controversy on student achievement and attitude in online cooperative learning environments. *Computers in Human Behavior, 37*, 237–248. https://doi.org/10.1016/j.chb.2014.05.007

Nissenbaum, H. (2004). Privacy as contextual integrity. *Washington Law Review, 79*(1), 119–157.

Pardo, A., & Siemens, G. (2014). Ethical and privacy principles for learning analytics. *British Journal of Educational Technology*. https://doi.org/10.1111/bjet.12152

Park, Y., & Jo, I.-H. (2015). Development of the learning analytics dashboard to support students' learning performance. *Journal of Universal Computer Science, 21*(1), 110–133.

Pistilli, M. D., & Arnold, K. E. (2010). Purdue signals: Mining real-time academic data to enhance student success. *About Campus: Enriching the Student Learning Experience, 15*(3), 22–24.

Prinsloo, P., & Slade, S. (2014). Student data privacy and institutional accountability in an age of surveillance. In M. E. Menon, D. G. Terkla, & P. Gibbs (Eds.), *Using data to improve higher education. Research, policy and practice* (pp. 197–214). Rotterdam, The Netherlands: Sense Publishers.

Schiefele, U., Krapp, A., Wild, K. P., & Winteler, A. (1993). Der "Fragebogen zum Studieninteresse" (FSI). *Diagnostica, 39*(4), 335–351.

Schumacher, C., & Ifenthaler, D. (2018). Features students really expect from learning analytics. *Computers in Human Behavior, 78*, 397–407. https://doi.org/10.1016/j.chb.2017.06.030

Sclater, N., & Bailey, P. (2015). *Code of practice for learning analytics*. Bristol, UK: Joint Information Systems Committee (JISC).

Slade, S., & Prinsloo, P. (2013). Learning analytics: Ethical issues and dilemmas. *American Behavioral Scientist, 57*(10), 1510–1529. https://doi.org/10.1177/0002764213479366

Solove, D. J. (2004). *The digital person: Technology and privacy in the information age*. New York, NY: New York University Press.

Trepte, S., Dienlin, T., & Reinecke, L. (2013). *Privacy, self-disclosure, social support, and social network site use*. Research report of a Three-Year Panel Study.

Warren, S. D., & Brandeis, L. D. (1890). The right to privacy. *Harvard Law Review, 4*(5), 193–220.

West, D., Huijser, H., & Heath, D. (2016). Putting an ethical lens on learning analytics. *Education Technology Research and Development, 64*(5), 903–922. https://doi.org/10.1007/s11423-016-9464-3

Dirk Ifenthaler is Professor and Chair of Learning, Design and Technology at University of Mannheim, Germany and UNESCO Deputy Chair of Data Science in Higher Education Learning and Teaching at Curtin University, Australia. His research focuses on the intersection of cognitive psychology, educational technology, data analytics, and organisational learning. Dirk's research outcomes include numerous co-authored books, book series, book chapters, journal articles, and international conference papers, as well as successful grant funding in Australia, Germany, and USA. He is the Editor-in-Chief of the Springer journal *Technology, Knowledge and Learning* (www.ifenthaler.info).

Clara Schumacher is a Research Associate at the chair of Economic and Business Education—Learning, Design and Technology at the University of Mannheim. Her research interests focus on educational technology, self-regulated learning, learning analytics, and informal learning.

Chapter 2
Measurement Challenges of Interactive Educational Assessment

David C. Gibson, Mary E. Webb, and Dirk Ifenthaler

Abstract This chapter discusses four measurement challenges of data science in educational assessments that are enabled by technology: (1) Dealing with change over time. (2) How a digital performance space's relationships interact with learner actions, communications and products. (3) How layers of interpretation are formed from translations of atomistic data into meaningful larger units suitable for making inferences about what someone knows and can do. (4) How to represent the dynamics of interactions between and among learners who are being assessed by their interactions with each other as well as with digital resources and agents in digital performance spaces. Because of the movement from paper-based tests to online learning, and in order to make progress on these challenges, the authors advocate the restructuring of training of the next generation of researchers and psychometricians in technology-enabled assessments.

D. C. Gibson
Curtin University, Perth, WA, Australia
e-mail: david.c.gibson@curtin.edu.au; https://staffportal.curtin.edu.au/staff/profile/view/David.C.Gibson

M. E. Webb
School of Education, Communication and Society, King's College London, London, UK
e-mail: mary.webb@kcl.ac.uk; https://www.kcl.ac.uk/sspp/departments/education/people/academic/webbm.aspx

D. Ifenthaler (✉)
Curtin University, Perth, WA, Australia

Economic and Business Education, Learning, Design and Technology, University of Mannheim, Mannheim, Germany
e-mail: dirk@ifenthaler.info; http://www.ifenthaler.info

D. Sampson et al. (eds.), *Learning Technologies for Transforming Large-Scale Teaching, Learning, and Assessment*, https://doi.org/10.1007/978-3-030-15130-0_2

1 Introduction

Assessment and learning analytics challenges have dramatically increased since new digital performance affordances, interactive user interfaces and the targets of technology-enabled assessments have become more complex. The increased complexity is due in part to technology's capabilities and roles in presenting interactive learning experiences and collecting rich data (de Freitas, 2014; Quellmalz et al., 2012) which is leading to the infusion of data science methods and techniques into learning and behavioural science research (Gibson & Knezek, 2011; Kozleski, Gibson, & Hynds, 2012). These changes require new quantitative methods as well as a reconceptualization of mixed methods (Tashakkori & Teddlie, 2003) that include domain experts as well as stakeholders in the construction of knowledge of such complex systems (Gibson & Ifenthaler, 2017).

In technology-enhanced assessments, the emergence of 'big data'—which at a minimum are defined as data with a large numbers of records, of widely differing data types, that are rapidly collected for immediate action (IBM, 2015; Margetts & Sutcliffe, 2013)—underscores the need to develop assessment literacy (Stiggins, 1995) in teachers, learners and other audiences of assessment. Assessment literacy has become more important than ever for understanding how technology influences and impacts assessment types and processes and especially for developing confidence in creating and analysing arguments from evidence, based on a user's current understanding of validation (Black, Harrison, Hodgen, Marshall, & Serret, 2010).

This chapter discusses four key challenges associated with applying data science methods to address aspects of an interactive digital media assessment's psychometric properties; time sensitivity; digital performance and the problem space for analysis; the hierarchy of tasks, turns and translations between different levels and the dynamics of interrelationships in assessment systems. First, in traditional assessments such as quizzes, tests and on-demand performances, change over time (e.g. whether a learner has newly acquired knowledge or skill, or has learned) is a matter of comparing a series of summative results. But in interactive digital media learning, acquisition of knowledge or skill may be evident during the learner's dynamic engagement with the media (Quellmalz et al., 2012). Second, the problem space in a traditional assessment is designed around the concept of a valid construct (Cronbach & Meehl, 1955); whereas in interactive digital media, it is perhaps more relevant to speak of an authentic performance (Wiggins, 1989). Third, in traditional assessments, a relatively static model pre-exists as the backdrop for the relationship of the test taker's task to the construct being measured (Fischer & Molenaar, 2012); while in interactive assessments, unexpected performances, resource utilizations and therefore interpretation models can dynamically emerge. Finally, in traditional assessments, the relationship of a learner's performance to the construct (including any error) is treated as invariant, but in interactive assessments, the challenges of longitudinal data analysis are evident (Hedeker & Gibbons, 2006).

In this chapter, the OECD (Organisation for Economic Co-operation and Development) PISA (Programme for International Student Assessment) plan for assessing complex problem-solving (CPS) is used as an example to explain these challenges in relation to a complex problem space. The chapter then illustrates a learning analytics case that shows how the identified challenges have been addressed in the development of assessments.

2 Background

There is uncertainty as to whether and how different perspectives on assessment—providing feedback information, supporting improvement decisions, identifying the degree of engagement and understanding, and making value judgments—can co-exist to the benefit of learners (Webb, Gibson, & Forkosh-Baruch, 2013). Even with the increased possibilities that information technology provides there is not yet a way to say confidently that the multiple purposes for which some assessments have been used (Mansell, James, & The Assessment Reform Group, 2009) can or should be supported through the same assessment systems. This is because *the impacts of some purposes interact with the validation processes of others* (Messick, 1994). For example, the validity of an assessment for a learner may be related to its relevance to knowledge needed immediately to improve performance, but the purpose of the assessment might have been designed to provide information about program effectiveness to a school authority. The test taker, not seeing the relevance, might not perform as well as possible. Therefore, in considering assessment design for multiple purposes for example for formative as well as summative purposes, assessment designers need to examine potential impacts carefully in order to minimise negative consequences on learning and learners.

Developing theory for the application of data science methods in educational research is important for two primary reasons. First, assessment of virtual performance presents new challenges for psychometrics (Clarke-Midura & Dede, 2010; Ifenthaler, Eseryel, & Ge, 2012; Quellmalz et al., 2012). Secondly, new tools are needed for discovery of patterns and drivers in complex systems for working with 'big data' in educational research preparation and practice (Gibson, 2012; Ifenthaler, 2015; Patton, 2011). Indicators of progress in theory development would be an increase in research exploring and articulating the use of data science methods in learning analytics to improve learning and achievement; and the expansion of methods beyond traditional statistics and qualitative approaches in educational research, to include data mining, machine learning and, in general, the methods of data science.

3 Four Psychometric Challenges

Psychometrics is the branch of psychology that deals with the design, administration and interpretation of quantitative tests for the measurement of psychological variables such as intelligence, aptitude and personality traits ("Psychometrics",

2014). A good psychometric test is "internally consistent, reliable over time, discriminating and of demonstrated validity in respect of its correlations with other tests, its predictive power and the performance of various criterion groups. It also has good norms" (Kline, 1998, p. 92).

Until recently, the field dealt almost exclusively with the construction and validation of measurement instruments such as questionnaires, tests and personality assessments. However, there is now a need to expand to include highly interactive digital learning and adaptive test experiences, such as the OECD PISA assessment of CPS. In brief, PISA is a triennial international survey that aims to evaluate education systems worldwide by testing the skills and knowledge of 15-year-old students in order to determine the extent to which they can apply their knowledge to real-life situations and hence are prepared for full participation in society. To constrain the quite complex variables that would be involved if the collaboration was among a set of real people, the OECD PISA CPS assessment utilizes the computer to play roles as collaborators in a *virtual performance assessment* (Clarke-Midura, Code, Dede, Mayrath, & Zap, 2012; Zervas & Sampson, 2018). The PISA assessment plan incorporates a complex behaviour space that illustrates some of the new demands on psychometrics.

The challenge with technology-enabled assessments that produce big data is to evolve the procedural foundations of psychometrics, which until recently have been primarily based on population statistics and static snapshots of data. Elements of a new foundation outlined here highlight the need to include time sensitivity, digital performance space relationships, multiple layers of aggregations at different scales and representations of the dynamics of a complex behaviour space (Gibson & Jakl, 2013; Quellmalz et al., 2012).

3.1 Time Sensitivity

In the OECD PISA CPS assessment, time is controlled as a boundary variable of the test and the computer is used to prompt the test taker to 'move on' when the evidence rule system detects that the student needs to be rescued from an unproductive problem-solving path. The decision to redirect appears natural to the situation because the computer is playing the role of one or more collaborators, so the suggestion to move on comes from a simulated peer. This situation illustrates that a technology-enabled assessment might well give the student perceived or actual control over time, compared to an assessment that only displays test item prompts in a timed test. In some virtual performance assessments, time is open-ended, and the use of item resources (e.g. in what order, with or without returning to the resources multiple times, time spent with each resource, timing of the appropriate use of a resource and total time to utilize the appropriate resources to accomplish the task) may be critical to the classification of the learner's response (Gibson & Jakl, 2013; Stevens & Palacio-Cayetano, 2003).

Table 2.1 Domain model for assessing collaborative problem-solving

	(1) Establishing and maintaining shared understanding	(2) Taking appropriate action to solve the problem	(3) Establishing and maintaining team organisation
(A) Exploring and understanding	(A1) Discovering perspectives and abilities of team members	(A2) Discovering the type of collaborative interaction to solve the problem, along with goals	(A3) Understanding roles to solve problem
(B) Representing and formulating	(B1) Building a shared representation and negotiating the meaning of the problem (common ground)	(B2) Identifying and describing tasks to be completed	(B3) Describe roles and team organisation (communication protocol/ rules of engagement)
(C) Planning and executing	(C1) Communicating with team members about the actions to be/being performed	(C2) Enacting plans	(C3) Following rules of engagement (e.g., prompting other team members to perform their tasks)
(D) Monitoring and reflecting	(D1) Monitoring and repairing the shared understanding	(D2) Monitoring results of actions and evaluating success in solving the problem	(D3) Monitoring, providing feedback and adapting the team organisation and roles

The OECD PISA CPS assessment solves the time sensitivity problem by parsing time into critical events and then monitoring the event patterns to detect the level of evidence of the competencies in the domain model (see Table 2.1). This is a form of *time segmentation*, because some events cannot happen until other events have occurred (e.g. establishing and maintaining team organisation must occur after establishing a shared vision, and while maintaining that vision and taking appropriate action to solve the problem). A planned sequence of activities and timed release of testing resources, known in game-based learning as a 'branching storyline' (Aldrich, 2005) is a method for controlling the evolution of a process.

Other problem-solving contexts, such as coordination of group actions needed for scientific inquiry and experimentation, require simultaneous actions mixed with sequences of actions. The classification system of the assessment has to handle *patterns of simultaneous and sequential interactions* in order to make valid links to time-sensitive evidence rules within the conceptual assessment framework (CAF), which is a key component of evidence-centred design (Mislevy, Steinberg, & Almond, 1999), an approach that is becoming increasingly prominent in assessment design and on which this analysis is based. The CAF has three core components: the student model, task model and evidence model (Mislevy et al., 1999; Mislevy, Steinberg, & Almond, 2003) within and among which the time-sensitive relationships adhere.

3.2 *Digital Performance Space Relationships*

A learning experience entails a designed structure of knowledge and action (Jonassen, 1997) and when that experience is interactive and digital there are many measurement challenges (Quellmalz et al., 2012). The emerging varieties of network analysis (e.g. social networks, visualization, artificial neural networks, decision trees) have arisen as new analytical tools and methods for understanding the structural relationships in technology-enhanced learning (Choi, Rupp, Gushta, & Sweet, 2010; Shaffer et al., 2009). In addition, the traces of knowledge and action (i.e., the actions, communications and products) created by a learner during the course of interacting with a digital learning application bear a relationship to that person's mental representations of the problem (Newell & Simon, 1972) and the knowledge and capability they acquired, accessed and utilized during the interaction (Ifenthaler, 2014; Pirnay-Dummer, Ifenthaler, & Spector, 2010; Thagard, 2010). This set of ideas are referred to here as '*digital performance space relationships*' which will be shown to be similar to 'items' and 'constructs' in classical test theory.

An interactive digital performance space can support several scenarios, each with one or more classification challenges for inferring what the test taker knows and can do. In the OECD PISA CPS assessment, for example, the scenarios presented to the student are designed to sample the digital performance space construct of 'collaborative problem-solving.' Each scenario allows the classification of the test taker into one or more cells of a matrix created by the intersection of three stages of 'collaboration' with four stages of 'problem-solving' (see Table 2.1). In classical test theory, the 'construct' plays a similar role to the digital performance space; several test items are used to make multiple measures of the construct. A review of the historical idea of a valid construct is helpful for making the bridge from classical testing to the digital age.

A valid construct was thought of as an *inductive summary* and as *part of a series* of validity investigations that included concurrent, predictive and content considerations. In addition, the *construct can change* and *become more elaborated over time*, as Cronbach noted (Cronbach & Meehl, 1955): When a construct is fairly new, there may be few specifiable associations by which to pin down the concept. As research proceeds, the construct sends out roots in many directions, which attach it to more and more facts or other constructs. Finally, the construct acquired validity through the idea of a *nomological network* which is a collection of overlapping *mappings* from (a) observable properties or quantities to one another; (b) different theoretical ideas to one another, or (c) theoretical constructs to observables (ibid). A single mapping might include examples of all these relations, as a construct might be a complex set of factors that interact with one another. The idea of a network of ideas and relationships was a fairly abstract philosophical idea in the 1950s but today has a renewed and concrete meaning that has become known as network theory in social science (Borgatti & Halgin, 2011) and network analysis in computational sciences, both of which are applied graph theory from mathematics (Brandes & Erlebach, 2005). This history outlines a bridge of ideas that carries forward into today when digital media learning spaces can record a network of traces of the actions of a learner.

Digital media learning presents problems as well as prompts for learner performance (e.g. problem-solving, collaboration) in a space that is characterized by hyperlinked resources that can be represented as nodes and relations in a network (Clarke-Midura et al., 2012; Quellmalz et al., 2012; Stevens, 2006). As a learner uses such a space to learn and perform (e.g. interacting with the resources to solve a problem, adding new information, re-arranging resources into new relationships) a new network can be created that represents the learner's response, a time-specific performance path through the digital performance space (Ifenthaler et al., 2012). The learner's performance network is a constructed knowledge structure that needs to be taken into account in assessment (Gijbels, Dochy, Van den Bossche, & Segers, 2005). The digital performance space and the constructed knowledge structure of the learner hold the same kind of relationship as the nomological network does to a demonstrated construct; the digital performance space holds the learning designer's view of the construct (e.g. what it means to act like a scientist in a given situation) and the constructed knowledge structure (e.g. what the learner did in this instance) holds evidence of the processes and products of knowing and doing.

The terms of the nomological network inference, which underpins a claim of construct validity, bear a similarity to the rules of a chain of a reasoned argument, which can lead to a claim concerning what a learner knows and can do as used in Evidence-Centered Design (ECD). In ECD, an argument has constituent claims, data, warrants and backing and must take account of alternative explanations. In a nomological network by comparison, there are observations, ideas and relationships, and a chain of inference must be used in order to establish a claim that a particular test is a measure of the construct.

The relationships and nodes of a network representation of the traces of learner interactions can be compared to the digital performance space resources and relationships to enable inferences about what the learner knows and can do (Al-Diban & Ifenthaler, 2011; Ifenthaler, 2010; Quellmalz, Timms, & Schneider, 2009). Network measures such as similarity, centrality, clusters and pattern matching are used in such inferences, where the patterns of the network imply functional and structural connectivity (Sporns, 2011). Digital performance space relationships examined with time-sensitive network analysis has increased the ability of research to characterise and make comment on processes, products, knowledge and know-how, and their complex entanglements in authentic performance settings.

3.3 *Layers of Aggregations and Translations*

In the OECD PISA CPS assessment, aggregations of events into tasks takes place in a hierarchy that begins at the top with a scenario and ends within each task of the scenario at the level of a 'turn'—a game-based learning concept that updates the state of the scenario based on the learner's input.

Each problem scenario (unit) contains multiple tasks. A task, for example, consensus building, is a particular phase within the scenario, with a beginning and an end. A task consists of a number of turns (exchanges, chats, actions, etc.) between the participants in the team. A finite number of options leading onto different paths are available to the participants after each turn, some of which constitute a step towards solving the problem. The end of a task forms an appropriate point to start the next task. Whenever the participants fail to reach this point a 'rescue' is programmed to ensure that the next task can be started (PISA, 2013).

With this hierarchy in mind (e.g. scenarios containing tasks that contain turns) the challenge of aggregating with time sensitivity and translating from one level of analysis to another can be addressed with moving averages, sliding time windows and event recognition. The OECD PISA CPS assessment uses event recognition, in which an action, communication or product of the test taker triggers a reaction by the test engine to update the scenario, which might include rescuing the test taker. In a moving average, some window of time is selected (e.g. every second, or after every three turns) and an average is performed to form an abstracted data layer that preserves some of the shape of the data movement over time. In the sliding time window (Choi et al., 2010; Han, Cheng, Xin, & Yan, 2007), a combination of event recognitions and moving averages, or some configuration of either, might be performed and then used as an abstracted data layer. In the example case summarized below, for example, the time stamps of every action were subtracted from each other to compute duration, which was then applied to each action, to nearby action-pairs and to action-n-grams (motifs) for further analysis.

Within any slice of time, or when comparing two or a few slices of time, standard statistical procedures and aggregations apply (e.g., means testing, correlations, regressions), but when high-resolution data is involved (e.g. many data points per record per unit of time) and where there are complex aggregations (e.g., widely varying sources of data and different units of measure) then data mining techniques are more applicable. Of note, regression techniques in data mining are not equivalent to the same methods in statistics, even though the terms sound and look the same. In data mining, regression represents a search within a complex nonlinear space for patterns and representations of structure and causal dynamic relationships, rather than the reduction of error of a linear model (Schmidt & Lipson, 2009). Thus, aggregations in the two approaches are also of different lineage and need to be considered as separate entities with separate representational functions, meaning and purposes (Bates & Watts, 1988).

3.4 Representations of Dynamics

Systems dynamics (Bar-Yam, 1997; Sterman, 1994) involves a mathematical modeling technique for framing, understanding and discussing the issues of time, digital performance space relationships and aggregation-translation in highly interactive technology-enhanced assessments. Field experiments with systems dynamics methods have, for example, focused on mid-level model-based theory building in an assessment context (Kopainsky, Pirnay-Dummer, & Alessi, 2010). The process of building a model from snapshots of a dynamic system is called a 'nonlinear state space reconstruction' (Sugihara et al., 2012). In such a state space equivalent to a network all the data fall within a finite band or manifold of behaviour. That is, every state of the system will be in one of the spaces created by the finite possibilities for each variable at some point in time. Such reconstructions of the underlying manifold governing the dynamics of a system can map to and uncover the causal relationships in a complex system (Schmidt & Lipson, 2009) including those that support inferences concerning what a user knows and can do.

Visualizing the current status of a learner's progress on an assessment is an example of representing a state of a dynamic system, as is visualizing the progress of the learner in relation to a domain model driving the assessment's evidence collection processes. The Khan Academy (Khan, 2011), for example, charts progress in learning mathematics or science content against a visualization of the content hierarchy. If the learner has mastered division, a visual tree shows how mastery fits with addition and subtraction and allows access to the next higher level of math skill. More dynamic and fine-grained visualizations are also possible, for example, that would trace the process steps of a solution, or document the details of a constructive process. Visualizations can aide pattern discovery involving both nonverbal and verbal expressions; for example, from bodies of text, from online student discussion forums, and from cognitive and mental model representations (Pirnay-Dummer et al., 2010).

To date the developments in learning analytics that provide visualisations of learning traces for learners and teachers have been represented by learning analytics dashboards. Such dashboards have been developed that keep track of time, social interactions for insights into collaboration, the use of documents and tools and the artefacts produced by students (Verbert, Duval, Klerkx, Govaerts, & Santos, 2013). While these dashboards currently fall far short of the detailed traces of assessment data that are possible to create, even these more limited opportunities for analysing their learning have been found to support learners' reflection and improve self-assessment as well as increasing course satisfaction (Verbert et al., 2013).

Examples of the more highly detailed traces are readily found in serious games, as well as casual games that are designed to be immersive and emotionally engaging rather than a simple pastime (Aldrich, 2005). In these game-based examples, the high-resolution feedback is always on, giving the player an up-to-date view of progress, hints about upcoming challenges, and a view to the longer-term goal (Prensky, 2001). Clearly educators and researchers might want to promote to policymakers the importance of researching the methods and impacts of presenting visualisations of data to teachers and learners along with developments in data processing that will better enable judgements of student performances.

Perhaps the biggest unresolved issue of representation of collaborative learning (and perhaps any learning progress during a complex process) is how to represent the moving and evolving quality of change over time. 'Movies' of dynamic educational processes have not yet been documented in many cases, and if existing, have not been widely disseminated into common practice. This lack of a practice base and experience hampers theory as well as practice in technology-enhanced assessments, and points to the need illustrated by the case in the next section, for future research and practice to create a shared understanding of the methods of data science in educational research.

4 Case Story: Virtual Performance Assessment

A case story illustrates how technology-enabled educational assessment can produce a large number of records, how time and process can be an included mediating factor in analysis and how machine learning and data mining methods are needed to support the rapid simultaneous testing of multiple hypotheses.

A game-based assessment of scientific thinking was created at Harvard (Clarke-Midura et al., 2012) and analysed by one of the authors (Gibson & Clarke-Midura, 2013) to ascertain the abilities of middle school students to design a scientific investigation and construct a causal explanation. A summary of the data science findings and issues included the observation of two of the three aspects of big data: volume (~821,000 records for 4000 subjects, or 205 records per subject); and variety of data (user actions, decisions and artefacts provided evidence of learning and thought processes). The third element of big data, velocity, was less important in this case; because the flow of data was not used in near-real time to give hints, correct mistakes, or inform the learner during the experience, so the data was streamed off to storage for later analysis.

This case illustrates several of the features of big data in educational assessment. First, the context was captured along with the learner action, decision and product, but that context needed to be effectively constructed from the smallest items of data into larger clusters of information. For example, a data element named 'opened door' by itself was relatively meaningless compared to knowing that it was a particular door, opened after another significant event such as talking to a scientist. Thus, patterns of action were transformed into *n-grams* (Scheffel, Niemann, & Leony, 2012) or *motifs*, which then became the transformed units of analysis. This concept of the unit of analysis containing the semantic, time and space contexts for lower levels of aggregation may be a new methodological requirement of digital assessments, and needs further study.

Second, as a large number of users traverse through the network of possibilities in a digital performance space, key movements of the population within the network can be counted and then used as the basis for *empirical prior probabilities* which assist in creating Bayesian inferences about the scientific problem-solving pathmaps of learners (Stevens, Johnson, & Soller, 2005). In particular, each pathway in such a network can be further characterized or specified with a predictive nonlinear mathematical relationship (Gibson & Clarke-Midura, 2013), for example, found through *symbolic regression* an evolutionary machine learning technique (Schmidt & Lipson, 2009). Or, alternatively an *association rule network* can be created that distinguishes user action patterns and motifs according to the prevalence of utilizing one resource compared to another. For example, if 100% of the population goes to resource 3 after resource 1 (skipping over and not utilising resource 2), then with a very high probability, if the sample is a good sample of the greater population, the next user entering the system will follow that path and the inference system can make a highly probable educated guess about what the person now using resource 1 will do next.

The third feature is that the complex set of relationships in various analyses such as those just mentioned, bear a structural relationship to something meaningful about the digital performance space as outlined above. For example, a *cluster analysis* can reveal that some resources are critical to success and others are ignored and not important to the most successful learners (Quellmalz et al., 2012) or a *network visualization* can highlight how people relate to each other or to a task such as quoting and using scientific resources (Bollen et al., 2009).

5 Conclusion and Implications

This chapter has introduced four challenges of big data in educational assessments that are enabled by technology: how to deal with change over time and time-based data; how a digital performance space's relationships interact with learner actions, communications and products; how layers of interpretation are formed from translations of atomistic data into meaningful larger units; and how to represent the dynamics of interactions between and among learners who are being assessed by their interactions in digital performance spaces. The chapter linked the big data challenges to solutions offered in the OECD PISA CPS assessment of collaborative problem-solving, and then reviewed some of the same issues by briefly summarizing a particular case.

The challenges and issues discussed in this chapter reveal the requirements for developments in theory as well as some of the practical challenges that will need to be overcome if educators are to achieve the vision of providing learners and teachers with a 'quiet assessment' system in which the impact can be turned up at the request of learners and teachers as they seek to understand the progress of learning. This joint approach which emphasises assessment AS, FOR and OF learning (Bennett, 2010) is discussed further in the following publications (Gibson & Webb, 2015; Webb & Gibson, 2015; Webb & Ifenthaler, 2018). In moving forward to embrace the opportunities that could be provided by technology-enhanced assessments the challenges that remain to be addressed must not be underestimated before educators can use automated assessments of complex skills and understanding with confidence.

References

Al-Diban, S., & Ifenthaler, D. (2011). Comparison of two analysis approaches for measuring externalized mental models. *Educational Technology & Society, 14*(2), 16–30.

Aldrich, C. (2005). *Learning by doing: The essential guide to simulations, computer games, and pedagogy in e-learning and other educational experiences*. San Francisco, CA: Jossey-Bass.

Black, P., Harrison, C., Hodgen, J., Marshall, M., & Serrett, N. (2010). Validity in teachers' summative assessments. *Assessment in Education: Principles, Policy & Practice, 17*(2), 215–232.

Bar-Yam, Y. (1997). *Dynamics of complex systems*. Reading, MA: Addison-Wesley.

Bates, D. M., & Watts, D. G. (1988). *Nonlinear regression analysis and its applications* (Vol. 32). New York, NY: John Wiley & Sons. https://doi.org/10.2307/2289810

Bennett, R. (2010). Cognitively based assessment of, for, and as learning (CBAL): A preliminary theory of action for summative and formative assessment. *Measurement: Interdisciplinary Research & Perspective, 8*(2–3), 70–91. Retrieved from http://www.tandfonline.com/doi/abs/10.1080/15366367.2010.508686

Bollen, J., Van de Sompel, H., Hagberg, A., Bettencourt, L., Chute, R., Rodriguez, M. A., & Balakireva, L. (2009). Clickstream data yields high-resolution maps of science. *PLoS One, 4*, e4803. https://doi.org/10.1371/journal.pone.0004803

Borgatti, S. P., & Halgin, D. S. (2011). On network theory. *Organization Science, 22*, 1168–1181. https://doi.org/10.1287/orsc.1100.0641

Brandes, U., & Erlebach, T. (2005). *Network analysis: Methodological foundations* (Lecture notes in computer science) (Vol. 3418). Berlin, Germany: Springer. https://doi.org/10.1007/b106453

Choi, Y., Rupp, A., Gushta, M., & Sweet, S. (2010). Modeling learning trajectories with epistemic network analysis: An investigation of a novel analytic method for learning progressions in epistemic games. In *National Council on Measurement in Education* (pp. 1–39).

Clarke-Midura, J., Code, J., Dede, C., Mayrath, M., & Zap, N. (2012). Thinking outside the bubble: Virtual performance assessments for measuring complex learning. In *Technology-based assessments for 21st Century skills: Theoretical and practical implications from modern research* (pp. 125–148). Charlotte, NC: Information Age Publishers.

Clarke-Midura, J., & Dede, C. (2010). Assessment, technology, and change. *Journal of Research in Teacher Education, 42*(3), 309–328.

Cronbach, L. J., & Meehl, P. E. (1955). Construct validity in psychological tests. *Psychological Bulletin, 52*(4), 281–302. https://doi.org/10.1037/h0040957

de Freitas, S. (2014). *Education in computer generated environments*. London, UK: Routledge.

Fischer, G. H. E., & Molenaar, I. W. E. (2012). *Rasch models: Foundations, recent developments, and applications*. New York, NY: Springer. https://doi.org/10.1007/978-1-4612-4230-7

Gibson, D. (2012). Game changers for transforming learning environments. In F. Miller (Ed.), *Transforming learning environments: Strategies to shape the next generation* (Advances in educational administration) (Vol. 16, pp. 215–235). Bingley, UK: Emerald Group Publishing Ltd. https://doi.org/10.1108/S1479-3660(2012)0000016014

Gibson, D., & Clarke-Midura, J. (2013). Some psychometric and design implications of game-based learning analytics. In D. Ifenthaler, J. Spector, P. Isaias, & D. Sampson (Eds.), *E-Learning systems, environments and approaches: Theory and implementation*. London, UK: Springer.

Gibson, D., & Ifenthaler, D. (2017). Preparing the next generation of education researchers for big data in higher education. In B. Kei Daniel (Ed.), *Big data and learning analytics: Current theory and practice in higher education* (pp. 29–42). New York, NY: Springer.

Gibson, D., & Jakl, P. (2013). *Data challenges of leveraging a simulation to assess learning*. West Lake Village, CA: Pragmatic Solutions. Retrieved from http://www.curveshift.com/images/Gibson_Jakl_data_challenges.pdf

Gibson, D., & Knezek, G. (2011). Game changers for teacher education. In P. Mishra & M. Koehler (Eds.), *Proceedings of Society for Information Technology & Teacher Education International Conference 2011* (pp. 929–942). Chesapeake, VA: AACE.

Gibson, D., & Webb, M. E. (2015). Data science in educational assessment. *Education and Information Technologies*. https://doi.org/10.1007/s10639-015-9411-7
Gijbels, D., Dochy, F., Van den Bossche, P., & Segers, M. (2005). Effects of problem-based learning: A meta-analysis from the angle of assessment. *Review of Educational Research, 75*, 27–61.
Han, J., Cheng, H., Xin, D., & Yan, X. (2007). Frequent pattern mining: Current status and future directions. *Data Mining and Knowledge Discovery, 15*(1), 55–86. https://doi.org/10.1007/s10618-006-0059-1
Hedeker, D., & Gibbons, R. D. (2006). *Longitudinal data analysis*. Hoboken, NJ: John Wiley & Sons. https://doi.org/10.1002/0470036486
IBM. (2015). *Big data*. Retrieved from http://www-01.ibm.com/software/au/data/bigdata/
Ifenthaler, D. (2010). Scope of graphical indices in educational diagnostics. In D. Ifenthaler, P. Pirnay-Dummer, & N. M. Seel (Eds.), *Computer-based diagnostics and systematic analysis of knowledge* (pp. 213–234). New York, NY: Springer.
Ifenthaler, D. (2014). AKOVIA: Automated knowledge visualization and assessment. *Technology, Knowledge and Learning, 19*(1–2), 241–248. https://doi.org/10.1007/s10758-014-9224-6
Ifenthaler, D. (2015). Learning analytics. In J. M. Spector (Ed.), *The SAGE encyclopedia of educational technology* (Vol. 2, pp. 447–451). Thousand Oaks, CA: SAGE.
Ifenthaler, D., Eseryel, D., & Ge, X. (2012). Assessment for game-based learning. In D. Ifenthaler, D. Eseryel, & X. Ge (Eds.), *Assessment in game-based learning. Foundations, innovations, and perspectives* (pp. 3–10). New York, NY: Springer.
Jonassen, D. H. (1997). Instructional design models for well-structured and ill-structured problem-solving learning outcomes. *Educational Technology Research and Development, 45*, 65–90. https://doi.org/10.1007/BF02299613
Khan, S. (2011). *Khan Academy*. Retrieved from http://www.khanacademy.org/
Kline, P. (1998). *The new psychometrics: Science, psychology, and measurement*. London, UK: Routledge.
Kopainsky, B., Pirnay-Dummer, P., & Alessi, S. M. (2010). Automated assessment of learner's understanding in complex dynamic systems. In *28th International Conference of the System Dynamics Society, Seoul* (pp. 1–39).
Kozleski, E., Gibson, D., & Hynds, A. (2012). Changing complex educational systems: Frameworks for collaborative social justice leadership. In C. Gersti-Pepin & J. Aiken (Eds.), *Defining social justice leadership in a global context* (pp. 263–286). Charlotte, NC: Information Age Publishing.
Mansell, W., James, M., & The Assessment Reform Group. (2009). *Assessment in schools. Fit for purpose? A Commentary by the Teaching and Learning Research Programme*. London. Retrieved from http://www.tlrp.org/pub/documents/assessment.pdf
Margetts, H., & Sutcliffe, D. (2013). Addressing the policy challenges and opportunities of "Big data". *Policy & Internet, 5*(2), 139–146. https://doi.org/10.1002/1944-2866.POI326
Messick, S. (1994). The interplay of evidence and consequences in the validation of performance assessments. *Educational Researcher, 23*(2), 13–23.
Mislevy, R., Steinberg, L., & Almond, R. (1999). *Evidence-centered assessment design*. Educational Testing Service. Retrieved from http://www.education.umd.edu/EDMS/mislevy/papers/ECD_overview.html
Mislevy, R., Steinberg, L., & Almond, R. (2003). On the structure of educational assessments. *Russell: The Journal of the Bertrand Russell Archives, 1*(1), 3–62.
Newell, A., & Simon, H. (1972). *Human problem solving*. Englewood Cliffs, NJ: Prentice-Hall.
Patton, M. (2011). *Developmental evaluation: Applying complexity concepts to enhance innovation and use*. New York, NY: The Guilford Press.
Pirnay-Dummer, P., Ifenthaler, D., & Spector, M. (2010). Highly integrated model assessment technology and tools. *Educational Technology Research and Development, 58*(1), 3–18.
PISA. (2013). *Draft collaborative problem solving framework*. Paris, France: PISA.
Prensky, M. (2001). *Digital game-based learning*. New York, NY: McGraw-Hill.
Psychometrics. (2014). In *American heritage dictionary*. Boston, MA: Houghton-Mifflin Company.

Quellmalz, E., Timms, M., Buckley, B., Davenport, J., Loveland, M., & Silberglitt, M. (2012). 21st century dynamic assessment. In M. Mayrath, J. Clarke-Midura, & D. Robinson (Eds.), *Technology-based assessments for 21st Century skills: Theoretical and practical implications from modern research* (pp. 55–90). Charlotte, NC: Information Age Publishers.

Quellmalz, E., Timms, M., & Schneider, S. (2009). *Assessment of student learning in science simulations and games*. Washington, DC: National Research Council.

Scheffel, M., Niemann, K., & Leony, D. (2012). Key action extraction for learning analytics. *21st century learning* ... (pp. 320–333). Retrieved from http://link.springer.com/chapter/10.1007/978-3-642-33263-0_25

Schmidt, M., & Lipson, H. (2009). Symbolic regression of implicit equations. In *Genetic programming theory and practice* (Vol. 7, pp. 73–85). New York, NY: Springer.

Shaffer, D., Hatfield, D., Svarovsky, G., Nash, P., Nulty, A., Bagley, E., … Mislevy, R. (2009). Epistemic network analysis: A prototype for 21st-century assessment of learning. *International Journal of Learning and Media, 1*(2), 33–53. Retrieved from http://www.mitpressjournals.org/doi/abs/10.1162/ijlm.2009.0013

Sporns, O. (2011). *Networks of the brain*. Cambridge, MA: MIT Press.

Sterman, J. D. (1994). Learning in and about complex systems. *System Dynamics Review, 10*(2/3), 291.

Stevens, R. (2006). Machine learning assessment systems for modeling patterns of student learning. In D. Gibson, C. Aldrich, & M. Prensky (Eds.), *Games and simulations in online learning: Research & development frameworks* (pp. 349–365). Hershey, PA: Idea Group.

Stevens, R., Johnson, D., & Soller, A. (2005). Probabilities and predictions: Modeling the development of scientific problem-solving skills. *Cell Biology Education, 4*(1), 42–57. https://doi.org/10.1187/cbe.04-03-0036

Stevens, R., & Palacio-Cayetano, J. (2003). Design and performance frameworks for constructing problem-solving simulations. *Cell Biology Education, 2*(Fall), 162–179.

Stiggins, R. J. (1995). Assessment literacy for the 21st century. *Phi Delta Kappan, 77*(3), 238–245.

Sugihara, G., May, R., Ye, H., Hsieh, C., Deyle, E., Fogarty, M., & Munch, S. (2012). Detecting causality in complex ecosystems. *Science (New York, N.Y.), 338*(6106), 496–500. https://doi.org/10.1126/science.1227079

Tashakkori, A., & Teddlie, C. (2003). *Handbook of mixed methods in social & behavioral research*. Thousand Oaks, CA: SAGE. Retrieved from http://books.google.com/books?id=F8BFOM8DCKoC&pgis=1

Thagard, P. (2010). *How brains make mental models*. Retrieved from cogsci.uwaterloo.ca/Articles/Thagard.brains-models.2010.pdf

Verbert, K., Duval, E., Klerkx, J., Govaerts, S., & Santos, J. L. (2013). Learning analytics dashboard applications. *American Behavioral Scientist*. https://doi.org/10.1177/0002764213479363

Webb, M. E., Gibson, D. C., & Forkosh-Baruch, A. (2013). Challenges for information technology supporting educational assessment. *Journal of Computer Assisted Learning, 29*(5), 451–462. https://doi.org/10.1111/jcal.12033

Webb, M., & Gibson, D. (2015). Technology enhanced assessment in complex collaborative settings. *Education and Information Technologies*. https://doi.org/10.1007/s10639-015-9413-5

Webb, M., & Ifenthaler, D. (2018). Assessment as, for and of 21st Century learning using information technology: An overview. In J. Voogt, G. Knezek, R. Christensen, & K.-W. Lai (Eds.), *International handbook of IT in primary and secondary education* (2nd ed., pp. 1–20). Cham, Switzerland: Springer.

Wiggins, G. (1989). Teaching to the (authentic) test. *Educational Leadership, 46*, 41–46.

Zervas, P., & Sampson, D. G. (2018). Supporting reflective lesson planning based on inquiry learning analytics for facilitating students' problem solving competence: The inspiring science education tools. In T.-W. Chang, R. Huang, & Kinshuk (Eds.), *Authentic learning through advances in technologies* (pp. 91–114). New York, NY: Springer.

David C. Gibson Director of Learning Futures at Curtin University in Australia and UNESCO Chair of Data Science in Higher Education Learning and Teaching, received his doctorate (Ed.D. Leadership and Policy Studies) from the University of Vermont in 1999 based on a study of complex systems modeling of educational change. His foundational research demonstrated the feasibility of bridging from qualitative information to quantifiable dynamic relationships in complex models that verify trajectories of organizational change. He provides thought leadership as a researcher, professor, learning scientist and innovator. He is the creator of simSchool, a classroom flight simulator for preparing educators, and eFolio an online performance-based assessment system, and provides vision and sponsorship for Curtin University's Challenge, a mobile, game-based learning platform for individuals and teams. He consults with project and system leaders, formulates strategies, and helps people articulate their vision for innovation; then helps connect people with the resources needed to fulfil their aspirations. His research has extended from learning analytics, complex systems analysis and modeling of education to application of complexity via games and simulations in teacher education, web applications and the future of learning. Dr. Gibson has also advanced the use of technology to personalize education via cognitive modeling, design and implementation.

Mary E. Webb is Reader in Information Technology in Education at King's College London. Mary is on the International Federation of Information processing (IFIP) Education Executive Committee and leads the Task Force on Computer Science in the Curriculum. Mary is internationally recognised for her research on pedagogy and formative assessment across both Computer Science as a subject and the uses of new technologies for learning. Mary's research has resulted in over 150 publications. Mary is joint editor of the Section: Using Information Technology for Assessment: Issues and Opportunities in the International Handbook entitled the use of IT in primary and Secondary Education which formed the foundation of the EDUsummITs. Mary is joint editor of: Tomorrow's learning: involving everyone, selected papers from World Conference on Computers in Education 2017.

Dirk Ifenthaler is Professor and Chair of Learning, Design and Technology at University of Mannheim, Germany and UNESCO Deputy Chair of Data Science in Higher Education Learning and Teaching at Curtin University, Australia. His previous roles include Professor and Director, Centre for Research in Digital Learning at Deakin University, Australia, Manager of Applied Research and Learning Analytics at Open Universities, Australia, and Professor for Applied Teaching and Learning Research at the University of Potsdam, Germany. He was a 2012 Fulbright Scholar-in-Residence at the Jeannine Rainbolt College of Education, at the University of Oklahoma, USA. Dirk's research focuses on the intersection of cognitive psychology, educational technology, data analytics and organisational learning. His research outcomes include numerous co-authored books, book series, book chapters, journal articles and international conference papers, as well as successful grant funding in Australia, Germany and USA—see Dirk's website for a full list of scholarly outcomes at www.ifenthaler.info. He is the Editor-in-Chief of the Springer journal *Technology, Knowledge and Learning* (www.springer.com/10758).

Chapter 3
Integrated e-Learning Paradigm in the Twenty-First Century: Management Education

Barbara K. Son

Abstract Since the early 2000s, online degree programs have been rapidly growing nationally and globally. Even traditional universities have been adopting learning-management systems to offer flexible, hybrid, and online classes. Concomitantly, textbook publishers have been improving e-Learning platforms and add-ons. The plethora of interactive e-Learning materials has produced a profound shift in the ways today's students acquire and apply knowledge, and poses growing challenges for online programs, instructional designers, and instructors to customize e-Learning materials for different learning styles. To fit students' learning needs, tailored instruction should be equipped with high-performing adaptable multimedia tools. We see the growing impact of live e-Learning and web collaboration technologies on the constructivist- and connectivist-based pedagogies. Accordingly, curricula of the twenty-first century digital age should foster collaborative learning, experiential learning, multimedia learning, and active learning. This chapter proposes a learner-centered integrated e-Learning paradigm that consists of these four interwoven learning components. Using the example of a global online MBA course, we also closely examine innovative e-Learning strategies that are vital to cultivating highly engaging and applied learning in the twenty-first century. Finally, we consider the implications of an integrated e-Learning paradigm in management education, discussing the most effective uses of pedagogical techniques.

1 Introduction

In today's technologically enhanced society, we need to close the gap between teachers' knowledge about technology and the integration of technology in their classes. Technology has impacted pedagogies significantly as flexible technology-based instructional design is a critical factor in the creation of an effective

B. K. Son (✉)
Anaheim University, Anaheim, CA, USA
e-mail: bson@anaheim.edu

D. Sampson et al. (eds.), *Learning Technologies for Transforming Large-Scale Teaching, Learning, and Assessment*, https://doi.org/10.1007/978-3-030-15130-0_3

e-Learning environment. This requires a significant commitment of teachers' effort and time so that they can acquire technological skills, develop technology-based classes, and deliver relevant and customized education. Rapid progress in educational software, mobile devices, and learning-management systems can help teachers customize their lessons to fit each student's learning style. This customized education is vital in developing students' twenty-first century skills.

Curriculum is an integral part of the customized and applied learning of the modern world. The constructivist pedagogy, which has been dramatically impacted by technology, stresses the role of teachers as facilitators in the learning process, while assigning learning responsibilities to students. In our previous studies, we examined these challenges by closely looking at innovative interactive learning approaches (Son & Goldstone, 2012; Son & Simonian, 2013, 2016). In this chapter, we will discuss how learner-centered innovative pedagogical techniques should be designed to improve these approaches. In particular, we will address how the twenty-first century pedagogies should meet online learners' needs by evolving e-Learning technologies (Kolb, 2015; Veletsianos & Shepherdson, 2016). Accordingly, we will explore integrated e-Learning strategies using the twenty-first century management education as the subject matter. We'll conclude with the practical implications and future potential of these strategies in modern classrooms.

2 New Paradigm in Twenty-First Century e-Learning

Rapidly evolving learning technologies are transforming teaching methods, learning design, and learning analytics at large. Popular open source learning management systems (LMS) such as Moodle (Modular Object-Oriented Dynamic Learning Environment) and Canvas embody collaborative learning and active learning pedagogies. The Moodle LMS offers an excellent e-Learning portal and development platform to build communities of learners. Students can use discussion forums, wikis, glossaries, and messaging to network with fellow students. This encourages them to build knowledge through collaborative learning and active learning. Meanwhile, asynchronous activities allow students to collaborate at different times. Hence, social constructivism-based Moodle triggers learners to contribute to learner-centric collaborative learning environments (Al-Ani, 2013).

Similarly, the Canvas LMS is designed to enhance collaborative learning through flexible customized educational tools. Its intuitive app allows teachers to cater to a wide variety of learning needs, while monitoring their students' performance. They can explore the active learning pedagogical approach by disseminating their courses through diverse learning channels, including videos, blogs, and wikis (Johnson & Sanders, 2015). Moreover, the Canvas platform, which fosters pedagogical flexibility, can enhance connectivist cognitive presence in blogs, social media posts, and webcasts. Learning through social networks requires a cognitive process. Connectivism is based on a constructivist model of learning, and its pedagogical foundation is that learning happens as learners connect newly acquired knowledge to their previous knowledge (Anderson & Dron, 2011).

Massive open online courses (MOOCs) based on connectivism also offer collaborative social learning tools, such as blogs, chat, forums, and group activities. As students in a MOOC develop problem-solving skills through case studies, constructivism-based MOOCs can persuade learners to contribute to discovery-learning environments (Ross, Sinclair, Knox, Bayne, & Macleod, 2014). Furthermore, MOOC providers can facilitate learning swarms through open pedagogy strategies such as Open Educational Resources (OER). However, MOOCs face a huge challenge of engaging all their students in order to prevent massive dropout rates (Spector, Ifenthaler, & Sampson, 2016). Pedagogical innovation that promotes high levels of interaction is vital to overcoming these challenges.

We see the growing impact of live e-Learning and web collaboration technologies on the constructivist- and connectivist-based pedagogies (Veletsianos & Shepherdson, 2016). Accordingly, the student-centered pedagogy of the modern digital age must address four vital learning components: collaborative learning, experiential learning, multimedia learning, and active learning. Hence, this chapter proposes a learner-centered integrated e-Learning paradigm that consists of these four interwoven learning components, as depicted in Fig. 3.1. Under the Integrated e-Learning approach, learners are able to:

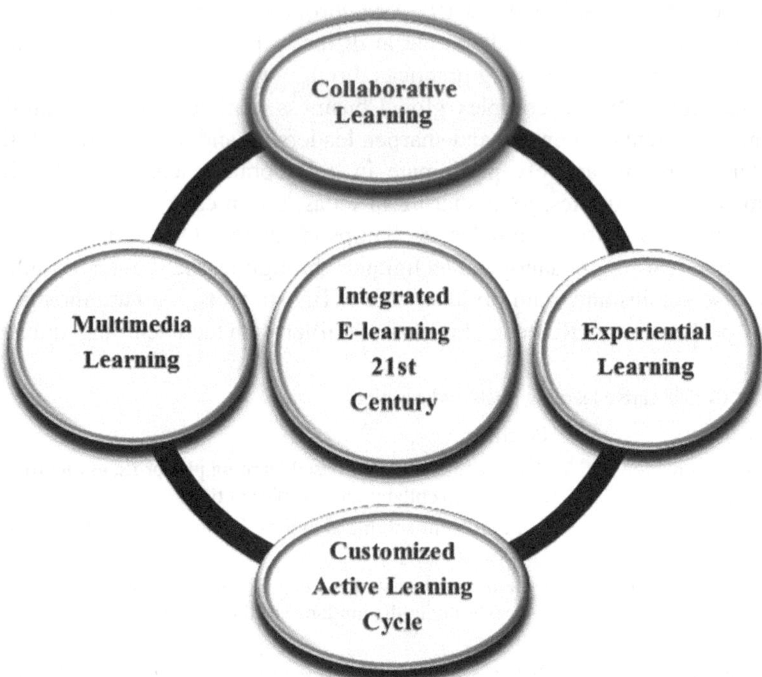

Fig. 3.1 Integrated e-Learning in the twenty-first century

- Develop collaborative learning through diverse applied e-learning activities.
- Develop experiential learning through continuous practice in areas that are related to the student's learning goals and experiences.
- Develop multimedia learning by applying different learning tools flexibly.
- Contribute to the active learning cycle by utilizing integrated active-learning modalities.

Using the example of our MBA class at Anaheim University, we look at the integrated e-Learning components in more detail. We also relate them to innovative flipped-learning strategies that are vital to cultivating highly engaging and applied learning in the twenty-first century.

2.1 Collaborative Learning

Table 3.1 highlights the goals and practices of collaborative learning. Collaborative knowledge creation is facilitated by social constructivism-based learning platforms such as Moodle and Canvas. The situated learning theory and expectancy-value theory see learning as more effective through challenging interactive activities that facilitate learner participation in practicing communities (Cook & Artino, 2016). The constructivist learning theory observes that interactivity leads to deeper learning (Krippel, McKee, & Moody, 2010). Asynchronous activities on flexible learning platforms allow students to collaborate at different times. In our MBA class, we emphasize collaborative learning practices through which our active learners share their perspectives toward complex global business markets, analyze multidimensional management challenges, and sharpen leadership and management skills.

Students have to actively participate in collaborative learning through joint problem-solving activities, joint sharing of ideas, group case studies, and projects (Al-Ani, 2013; Spector, Ifenthaler, & Sampson, 2016). Our MBA class adopts collaborative-learning pedagogical techniques through learner-centered multidisciplinary case studies and team projects. Our MBA students, who are mostly global business professionals (Reuters, 2008), are familiar with team learning and projects

Table 3.1 Collaborative learning goals and practices

Goals	Practices
Collaborative creation of knowledge	Social constructivism-based learning platforms, asynchronous activities to collaborate at different times
Students' learning responsibilities	Joint problem-solving activities, joint sharing of ideas, group case studies, and projects
Communities of learners	Collaboration of students on authentic tasks and on a common endeavor under the guidance of their teachers/facilitators of learning
Dynamic and interactive learning environment	Networking through collaborative social learning tools, such as blogs, chat, discussion forums, social media sites, wikis, and glossaries

in multinational and multicultural organizations. To build high-order entrepreneurial thinking and analytical skills, they are required to perform an analysis of the practical applications of entrepreneurship in our innovation and entrepreneurship class. To promote these learning outcomes, we created the following team activity:

Each team participates in the study of successful entrepreneurship. The team members conduct research on successful entrepreneurship strategies and prepare a "Successful Entrepreneurship" document.

The document must discuss each of the following aspects:

- Entrepreneurship successes and failures
- Key implementation steps
- Entrepreneurship resources
- Entrepreneurship opportunities

The written submission should then reflect their team study experiences.

As organizational complexity grows, global management education has to prepare students to be effective leaders who drive organizational performance and competitiveness. To build communities of learners, students have to construct their knowledge, build self-directed learning skills, and collaborate on authentic tasks and on a common endeavor under the guidance of their teachers, who are facilitators of learning.

Students' cognitive load is reduced by scaffolded learning, which helps them investigate and solve complex problems. Scaffolded learning is very useful for problem-based learning, inquiry learning, and self-directed learning (Hmelo-Silver, Duncan, & Chinn, 2007). We apply the scaffolded learning model in our class as weekly student hosts take responsibility for promoting active discussion in the discussion forum during the entire week, while receiving guidance and feedback from professors. Scaffolded collaborative learning is facilitated by weekly student hosts who motivate and encourage their peers to share knowledge and experiences together on the assigned topics.

Technology facilitates constructivist pedagogy and collaborative learning as learners engage in social interaction (Spector, Ifenthaler, Sampson, & Isaias, 2016). They network through collaborative social learning tools, such as blogs, chat, discussion forums, social media sites, wikis, and glossaries (Veletsianos & Shepherdson, 2016). Social media tools may improve collaborative learning when students share ideas and learning materials and collaborate virtually with each other for joint problem-solving. In our class, students utilize various collaborative tools such as chat and discussion forums for sharing and building knowledge, which creates a dynamic and interactive learning environment.

2.2 *Experiential Learning*

According to the experiential learning theory, experience is involved in all learning cycles of grasping experience and transforming experience. Accordingly, learners' experiences are not just limited to experiential exercises, games, and internships.

Table 3.2 Experiential learning goals and practices

Goals	Practices
Critical reasoning skills	Explore real-life issues and develop greater skills to solve unfamiliar problems in experiential settings
Diverse multiple perspectives	Interact with people who have different perspectives, backgrounds, and cultures in experiential settings
Lifelong learning	Lifelong learning related to academic and career interests in experiential settings
Social responsibility	Understanding social and environmental issues and participating in social action

Their experiences also include abstract experience, reflective observations, and active experiments (Kolb, 2015). According to the 2015 Global Management Education Survey, business school students prefer experiential learning (Plompen, 2015).

As Table 3.2 summarizes, the first goal of experiential learning is developing critical reasoning skills. To achieve this goal, students must explore real-life issues and develop greater skills to solve unfamiliar problems in experiential settings. Working students generally are interested in applying their work and life experiences to learning and also in applying their classroom learning to their work lives. There is a reciprocal relationship between work-life experiences and class learning. Hence, instructors need to deliver practical experiential learning that extends into the real workplace (Son & Goldstone, 2012).

To embed experiential learning in our innovation and entrepreneurship class, we draw on our work and life experiences to apply experiential learning methods such as real case studies, consulting exercises, and multinational group collaborations. Through these methods, we help MBA students become critical and creative thinkers and problem solvers, and also help them build management competencies (Caligiuri & Tarique, 2012). Through digitally networked learning, our students are also able to cocreate knowledge with professors. Learners' digital-network experience is becoming an increasingly important form of experiential learning in the twenty-first century (Campbell, 2016).

Building multiple diverse perspectives is the second goal of experiential learning, which is facilitated by interacting with people who have different perspectives, backgrounds, and cultures in experiential settings (Ifenthaler, Masduki, & Seel, 2011). Today's leaders are called upon to develop diverse and inclusive workplaces. It is critical for them to build cultural intelligence (Gutierrez, Spencer, & Zhu, 2012). Accordingly, MBA curriculums in the twenty-first century must address experiential learning so that students learn and build these leadership skills in experiential settings. The third goal of experiential learning is lifelong learning, which calls for a culture of continuous improvement. We see students seeking advanced degrees and certifications. In the rapidly changing technology-driven world, as teachers engage in a lifelong learning process through their professional development, they can better help their students become lifelong learners. We apply this approach to our class as the professor and students are lifelong learners. We promote lifelong learning related to academic and career interests in experiential settings. Our experienced middle- and senior-level manager students clearly understand the culture of continuous improvement.

Social responsibility is the last goal of experiential learning. This goal is enhanced by students learning about and understanding social and environmental issues, and by their participation in social action. As the United Nations' Principles for Responsible Management Education advocates, today's management curriculums must address corporate social responsibility and sustainable management (Alcaraz & Thiruvattal, 2010). Interdisciplinary pedagogies are further required to facilitate positive social changes and social action. Our innovation and entrepreneurship class examines the broad impacts of these values and sustainable management practices in multinational organizations. We also explore social responsibility, social entrepreneurship, and sustainability issues in the case studies, reflective exercises, and group practices.

2.3 Multimedia Learning

The cognitive theory of multimedia learning suggests that cognitive load should be a key factor in multimedia instruction (Mayer & Moreno, 2003). According to Moreno and Mayer (2007), interactive multimodal learning environments alone do not produce meaningful learning. Since multimedia technologies are just tools, effective learning relies on the successful integration of customized multimedia materials into course activities. The Astleitner and Wiesner model expanded on Mayer's cognitive model and suggested different components of motivation. In the view of a cognitive theory of motivation, video information results in higher learning motivation than just audio information (Astleitner & Wiesner, 2004). As shown in Table 3.3, the first goal of multimedia learning is effective and engaged learning (Neo, 2007). To pursue this goal, learner-centered multimedia designs must be customized based on students' learning styles. According to the expectancy-value theory, learning motivation increases with relevant learning materials and meaningful and challenging activities (Leacock & Nesbit, 2007). Instructors must make their course lessons more connected, more relevant, and more interesting. In addition, they need to offer interactive and challenging activities to facilitate learner

Table 3.3 Multimedia learning goals and practices

Goals	Practices
Effective and engaged learning	Learner-centered multimedia designs and interactive and challenging activities that facilitate learner participation
Support system for learning through doing	Collaborative multimedia applications and practices
Flexible learning	Provide wide choices of flexible multimedia tools including tutorials
Adapted learning	Adapt multimedia design materials to learners' characteristics

participation. The overall effectiveness of this approach has been documented (Son, 2016; Son & Simonian, 2016). Customized multimedia learning tools can help motivate students through learner-centered applications and practices (Son & Simonian, 2013, 2014).

The cultural historical activity theory views learning technologies as representing a support system for learning through doing. Accordingly, successful learning through doing depends on how teachers and learners use learning technologies (DeVane & Squire, 2012). The pedagogies associated with the activity theory have been increasingly impacted by technology's influence on learning components. To promote learning through doing with the support of technology, teachers must commit a heavy investment of time and effort to preparing collaborative multimedia applications and practices on the learning platforms. Applications are shared on electronic whiteboards, which stirs collaborative visual learning (Son, 2016). Learners should be treated as actors who manage their own learning processes. In our class, students can view lectures and videos on their own time before joining the real-time live seminars through a customized web-based portal. We offer our global manager students live session platforms for project discussion and collaborative problem-solving (Anaheim University, 2015). In real-time online classes, we encourage engaged and collaborative learning through the latest high-definition video webcam technology (Gutierrez et al., 2012).

The third goal of multimedia learning is flexible learning, in which learners have wide choices of flexible multimedia tools including hypermedia and adaptive tutorials (Beetham, 2007). In addition to the intrinsic benefits of this flexibility, learners still need to receive feedback and support from teachers who facilitate deeper learning. Accordingly, we embed learning materials in appropriate graded activities in our innovation and entrepreneurship class. We adopt flexible multimedia learning tools. Our students, who are mostly global business professionals, can engage in discussion, seminars, and project forums through iPod, DVD, streaming video webcast, and video podcasts (Anaheim University, 2015). We help them practice different learning tools flexibly in order to comprehend complex management issues.

Adaptive learning is the last goal of multimedia learning. As learning facilitators, we need to adapt learning materials to learners' characteristics. Diagnostic tools such as analytics in Canvas offer the possibility of adapting materials to learner characteristics (Brown, Dehoney, & Millichap, 2015; Ifenthaler, Demetrios, Sampson, & Spector, 2018). Through examining learners' behavior in terms of participation, submissions, and scores, instructors can not only lend individual support to struggling students but also can adjust learning activities per learning needs. New innovative video platforms such as Arc also offer analytics. This enables instructors to examine their learners' video-based learning behavior to create more effective videos. This approach promotes the adaptive learning goal. In addition, Arc allows two-way interaction between instructors and learners through a commenting feature, which facilitates collaborative engaged learning ("Instructure", 2016). Meanwhile, adaptive and personalized mobile learning systems are becoming more important due to the growing demand for customized mobile applications for colleges (Sampson & Zervas, 2013; Son & Simonian, 2014). It is easy to customize mobile applications through iMobileU (Keller, 2011), while the jQuery Mobile platform automatically adjusts "the video content for the device it is viewed on, extending clear video functionality to all mobile visitors" (Duo Consulting, 2012, p. 1).

To match the more interactive and engaging digital content available to students outside of the classroom, multimedia learning tools can assist and help motivate students by supplementing traditional teaching modalities with learner-centered learning, through application and practice. The evolving mobile learning technology of the twenty-first century requires innovative and flexible adaptation of the students' learning behavior, which leads to higher learning effectiveness and learner satisfaction (Son & Simonian, 2016; Su & Yeh, 2015).

2.4 Active Learning Cycle

Active learning is based on the social constructivism theory, which emphasizes interactivity. According to the theory, learners build knowledge primarily through social interaction (Krippel et al., 2010). Active learning is also consistent with an inquiry-based, constructivist learning theory that relies on the principles of discovery learning through problem-solving, experimenting, and experiences (Bell, Urhahne, Schanze, & Ploetzner, 2010). Active learning demands online instructors who are committed to a constructive approach that facilitates learners through student-centered collaborative-learning activities (Son & Simonian, 2014, 2016). Facilitative instructors need to constantly draw forth learning feedback to support continuous inquiry-based active learning. As shown in Table 3.4, the learner-centered active learning cycle enables bridging the gap between theory and practice. This cycle is further facilitated by learner-centered active teaching, which is the second goal of active learning. Teachers and active learners have to be active-learning partners to keep the "active learning cycle" (Fig. 3.2) moving forward.

Table 3.4 Active learning goals and practices

Goals	Practices
Bridging the gap between active learning theory and practice	Learner-centered active learning cycle
Learner-centered active teaching	Interactive learning, practice planner and active coach; discussion/participation facilitator and motivator; and facilitator of discovery learning and applied learning
Thought-stimulating active learning	Thought-stimulating activities, problem-solving exercises/presentations, debating, brainstorming, cooperative group work/presentations, customized interactive multimedia exercises, case studies/presentations, role-playing exercises, and reflection exercises
Active assessments	Self-reflection with teacher assessment, peer assessment, sharing of assessment criteria, active feedback, and adapting teaching to assessment results

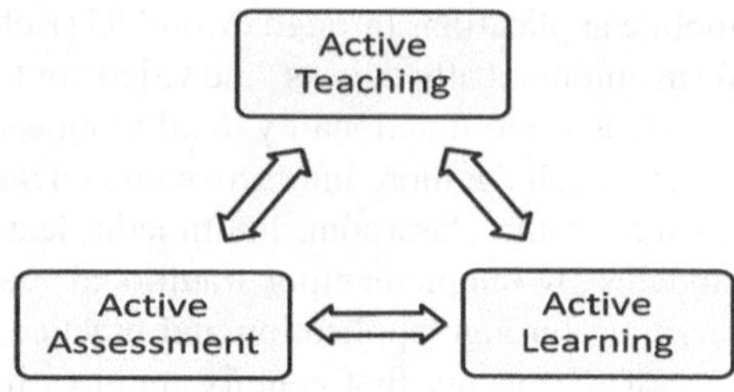

Fig. 3.2 Active learning cycle

Teachers must act as mentors and active learning facilitators to guide students to expand their knowledge and to practice experiential applied learning (Ash & Clayton, 2009). Concomitantly, they have to be engaged in active teaching to successfully apply student-centered innovative pedagogical techniques. Active teaching methods require facilitative instructors to act as interactive learning and practice planners, active coaches, discussion and participation motivators, and facilitators of discovery learning and applied learning. By being proactively involved and encouraging, instructors can nurture an active learning environment and can expand collaborative discovery learning (Son & Goldstone, 2010). They need to prepare effective teaching materials, facilitate learner-centered active learning, and provide rich feedback through active learning assessments, which creates a continuous active learning cycle. To facilitate this cycle, we apply the following active teaching techniques in our class, utilizing integrated active learning modalities:

- Serve as a coach and a learning facilitator
- Use questions to help learners explore, reflect on, understand, practice, and apply what they have learned
- Facilitate critical-thinking questions and active discussion

As described in Table 3.4, thought-stimulating active learning is the third goal of active learning. To facilitate this goal, innovative pedagogical techniques must be incorporated into modern online education curricula. Accordingly, teachers have to facilitate the following practices to foster thought-stimulating active learning: problem-solving exercises, debating, brainstorming, cooperative group work and presentations, interactive multimedia exercises, case studies, simulations, games, role-playing exercises, and reflection exercises (Shaw, 2010; Son, 2017). We apply flipped-learning pedagogical techniques through collaborative and active learning in our class. Flipped learning is consistent with the constructivist learning theory, which promotes discovery learning, and the practice-based behaviorist learning theory (Roach, 2014).

In the evolving complex global environment, the scope of management education has to be broadened, and active learning needs to be incorporated into the student-centered nurturing pedagogy (Son, 2017). Our global management students realize the actual roles they collectively play in the class.

To facilitate their active learning cycle, we apply the following active learning techniques in our class:

1. Reflection exercises and presentations.
2. Students seeing the material in context and exploring their own beliefs.
3. Application of course material to practical contexts.
4. Brainstorming in group activities and discussions.
5. Working on continuous solutions in a cooperative group.
6. Students identifying and organizing information and establishing meaningful relationships between the pieces of information.

We encourage students' critical reflections about their experiences and various aspects of the strategies and techniques that drive successful entrepreneurship. Critical reflections serve as an effective active learning tool for students to add their creative insights to the body of knowledge (Ash & Clayton, 2009; Son, 2017). In addition, brainstorming and presentations through flexible interactive tools encourage engaged learning and critical thinking skills. To help students understand the theoretical and practical arguments underlying many of the global management issues, we tailor customized active learning activities to a variety of contexts. To draw from students' rich perspectives, we look into the relevant theories, cases, and testimonials. Through rigorous critical thinking activities, our students analyze and explain interwoven complex entrepreneurship issues. Active teaching and active learning principles are incorporated into customized concept-application lectures in a variety of global management contexts. We need to actively research to create customized lecture materials that include entrepreneurship case exercises and scaffolding of activities. We carefully develop them to instill responsible and experiential educational values in entrepreneurial management (Dean & Forray, 2017). We explore complex entrepreneurship challenges and integrate ethical leadership and corporate social responsibility issues in the case studies, reflective exercises, and group practices.

The last goal of active learning is active and systematic assessment. Teachers have to find creative avenues to provide active learners with continuous active assessments (Eseryel, Ifenthaler, & Ge, 2011). They can creatively apply knowledge maps to assess students' performances in relation to their peers (Ifenthaler et al., 2011). As described in Table 3.4, they should flexibly adopt the following active assessment tools that are central to connectivist pedagogy: self-reflection with teacher assessment, peer assessment, sharing of assessment criteria, active feedback, and adapting teaching to assessment results (Veletsianos & Shepherdson, 2016). The following are some of the assessment tools we use in our class:

- Students' self-assessment and surveys
- Giving students more time to answer challenging questions
- Using suggested questions from the students to model the most effective assignment questions
- Setting group activities aimed at getting students to assess their own views

As depicted in Fig. 3.2, reciprocal linkages between active teaching, active learning, and active assessment complete the full active learning cycle. Under the active assessment approach, teachers should adopt real-life assessments that are pivotal for nurturing applied learning in real-world contexts.

3 Integrated e-Learning Environment in the Twenty-First Century

In the previous section, we closely examined the learner-centered integrated e-Learning paradigm in the twenty-first century, which consists of four interwoven components: collaborative learning, experiential learning, multimedia learning, and active learning. These components are facilitated by the continuous progress in e-Learning portal-development platforms. Social constructivism-based learning platforms that foster connectivist cognitive presence allow students to develop collaborative learning through diverse applied e-Learning activities (Veletsianos & Shepherdson, 2016). As flexible learning platforms facilitate learners' digital network experience, pedagogical techniques must facilitate practical experiential learning for twenty-first century students (Campbell, 2016; Consiglio & Van der Veer, 2015). The pedagogies associated with the cognitive theory of multimedia learning have been increasingly impacted by multimedia technologies. Accordingly, wide choices of flexible multimedia and diagnostic tools foster adaptive multimedia learning (Son & Simonian, 2016). Flipped-learning pedagogical techniques facilitate active learning, which promotes practice-based discovery learning (Roach, 2014).

The learner-centered integrated e-Learning paradigm in the twenty-first century requires an integrated e-Learning environment in which instructors and students take on higher responsibilities to enhance collaborative, experiential, multimedia, and active learning processes. Active teaching and learning in our innovation and entrepreneurship class require instructors and global manager students to take higher responsibilities towards an integrated e-Learning environment. Online instructors and active learners have to be active learning partners to keep the integrated learning environment moving forward. Active learners must acquire cognitive learning that enhances analytical and decision-making skills as well as affective learning, from which they gain diverse perspectives toward complex issues. We integrate innovative case exercises into interactive and collaborative lessons to deliver an integrated learning environment. Our students realize the actual roles they collectively play in global management affairs. We emphasize integrated learning from which active learners can gain perspective on tightly interwoven global issues, have empathy for others, and develop insights into others' challenges (Gutierrez et al., 2012). We encourage students' critical reflections about their own experiences and critical views about various aspects of entrepreneurship. Critical reflections are central to applied learning pedagogies based on reflective, experiential learning (Son, 2017).

As entrepreneurship encompasses a wide range of areas, students must acquire multidisciplinary learning and develop communication and creative and analytical skills to explore innovative ideas and understand complex interwoven issues. To facilitate these skills and learning outcomes, active teaching and learning in our class require everyone to commit high levels of learning activity preparation and participation. We then contribute our enthusiasm to a quality learning environment.

This has led to very high learning satisfaction. For example, when we surveyed 24 MBA students during 2011–2012, all of them responded that they achieved the learning goals they had when they started our entrepreneurship course. What they gained most from our integrated learning environment was how to use innovative entrepreneurial thinking to produce a real plan that includes the concept, development, funding, and reduction of risks and uncertainties (Son, 2017). As can be seen from students' learning experiences, our learning strategies help students understand the entrepreneurial environment in which entrepreneurial managers must operate and thrive to succeed. Students need to grasp the elements of essential entrepreneurial skills to deal with challenges of the entrepreneurial environment. Ultimately, they can succeed in building and developing entrepreneurship in practice.

4 Conclusion

Curriculum plays an integral part in the highly engaging and applied learning of the twenty-first century. From our close examination, we can see that the curricula of the twenty-first century digital age should foster collaborative learning, experiential learning, multimedia learning, and active learning. We explored the learner-centered integrated e-Learning paradigm, which consists of these four interwoven learning components. However, there exist several limitations to our proposed paradigm for modern management education using the example of our online MBA course. Firstly, we can gain more insight into the learning outcomes of our proposed pedagogical techniques with greater data scope. As teaching styles and learners' characteristics vary, sharing of pedagogical feedback and learner experiences add depth to our proposed paradigm. Secondly, there are potential challenges in fully implementing the proposed e-Learning paradigm, which requires strong support from administrators and faculty members. Thirdly, faculty and students have to undergo training for technology-integrated active learning. Lastly, the learning management system must be customized to foster innovative and effective managerial thinking, knowledge, and skills vital to success in the global business environment.

Bearing these limitations in mind, our proposed integrated e-Learning paradigm consisting of the four interwoven learning components raises a number of implications for modern management classrooms, where applications promote collaborative visual learning, and the learner's digital network experience becomes an increasingly important form of experiential learning (Campbell, 2016). Concomitantly, distance education interaction moves beyond activities in online classrooms and toward the e-Learning community through blogs, webcasts, and social media posts. Teachers are increasingly equipped with flexible multimedia learning tools thanks to the progress in live e-Learning and web collaboration technologies. These tools that are integrated into collaborative lessons help teachers promote an integrated e-Learning environment. Teachers as facilitators of communities of practice need to guide learners to find and apply knowledge (Spector,

Ifenthaler, Sampson, & Isaias, 2016; Veletsianos & Shepherdson, 2016). As demonstrated in Fig. 3.2, the presented paradigm facilitates the active process of co-constructing knowledge between teachers and active learners. The active learning cycle is designed to constantly draw forth active learning feedback to facilitate learner-centered management classrooms. To facilitate this process, instructors need to integrate various active learning modalities into customized activities to fit each student's learning style. Personalized and exploratory learning in twenty-first century can be deepened by the progress in learning analytics and adaptive learning technology in learning management systems (Brown et al., 2015; Ifenthaler et al., 2018). Active management learners need to be adaptive and explore creative and flexible solutions to rising complex management challenges (Balaji, 2013; Schlenker & Chantelot, 2016). To facilitate these learning outcomes, innovative pedagogical techniques must be incorporated into management curricula in twenty-first century.

Open educational resources with the support of an open participatory learning infrastructure support diverse ecosystems of people and learning environments (Wiley, Webb, Weston, & Tonks, 2017). Evolving mobile learning systems require flexible adaptation of students' learning behavior, which leads to higher learning effectiveness (Sampson & Zervas, 2013; Son & Simonian, 2014). Hence, the best online pedagogies are those that support evolving e-Learning environments that encompass a spectrum of course designs (Becker, Winn, & Erwin, 2015). Collaboration, innovation, and creativity are vital components in modern classrooms. Using the example of our MBA class, we looked at them in more detail. In today's fast-moving global environment, MBA curricula must continue to foster pedagogical flexibility and address interdisciplinary pedagogies so that students learn and build management skills from diverse perspectives through integrated e-Learning. As we examined, higher learning outcomes from this approach are reinforced by the creative, innovative, and flexible adaptation of interconnected pedagogical techniques.

References

Al-Ani, W. T. (2013). Blended learning approach using Moodle and student's achievement at Sultan Qaboos University in Oman. *Journal of Education and Learning, 2*(3), 96–110.

Alcaraz, J., & Thiruvattal, E. (2010). The United Nations' principles for responsible management education: A global call for sustainability. *Academy of Management Learning & Education, 9*(3), 542–550.

Anaheim University. (2015). *Student Resources*. Retrieved from https://www.anaheim.edu/student-resources/online-discussion-forum

Anderson, T., & Dron, J. (2011). Three generations of distance education pedagogy. *International Review of Research in Open and Distance Learning, 12*(3), 80–97. Retrieved from http://www.irrodl.org/index.php/irrodl/article/view/890/1663

Ash, S., & Clayton, P. (2009). Generating, deepening, and documenting learning: The power of critical reflection in applied learning. *Journal of Applied Learning in Higher Education, 1*, 25–48.

Astleitner, H., & Wiesner, C. (2004). An integrated model of multimedia learning and motivation. *Journal of Educational Multimedia and Hypermedia, 13*(1), 3–21. Retrieved from http://www.editlib.org/p/5049

Balaji, R. (2013). Trends, issues and challenges in management education. *International Journal of Innovative Research in Science, Engineering and Technology, 2*(4), 1257–1262.

Becker, M., Winn, P., & Erwin, S. (2015). Student-centered, e-learning design in a university classroom. In P. Isaias, J. M. Spector, D. Ifenthaler, & D. G. Sampson (Eds.), *E-Learning systems, environments and approaches* (pp. 229–246). New York, NY: Springer.

Beetham, H. (2007). An approach to learning activity design. In H. Beetham & R. Sharpe (Eds.), *Rethinking pedagogy for a digital age* (pp. 26–40). New York, NY: Routledge.

Bell, T., Urhahne, D., Schanze, S., & Ploetzner, R. (2010). Collaborative inquiry learning: Models, tools, and challenges. *International Journal of Science Education, 32*(3), 349–377.

Brown, M., Dehoney, J., & Millichap, N. (2015). The next generation digital learning environment. A report on research. Educause Learning Initiative paper. *EDUCAUSE Learning Initiative* (pp. 1–11).

Caligiuri, P., & Tarique, I. (2012). Dynamic cross-cultural competencies and global leadership effectiveness. *Journal of World Business, 47*, 612–622. https://doi.org/10.1016/j.jwb.2012.01.014

Campbell, G. (2016). Networked learning as experiential learning. *Educause Review, 51*(1), 70–71. Retrieved from http://er.educause.edu/articles/2016/1/networked-learning-as-experiential-learning

Consiglio, T., & Van der Veer, G. (2015). ICT support for collaborative learning—A tale of two cities. In P. Isaias, J. M. Spector, D. Ifenthaler, & D. G. Sampson (Eds.), *E-Learning systems, environments and approaches* (pp. 147–164). New York, NY: Springer.

Cook, D. A., & Artino, A. R. (2016). Motivation to learn: An overview of contemporary theories. *Medical Education, 50*, 997–1014. https://doi.org/10.1111/medu.13074

Dean, L., & Forray, J. M. (2017). *Seeding the scholarship of teaching and learning garden* (pp. 1–5). Thousand Oaks, CA: SAGE. Retrieved from http://journals.sagepub.com/doi/pdf/10.1177/1052562917722802

DeVane, B., & Squire, K. D. (2012). Activity theory in the learning technologies. In S. Land & D. Jonassen (Eds.), *Theoretical foundations of learning environments* (2nd ed., pp. 242–267). New York, NY: Routledge.

Duo Consulting. (2012). DeVry University. Retrieved from http://www.duoconsulting.com/portfolio/devry-university-mobile-website.

Eseryel, D., Ifenthaler, D., & Ge, X. (2011). Alternative assessment strategies for complex problem solving in game-based learning environments. In D. Ifenthaler, P. Kinshuk, D. Isaias, G. Sampson, & J. M. Spector (Eds.), *Multiple perspectives on problem solving and learning in the digital age* (pp. 159–178). New York, NY: Springer.

Gutierrez, B., Spencer, S. M., & Zhu, G. (2012). Thinking globally, leading locally: Chinese, Indian, and Western leadership. *Cross Cultural Management, 19*(1), 67–89. https://doi.org/10.1108/13527601211195637

Hmelo-Silver, C. E., Duncan, R. G., & Chinn, C. A. (2007). Scaffolding and achievement in problem-based and inquiry learning: A response to Kirschner, Sweller, and Clark (2006). *Educational Psychologist, 42*(2), 99–107.

Ifenthaler, D., Demetrios, G., Sampson, J., & Spector, M. (2018). Linking analytics data and digital systems for supporting cognition and exploratory learning in 21st Century. *Computers in Human Behavior, 78*, 348–350.

Ifenthaler, D., Masduki, I., & Seel, N. M. (2011). The mystery of cognitive structure and how we can detect it. Tracking the development of cognitive structures over time. *Instructional Science, 39*(1), 41–61. https://doi.org/10.1007/s11251-009-9097-6

Instructure. (2016, October 25). Instructure announces general availability of arc video platform that seamlessly integrates with canvas. *PR Newswire*. Retrieved from http://www.prnewswire.com/news-releases/instructure-announces-general-availability-of-arc-video-platform-that-seamlessly-integrates-with-canvas-300350356.html

Johnson, H. K., & Sanders, N. (2015, January 30). *Canvas as a pedagogical platform*. Center for Teaching & Learning Excellence. The University of Utah. Retrieved from http://ctle.utah.edu/tws/workshop-ppts/Canvas.pdf

Keller, J. (2011, January 23). As the web goes mobile, colleges fail to keep up. *The Chronicle of Higher Education*. Retrieved from http://michellepacanskybrock.visibli.com/d698a20f95a1e0f0/?web=1abcc5&dst=http%3A//chronicle.com/article/Colleges-Search-for-Their/126016/

Kolb, D. A. (2015). *Experiential learning: Experience as the source of learning and development* (2nd ed.). Upper Saddle River, NJ: Pearson.

Krippel, G., McKee, A. J., & Moody, J. (2010). Multimedia use in higher education: Promises and pitfalls. *Journal of Instructional Pedagogies, 3*(2), 1–8.

Leacock, T. L., & Nesbit, J. C. (2007). A framework for evaluating the quality of multimedia learning resources. *Educational Technology & Society, 10*(2), 44–59.

Mayer, R., & Moreno, R. (2003). Nine ways to reduce cognitive load in multimedia learning. *Educational Psychologist, 38*(1), 43–52.

Moreno, R., & Mayer, R. (2007). Interactive multimodal learning environments. *Educational Psychology Review, 19*(3), 309–326.

Neo, M. (2007). Learning with multimedia: Engaging students in constructivist learning. *International Journal of Instructional Media, 34*(2), 149–158.

Plompen, M. (2015). Global management education: Return on investment and employment outlook. *EFMD*. Retrieved from https://www.efmd.org/efmd-deans-across-frontiers/view/869-global-management-education-return-on-investment-and-employment-outlook

Reuters. (2008). Anaheim University Ranks #1 in Japan's Nikkei BP MBA Rankings. Retrieved from http://www.reuters.com/article/pressRelease/idUS110001+12-May-2008+MW20080512

Roach, T. (2014). Student perceptions toward flipped learning: New methods to increase interaction and active learning in economics. *The International Review of Economics Education, 17*, 74–84.

Ross, J., Sinclair, C., Knox, J., Bayne, S., & Macleod, H. (2014). Teacher experiences and academic identity: The missing components of MOOC pedagogy. *Journal of Online Learning and Teaching, 10*(1), 57–69.

Sampson, D. G., & Zervas, P. (2013). Context-aware adaptive and personalized mobile learning systems. In D. Sampson, P. Isaias, D. Ifenthaler, & J. Spector (Eds.), *Ubiquitous and mobile learning in the digital age* (pp. 3–17). New York, NY: Springer.

Schlenker, L., & Chantelot, S. (2016). DSIGN4CHANGE: 4Ps for improving management education. In J. Spector, D. Ifenthaler, D. Sampson, & P. Isaias (Eds.), *Competencies in teaching, learning and educational leadership in the digital age* (pp. 259–270). Cham, Switzerland: Springer.

Shaw, C. M. (2010). Designing and using simulations and role-play exercises. In R. A. Denemark (Ed.), *The international studies encyclopedia*. London, UK: Blackwell Publishing.

Son, B. K. (2016). Innovative collaborative learning strategies for integrated interactive E-learning in the 21st century. In D. G. Sampson, J. M. Spector, D. Ifenthaler, & P. Isaías (Eds.), *Proceedings of CELDA 2016: 13th International Conference on Cognition and Exploratory Learning* (pp. 315–318). Mannheim, Germany: IADIS.

Son, B. K. (2017). Integrated collaborative E-learning for the global management education in the 21st century. In D. G. Sampson, J. M. Spector, D. Ifenthaler, & P. Isaías (Eds.), *Proceedings of CELDA 2017: 14th International Conference Cognition and Exploratory Learning in Digital Age* (pp. 311–314). Vilamoura, Portugal: IADIS.

Son, B., & Goldstone, B., (2010). Innovative approaches to quality delivery: Best practices at the top-ranked global MBA online program in Japan. *Global Learn Asia Pacific 2010 Conference, Malaysia*.

Son, B., & Goldstone, B. (2012). Innovative live lecture strategies for integrated interactive e-learning at DeVry online. In *Proceedings of Global TIME 2012—Online Conference on Technology, Innovation, Media & Education* (pp. 184–190). Chesapeake, VA: Association for the Advancement of Computing in Education (AACE). Retrieved from http://www.editlib.org/p/39421

Son, B., & Simonian, M. (2013). Using integrated multimedia learning in cyber-classrooms: Transforming "dull economics" into "fun" economics." *E-LEARN 2013–World Conference on E-Learning, Las Vegas, Nevada* (pp. 21–24).
Son, B., & Simonian, M. (2014). Using mobile learning to enhance innovative interactive learning at DeVry online. *EdMedia—World Conference on Educational Multimedia, Hypermedia and Telecommunication, Chesapeake, VA* (pp. 546–552).
Son, B., & Simonian, M. (2016). An integrated multimedia learning model vs. the traditional face-to-face learning model: An examination of college economics classes. *Journal of Educational Multimedia and Hypermedia, 25*(4), 305–321.
Spector, J. M., Ifenthaler, D., & Sampson, D. G. (2016). Digital systems supporting cognition and exploratory learning in twenty- first century: Guest editorial. *Journal of Computing in Higher Education, 28*(3), 301–306.
Spector, J. M., Ifenthaler, D., Sampson, D. G., & Isaias, P. (2016). *Competencies in teaching, learning and educational leadership in the digital age*. New York, NY: Springer.
Su, K.-D., & Yeh, S.-C. (2015). Effective assessments of integrated animations to explore college students' physics learning performances. *Procedia – Social and Behavioral Sciences, 176*, 588–595.
Veletsianos, G., & Shepherdson, P. (2016). A systematic analysis and synthesis of the empirical MOOC literature published in 2013–2015. *International Review of Research in Open and Distance Learning, 17*(2), 198–221. Retrieved from http://www.irrodl.org/index.php/irrodl/article/view/2448
Wiley, D., Webb, A., Weston, S., & Tonks, D. (2017). A preliminary exploration of the relationships between student-created OER, sustainability, and students success. *International Review of Research in Open and Distributed Learning, 18*(4). https://doi.org/10.19173/irrodl.v18i4.3022

Barbara K. Son is a professor of business and sustainable management at Anaheim University. Her current research focuses on global health, the healthcare industry, and management education. She has authored scholarly publications in healthcare, business services, and online education. She was vice president and cofounder of the International Association Management Group. She served as a site reviewer of business-degree and online programs for the California Bureau for Private Post-Secondary and Vocational Education.

Part II
Analytics for Improving Learning Experiences

Chapter 4
Building a Learning Experience: What Do Learners' Online Interaction Data Imply?

Mehmet Kokoç and Arif Altun

Abstract It is still under debate whether learners' interaction data within e-learning and/or open learning environments could be considered as reflections of their learning experiences to be effective or not. Therefore, it is meaningful to explore the nature of these interactions and to make meaningful conclusions. The purpose of this study is to model learners' learning experiences based on their interaction data in an LMS. The study was designed to understand the nature of interactions and to observe whether interaction types display an observable meaningful pattern. For this purpose, a course titled Computer Networks and Communication was designed and taught in a learning management system, where learners could receive real-time responses and monitor their process through dashboards as recommendations for their learning process. Thirty-one metrics were gathered from database records, which yielded a common factor with six subfactors, where the highest correlation was between learners–learning dashboards interactions and learners–learning objects. In addition, this factorial structure could be considered a holistic view of a learning experience based on the interaction data within a learning management system. Another finding of this study indicated that learners' interaction with learning dashboards had been a meaningful dimension of their overall learning experiences. The results of this study present instructional design cues and pedagogical outcomes.

M. Kokoç (✉)
Department of Computer Education and Instructional Technologies,
Fatih Faculty of Education, Trabzon University, Trabzon, Turkey
e-mail: kokoc@trabzon.edu.tr; http://www.ontolab.hacettepe.edu.tr/en

A. Altun
Department of Computer Education and Instructional Technologies, College of Education,
Hacettepe University, Ankara, Turkey
e-mail: altunar@hacettepe.edu.tr; http://www.ontolab.hacettepe.edu.tr/en

D. Sampson et al. (eds.), *Learning Technologies for Transforming Large-Scale Teaching, Learning, and Assessment*, https://doi.org/10.1007/978-3-030-15130-0_4

1 Introduction

In recent years, interest in Learning Management Systems (LMSs) has been increasing dramatically. Courses delivered via LMSs have widely used in universities. Availability of online courses in different subjects, with space and time flexibility, has led to an increase in demand through LMSs where learners can dive into a learning experience individually and/or collaboratively. Previous studies have shown that learning experiences in LMSs differ from face-to-face or traditional digitally mediated courses (Milligan & Griffin, 2016). Online courses provide learners different contexts and settings from face-to-face environment. These differences have also transformed the characteristics of pedagogy on the internet (Gros, Suárez-Guerrero, & Anderson, 2016), among which are self-regulation skills of learners, learner activities, and quality of interaction (Cerezo, Sánchez-Santillán, Paule-Ruiz, & Núñez, 2016; Friesen & Kuskis, 2013). Thus, online learning experiences need to be analyzed based on interaction data in online learning. This study attempts to show that how learners' interaction pattern emerge within an LMS and whether this pattern would be indicative of online learning experiences.

1.1 Online Learning Experience

Term of learning experience is defined from various perspectives in the literature. Roth and Jornet (2014) state that learning in and through experience is a mere truism. Forlizzi and Ford (2000) use the term "experience" to refer to designing and developing interactions between users and products. From social-cognitive perspectives (Bandura, 1989), it can be said that one of the essential elements that has effect on learning is the sole interaction among individual capacities, behaviors and environment. Driscoll (2013) emphasize that learning comes about a learners' experience through interactions whether within a traditional learning setting or not. Considering these definitions, a learning experience can be defined as interactive and complex process in which learning takes place among learners, instructors and learning resources not only in face-to-face environments but also in online learning environments like in LMSs.

Online learning experience can be varied based on learning context and interaction opportunities in an online learning environment. Features and tools of an online learning environment have diversified the ways in which learning experiences occur considering media effect (Friesen & Kuskis, 2013). LMSs can support learners by providing learning materials (content online, videos etc.), learning tasks, discussion forums, quizzes, assignment, and assessment activities (Piña, 2010). In other words, a packaged set of intended learning experience can be delivered via LMSs through multiple course content and learning activities (Park, 2015). After enrolling in a course, online learning experience start by learners' access and interaction with learning materials/activities within LMSs. Learners can read course content, watch lecture videos, participate in discussions, share their opinions with other learners and instructor, engage in learning activities, complete learning tasks and assignments according to learning goal of the course. Also, learners can freely select course content and control their learning pace (Li & Tsai, 2017). As an important feature, LMSs automatically record those interaction data in a database, such as number of views for course content, text in discussion boards, and total time spent online. With these indicators, learners' every action and interaction from course starting date to course end date form their online learning experiences in LMSs. In the same vein, Park (2015) notes that overall online learning experience is made up for a lot of smaller experiences in online learning environment.

Learning experiences of learners should be effective and optimized to have high learning performance in online learning. What is important at this point is to determine which of those indicators could be investigated to better understand their learning experiences. Interaction data derived from LMS logs, for example, have also been used as essential indicators of online learning experiences in the field of learning analytics (You, 2016; Park, 2015). These interaction data provide a wealth of information about learning process (Doleck, Basnet, Poitras, & Lajoie, 2015; Joksimović, Gašević, Loughin, Kovanović, & Hatala, 2015). Thus far, a number of studies have revealed significantly an association between interaction patterns of learners and online learning outcomes (Akçapınar, Altun, & Aşkar, 2015; Cerezo et al., 2016; Li & Tsai, 2017; You, 2016). For example, Akçapınar et al. (2015) have found that students' login counts and durations, participation in online discussions, writing reflections and tagging these reflections predict students' academic performance significantly. In their detailed analysis, Cerezo et al. (2016) concluded that the different patterns of interaction with the LMS were associated with learning performances of learners. Similarly, Li and Tsai (2017) found that three behavior patterns, which were clustered based on learners' viewing behaviors, were also associated with learning performances. In another study, You (2016) revealed that learners' regular study, late submissions of assignments, number of logins, and replies significantly predicted learners' course achievement. These studies clearly indicate that there is a strong relationship between LMSs interaction data and learning performance. Thus, more insight into interaction pattern indicating learning behaviors of learners is essential to understanding effective online learning experience in LMSs.

1.2 Interaction in Online Learning

There are multiple definitions of interaction that are varying depending on various theoretical perspectives and learning context as a term. Moore (1989) and Wagner (1994) define interaction as reciprocal events occuring between two objects and two actions. They emphasize that interaction involves behaviors where individuals and groups directly influence one another. Similarly, interaction is, for Muirhead and Juwah (2005), the event which occurs between two or more objects and participants synchronously and/or asynchronously. It is expected that interaction results in a change in terms of behavior or cognition. Considering learning context, Thurmond and Wambach (2004) state that "*the goal of interaction is to increase understanding of the course content or mastery of the defined goals.*" (p. 4).

Frameworks of interaction in the literature have been explained by taking into account multiple types of interaction. As commonly used framework in studies in online learning, Moore (1989) proposes three types of interactions: (1) student–student, (2) student–instructor, and (3) student–content interaction types. Emerging new types of interactions according to contemporary technological affordances and ICT tools that are used in online learning environment have expanded the Moore's interaction framework. For example, Hillman, Willis, and Gunawardena (1994) explain a type of interaction called "learner–interface interaction," which is a process of manipulating tools to accomplish a task. Sutton (2000) describes another type of interaction called "vicarious interaction" that is defined as "vicarious interaction takes place *when a student actively observes and processes both sides of a direct interaction between two other students or between another student and the instructor*" (p. 4). Considering the context of e-learning and new technologies, Bouhnik and Marcus (2006) propose a model with four types of interaction built on Moore's framework. They identify a new type of interaction that they refer to as "*interaction with the system.*" They emphasize close relationship between types of interactions that take place in the same learning medium. Besides, separating different types of interactions is difficult due to developments in academic analytics and social networking (Friesen & Kuskis, 2013).

The proposed types of interaction defined by researchers have contributed to improve our conceptual understanding of how interaction occurs and relates learning experience in online learning environment. Considering definition of interaction and interaction types, it can be said that there is a consensus regarding learning that occurs when a learner interacts with a learning environment or with other learners (Tirri & Kuusisto, 2013). To have effective learning experiences, interaction is a fundamental component in online learning environments in terms of learners, teachers, and learning context (Arbaugh & Benbunan-Fich, 2007; Joksimović et al., 2015). There are evidences in the literature that interaction plays a crucial role in learner satisfaction (Lee & Rha, 2009), learning outcomes (Agudo, Iglesias-Pradas, Conde-González, & Hernández-García, 2014), and efficacy of online learning (Nandi, Hamilton, & Harland, 2012). Moreover, learners' interactions with components and resources of an online learning environment yield the emergence of online learning experiences (Parrish, 2009). It is further emphasized that learners' learning experiences rely heavily on the interactions within online learning environment (Agudo et al., 2014; Duval, 2011). Thus, understanding how learning experiences build based on interaction pattern in online learning environment may give instructors, researchers, and practitioners useful information to improve learning process and support learning performance of learners. What matters at this point is how to measure interaction in online learning environment. LMSs tools enable to measure objective data (trace data) together with subjective data (perceived interaction level). Joksimović et al. (2015) revealed that the trace data can be used to measure the interaction in LMSs. LMSs record learners' online behavioral action and traces during learning process in system logs and provide log data to teachers, learners, and researchers to improve online teaching and learning. Studies in learning analytics and educational data mining show that the log data of learners can be transformed to actionable knowledge for improving quality of learning experiences (Duval, 2011; Gašević, Dawson, Rogers, & Gasevic, 2016). In this context, it is very important to gain in-depth insight into learning experiences reflecting learners' online behaviors based on interactions in LMSs (Cerezo et al., 2016).

A considerable amount of literature has been published investigating the effects of interaction types and the relations between interaction data and learner characteristics in LMSs. These studies showed that learners could be clustered based on certain characteristics, and academic performance could be predicted by using learners' interaction data (Cerezo et al., 2016; You, 2016) mostly by using self-report measurement tools. Thus far, few studies have utilized objective measures. For instance, in a study conducted by Joksimović et al. (2015), it was found that their analysis of learner interaction data depending on interaction types proposed by Moore (1989) and Hillman et al. (1994) showed the association between different interaction types and learning outcomes. In another study, Park (2015) examined online learning experience using experience sampling method and web log data. To the best of our knowledge, no study has reported new interaction types of learners based on interaction data within LMSs.

When research in learning analytics, academic analytics, and informal learning networks are reviewed, one could easily observe the difficulties in productive analysis to forecast the possible interactions simply by using the interaction types. Although this interaction is paramount; yet, it is not enough to infer whether learning happens or not (Friesen & Kuskis, 2013; Simonson, 2012). Furthermore, there is no consensus yet to point out which interaction type is more important to choose during running learning analytics (Duval & Verbert, 2012). Furthermore, more research is needed to define learning experiences within interaction pattern in LMSs.

Therefore, the purpose of this study, first, is to model learners' learning experiences based on their interaction data in an LMS. The study was designed to understand the nature of interactions and to observe whether emerged interaction types display an observable and meaningful pattern with the following guiding questions:

1. What is the nature of learners' interactions within an LMS? In other words, how do learners' interaction pattern emerge within an LMS?
2. What is the relationship between interaction types of learners?
3. Would interaction pattern of learners yield a meaningful learning experience as a structure?

This study proposes a way to use LMS datasets as a factor to predict learning success by analyzing what the major types of interactions are among learners and which patterns would be indicative of learning experiences. It can provide valuable insights regarding online learning experiences and help us provide relevant recommendations to instructional designers to encourage specific types of interaction during online learning. We hope that the interaction pattern and types modeling learners' learning experiences would be applicable to be used in a larger multivariable predictive model to provide finer-grained predictions of learners' academic performances.

2 Method

2.1 *Participants*

The participants in this study were 126 undergraduate learners (prospective teachers) attending Computer Networks and Communication course in two major state universities during the Spring 2015 semester. Among the participants, 67 were male and 59 were female. The average age was 21.57 (SD: 0.51). All the participants voluntarily participated in the study. Prior to the study procedure, the institutional ethics committee approval was sought. All participants in the study interacted within the same e-learning environment at the same time period.

2.2 *Context*

The context of this study is a formal course titled Computer Networks and Communication. The 12-week-long hybrid course was delivered via Moodle (v. 2.8). The participants attended face-to-face meetings for 2 h each week in a Computer Networks Laboratory where each student had computers with internet connection. The expected outcome of the Computer Networks and Communication course was to comprehend the foundations of computer networks, to design computer networks, and practice in running and maintaining networks. When designing the learning objects and allocate resources for the course, these expected outcomes were taken into account. Content was designed as learning objects where each learning object was designed in accordance with SCORM V.3 in the form of digital book chapters, course video recordings, educational games, and educational videos. In addition, discussion activities and learning tasks were provided through the Moodle environment. The Moodle stores all participants' clicking events in database logs as raw data. But raw data could not provide usable information to measure variables reflecting any learning behaviors like time spent. Thus, the Moodle database was redesigned to gather the necessary data for the purpose of this study. Furthermore, personalized learning dashboards were embedded in the Moodle environment, through which students were presented information and recommendations about their learning process in order to improve their learning performances. These learning dashboards were voluntarily available to students and each dashboard displayed data calculated through a learning analytics process (data extraction, preprocessing, visualization, action, and improvement).

2.3 Data Sources

Date and time stamps for each learner activity in the Moodle were stored in the system database. During data processing phase, 31 additional metrics were extracted from the LMS log data considering learning actions of learners and features of the LMS environment. These data were queried through MySQL queries. These metrics were related to certain learning activity and online behavioral data in the course. Name of the interaction variables with their description are presented in Table 4.1.

Table 4.1 Name of interaction variables and their description

No	Name	Description
1	v_lectureslides	Total number of lecture slides views
2	t_lectureslides	Total time spent on lecture slides (min)
3	a_lectureslides	Total number of each access of lecture slides
4	c_forumpages	Total number of forum pages clicks
5	t_forumpages	Total time spent in forum pages (min)
6	v_discussionpost	Total number of discussion posts views
7	s_discussionthread	Total number of discussion thread starts
8	s_discussionreply	Total number of replies written in discussions
9	r_discussionpost	Total number of discussion posts rated
10	c_messagepages	Total number of messages pages clicks
11	p_personalmessage	Total number of personal messages posted
12	p_messageinstructor	Total number of messages posted to instructor
13	e_onlinechats	Total number of online chats engaged in
14	v_glossarypages	Total number of glossary pages views
15	ad_glossaryentry	Total number of glossary entry added
16	v_videolectures	Total number of video lectures views
17	v_additionalresources	Total number of additional course resources views
18	v_scormpackages	Total number of SCORM packages views
19	t_scormpackages	Total time spent on SCORM packages (min)
20	v_assignmentpages	Total number of assignments pages views
21	st_assignment	Total number of assignments submitted
22	v_quizzespages	Total number of quizzes pages views
23	ct_quizzes	Total number of quizzes completed
24	t_quizzes	Total time spent on quizzes (min)
25	v_quizzesfeedback	Total number of feedback views
26	a_learningdashboard	Total number of PLD accessed
27	v_learningdashboard1	Total number of first section of PLD views
28	v_learningdashboard2	Total number of second section of PLD views
29	v_learningdashboard3	Total number of third section of PLD views
30	v_learningdashboard4	Total number of fourth section of PLD views
31	t_learningdashboards	Total time spent on PLD (min)

2.4 *Data Analysis*

In order to explore the interaction pattern, as a feature selection method, principal component analysis (PCA) was executed (Kantardzic, 2011). This analysis initiates the process by m times of variables in the dataset, runs reduction and rotation analysis, and yield k times linear components ($k < m$). Given the learning trajectory of learners and the modules of the Moodle, an initial analysis indicated a correlation among 31 variables; therefore, the rotation in PCA was chosen to be direct oblique rotation (see, Alpar, 2011; Field, 2009). In order to explore the relations between factors, a correlation analysis was run. Then, in order to observe whether these learning experiences are hidden within the navigational patterns embedded in the related factors, a hierarchical factorial analysis was run. Finally, the corresponding fit indices were reviewed (RMSEA, CFI, GFI, NNFI) to check whether the model fitted with the data.

3 Results

3.1 *The Nature of Learners' Interactions in an e-Learning Environment*

This study is designed to investigate learners' interactional behaviors in an e-learning environment to infer to what extent this experience carries meaning about their learning processes. A total of 31 metrics (variables) related to their interaction and behaviors were generated to be analyzed. PCA was executed over 31 interactional data with 126 observations. Before the analysis, Kaiser–Meyer–Olkin (KMO) analysis was checked to see whether the sampling is acceptable, and it was found that the results were above the acceptable range (KMO = 0.89) (Field, 2009). Barlett Sphericity test also indicated that the correlation between items was acceptable for factor analysis ($\chi^2(465) = 6003.66, p < 0.001$) (Table 4.2).

PCA results indicated there were six factors with an eigenvalue greater than 1 and the factor loadings greater than 0.35. The overall variation explained was found to be 82.35%. These factors and their related items are described below:

- Factor 1 (F_1), consists of five items related to learners' behavioral data related to their interaction with dashboards, thus, named as "*learner–prescriptive learning dashboards interaction.*"
- Factor 2 (F_2), consists of six items related to learners' interaction data in Forum discussions, thus named as "*learner–learner interaction.*"
- Factor 3 (F_3), consists of seven items related to learners' interaction data in accessing learning objects, and one item related to examination feedback, and one related to navigation between learning tasks. Exam feedback was provided as a response to their quizzes, embedded within learning tasks. This feedback information is provided with a button interaction, available for learners on a

Table 4.2 Results of the PCA

	Factor loadings					
Metrics	Factor 1	Factor 2	Factor 3	Factor 4	Factor 5	Factor 6
v_learningdashboard3	0.959					
v_learningdashboard2	0.943					
v_learningdashboard4	0.937					
a_learningdashboard	0.895					
v_learningdashboard1	0.843					
t_learningdashboards	0.513					
s_discussionthread		0.624				
v_discussionpost		0.589				
r_discussionpost		0.577				
c_forumpages		0.425				
t_forumpages		0.389				
v_discussionpost		0.369				
t_scormpackages			0.997			
v_scormpackages			0.953			
v_lectureslides			0.890			
t_lectureslides			0.874			
a_lectureslides			0.850			
v_videolectures			0.530			
v_quizzesfeedback			0.468			
v_additionalresources			0.467			
v_assignmentpages			0.388			
ad_glossaryentry				0.970		
v_glossarypages				0.952		
p_messageinstructor					0.909	
e_onlinechats					0.638	
p_personalmessage					0.562	
c_messagepages					0.518	
t_quizzes						0.768
ct_quizzes						0.734
st_assignment						0.515
v_quizzespages						0.510
Eigenvalues	16.36	3.15	2.04	1.57	1.31	1.08
Explained variances %	52.78	10.18	6.58	5.07	4.22	3.50

voluntarily base. As to the learning tasks, each learning task was provided to learners within the course materials and is available to them when more details are sought.

- Therefore, this factor is titled as "*learner–learning object interaction*."
- Factor 4 (F_4), consists of two items related to learners' interactional data with the glossary; thus, named as "*learner–glossary interaction*."
- Factor 5 (F_5), consists of six items related to learners' interactional data during messaging with each other; thus, named as "*learner–messaging interaction*."

Table 4.3 The correlation matrix

	F_1	F_2	F_3	F_4	F_5	F_6
F_1	1.000					
F_2	0.211[a]	1.000				
F_3	0.580[b]	0.163	1.000			
F_4	0.375[b]	0.178[a]	0.441[b]	1.000		
F_5	0.251[b]	0.195[a]	0.347[b]	0.273[b]	1.000	
F_6	0.389[b]	0.066	0.297[b]	0.063	0.079	1.000

[a]Correlation is significant at the 0.05 level
[b]Correlation is significant at the 0.01 level

- Factor 6 (F_6), consists of three items related to learners' interactional data with short exams, and one item related to their submission task. Since these data are related to their assessment experiences, this factor is named as "*learner–assessment interaction.*"

3.2 *The Relationship Between Interaction Types*

The correlation matrix obtained from the measurement model is presented in Table 4.3.

When the correlation matrix is considered, the highest correlation was between factor 1 and 3; and, factor 3 and 4; the lowest, on the other hand, was between factor 2 and 6, and factor 4 and 6. These findings indicate that learner–learning object interaction has a positive and medium-level correlation with learner–learning dashboards and learner–glossary interaction. Furthermore, learner–assessment interaction has a positive yet low correlation with learner–learner interaction and learner–glossary interaction.

PCA results indicated six different factors available when understanding the learning experiences in this particular context. This result is an expected outcome in an e-learning environment when considering that learners navigate among the learning sources, initiate and continue with mutual messaging among peers, and engage in learning related activities.

3.3 *Would Interaction Pattern of Learners Yield a Meaningful Learning Experience as a Structure?*

In order to observe whether the interaction patterns seem to indicate a constructive learning experience, a hierarchical factor analysis was run. The analysis results are presented in Fig. 4.1.

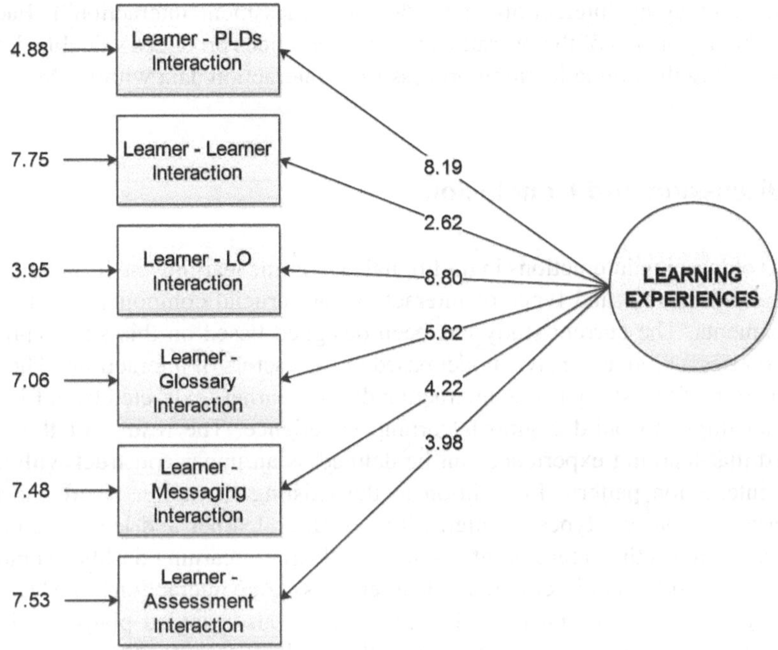

Fig. 4.1 *t*-Values in hierarchical factor analysis

Table 4.4 Fit indices

Fit indices	Acceptable values	Analysis results
CFI	CFI > 0.90	0.97
GFI	GFI > 0.90	0.97
NNFI	NNFI > 0.90	0.96
RMSEA	RMSEA < 0.08	0.062

In order to see the model-data fit in the structural model, the fit indices and acceptable values proposed by Jöreskog, Olsson, and Wallentin (2016) are presented in Table 4.4.

When the structure in Fig. 4.1 and the values in Table 4.4 are reviewed, it can be concluded that the fit indices are within the acceptable range and the model-fit indices are established.

These findings indicate that when learners' interactions in an e-learning environment are examined, it can be concluded that their behavioral patterns indicate that they develop a learning experience within this context, consisting of six different components (i.e., "learner–learning dashboard interaction," "learner–learner interaction," "learner–learning object interaction," "learner–glossary interaction," "learner–messaging interaction," and "learner–assessment interaction"). Each of these subcomponents of the overall learning experiences produces valuable data for understanding the online learning process from interaction data within LMS.

4 Discussion and Conclusion

Studies of learning interactions in traditional and online learning environments indicate that interaction and types of interactions are crucial components in learning environments. The current study has been designed based on this strong premise and proposes a more extensive model based on six factors of interactions. The main contribution of this study is that interaction data of learners extracted from LMS log data can imply to build a global learning experience. The results of this study showed that learning experience can be defined as an upper construct with a six-factor interaction pattern. In addition to the existing literature, where the main emphasis was on two types of interactions (learner–learner and learner–content), this study extends the nature of interactions to "learner–learning dashboard interaction," "learner–glossary interaction," "learner–messaging interaction," and "learner–assessment interaction." Factor reduction analyses also yielded plausible data to help us predict learners' interaction during their online learning process.

Given the analyses' results, we can create a predictive model to predict learners' future interactions.

Hierarchical factor analysis yielded these six subfactors could be an indicator of an upper construct. This finding supports the theoretical framework in that learners' experience is shaped through connections in social context; moreover, they take charge of their learning process (Macfadyen & Dawson, 2010; Vygotsky, 1978). In addition, this finding also supports the existing assumptions in learning analytics research findings in that learners' interactions within a learning environment represent their learning experiences (Bousbia & Belamri, 2014; Dyckhoff, 2012; Tempelaar, 2015).

This study also found that learners' interaction with learning dashboards is a subcomponent of their global learning, in general. This finding has various insights for learning analytics researchers. Learning dashboards enable learners to monitor their own learning experiences; therefore, when designing instruction, emphasis should be placed on designing and developing interactional opportunities with learning dashboards.

It is interesting to note that the highest correlation was found to be between learner–learning object and learner–learning dashboards in the current study. This relationship might be an indicator of a tendency toward using learning dashboards, if students are in interaction with learning objects. Although existing literature reports that learner–content interaction is the highest predictor of success (Bernard et al., 2009), there are some contradictory findings in predicting success (Agudo et al., 2014; Joksimović et al., 2015). Furthermore, in the literature, researchers have reported that learners spend most of their time in interacting with content (Macfadyen

& Dawson, 2010). This study also supported this finding in that learners had spent significant time interacting with learning objects compared to others. Therefore, regardless of their achievement, we can speculate that as learners interact more with learning objects, they tend to use learning dashboards accordingly. On the other hand, it can also be argued that as they spend more time with learning objects, they get engaged with personal activities; thus, leading to lessen their interaction time with their peers (Dennen, 2013).

The overall purpose of this study was to model learners' learning experiences based on their interactions within an LMS and to propose design ideas as well as pedagogical cues for online course instructors. The emerged interactional patterns could be a source when designing online learning course modules (Pardo, 2014; Pistilli, 2014). Furthermore, the relationship between learning experiences and outcomes could be further explored when designing personalized learning environments (Greller & Drachsler, 2012; Siemens, 2013; Spector, 2013). To conclude, these interactional patterns could be explored in various contexts with several learner characteristics considering social and/or cognitive individual differences of learners.

5 Limitations and Future Studies

This study has several limitations. First, learning experience was limited only to learners' behavioral data extracted from the LMS logs. Whereas, learning experience was also formed by emotional and motivational experiences of learners (Park, 2015). Future studies can investigate the relations between online learning experience and interaction taking multiple aspects of learning experiences into consideration.

Second, we have performed an exploratory analysis with interaction data from one course. The measurement in the study focused on quantitative data. In addition, the results were limited to design and educational features of the Moodle environment prepared for one course. Therefore, future studies should be employed to ensure the generalizability of the results in various learning contexts with larger learners group. Thus, further studies can be designed to explore various types of online learning environment (Canvas, Blackboard, edX) investigating long-term learning experiences of learners.

Third, principal component analysis has been used to explore interaction pattern based on behavioral data of learners within LMS. Educational data mining methods such as sequential pattern mining and other feature reduction methods can be used to analyzing online learning experiences based on interaction data of learners in future studies.

Acknowledgments This chapter is a part of the first author's PhD thesis done under the supervision of the second author.

References

Agudo-Peregrina, Á. F., Iglesias-Pradas, S., Conde-González, M. Á., & Hernández-García, Á. (2014). Can we predict success from log data in VLEs? Classification of interactions for learning analytics and their relation with performance in VLE-supported F2F and online learning. *Computers in Human Behavior, 31*, 542–550. https://doi.org/10.1016/j.chb.2013.05.031

Akçapınar, G., Altun, A., & Aşkar, P. (2015). Modeling students' academic performance based on their interactions in an online learning environment. *Elementary Education Online, 14*(3), 815–824. https://doi.org/10.17051/io.2015.03160

Alpar, R. (2011). *Applied multivariate statistical methods*. Ankara, Turkey: Detay Publishing.

Arbaugh, J. B., & Benbunan-Fich, R. (2007). The importance of participant interaction in online environments. *Decision Support Systems, 43*(3), 853–865. https://doi.org/10.1016/j.dss.2006.12.013

Bandura, A. (1989). Human agency in social cognitive theory. *American Psychologist, 44*(9), 1175–1184. https://doi.org/10.1037/0003-066X.44.9.1175

Bernard, R. M., Abrami, P. C., Borokhovski, E., Wade, C. A., Tamim, R. M., Surkes, M. A., & Bethel, E. C. (2009). A meta-analysis of three types of interaction treatments in distance education. *Review of Educational Research, 79*(3), 1243–1289. https://doi.org/10.3102/0034654309333844

Bouhnik, D., & Marcus, T. (2006). Interaction in distance-learning courses. *Journal of the American Society for Information Science and Technology, 57*(3), 299–305. https://doi.org/10.1002/asi.20277

Bousbia, N., & Belamri, I. (2014). Which contribution does EDM provide to computer-based learning environments? In A. Peña-Ayala (Ed.), *Educational data mining* (pp. 3–28). Cham, Switzerland: Springer International Publishing.

Cerezo, R., Sánchez-Santillán, M., Paule-Ruiz, M. P., & Núñez, J. C. (2016). Students' LMS interaction patterns and their relationship with achievement: A case study in higher education. *Computers & Education, 96*, 42–54. https://doi.org/10.1016/j.compedu.2016.02.006

Dennen, V. P. (2013). Activity design and instruction in online learning. In M. G. Moore (Ed.), *Handbook of distance education* (pp. 282–298). London, UK: Routledge.

Doleck, T., Basnet, R. B., Poitras, E. G., & Lajoie, S. P. (2015). Mining learner–system interaction data: Implications for modeling learner behaviors and improving overlay models. *Journal of Computers in Education, 2*(4), 421–447. https://doi.org/10.1007/s40692-015-0040-3

Driscoll, M. P. (2013). Learning. In R. C. Richey (Ed.), *Encyclopedia of terminology for educational communications and technology* (p. 181). New York, NY: Springer.

Duval, E. (2011). Attention please! Learning analytics for visualization and recommendation. In *Proceedings of the First International Conference on Learning Analytics and Knowledge LAK'11* (pp. 9–17).

Duval, E., & Verbert, K. (2012). Learning analytics. *ELEED: E-Learning and Education, 8*(1). Retrieved from www.eleed.campussource.de/archive/8/3336

Dyckhoff, A. L. (2012). Design and implementation of a learning analytics toolkit for teachers. *Journal of Educational Technology & Society, 15*(3), 58–76.

Field, A. (2009). *Discovering statistics using SPSS* (3rd ed.). Thousand Oaks, CA: Sage Publications.

Forlizzi, J., & Ford, S. (2000). *The building blocks of experience: An early framework for interaction designers*. Paper presented at the Proceedings of the 3rd conference on Designing Interactive Systems: Processes, Practices, Methods, and Techniques, New York City, New York, USA.

Friesen, N., & Kuskis, A. (2013). Modes of interaction. In M. G. Moore (Ed.), *Handbook of Distance Education* (3rd ed., pp. 351–371). London, UK: Routledge.

Gašević, D., Dawson, S., Rogers, T., & Gasevic, D. (2016). Learning analytics should not promote one size fits all: The effects of instructional conditions in predicting academic success. *The Internet and Higher Education, 28*, 68–84. https://doi.org/10.1016/j.iheduc.2015.10.002

Greller, W., & Drachsler, H. (2012). Translating learning into numbers: A generic framework for learning analytics. *Educational Technology & Society, 15*(3), 42–57.

Gros, B., Suárez-Guerrero, C., & Anderson, T. (2016). The internet and online pedagogy editorial. *International Journal of Educational Technology in Higher Education, 13*(1), 38. https://doi.org/10.1186/s41239-016-0037-7

Hillman, D. C. A., Willis, D. J., & Gunawardena, C. N. (1994). Learner-interface interaction in distance education: An extension of contemporary models and strategies for practitioners. *American Journal of Distance Education, 8*(2), 30–42. https://doi.org/10.1080/08923649409526853

Joksimović, S., Gašević, D., Loughin, T. M., Kovanović, V., & Hatala, M. (2015). Learning at distance: Effects of interaction traces on academic achievement. *Computers & Education, 87*, 204–217. https://doi.org/10.1016/j.compedu.2015.07.002

Jöreskog, K. G., Olsson, U. H., & Wallentin, F. Y. (2016). *Multivariate analysis with Lisrel.* Cham, Switzerland: Springer International Publishing.

Kantardzic, M. (2011). *Data mining: Concepts, models, methods, and algorithms*. Totowa, NJ: IEEE Press.

Lee, H. J., & Rha, I. (2009). Influence of structure and interaction on student achievement and satisfaction in web-based distance learning. *Educational Technology & Society, 12*(4), 372–382. Retrieved from www.jstor.org/stable/jeductechsoci.12.4.372

Li, L.-Y., & Tsai, C.-C. (2017). Accessing online learning material: Quantitative behavior patterns and their effects on motivation and learning performance. *Computers & Education, 114*, 286–297. https://doi.org/10.1016/j.compedu.2017.07.007

Macfadyen, L. P., & Dawson, S. (2010). Mining LMS data to develop an "early warning system" for educators: A proof of concept. *Computers & Education, 54*(2), 588–599. https://doi.org/10.1016/j.compedu.2009.09.008

Milligan, S., & Griffin, P. (2016). Understanding learning and learning design in MOOCs: A measurement-based interpretation. *Journal of Learning Analytics, 3*(2), 8–15.

Moore, M. G. (1989). Three types of interaction. *American Journal of Distance Education, 3*(2), 1–6.

Muirhead, B., & Juwah, C. (2005). Interactivity in computer-mediated college and university education: A recent review of the literature. *Journal of Educational Technology & Society, 7*(1), 12–20.

Nandi, D., Hamilton, M., & Harland, J. (2012). Evaluating the quality of interaction in asynchronous discussion forums in fully online courses. *Distance Education, 33*(1), 5–30. https://doi.org/10.1080/01587919.2012.667957

Pardo, A. (2014). Designing learning analytics experiences. In J. A. Larusson & B. White (Eds.), *Learning analytics: From research to practice* (pp. 15–38). New York, NY: Springer.

Park, S. (2015). Examining Learning Experience in Two Online Courses Using Web Logs and Experience Sampling Method (ESM). In B. Hokanson, G. Clinton, & M. W. Tracey (Eds.), *The Design of Learning Experience: Creating the Future of Educational Technology* (pp. 269–287). Cham: Springer International Publishing.

Parrish, P. E. (2009). Aesthetic principles for instructional design. *Educational Technology Research and Development, 57*(4), 511–528. https://doi.org/10.1007/s11423-007-9060-7

Piña, A. A. (2010). An overview of learning management systems. In Y. Kats (Ed.), *Learning management system technologies and software solutions for online teaching* (pp. 1–19). Hershey, PA: Information Science Reference.

Pistilli, M. D. (2014). Analytics through an Institutional Lens: Definition, theory, design, and impact. In J. A. Larusson & B. White (Eds.), *Learning analytics: From research to practice* (pp. 79–102). New York, NY: Springer.

Roth, W.-M., & Jornet, A. (2014). Toward a theory of experience. *Science Education, 98*, 106–126.

Siemens, G. (2013). Learning analytics: The emergence of a discipline. *American Behavioral Scientist, 57*(10), 1380–1400. https://doi.org/10.1177/0002764213498851

Simonson, M. (2012). *Teaching and learning at a distance: Foundations of distance education.* Boston, MA: Pearson.

Spector, J. M. (2013). Emerging educational technologies and research directions. *Educational Technology & Society, 16*(2), 21–30.
Sutton, L. A. (2000, April). *Vicarious interaction: A learning theory for computer-mediated communications.* Paper presented at the Annual Meeting of the American Educational Research Association. New Orleans, LA.
Tempelaar, D. T. (2015). In search for the most informative data for feedback generation: Learning analytics in a data-rich context. *Computers in Human Behavior, 47*, 157–167. https://doi.org/10.1016/j.chb.2014.05.038
Thurmond, V. A., & Wambach, K. (2004). Understanding interactions in distance education: A review of the literature. *Journal of Instructional Technology and Distance Learning, 1*, 9–33.
Tirri, K., & Kuusisto, E. (2013). *Interaction in educational domains.* Rotterdam, The Netherlands: Sense Publishers.
Vygotsky, L. S. (1978). *Mind in society: The development of higher psychological processes.* Cambridge, MA: Harvard University Press.
Wagner, E. D. (1994). In support of a function definition of interaction. *The American Journal of Distance Education, 8*(20), 6–29.
You, J. W. (2016). Identifying significant indicators using LMS data to predict course achievement in online learning. *The Internet and Higher Education, 29*, 23–30. https://doi.org/10.1016/j.iheduc.2015.11.003

Mehmet Kokoç is currently a PhD researcher at the Department of Computer Education and Instructional Technologies, Trabzon University. He holds a PhD in Computer Education and Instructional Technology, Hacettepe University at December, 2015. His research projects and publications have mainly focused on exploring how emerging technologies enhance individual learning. His research interests include learning analytics, cognitive profiling, social media and video use in open and distance learning.

Arif Altun has been offering courses at both undergraduate and graduate levels at the Department of Computer Education and Instructional Technology at Hacettepe University. His lectures and research are on the issues related to cognition and computers. He has conducted several experimental studies primarily on cognitive process in e-learning environments in ONTOLAB, which was established for multidisciplinary studies in relevant fields. He has employed both qualitative and quantitative methods to address the development and evaluation of ontologies based on cognitive profiles, development of measures to adapt neuropsychological tests on computer-aided environments, cognitive profiling for e-learning environments, learning analytics and cognitive elements in learning process. He has contributed many national and international articles, papers, and book chapters addressing these topics.

Chapter 5
Evaluating the Usefulness of the Visualization Tool SimReal+ for Learning Mathematics: A Case Study at the Undergraduate Level

Said Hadjerrouit and Harald H. Gautestad

Abstract Research on visualization tools is a topic of current concern. SimReal+ is a new visualization tool that is used to teach a wide range of mathematical topics spanning from school to higher education. However, SimReal+ has not been fully evaluated with respect to its potentialities and constraints in educational settings. While technical issues are self-evident requirements, pedagogical and mathematical aspects are much less frequently explored. The aim of this chapter is to assess the usefulness of SimReal+ in an undergraduate mathematics course for engineering students. It uses a set of criteria that cover technical, pedagogical, and mathematical issues.

1 Introduction

The visualization tool SimReal+ can be used both face-to-face and online for a large number of students in mathematics education. However, despite the potentialities of SimReal+, there are few research studies to assess its usefulness in educational settings. Moreover, there is a lack of powerful theoretical approaches to address the usefulness of visualization tools in mathematics education. Artigue, Cerulli, Haspekian, and Maracci (2009) and Drijvers et al. (2010) suggest several approaches, but no one is ready-made for the purpose of this work. However, according to Cobb (2007), elements of different theoretical perspectives can be adapted and combined for the concerns of a research study as a source of ideas. This work uses the theory of instrumental approach and the notion of usefulness to evaluate SimReal+ at the

S. Hadjerrouit (✉)
University of Agder, Kristiansand, Norway
e-mail: Said.Hadjerrouit@uia.no

H. H. Gautestad
Tangen Upper Secondary School, Kristiansand, Norway

D. Sampson et al. (eds.), *Learning Technologies for Transforming Large-Scale Teaching, Learning, and Assessment*, https://doi.org/10.1007/978-3-030-15130-0_5

undergraduate level. From the instrumental theoretical point of view, visualization tools are considered as artifacts with potentialities and constraints that may hinder or promote student engagement with mathematics (Trouche, 2004). The notion of usefulness can be used to assess the potentialities and constraints of visualization tools.

The intention of this chapter is to assess the usefulness of SimReal+ using technical, pedagogical, and mathematical criteria.

The chapter is structured as follows. First, the visualization tool SimReal+ is presented. Secondly, the theoretical framework is outlined. The research design and methods are then described, followed by the results. Finally, some general remarks conclude the chapter.

2 Visualizations in Mathematics Education

2.1 The Notion of Visualization

There has been an increased interest in visualizations in mathematics education (Hoffkamp, 2011; McKenzie & Clements, 2014; Natsheh & Karsenty, 2014; Presmeg, 2014). Textbooks are filled with pictures, figures, diagrams, and graphs. Graphing calculators have become integral part of mathematics education. Likewise, there is an increased number of studies that focus on visualizations in mathematics education across various topics such as computational modeling (Liu, 2005), dynamic geometry using GeoGebra (Fahlberg-Stojanovska & Stojanovski, 2009; Haciomeroglu, 2011), calculus using the graphing calculator by Texas Instruments called NSpire (Leng, 2011), linear algebra using various resources (Souto-Rubio, 2015), or statistics using diverse digital tools (Forbes et al., 2014). These are some examples of the rich area of visualization support for learning mathematics. According to Souto-Rubio (2015), visualizations are unavoidable in mathematics education, but there are obstacles that make difficult their use in class, such as visualizations are cognitively demanding, and they are hard to communicate (pp. 751–752).

There is no clear definition of the notion of visualization. Presmeg (2014) includes processes of construction and transformation of visual mental images and inscriptions of a spatial nature that may be implicated in doing mathematics. According to Arcavi (2003), visualization is the ability to use and reflect upon pictures, graphs, animations, images, and diagrams with digital tools or on paper with the aim of communicating information, thinking about and advancing understandings. Visualizations incorporate both the process and product of creation, and reflection upon pictures, images in the mind internally, and on paper or with digital tools externally.

Another use of the notion is visual representation. Visualizations also refer to the terms "representation" and "inscriptions," and some researchers do not make a difference between mathematical visualizations (pictures, images, and diagrams) and mathematical representations (verbal, graphical, and symbolical). Hence, the notion of visualization is complex, and there is little empirical support for exploring tools incorporating different types of visualizations in mathematics education (Macnab, Phillips, & Norris, 2012).

2.2 *The Visualization Tool SimReal+*

In contrast to specific visualization tools such as GeoGegra, SimReal+ is a generic tool for teaching and learning mathematics for a wide range of mathematical subjects. SimReal+ contains a combination of video lessons, live streaming of lectures, video simulations, interactive simulations, exercises, and applications. SimReal+ uses an advanced graphic calculator with a wide range of mathematical functions. It also includes pre-prepared applications and a combination of programming in JavaScript, Python, and MATLAB (Hogstad, n.d.). SimReal+ has more than 5000 applications and tasks in various areas of mathematics (Brekke & Hogstad, 2010). The tool can be divided in small subsets, while keeping the same structure and basic user interface. According to Hogstad, Ghislain, and Vos (2016), a subset of SimReal+ called Sim2Bil provides four windows for visualizations: simulation, graph, formula, and menu window.

There are few studies on SimReal+ in higher education. Brekke and Hogstad (2010) reported on positive attitudes towards the use of SimReal+ and its usefulness in difficult and abstract mathematical areas. Students considered SimReal+ as a positive supplement to ordinary teaching, and encountered few challenges. These studies used quantitative and qualitative methods to assess students' perceptions of SimReal+. Another study used SimReal+ in a technology-based course in teacher education (Hadjerrouit, 2015). The notion of usability is used in this work to address the potentialities and constraints of SimReal+. Hogstad et al. (2016) studied a subset of SimReal+ called Sim2bil that aims at exploring how engineering students use visualizations in their mathematical communication. Finally, Hadjerrouit (2017) designed a framework based on the notion of affordances to evaluate the educational quality of SimReal+.

3 Theoretical Framework

The framework used for evaluating SimReal+ is rooted in two approaches that are particularly pertinent to this study. The first one is the instrumental approach and the distinction between artifact and instrument, and how to transform an artifact to an instrument through the processes of instrumental genesis (Trouche, 2004). Artifacts have potentialities and constraints. These can be explored using the notion of usefulness.

3.1 Instrumental Approach

Trouche (2004) considers digital tools as artifacts that can be transformed to instruments. An instrument is then the result of a construction by a subject on the basis of a given artifact through a process called "instrumental genesis." This consists of two interrelated processes: An instrumentalization process that is directed towards the artifact and an instrumentation process that is directed towards the subject.

Instrumentation is the process by which the artifact impacts the subject, e.g., allows him/her to develop an activity within the potentialities and constraints of the artifact. Instrumentalization is the component of instrumental genesis directed towards the artifact. It can go through different stages, that is, a stage of discovery and selection of the relevant functions, a stage of personalization, and a stage of transformation of the artifact. In other words, instrumentalization is a differentiation process directed towards the artifact itself. The instrumental approach has been used to integrate digital tools in mathematics education (Haspekian, 2005).

3.2 The Notion of Usefulness

The notion of usefulness is used to address the potentialities and constraints of digital tools within the framework of the instrumental approach. The notion is defined differently in the research literature. Nielsen (1993) states that the term usefulness can be further divided into utility and usability. Utility refers to the ability of the tool to provide a functionality that corresponds with the needs of the users, and usability refers to how well the users are able to use the functions offered by the tool. In other words, the term utility refers to pedagogical usability, and the general term usability is associated with technical usability.

Other studies differ in the definition of usefulness, but they have much in common. Hadjerrouit (2010) used three technical criteria to evaluate Web-based learning tools: Easy-to-use, easy-to-understand, and easy-to-navigate. In addition, 12 pedagogical criteria were used: Understanding, usefulness, learning objectives, time, interaction, multimedia, motivation, differentiation, flexibility, autonomy, cooperation and variety. Nokelainen (2006) elaborated the following criteria to assess digital tools: Pupil control, student activity, collaborative learning, learning, utility, added value, motivation, evaluation of prior learning, flexibility, and feedback. Leacock and Nesbit (2007) applied a set of similar criteria to evaluate multimedia tools: Content quality, feedback and adaptation, motivation, design, interaction usability, accessibility, recycling and use of standards.

The criteria from the literature described above apply to most digital tools in educational settings, but there are also studies that relate specifically to digital tools in mathematics education (Artigue et al., 2009; Bokhove & Drijvers, 2010; Yağmur & Çağıltay, 2013). Bokhove and Drijvers (2010) used four main criteria: Algebra, tools, assessment, and general criteria. Algebra criteria are about students working with algebra, and how well digital tools can be used the same way with pen and paper. Tool criteria refer to technical usability issues. Accordingly, digital tools should offer an intuitive user interface that provides a trouble-free interaction to free more resources for the learning process. The assessment criteria measure the extent to which a digital tool provides feedback to the student. General criteria are related to costs of digital tools, technical support, stability, etc. These main criteria are divided into several subcategories.

3.3 Evaluation Criteria

Three main categories of evaluation criteria have emerged from the research literature to assess the usefulness of SimReal+ in mathematics education: Technical, pedagogical, and mathematical usefulness criteria. These categories are divided into a set of sub-criteria that are intimately related to each other to form an overall evaluation instrument.

Technical usefulness is a self-evident requirement for any digital tool in mathematics education. It provides a foundation for pedagogical usefulness, but an inappropriate technical use of the tool can obstruct its pedagogical quality in mathematics education. In contrast, pedagogical usefulness and its actualization are less evident in educational settings (Artigue et al., 2009; Hadjerrouit, 2015; Nokelainen, 2006; Pierce & Stacey, 2010). Moreover, the impact of technical usefulness is limited when it comes to pedagogical use of the tool in educational settings, mostly because digital tools are not designed with an explicit pedagogy that guides their use in teaching and learning. Basically, technical usefulness ensures a trouble-free interaction with the digital tool while pedagogical usefulness aims at supporting the teaching and learning of mathematics.

A third main criterion that builds the ground for SimReal+ is the mathematical content in terms of correctness of notations and congruence with paper and pencil techniques. Moreover, the content provided by SimReal+ must be mathematically sound and help students gain knowledge that is otherwise difficult to acquire using textbooks.

3.3.1 Technical Usefulness Criteria

Technical usefulness measures the extent to which the tool is convenient, practicable, and usable for the users:

- *Easy-to-use*. This criterion describes the extent to which SimReal+ is easy to use in terms of layout, graphics, illustrations, and accompanying figures.
- *Easy-to-understand*. This criterion describes the extent to which it is easy to understand the mathematics provided by SimReal+ and how easy it is to access and work with the mathematical content.

- *Easy-to-navigate*. This criterion assesses how easy it is for a user to navigate through the menus, links, and screens of the tool.

3.3.2 Pedagogical Usefulness Criteria

Pedagogical usefulness criteria can be divided in two main categories: General and specific pedagogical criteria. General criteria are motivation, learning, variation, collaboration, and supplementary resource.

- *Motivation*. This criterion measures the extent to which SimReal+ is attractive to use, adapted to the students' age, knowledge level, and development, as well as tied to the students' other activities and tasks.
- Using SimReal+ should be a motivational factor for learning mathematics.
- *Variation*. This criterion aims at presenting the mathematical content of the tool in several ways. Variation should facilitate diverse activities for students, and the tool may be used in combination with textbooks and online teaching material. Moreover, SimReal+ should be used as an alternative to achieve variation in teaching.
- *Collaboration*. SimReal+ should provide opportunities to stimulate group work and collaboration. This presupposes that SimReal+ contains collaborative tasks and communication tools as integral part of the tool.
- *Learning*. SimReal+ should promote the learning of mathematics and provide support for students to achieve the intended learning outcomes.
- *Supplementary resource*. The criterion describes the extent to which SimReal+ can be used as supplementary resource to textbooks, pen and paper techniques, or online teaching material.

In addition to general pedagogical principles, the usefulness of SimReal+ covers opportunities provided for online students and large-scale education for a large number of students who cannot attend classroom lectures. These opportunities are live streaming of lessons, video lessons, interactive simulations, exercises, applications, and their combination.

3.3.3 Mathematical Usefulness Criteria

Mathematical usefulness includes several criteria. Firstly, SimReal+ should provide a rich mathematical content that is sound to the underlying mathematical properties. Secondly, it should support conceptual understanding, that is, comprehension of mathematical concepts and symbols, operations, and relationships. Thirdly, it should enable flexibility, accuracy, and efficiency in manipulating mathematical concepts (Bokhove & Drijvers, 2010). Then, SimReal+ should ensure a good representation of mathematical concepts, symbols, operations, and formulas. Likewise, another important criterion is the congruence between the tool features and paper and pencil techniques to capture both mathematical concepts and procedural skills.

- *Mathematical content*. The mathematical concepts, tasks, exercises, and problems provided by SimReal+ should be of high quality. The content should be mathematically sound and faithful to the underlying mathematical properties.
- *Correctness*. SimReal+ should display formulas correctly and help students gain knowledge that is otherwise difficult to acquire.
- *Conceptual understanding*. SimReal+ should support conceptual understanding and metacognition.
- *Congruence between SimReal+ mathematics and paper and pencil techniques*. SimReal+ should enable the student to apply his/her own paper and pencil technique reasoning steps and strategies, and express mathematical ideas, as well as facilitate students' mathematical activities.

4 Methodology

4.1 The Setting of the Study

The study was conducted at the University of Agder in the context of a mathematics-based course for engineering students. Participants were first-year students taking an engineering course with mathematical focus. The mathematical topics being studied were differentiation and integration. Six hundred and seven (607) students were registered for this course. For some reasons, many students were not able to attend lectures in classroom, but they had access to online lessons by means of live streaming of lectures.

4.2 Research Purpose and Questions

The study aims at exploring the usefulness of SimReal+ for mathematical learning in an engineering-based course at the university level. The research questions are of exploratory nature. By investigating SimReal+ from the usefulness perspective, some opportunities and constraints for the learning of mathematics can be revealed. The study draws on a master thesis performed in 2015 (Gautestad, 2015; Hadjerrouit and Gautestad, 2016). The first aim of the study is to evaluate the students' perceptions of SimReal+ using a set of technical, pedagogical, and mathematical criteria based on the notion of usefulness. The second aim is to assess which of the criteria are met, and suggest some educational implications for a large number of students. Given this background, this work addresses two research questions:

- What are the students' perceptions of the usefulness of SimReal+?
- What criteria are met?

4.3 Methods

This work is a single case study. Both quantitative and qualitative methods were used to collect and analyze students' responses to a survey questionnaire with open-ended questions. The survey questionnaire used a five-point Likert scale from 1 to 5, where 1 was coded as the highest and 5 as the lowest (1 = "Strongly Agree"; 2 = "Agree"; 3 = "Neither Agree nor Disagree"; 4 = "Disagree"; 5 = "Strongly Disagree"). The results show the percentage of students (%) who responded to the survey. The responses to open-ended questions were analyzed qualitatively. The survey included 29 items that were distributed as follows: Technical usefulness (5 items), pedagogical usefulness (18 items), and mathematical usefulness (6 items). The students were asked to respond to the survey using the five-point Likert scale, and comment each of the items in their own words. In addition, the students were asked to provide written answers to open-ended questions. The presentation of the comments and responses to open-ended questions were guided by the notion of usefulness and instrumental approach, and some open-coding to bring to the fore information that was not covered by the framework. One-hundred twenty-seven (127) out of 607 responded to the survey questionnaire.

5 Results

This section presents the results achieved by means of the survey questionnaire, and how the students addressed the evaluation criteria. Some responses are difficult to interpret, especially those corresponding to the category of the Likert scale "Neither Agree or Disagree," which can be considered as a neutral response. However, depending on the context, a neutral response can either be perceived as a negative or positive response.

5.1 Technical Usefulness

The results (Table 5.1) show that less than the majority of the students believed that SimReal+ is easy to use (Item 1), and that 63% of the students disagree or strongly disagree that SimReal+ cannot be used due to frequent technical problems (Item 3). In contrast, 80% of the students strongly agree or agree that the technical quality of the video lectures is good (Item 4). Likewise, 81% of the students strongly agree or agree that the technical quality of video simulations is good. Looking at item 2, no clear answer is given, but the supplementary comments suggest that some students think that the navigation should be more intuitive. Some requested more help from SimReal+, for example in terms of explanatory text when using the menu with various options. It may be that only those who answered negatively have commented

Table 5.1 Technical usefulness

Item	Strongly agree	Agree	Neither agree nor disagree	Disagree	Strongly disagree
1. SimReal+ is easy to use	2	42	28	39	9
2. It is easy to navigate through the tool	4	28	33	26	11
3. SimReal+ cannot be used effectively due to technical problems	2	9	26	36	27
4. The technical quality of the video lectures is good	15	65	14	5	1
5. The technical quality of the video simulations is good	18	63	14	2	2

these points in their own words. Despite these critical comments, the positive side of SimReal+ is that the video lectures and simulations are of good quality.

5.2 *Pedagogical Usefulness*

Table 5.2 shows the results achieved in terms of pedagogical usefulness. Item 6 and 7 provide no clear answer, but it seems that there are more students responding Agree or Strongly Agree than Disagree or Strongly Disagree. Looking at item 8, it appears that 55% of the students agree or strongly agree that SimReal+ makes mathematics more motivating and interesting because of the visualizations, and combination of different representations. This item does not stand very clearly for a positive response, but there are more students who strongly agree or agree than disagree or strongly disagree. This item can be considered as an understatement of item 6, and it is not surprising that the results are somewhat different.

Item 13, 14, and 15 are associated with collaboration and group discussion. The results show that a large percentage of the students responded Neither Agree nor Disagree, ranging from 42% to 55%. Clearly, it is not easy to interpret this apparently neutral response, and whether it can be assessed as a positive or negative answer.

Furthermore, 71% of the students strongly agree or agree that SimReal+ is a good supplement to the textbook (Item 11). Likewise, 63% of the students answered that they strongly agree or agree that SimReal+ is a good supplement to mathematics with pen and paper (Item 12). Further, students responded evenly to item 9. In this case, it cannot be concluded that they learn better by solving tasks with SimReal+. The same interpretation applies to item 10 indicating that 39% think that the textbook is more important than SimReal+.

Finally, the results show that the students think that SimReal+ provides variation and it is a good supplement to learning mathematics. However, it does not come up with any clear answer as to whether SimReal+ makes learning of mathematics more

Table 5.2 General pedagogical usefulness

Item	Strongly agree	Agree	Neither agree nor disagree	Disagree	Strongly disagree
6. SimReal+ contributes to enhance motivation for learning mathematics	9	35	27	15	15
7. SimReal+ is confusing because the navigation is not straightforward	14	21	29	25	12
8. SimReal+ visualizations make mathematics more motivating	16	39	22	15	7
9. I learn much when solving tasks and exercises	3	29	30	23	14
10. The textbook is more important than SimReal+	12	27	29	22	10
11. SimReal+ is a good supplement to the textbook	24	47	21	2	5
12. SimReal+ is a good supplement to mathematics with pen and pencil	22	41	20	11	6
13. SimReal+ contributes to discussion	2	22	48	20	7
14. SimReal+ does not enhance collaborative work	5	16	55	15	5
15. I spend less time to questions and discussion when SimReal+ is used	5	20	42	27	5

engaging. Likewise, no clear answer is given regarding whether SimReal+ contributes to increased collaboration and discussion. Some students commented that they do not want spending time familiarizing themselves with SimReal+ because they were not allowed to use the tool in exams. They choose instead to perform exercises with pen and paper.

Table 5.3 shows an overview of students' responses to issues related to live steaming, video lessons, and simulations. It appears that the majority of the students think that they would rather attend classroom lectures instead of being home and follow live streaming (Item 16 and 17). Further, most students dislike postponing the learning process even though they could watch lectures by means of live streaming (Item 18). The majority of the students responded that they understand a lot by watching video lectures and video simulations (item 19 and 20). Fifty-seven percent (57%) agree or strongly agree with these statements, but there is a relatively high percentage corresponding to Neither Agree nor Disagree.

Furthermore, 60% of the students indicated that they disagree or strongly disagree that they understand better by watching video streaming at home (item 21). Finally, the majority of the students pointed out that they agree that SimReal+ helps to improve their thinking and reflect on their understanding of mathematics (Item 23), but there is a relatively high percentage of neutral responses (30%).

Table 5.3 Pedagogical usefulness criteria for online students

Item	Strongly agree	Agree	Neither agree nor disagree	Disagree	Strongly disagree
16. I prefer doing mathematics outside classroom because of live streaming lectures	8	11	21	22	38
17. I prefer attending lectures even though these are live streamed	44	32	17	6	1
18. I postpone the learning of mathematics because of live streaming	1	6	8	29	56
19. My understanding of mathematics is enhanced when using video lectures	9	48	36	5	2
20. My understanding of mathematics is enhanced when using video simulations	8	49	27	12	4
21. My understanding of mathematics is enhanced by streaming of lessons	2	9	29	48	12
22. The combination of video lectures, simulations, and live streaming stimulates learning	25	49	15	8	3
23. SimReal+ stimulates reflection and higher order thinking skills	12	42	30	12	4

5.3 *Mathematical Usefulness*

Table 5.4 shows the results for mathematical usefulness. Item 24 and 25 deal with differentiation and integration, and there is no clear answer as to whether the students think that SimReal+ is useful. The percentage of the students who neither agree nor disagree is high (43%). Fifty-four percent (54%) of the students strongly agreed or agreed that SimReal+ provides more opportunities to explain integration and derivation (Item 26). This is not a clear distinction, but the percentage of those who strongly disagree or disagree is small. Item 27 provides no clear answer, but the percentage of those responding Agree or Strongly Agree is larger than the proportion corresponding to Disagree or Strongly Disagree. Eighty percent (80%) of the students think that they have benefited greatly from rotation simulations (Item 28). This shows that SimReal+ can be useful for learning difficult mathematical topics. Sixty percent (60%) strongly disagree or disagree that there is no need for a visualization tool for understanding the subject matter (Item 29). This may indicate that SimReal+ is a useful tool for students learning advanced mathematics.

Table 5.4 Mathematical usefulness

Item	Strongly agree	Agree	Neither agree nor disagree	Disagree	Strongly disagree
24. It is easy to solve derivation problems using SimReal+	4	34	43	16	2
25. It is not easy to solve integration problems using SimReal+	1	19	43	14	4
26. SimReal+ provides more opportunities for explaining derivation and integration	14	40	36	6	2
27. SimReal+ contributes to conceptual understanding of derivation	8	33	43	13	3
28. Rotation simulation with velocity and acceleration enhances learning	30	50	13	5	2
29. There is no need for a visualization tool to understand the subject matter	1	10	29	43	17

5.4 Summary of Results

In terms of technical usefulness, many students think that it is difficult to navigate through the interface of the tool. They recommend making the interface more intuitive. In contrast, the students were satisfied with the technical quality of the video lectures and simulations. The results also indicate that the use of SimReal+ is time-consuming and demanding in terms of efforts and that there is a need for more training from the very start of the course. It seems that many students lack sufficient digital competencies and did not automatically understand what is going on when the teacher uses SimReal+. Nevertheless, most students have rarely or never experienced that they could not use SimReal+ because of technical problems.

In terms of pedagogical usefulness, most students were motivated and engaged when the mathematical subject is repeated using SimReal+. The students indicated that SimReal+ is very useful for the preparation of lectures, and particularly useful to visualize problems because it provides a more realistic view of mathematics. This perception is clearly confirmed by the results, which show that video lectures and simulations constitute a positive element of learning mathematics. Likewise, the combination of video, live streaming, and simulations provides the most useful way of learning mathematics. The results also show that interactions with the teacher and collaboration between students are important. Moreover, it appears that the combination of SimReal+ with pen and paper techniques enhances the problem-solving process. Finally, the students prefer attending classroom lectures even though these are live streamed. Hence, video live streaming seems to play a minor role in the learning process, but it can be useful for repetition even though few used it. Further, the students think that questions that come up in classroom are useful and instructive, but discussions were rare.

In terms of mathematical issues, it appears that SimReal+ plays a small role in learning differentiation and integration. Several students pointed out that this subject is well known, and therefore it was considered as a repetition. Nevertheless, it may be useful to visualize dynamically the concept of derivation with SimReal+. This can lead to conceptual understanding according to some students. It is unclear whether SimReal+ is useful when students work with the concept of velocity vectors and derivation. However, the visualization of rotations is particularly useful for some students. Globally, the students think SimReal+ is a useful tool that provides powerful visualizations.

6 Discussion

The theoretical framework of this work has proven to be useful for evaluating SimReal+ in terms of technical, pedagogical, and mathematical usefulness criteria. In this section, the results are discussed, and some implications are drawn for learning of mathematics.

6.1 Technical Usefulness

The results indicate that more than one-third of the students found it difficult to navigate through the menus of SimReal+. They experienced that it is hard to figure out how the user interface works, where they stand in the menu structure, and what to do next.

The validity of the above statement is strengthened, provided that many apparently neutral (and perhaps undecided) answers (Neither Agree nor Disagree) are interpreted as negative responses. This means that the students do not agree that it is easy to navigate through the menus. This is in line with several other supplementary comments and open-ended questions. The comments pointed out that the button-based navigation of SimReal+ is not straightforward and not intuitive enough, particularly for students having difficulties in understanding the meaning of the different menu options of the tool.

The students also pointed out that using SimReal+ is time-consuming due to the complexity of software tool. Some students reported that they do not have sufficient time to familiarize themselves with the technicalities of the tool. Students put time and efforts into many other subjects, and must therefore set priorities. If the goal is to use SimReal+ as a supplementary resource in mathematics education, then it is obvious that more technical demonstrations are needed. If students understand the technicalities of SimReal+, it might be easier to familiarize themselves with the tool when using it out of classroom on a large scale. It is also important to note that not all students had the same understanding of the user interface. Many students found SimReal+ easy to use, but it is nevertheless necessary to improve the tool so that it becomes more usable for all students.

Clearly, the technicalities of a digital tool have an impact on students' instrumental genesis. From the outset, SimReal+ can be regarded as an artifact or a set of artifacts. Trouche (2004) pointed out that instrumental genesis is a complex and time-consuming process and argues for the necessity of students' instrumental genesis to transform an artifact to an instrument for learning mathematics. In similar terms, Hadjerrouit (2015) pointed out that the technical usability of a tool is prerequisite for pedagogical usability and mathematical learning. Hence, the technicalities of SimReal+ can be an obstacle to students' instrumental genesis, if they have not received intensive training in using the tool.

6.2 Pedagogical Usefulness

The majority of the students think that the quality of the video lectures is good, and that the video clips contribute positively to mathematical learning. This is in line with the research literature. For example, Kay and Kletskin (2012) used video podcast with problem-based tasks within pre-calculus curriculum for first-year students. These were available in a period of 3 weeks. The students found the videos particularly useful for visualizing problems and getting explanations of the problem-solving process step by step.

Regarding motivational issues, it is be difficult to interpret students' responses on the basis of the questionnaire. Globally, many students claim that SimReal+ provides motivating exercises that appeal to engineering students, and this point is to some extent revealed in this study. However, it is difficult to interpret the perceptions of the majority of the students. Furthermore, the findings show that they liked the combination of simulations, visualizations, video lectures, and video streaming. This indicates that SimReal+ offers different ways of learning, and that variation in teaching motivates students. This is in line with research work that points out that variation in teaching plays a key role because students learn in different ways (Hadjerrouit, 2017). SimReal+ should therefore be used to achieve more variation in mathematics teaching and present the mathematical content in various ways. The findings support the view that SimReal+ contributes to varied teaching and representation of mathematics in several ways.

There is no clear-cut answer as to whether SimReal+ contributes to increased interaction and discussions. Based on observations in classroom, questions and discussions were rare. This is perhaps due to the large number of students attending the lectures, resulting in reluctance to ask questions in classroom. Even though discussions happened sometimes in classroom, it appears that SimReal+ does not contribute much to interactions in classroom, perhaps due to the lack of group tasks. It would therefore be important in future research to examine how and whether students work together in small groups when solving problems.

Research studies (Bokhove & Drijvers, 2010; Hadjerrouit & Bronner, 2014) argue that digital tools should provide formative feedback to the work students are doing, e.g., in the form of review modes, because feedback supports the learning process. However, SimReal+ lacks this kind of feedback on the mathematical work being performed. Likewise, SimReal+ cannot assess students' misunderstandings or misconceptions, and record their problem resolutions. It is possible that the students had found SimReal+ more useful if the tool had provided formative feedback so that they can follow the solution process step by step. On the other hand, visualizations give another type of feedback by showing mathematical concepts dynamically. This is the strength and added-value of visualization tools like SimReal+.

6.3 Mathematical Usefulness

The survey questionnaire does not give a clear answer on what the students think about derivation and integration problems using the visualizations of SimReal+.

Many students emphasized that these topics are known subjects, and therefore, there was no need for repetition. However, several comments indicate that SimReal+ can provide a deeper understanding of differentiation and integration by visualizing mathematical concepts.

Within the same mathematical context, Diković (2009) found that students using GeoGebra achieved a good understanding of differential calculus. Using GeoGebra, students got an intuitive feel of basic concepts of calculus by means of visualizations. The use of GeoGebra allowed students to explore a wide range of function types and gave them the opportunity to create links between symbolic and visual representations. This study is in line with similar research (Arbain & Shukor, 2015; Takači, Stankov, & Milanovic, 2015; Zarzycki, 2004; Zulnaidi & Zakaria, 2012).

In comparison to GeoGebra, SimReal+ provides more mathematical content and more visualization opportunities, and a wide range of mathematical topics. In this regard, SimReal+ seems to be a good aid, and the students clearly valued the opportunity to visualize rotations, which is a difficult topic for engineering students. Likewise, the students agreed that SimReal+ is a useful tool for visualizing problems related to velocity and acceleration vectors associated with particles in motion, and how the various vectors behave. As a result, the vast majority of the students think that SimReal+ is particularly useful to deal with difficult subjects in mathematics.

Finally, some students think that SimReal+ provides support for learning mathematical concepts, but it does not provide appropriate support for solving problems that requires procedural skills. This issue is linked to conceptual and procedural understanding of mathematics (Rittle-Johnson, Siegler, & Alibali, 2001). The results seem to indicate that SimReal+ provides more help for conceptual than procedural understanding. SimReal+ does provide formative feedback, and as a result, the tool is not able to assess students' procedural understanding. Despite this limitation, it appears that visualizations are helpful, and being able to visualize mathematical problems helps to create more sense of problem-solving. Meanwhile, it can be argued that visualizations may help to promote conceptual understanding, and that the lack of formative feedback is compensated by visualizations.

7 Conclusion

Despite the limitations of the study due to the number of participants ($N = 127$), and the data collection and analysis methods being used, it has been possible to gain some valuable insights into the role of the visualization tool SimReal+ in learning mathematics at the undergraduate university level. Firstly, the results show that SimReal+ provides technical, pedagogical, and mathematical opportunities for learning mathematics for a large number of students both in classroom and online. Secondly, the theoretical framework provides the necessary knowledge to assist designers and teachers in improving existing functionalities and introducing new features according to the notion of usefulness. Still, research remains to be done to make SimReal+ technically, pedagogically, and mathematically fully useful in mathematics education. Learning to use a new tool to deliver large-scale mathematics education is demanding in terms of efforts and time, making the process of instrumental genesis more complex (Trouche, 2004). The advantage of SimReal+ is that it can be used in various ways depending on students' needs and experiences with visualization tools, e.g. combining video lectures, simulations, and live streaming. Moreover, SimReal+ offers good opportunities for online students, provided that the user interface is made more intuitive and easy to use. More experimentations and studies will be carried out in future research work to ensure more reliability and validity. Supplementary data collection and analysis will be used for this purpose.

Acknowledgments We would like to express our special appreciation and thanks to Associate Professor Per Henrik Hogstad, Department of Engineering Sciences, University of Agder (Norway), and his involvement and great support in the teaching of mathematics using SimReal+.

References

Arbain, N., & Shukor, N. A. (2015). The effects of GeoGebra on students achievement. *Procedia – Social and Behavioral Sciences, 172*, 208–214.

Arcavi, A. (2003). The role of visual representations in the learning of mathematics. *Educational Studies in Mathematics, 52*(3), 215–241.

Artigue, M., Cerulli, M., Haspekian, M., & Maracci, M. (2009). Connecting and integrating theoretical frames: The TELMA contribution. *International Journal of Computers for Mathematical Learning, 14*, 217–240.

Bokhove, C., & Drijvers, P. (2010). Digital tools for algebra education: Criteria and evaluation. *International Journal of Computers for Mathematical Learning, 15*, 45–62.

Brekke, M., & Hogstad, P. H. (2010). New teaching methods—Using computer technology in physics, mathematics, and computer science. *International Journal of Digital Society (IJDS), 1*(1), 17–24.

Cobb, P. (2007). Putting philosophy to work: Coping with multiple theoretical perspectives. In F. K. Lester (Ed.), *Second handbook of research on mathematics teaching and learning* (pp. 3–38). Charlotte, NC: Information Age.

Diković, L. (2009). Applications GeoGebra into teaching some topics of mathematics at the college level. *Computer Science and Information Systems, 6*(2), 191–203.

Drijvers, P., Kieran, C., Mariotti, M.-A., Ainley, J., Andresen, M., Chan, Y., et al. (2010). Integrating technology into mathematics education: Theoretical perspectives. In C. Hoyles & J.-B. Lagrange (Eds.), *Mathematics education and technology—Rethinking the terrain* (Vol. 13, pp. 89–132). New York, NY: Springer.

Fahlberg-Stojanovska, L., & Stojanovski, V. (2009). GeoGebra—Freedom to explore and learn. *Teaching Mathematics and Its Applications, 28*, 69–76.

Forbes, S., et al. (2014). Use of data visualization in the teaching of statistics: A New Zealand perspective. *Statistics Education Research Journal, 13*(2), 187–201.

Gautestad, H. H. (2015). *Use of SimReal+ in mathematics at the university Level: A case study of teacher's orchestrations in relation to the usefulness of the tool for students*. Unpublished master thesis, University of Agder, Kristiansand, Norway

Haciomeroglu, E. S. (2011). Visualization through dynamic GeoGebra illustrations. In L. Bu & R. Schoen (Eds.), *Model-centered learning: Pathways to mathematical understanding using GeoGebra* (pp. 133–144). Rotterdam, The Netherlands: Sense Publishers.

Hadjerrouit, S. (2010). A conceptual framework for using and evaluating web-based learning resources in school education. *Journal of Information Technology Education, 9*, 53–79.

Hadjerrouit, S. (2015). Evaluating the interactive learning tool SimReal+ for visualizing and simulating mathematical concepts. In *Proceedings of the 12th International Conference on Cognition and Exploratory Learning in Digital Age (CELDA 2015)* (pp. 101–108).

Hadjerrouit, S. (2017). Assessing the affordances of SimReal+ and their applicability to support the learning of mathematics in teacher education. *Issues in Informing Science and Information Technology, 14*, 121–138.

Hadjerrouit, S., & Bronner, A. (2014). An instrument for assessing the educational value of Aplusix for learning school algebra. In M. Searson & M. Ochoa (Eds.), *Proceedings of Society for Information Technology & Teacher Education International Conference 2014* (pp. 2241–2248). Chesapeake, VA: AACE.

Hadjerrouit, S., & Gautestad, H.H. (2016). Using the interactive visualization tool SimReal+ to teach mathematics at the university level: An instrumental approach. In *Proceedings of the International Network for Didactic Research in University Mathematics (INDRUM 2016), Montpellier, France* (pp. 429–430).

Haspekian, M. (2005). An instrumental approach to study the integration of a computer tool into mathematics teaching: The case of spreadsheets. *International Journal of Computers for Mathematical Learning, 10*(2), 109–141.

Hoffkamp, A. (2011). The use of interactive visualizations to foster the understanding of concepts of calculus: Design principles and empirical results. *ZDM - The International Journal on Mathematics Education, 43*, 359–372.

Hogstad, P. H. (n.d.). *SimReal+/Video lectures—Simulations* [in Norwegian: SimReal+ Videoforelesninger—Simuleringer]. Retrieved from http://grimstad.uia.no/perhh/phh/video/video.htm

Hogstad, N. M, Ghislain, M., & Vos, P. (2016). Engineering students' use of visualizations to communicate about representations and applications in a technological environment. In *Proceedings of the International Network for Didactic Research in University Mathematics (INDRUM 2016), Montpellier, France* (pp. 211–220).

Kay, R., & Kletskin, I. (2012). Evaluating the use of problem-based video podcasts to teach mathematics in higher education. *Computers & Education, 59*, 619–627.

Leacock, T. L., & Nesbit, J. C. (2007). A framework for evaluating the quality of multimedia learning resources. *Educational Technology & Society, 10*, 44–59.

Leng, N. W. (2011). Using an advanced graphing calculator in the teaching and learning of calculus. *International Journal of Mathematical Education in Science and Technology, 42*(7), 925–938.

Liu, H. P. (2005). Mathematical Modeling and visualization: A preliminary course design for computational science curriculum. In *Proceeding of Frontiers in Education Conference, 2005*.

Macnab, J. S., Phillips, L. M., & Norris, S. P. (2012). Visualizations and visualization in mathematics education. In S. P. Norris (Ed.), *Reading for evidence and interpreting visualizations in mathematics and science education* (pp. 103–122). Rotterdam, The Netherlands: Sense Publishers.

McKenzie, K., & Clements, A. (2014). Fifty years of thinking about visualization and visualizing in mathematics education: A historical overview. In M. N. Fried & T. Dreyfus (Eds.), *Mathematics & mathematics education: Searching for common ground: Advances in mathematics education* (pp. 177–192). Berlin, Germany: Springer.

Natsheh, I., & Karsenty, R. (2014). Exploring the potential role of visual reasoning tasks among inexperienced solvers. *ZDM - The International Journal on Mathematics Education, 46*(1), 109–122.

Nielsen, J. (1993). *Usability Engineering*. Boston, MA: Academic Press.

Nokelainen, P. (2006). An empirical assessment of pedagogical usability criteria for digital learning material with elementary school students. *Educational Technology & Society, 9*, 178–197.

Pierce, R., & Stacey, K. (2010). Mapping pedagogical opportunities provided by mathematics analysis software. *International Journal of Computers for Mathematical Learning, 15*(1), 1–20.

Presmeg, N. (2014). Visualization and learning in mathematics education. In S. Lerman (Ed.), *Encyclopedia of mathematics education* (pp. 636–640). Berlin, Germany: Springer.

Rittle-Johnson, B., Siegler, R. S., & Alibali, M. W. (2001). Developing conceptual understanding and procedural skill in mathematics: An iterative process. *Journal of Educational Psychology, 93*, 346–362.

Souto-Rubio, B. (2015). Visualizing mathematics at university? Examples from theory and practice of a linear algebra course. In S. Cho (Ed.), *Selected Regular Lectures from the 12th International Congress on Mathematical Education* (pp. 731–753). Cham, Switzerland: Springer.

Takači, D., Stankov, G., & Milanovic, I. (2015). Efficiency of learning environment using GeoGebra when calculus contents are learned in collaborative groups. *Computers and Education, 82*, 421–431.

Trouche, L. (2004). Managing the complexity of human/machine interactions in computerized learning environments: Guiding students' command process through instrumental orchestrations. *International Journal of Computers for Mathematical Learning, 9*, 281–307.

Yağmur, S., & Çağıltay, K. (2013). A usability study of dynamic geometry software's interfaces. *Communications in Computer and Information Science, 373*, 175–179.

Zarzycki, P. (2004). From visualizing to proving. *Teaching Mathematics and Its Applications, 23*(3), 108–118.

Zulnaidi, H., & Zakaria, E. (2012). The effect of using GeoGebra on conceptual and procedural knowledge of high school mathematics students. *Asian Social Science, 8*(11), 202–206.

Said Hadjerrouit is Professor of Informatics Education and Computer Science at the University of Agder. Hadjerrouit holds a Ph.D. (1992) in Medical Expert Systems and Artificial Intelligence, and a master's (1985) in Software Engineering from the Technical University of Berlin (Germany). He has been working at the University of Agder in Kristiansand (Norway) since 1991. Hadjerrouit has teaching experience in informatics and society, philosophical and ethical issues of computing, object-oriented programming, Web engineering, software development, databases, didactics of informatics, ICT in mathematics education, ICT-based learning, and theories of learning in mathematics education. His current research work focuses on didactics of informatics, digital tools in mathematics education, theories of teaching and learning in mathematics education, technology-enhanced learning, Web-based learning resources, and social software. Hadjerrouit has published more than 150 articles in international journals and conferences proceedings.

Harald H. Gautestad is currently a teacher in mathematics at Tangen upper secondary school in Kristiansand (Norway). He completed his master's degree in mathematics education in 2015 at the University of Agder. The thesis investigated the role of the visualization tool SimReal+ in an undergraduate mathematics course for engineering students. Gautestad worked as student representative for MatRIC, The Center for Excellence in Mathematics Teaching at Higher Education in Norway.

Chapter 6
Participation and Achievement in Enterprise MOOCs for Professional Development: Initial Findings from the openSAP University

Marc Egloffstein and Florian Schwerer

Abstract MOOCs are an emerging trend in the field of professional learning and development. This chapter introduces openSAP, the MOOC offering of SAP SE, as a major example of an Enterprise MOOC provider. In order to gain insights on MOOCs in professional learning, five openSAP courses with a total sample of $n = 9994$ have been surveyed in an exploratory study. Participation in terms of participants' characteristics and intentions as well as actual achievement has been analyzed. Results indicate that Enterprise MOOCs can be a valuable tool for professional learning on a global scale. However, current usage does not necessarily focus on digital workplace learning. Moreover, Enterprise MOOCs seem to call for alternative perspectives on measuring achievement. Implications for future research are discussed.

1 Introduction

Massive Open Online Courses (MOOCs) have been a trending topic in online learning and especially in academic education over the recent years. Departing from enormous expectations (like no less than the democratization of the education sector through educational technology), academic MOOCs currently might just have overcome what is called the "trough of disillusionment" in the "Gartner Hype Cycle"-model (Bozkurt, Keskin, & de Waard, 2016; White, 2014). Quite a few MOOCs in academia fell short of their self-imposed targets, facing challenges like

M. Egloffstein (✉)
Learning, Design and Technology, University of Mannheim, Mannheim, Germany
e-mail: egloffstein@uni-mannheim.de; http://www.egloffstein.com

F. Schwerer
SAP SE, openSAP University, Walldorf, Germany
e-mail: Florian.Schwerer@sap.com; https://open.sap.com

D. Sampson et al. (eds.), *Learning Technologies for Transforming Large-Scale Teaching, Learning, and Assessment*, https://doi.org/10.1007/978-3-030-15130-0_6

unsatisfactory completion rates (Jordan, 2015) and questionable instructional quality (Margaryan, Bianco, & Littlejohn, 2015). However, there is a growing body of research on the design of MOOCs (Sergis, Sampson, & Pelliccione, 2017), and promising developments to reach the "plateau of productivity" are underway.

In this light, academic MOOC providers like Udacity (Ifenthaler & Schumacher, 2016) shifted their offerings away from the ideas of open education toward more business-oriented formats, while the corporate sector itself became aware of the MOOCs. As contemporary workplace learning calls for a reconceptualization of learning environments with a special focus on learning technologies (Noe, Clarke, & Klein, 2014), MOOCs can be seen as a promising option in technology-enhanced training and development (Egloffstein & Ifenthaler, 2017). MOOCs are associated with flexible, scalable and measurable knowledge transfer. They are expected to save costs and to promote lifelong learning. For professional development, MOOCs can suit the demands of corporations which have to deal with an increasingly complex and rapidly evolving business environment, shortened lifecycles of products and services, and a global stakeholder network in demand for highly topical job-relevant knowledge (Egloffstein & Ifenthaler, 2017). However, there are still only few substantial corporate MOOC initiatives, and little is known about MOOCs in professional learning and development (Castaño-Muñoz, Kreijns, Kalz, & Punie, 2017; Hamori, 2017). Therefore, this exploratory study aims to shed light on corporate MOOCs and their learners. For the example of openSAP, a major Enterprise MOOC platform, participants' characteristics and their intentions on using MOOCs are being analyzed with regard to actual achievement, leading to first insights on how MOOCs are currently utilized for professional learning.

The rest of the chapter is structured as follows. In Sect. 2, we briefly describe the concept of Enterprise MOOCs. Section 3 introduces openSAP as a major example of Enterprise MOOCs and as the research context of the study at hand. Section 4 covers the exploratory study and its research questions, methods, and results. The chapter closes with a conclusion and an outlook on future research.

2 Enterprise MOOCs in Professional Development

MOOCs are basically online courses with free and open registration that allow for large participant groups via the Internet. According to the different underlying pedagogies, two major categories of MOOCs can be differentiated (Ifenthaler, Bellin-Mularski, & Mah, 2015; Tu & Sujo-Montes, 2015): (1) connectivist MOOCs (cMOOCs) focus on collaboration and learner networks. They provide interactive learning environments, foster discussions, peer learning and assessment, and promote autonomy of educational objectives and social network engagement. cMOOCs do not rely on one single platform, but make use of different tools and applications like Twitter, Facebook, YouTube, and WordPress; (2) extended MOOCs (xMOOCs), on the other hand, are based on a traditional cognitive-behaviorist approach and focus primarily on scalable content delivery. Typical elements are lecture videos, integrated quizzes and short (mostly multiple-choice) online tests for automated assessment.

Corporate MOOCs mostly follow the xMOOC-model, but can differ from academic MOOCs in various aspects (Egloffstein & Ifenthaler, 2017): (1) They are mostly limited to employees, (2) they are only open within the organization, (3) they may include additional instructional elements (e.g. discussions), and (4) they may include custom-built content. Enterprise MOOCs[1] can be seen as an extension of this concept: Although they also deal with corporate knowledge or product-specific contents, they are not limited to a special target group within the organization. Instead, they are open to relevant stakeholders like suppliers, customers, the government, and the general public.

Recent studies indicate that employers tend to have a rather positive attitude towards the use of MOOCs in professional learning (Walton Radford et al., 2014). Likewise, openness as promoted in Enterprise MOOCs was not seen as a hindrance by managers and HR specialists, so that Enterprise MOOCs could be suitable for organized professional development (Olsson, 2016). In the following section, a major implementation of the Enterprise MOOC concept will be introduced.

3 Case Study: Enterprise MOOCs at openSAP

3.1 The openSAP University

The openSAP University (available at https://open.sap.com) claims to be the first Enterprise MOOC platform on the market (Renz, Schwerer, & Meinel, 2016). Since 2013, SAP SE offers online courses free of charge, providing basic knowledge about product and innovation topics in the area of business and information technology. Applying the xMOOC format, openSAP enables scalable knowledge transfer throughout its entire ecosystem, including partners and customers. The corresponding platform infrastructure (Xikolo Management System) is hosted and further developed by the Hasso Plattner Institute (HPI) based in Potsdam, Germany. This enables business adjustments and technical improvements in a co-innovative partnership. Within SAP, a dedicated team is responsible for managing the course portfolio and the platform instance, as well as the course production with all its associated tasks, e.g. instructional design, communication, quality management and operations. These well-defined processes enable a short time-to-market production cycle and thus a fast distribution of new knowledge to the respective stakeholders.

An overview of the most important indicators on key achievements of openSAP is given in Fig. 6.1. Until the third quarter of 2017, more than 125 courses have been delivered; excluding re-runs of courses, updates, and localized offerings (translation to languages other than English or German). On the openSAP platform, more than

[1] The term was coined by Clemens Link in establishing the openSAP learning format in 2014.

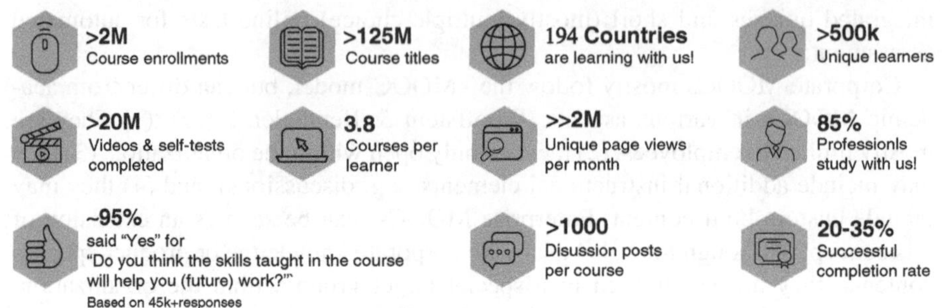

Fig. 6.1 openSAP key achievements (until mid 2017)

500k unique learners from over 194 countries have been registered. Learners take 3.8 courses on average, which has led to over 2 million course enrolments until mid-2017. More than 50% of the unique learners are located either in India, USA, or Germany. Most of the users are professionals (approx. 85%), with only a small amount among them being SAP internals (approx. 15%).

3.2 *Learning Environment and Instructional Design*

The openSAP platform provides learning anywhere, anytime on any device. The platform itself is available in five languages to ease navigation and ensure a global reach. The content is mostly produced in English. Some exceptions (e.g. courses in Mandarin) guarantee a standardized delivery to larger global audiences. The offering is open to anyone, free of charge and mostly free from knowledge prerequisites. To participate in a course, a registration with a valid email address is the only precondition. While it is possible to download all the course contents, assessments take place exclusively online. In addition, every openSAP course follows a well-defined structure. Thus, courses have a defined start and end date, and the content is divided into several weeks (in average 4–6) to provide a guiding structure for the learners. Regardless of the fixed course duration, it is possible to enroll in a course at any given time. Every week, new content is released to keep users in a similar learning pace. One course week includes various learning elements:

- Video lectures of approximately 15 min are released week-by-week throughout the course. Once they have been released, videos can be viewed any time or downloaded for offline viewing. Videos are complemented by elaborate transcripts and subtitles.
- After each video unit, the user has the opportunity to test his or her knowledge. These so-called self-tests are not graded, and they can be attempted several times.
- Wiki pages provide participants with text-based information about the course. They are adaptable for various use cases, e.g. to introduce a demo system used

for hands-on exercises, provide a summary of download links or other additional resources.

- At the end of each week, an assessment containing ten questions in a multiple answer or multiple response format is conducted. Participants have 60 min in total to answer the questions and only one attempt. To keep users motivated, all assignments have a weekly deadline for submission, so users have to learn continuously. The points collected in these weekly assignments and the final exam add up to the overall course performance.

The suggested average learning time is 4–6 h per week. At the end of each course, a final exam about the whole course contents is conducted in the same format as the weekly assignments, yet with more questions that have to be answered within 120 min. The overall points of the final exam equal the sum of all weekly assignments. As an alternative to the final exam, openSAP offers peer assessment for examination in selected courses. This is used primarily if a task cannot be evaluated in a computerized way and thus needs a more complex assessment format.

Participants can earn two kinds of certificates. To obtain a Confirmation of Participation (COP), learners need to work with at least 50% of the given learning materials. To earn a Record of Achievement (ROA), learners need to participate in the weekly assignments and the final exam and collect at least 50% of the overall points available. Outside the regular course runs, all content remains available, except for the graded assignments, final exams and peer assessments. Thus it is still possible to earn a COP, but not a ROA outside the regular course runs. Outside the regular runs, courses are labeled "self-paced courses."

Courses are complemented with additional features: Discussion forums aim at fostering exchange between learners. Course-specific weekly announcements help the users to keep track and to stay active over the weeks. Collaboration spaces enable smaller groups to jointly deepen their knowledge and go beyond the weekly contents. File sharing, online documents, a discussion board, and a video chat are implemented here as collaboration tools.

4 Participation and Achievement at openSAP

4.1 Purpose of the Study

Regardless of their potential benefits, MOOCs in corporate training and development have not been researched extensively yet. A survey study showed a comparatively low awareness for MOOCs among employers. However, once the concept was acknowledged, potentials for professional and workplace learning were identified (Walton Radford et al., 2014). On the other hand, studies highlight that most employers are unaware of their employees' participation in MOOCs (Castaño Muñoz, Kalz, Kreijns, & Punie, 2016). Although a learner's current context and professional role impacts learning in a MOOC (Hood, Littlejohn, & Milligan, 2015), there are still only few studies that characterize the learners taking part in MOOCs for professional development. Therefore, the purpose of this research is to explore the participation in Enterprise MOOCs, which involves participants' characteristics, their initial intentions on how to use the MOOCs and on what to achieve, and their actual achievement in the course. The following research questions are addressed:

- RQ1: Who is participating in Enterprise MOOCs at openSAP?
- RQ2: What are participants' MOOC-related experiences, intended usage contexts, and learning objectives for Enterprise MOOCs at openSAP?
- RQ3: What are participants' achievements in Enterprise MOOCs at openSAP?

4.2 Courses Analyzed

In total, five different courses on the openSAP Enterprise MOOC platform have been analyzed:

- "Next Steps in HANA Cloud Platform" (HC) is the successor of the introductory course "Introduction to HANA Cloud Platform." It comprises of 6 weeks and ran for the third time (second repeat). The course focused on the product SAP HANA Cloud Platform and how to develop native/HTML5 applications, apply advanced security features and develop widgets on the SAP HANA Cloud Portal. Therefore mainly application developers were targeted with this offering. For additional hands-on exercises, a trail system was provided. The use of this system was not mandatory and had no consequences on participants' course performance.
- "Introduction to SuccessFactors Solutions" (SF) is an introductory course and ran for the first time over 4 weeks. The course focused on the product SAP SuccessFactors and how this cloud-based solution supports the full HR lifecycle. The course was open to anyone interested and had no specific prerequisites or entry requirements.
- "Application Development for Business ByDesign" (AD) is a 6 weeks' introductory course and was conducted for the first time. The overall objective of the course was to enable participants to develop add-ons to meet specific business needs for the product SAP Business ByDesign. The target audience included mainly application developers.
- "SAP S/4HANA—Deep Dive" (S4) is the successor of the introductory course "SAP S/4 HANA in a Nutshell," comprises of 4 weeks and was delivered for the first time. The purpose of this deep dive course was to look at the product SAP S/4HANA in detail along the customer lifecycle. There were no prerequisites for this course.
- "Driving Business Results with Big Data" (BD) is a 5 weeks' course and ran for the first time on the platform. The course focused on the topic of big data, on what it takes to extract the value from big data, and presented solutions on how to acquire, store, analyze and act on big data. Within the course, SAP Rapid Deployment solutions, which help businesses adopt big data solutions and related technology, were presented. The target audience was anyone involved or interested in big data.

Table 6.1 Sample of the study

Sample metrics	HC	SF	AD	S4	BD	Total
Enrollments (half-way)[a]	5962	9620	3397	18,448	7993	45,420
Responses	687	2651	581	4529	1546	9994
Response rate (percentage)	11.5	27.6	17.1	24.6	19.3	22.0

[a]Enrollments half-way: number of enrollments after half of the course time including "no-shows." Participants still have the chance to fully reach the course objective (ROA) when starting from that point

4.3 *Sample and Method*

For the purpose of data collection, specifically designed short questionnaires had been coded and linked to the Xikolo learning management platform, so that the survey could be integrated in the course environment in a seamless manner. In the study at hand, participant demographics (six single-choice items, age classified due to privacy reasons) and data on previous MOOC experience, the intended usage context and the intended learning objective (one single-choice item each) have been merged with achievement data (actual credential achieved), and a sample of usable data sets was generated. Data was analyzed using Microsoft Excel 2010 and standard procedures of SPSS 23. While the number of responses seems considerably high in absolute terms, the pertaining response rates point towards a limited representativeness of the subsamples. Table 6.1 gives an overview on the population and the sample of the study.

4.4 *Results*

4.4.1 RQ1: Participant Characteristics

Table 6.2 shows participant characteristics for the five surveyed openSAP courses.

Participant characteristics present a consistent picture over the five courses. The vast majority of participants are in the medium age group "Experienced," and most of them are male. Only the "SF" MOOC shows a higher proportion of female participants. Geographically, people from all over the world take part in openSAP Enterprise MOOCs, with especially high participation rates from the Asia Pacific region. The vast majority of the participants have an academic background. With regard to professional status, most participants are employed and, not surprisingly, mostly working in the IT business.

4.4.2 RQ2: Participants' MOOC Experiences, Intended Usage Contexts, and Learning Objectives

Table 6.3 shows participants' MOOC-related previous experiences and intentions.

Table 6.2 Participant characteristics (percentages of the subsamples)

Characteristic	HC	SF	AD	S4	BD	Total
Age group[a]						
Juniors	18.3	13.4	21.9	13.2	19.5	15.1
Experienced	74.5	79.1	70.9	76.6	71.9	76.0
Seniors	7.1	7.5	7.2	10.2	8.7	8.9
Gender						
Female	14.6	31.2	16.2	16.2	19.1	20.5
Male	84.4	67.7	82.8	82.8	79.7	78.4
Location						
Americas	18.9	22.5	20.7	20.2	20.0	20.7
Asia Pacific	40.2	43.0	40.4	40.0	37.1	40.4
Europe	36.7	27.6	30.5	35.4	34.6	33.0
Middle East	3.2	6.1	7.2	3.5	6.9	4.9
Africa						
Academic back-ground						
None/other	6.6	6.5	6.7	6.2	6.7	6.4
Bachelor's degree	46.4	44.5	49.9	46.4	41.8	45.4
Master's degree	36.7	47.3	41.3	45.8	47.2	46.0
Doctoral degree	3.2	1.3	1.7	1.3	3.9	1.8
Professional Status						
Student	4.5	2.2	6.4	2.0	6.3	3.1
Employed	83.0	87.6	77.3	89.1	78.6	86.0
Self-employed	8.4	6.3	9.8	6.0	8.5	6.9
Not employed	3.8	3.3	5.7	2.2	6.0	3.4
Field of work						
IT	66.4	63.7	65.1	64.6	61.1	64.0
Not IT	33.6	36.3	34.9	35.4	38.9	36.0

Note. $n = 9994$; missing values not presented

[a]Age group: Juniors < 25 years, Experienced = 26–50 years, Seniors > 50 years

Looking at participants' previous experiences and intentions, results are also rather consistent over the courses surveyed. Most participants are aware of the MOOC concept and have relevant previous experience. Looking at the intentions, it becomes clear that participants are expecting to make use of openSAP Enterprise MOOCs mostly in times off their working hours. As a learning objective, the vast majority of participants are aiming at a full Record of Achievement.

4.4.3 RQ3: Participants' Achievements

With respect to participants' results, completion and achievement rates are displayed in Table 6.4. Achievement categories were calculated by comparing the intended learning objectives (cf. Table 6.3) with the actual achievements after finishing the course. When both variables match, participants are categorized as "Achievers."

Table 6.3 MOOC-related experiences and intentions (as percentages of the samples)

Experiences and intentions	HC	SF	AD	S4	BD	Total
Previous MOOC experience[a]						
None	13.2	35.9	26.0	26.0	16.2	23.7
Little	16.2	15.3	12.4	12.4	12.3	15.5
Medium	41.6	30.3	32.7	32.7	39.4	36.8
High	28.2	17.7	27.9	27.9	31.3	23.2
Intended usage context						
Working time	22.4	26.3	23.2	28.4	19.7	25.8
Leisure time	61.7	56.5	57.7	55.6	65.4	57.9
Travel time	3.3	2.0	2.1	2.7	2.7	2.5
Other occasions	11.5	12.6	15.0	11.7	10.9	12.0
Intended learning objective[b]						
ROA	86.6	85.6	80.9	85.3	85.4	85.2
COP	6.8	7.1	10.0	8.3	7.8	7.9
NC	3.9	5.2	5.5	4.0	3.8	4.4
N/A	2.6	2.1	3.6	2.4	3.0	2.5

Note. $n = 9994$; missing values not presented
[a]MOOC experience: Little = 1 MOOC, Medium = 2–5 MOOCs, High > 5 MOOCs
[b]Intended Learning Objective: ROA = Record of Achievement, COP = Confirmation of Participation, NC = No Certificate, N/A = Not Available

Table 6.4 Completion and achievement rates (as percentage of the samples)

	HC	SF	AD	S4	BD	Total
Completion categories						
ROA	38.7	47.5	31.5	47.8	40.0	45.0
COP	14.7	16.8	13.8	13.6	14.2	14.6
NC	46.6	37.7	54.7	38.6	45.8	40.4
Achievement categories						
Overachievers	1.5	3.7	2.6	3.6	2.3	4.2
Achievers	54.1	45.8	58.5	45.3	53.1	49.5
Underachievers	41.8	48.4	35.3	48.7	41.6	46.3

Note. $n = 9994$; missing values not presented

"Underachievers" are participants aiming at a ROA who only achieved a COP or NC, and participants aiming at a COP who only achieved NC—"Overachievers" vice versa. Participants with no intended learning objective N/A were categorized like those not aiming at any certificate (NC).

Table 6.4 shows high completion rates among the surveyed sample. It has to be noted that the actual ("official") course completion rates are notably lower, as they also take the "no-shows" into account which were not included in the sample. However, in the surveyed sample, almost 60% of the participants achieved a certificate which points towards a high level of motivation and/or the relevance of the contents.

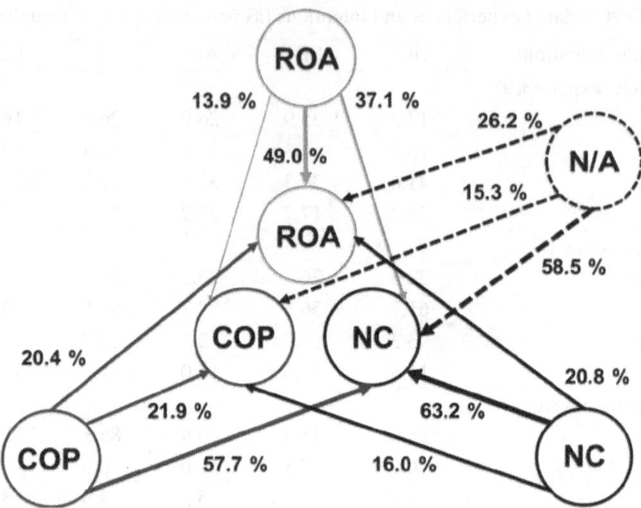

Fig. 6.2 Achievement patterns

Looking at achievement categories, more than half of the participants in the five courses reached or excelled their initial objectives. To gain a deeper understanding of the relationship between intended learning objectives and actual achievements, the achievement patterns for the total sample have been depicted in Fig. 6.2. Outer circles symbolize intended leaning objectives, inner circles actual achievement. Achievement patterns then can be described as transitions between intended learning objectives and the actual achievement. For example, 49.0% of the participants with the intended learning objective ROA (which made up 85.2% of the total sample) actually received this credential, classifying them as "Achievers."

Figure 6.2 shows that the highest transition rates relate to the "Achievers" category—with one notable exception, as the majority of the participants aiming at a COP fail to achieve anything. Generally, the number of people aiming at a full ROA is about ten times higher over all five courses (cf. Table 6.3). However, among the few people aiming at a COP, the majority do not reach their intended learning objective. Aiming at a COP is apparently not positively related to success, which questions the motivational value of that particular credential.

5 Conclusion

This chapter presented initial findings on participants in Enterprise MOOCs, their intentions and achievements by the example of openSAP. Results indicate that Enterprise MOOCs can be a valuable tool for professional learning and development, especially in technology-oriented domains where a quick access to up-to-date knowledge is crucial. The courses seem to suit the demands of highly qualified professional learners from all around the globe.

Looking at the intended usage context, it becomes clear that MOOCs are not primarily used in digital workplace learning, but rather in off- or near-the-job contexts. As this seems more of an organizational than a technical or instructional design aspect, awareness among employers and responsible HR managers should be raised, so that Enterprise MOOCs can become a fully accepted medium of corporate training instead of just an additional "nice-to-have." For MOOC designers, on the other hand, it might be worthwhile to consider building smaller self-paced courses which could then be better integrated in workplace learning settings.

With respect to completion rates, the study indicates that academic drop-out concepts do not fit too well within the enterprise context. When participants are looking for specific pieces of content without actually studying in lengthy academic-style courses, course completion rates might not be the best measures of success. Analyzing achievement patterns by comparing intended learning objectives and actual achievements might be a first step towards more reliable and realistic performance indicators. Additional micro-credentialing with badges or gamification mechanisms (Ifenthaler, Bellin-Mularski, & Mah, 2016) might better suit the learner demands for small-scale learning in professional contexts.

Apart from being merely descriptive, the study at hand has some methodological shortcomings, most notably an apparent sample bias. Completion rates within the sample are higher than the openSAP average, as users not taking part in the survey could not be included. Thus, achievement results must be interpreted with caution. Also, possible differences between the surveyed courses should be taken into account.

All in all, the study provides first insights into the relationships between intentions and achievement in Enterprise MOOCs. In future studies, these relationships should be investigated more thoroughly. A combination from additional sample data (e.g. on motivational variables) and system-generated performance data (e.g. from learning analytic tools) seems to be a promising approach here. Generally, the learning science perspective (Fischer, 2014) seems equally important to MOOCs in the corporate or enterprise context as it is in academic learning, so much additional research needs to be undertaken.

Acknowledgements The authors would like to thank openSAP for the fruitful cooperation and the ongoing support of a graduate research project. For extensive technical support especially with the data collection, we would also like to thank the Xikolo team at the Hasso Plattner Institute (HPI) in Potsdam, Germany.

References

Bozkurt, A., Keskin, N. O., & de Waard, I. (2016). Research trends in Massive Open Online Course (MOOC) theses and dissertations: Surfing the Tsunami wave. *Open Praxis, 8*(3), 203–222. https://doi.org/10.5944/openpraxis.8.3.287

Castaño Muñoz, J., Kalz, M., Kreijns, K., & Punie, Y. (2016). Influence of employer support for professional development on MOOCs enrolment and completion: Results from a cross-course survey. In M. Khalil, M. Ebner, M. Kopp, A. Lorenz, & M. Kalz (Eds.), *Proceedings of the European Stakeholder Summit on Experiences and Best Practices in and Around MOOCs - EMOOOCS 2016* (pp. 251–263). Graz, Austria: University of Graz.

Castaño-Muñoz, J., Kreijns, K., Kalz, M., & Punie, Y. (2017). Does digital competence and occupational setting influence MOOC participation? Evidence from a cross-course survey. *Journal of Computing in Higher Education, 29*(1), 28–46. https://doi.org/10.1007/s12528-016-9123-z

Egloffstein, M., & Ifenthaler, D. (2017). Employee perspectives on MOOCs for workplace learning. *TechTrends, 61*(1), 65–70. https://doi.org/10.1007/s11528-016-0127-3

Fischer, G. (2014). Beyond hype and underestimation: Identifying research challenges for the future of MOOCs. *Distance Education Journal, 35*(2), 149–158. https://doi.org/10.1080/01587919.2014.920752

Hamori, M. (2017). The drivers of employer support for professional skill development in MOOCs. In C. Delgado Kloos, P. Jermann, M. Pérez-Sanagustín, D. Seaton, & S. White (Eds.), *Digital education: Out to the world and back to the campus. EMOOCs 2017*. Cham, Switzerland: Springer. https://doi.org/10.1007/978-3-319-59044-8_24

Hood, N., Littlejohn, A., & Milligan, C. (2015). Context counts: How learners' contexts influence learning in a MOOC. *Computers & Education, 91*, 83–91. https://doi.org/10.1016/j.compedu.2015.10.019

Ifenthaler, D., Bellin-Mularski, N., & Mah, D.-K. (2015). Internet: Its impact and its potential for learning and instruction. In J. M. Spector (Ed.), *The SAGE encyclopedia of educational technology* (pp. 416–422). Thousand Oaks, CA: Sage. https://doi.org/10.4135/9781483346397.n176

Ifenthaler, D., Bellin-Mularski, N., & Mah, D.-K. (Eds.). (2016). *Foundation of digital badges and micro-credentials. Demonstrating and recognizing knowledge and competencies*. New York, NY: Springer. https://doi.org/10.1007/978-3-319-15425-1

Ifenthaler, D., & Schumacher, C. (2016). Udacity. In S. Danver (Ed.), *The SAGE encyclopedia of online education* (pp. 1149–1151). Thousand Oaks, CA: Sage. https://doi.org/10.4135/9781483318332.n372

Jordan, K. (2015). Massive open online course completion rates revisited: Assessment, length and attrition. *International Review of Research in Open and Distance Learning, 16*(3), 341–358. https://doi.org/10.19173/irrodl.v16i3.2112

Margaryan, A., Bianco, M., & Littlejohn, A. (2015). Instructional quality of Massive Open Online Courses (MOOCs). *Computers & Education, 80*, 77–83. https://doi.org/10.1016/j.compedu.2014.08.005

Noe, R. A., Clarke, A. D. M., & Klein, H. J. (2014). Learning in the twenty-first-century workplace. *Annual Review of Organizational Psychology and Organizational Behavior, 1*(1), 245–275. https://doi.org/10.1146/annurev-orgpsych-031413-091321

Olsson, U. (2016). Open courses and MOOCs as professional development—Is the openness hindrance? *Education + Training, 58*(2), 229–243. https://doi.org/10.1108/ET-01-2015-0006

Renz, J., Schwerer, F., & Meinel, C. (2016). openSAP: Evaluating xMOOC usage and challenges for scalable and open enterprise education. *International Journal of Advanced Corporate Learning, 9*(2), 34–39. https://doi.org/10.3991/ijac.v9i2.6008

Sergis, S., Sampson, D. G., & Pelliccione, L. (2017). Educational design for MOOCs: Design considerations for technology-supported learning at large scale. In M. Jemni, Kinshuk, & M. K. Khribi (Eds.), *Open education: From OER to MOOCs* (pp. 39–71). Heidelberg, Germany: Springer. https://doi.org/10.1007/978-3-662-52925-6_3

Tu, C. H., & Sujo-Montes, L. E. (2015). MOOCs. In R. Papa (Ed.), *Media rich instruction. Connecting curriculum to all learners* (pp. 287–304). New York, NY: Springer. https://doi.org/10.1007/978-3-319-00152-4_18

Walton Radford, A., Robles, J., Cataylo, S., Horn, L., Thornton, J., & Whitfield, K. E. (2014). The employer potential of MOOCs: A mixed-methods study of human resource professionals' thinking on MOOCs. *International Review of Research in Open and Distributed Learning, 15*(5), 1–25. https://doi.org/10.19173/irrodl.v15i5.1842

White, B. (2014). Is "MOOC-Mania" over? In S. K. S. Cheung, J. Fong, J. Zhang, R. Kwan, & L. F. Kwok (Eds.), *Hybrid learning. Theory and practice. ICHL 2014* (Lecture notes in computer science) (Vol. 8595, pp. 11–15). Cham, Switzerland: Springer. https://doi.org/10.1007/978-3-319-08961-4_2

Marc Egloffstein is a member of the Learning, Design and Technology group at the University of Mannheim, Germany (Professor Dirk Ifenthaler). Prior to that, he has been working in Economic and Business Education at the Universities of Bamberg, Konstanz, and Mannheim, in Mannheim's academic staff development department and as an instructional designer at Mannheim Business School. Current research interests include the design and evaluation of open online courses in higher education and professional development, digital workplace learning, and data-driven learning and instruction.

Florian Schwerer is a Knowledge Consultant at SAP SE in Walldorf with a focus on digital learning solutions. As part of the openSAP University, he is responsible for research and innovation projects in the context of scalable learning platforms.

Chapter 7
Online Learners' Navigational Patterns Based on Data Mining in Terms of Learning Achievement

Sinan Keskin, Muhittin Şahin, and Halil Yurdugül

Abstract The aim of this study is to explore navigational patterns of university students in a learning management system (LMS). After a close review of the literature, a scarcity of research on the relation between online learners' navigational patterns and their learning performance was found. To contribute to this research area, the study aims to examine whether there is a potential difference in navigational patterns of the learners in terms of their academic achievement (pass, fail). The data for the study comes from 65 university students enrolled in online Computer Network and Communication. Navigational log records derived from the database were converted into sequential database format. According to students' achievement (pass, failure) at the end of the academic term, these data were divided into two tables. Page connections of the users were transformed into interaction themes, namely homepage, content, discussion, messaging, profile, assessment, feedback, and ask the instructor. Data transformed into sequential patterns by the researchers were organized in navigational pattern graphics by taking frequency and ratio into consideration. The z test was used to test the significance of the difference between the ratios calculated by the researchers. The findings of the research revealed that although learners differ in terms of their achievement, they draw upon

S. Keskin (✉)
Faculty of Education, Computer Education and Instructional Technology, Hacettepe University, Beytepe, Ankara, Turkey

Faculty of Education, Van Yuzuncu Yil University, Van, Turkey
e-mail: sinan.keskin@hacettepe.edu.tr; http://yunus.hacettepe.edu.tr/~sinan.keskin/

M. Şahin
Faculty of Education, Computer Education and Instructional Technology, Hacettepe University, Beytepe, Ankara, Turkey

Faculty of Education, Ege University, İzmir, Turkey
e-mail: muhittin.sahin@hacettepe.edu.tr

H. Yurdugül
Faculty of Education, Computer Education and Instructional Technology, Hacettepe University, Beytepe, Ankara, Turkey
e-mail: yurdugul@hacettepe.edu.tr; http://yunus.hacettepe.edu.tr/~yurdugul/

D. Sampson et al. (eds.), *Learning Technologies for Transforming Large-Scale Teaching, Learning, and Assessment*, https://doi.org/10.1007/978-3-030-15130-0_7

similar processes in the online learning environments. Nevertheless, it was observed that students differ from each other when considering their system interaction durations. According to this, learning agents, interventional feedbacks, and leaderboards can be used to keep failed students in the online learning environment. Studies were also proposed on the ordering of these LMS navigational themes, which are important in the e-learning process. Findings from these studies can guide designers and researchers in the design of adaptive e-learning environments, which are also called next-generation digital learning environments.

1 E-Learning Environments and Interaction

E-learning can be defined as the process of building and strengthening knowledge through the use of synchronous and asynchronous communication technologies (Garrison, 2011). E-learning environments make it possible for learners to access the learning environment at any time and from anywhere. In today's world, when it comes to e-learning, web technology first comes to mind. The principal aim of educational web technologies is to support the learners' learning process and increase their learning performance (Richey, Silber, & Ely, 2008). Web technologies especially draw attention in terms of providing opportunities for time- and place-independent learning, supporting learners anywhere and anytime, updating teaching materials instantly, and having an adaptive nature in accordance with learners' needs (Ally, 2008; Hwang, 2014). Besides, traditional e-learning systems have some disadvantages. One of the most important disadvantages is the assumption that all learners who are involved in the learning environment learn in a similar way. However, because the characteristics (learning speed, motivation, achievement, etc.) and needs of learners are different from each other, they use e-learning environments in different ways. Traditional e-learning systems are failing to keep pace with advances to meet the needs and preferences of different individuals (Dagger, O'Connor, Lawless, Walsh, & Wade, 2007). With the development of intelligent and adaptive e-learning systems, it is possible to consider the different learning needs and characteristics. These systems keep data, called log records, about learners' e-learning processes. These log data are used to support learners' learning processes by making use of educational data mining techniques and learning analytics. With the help of intelligent, adaptive, and personalized learning environments, disadvantages of the traditional e-learning systems can be minimized through providing feedback and interventions appropriate for individual needs.

Web-based e-learning applications mostly utilize Learning Management Systems (LMS). In the traditional sense, these systems aim at reaching learners with learning materials. LMS are learning environments with advanced tools and features that are used to create interactive e-learning environments. As a matter of fact, some studies revealed that LMS are used for the distribution of course contents and file sharing (Malikowski, Thompson, & Theis, 2007). Beyond sharing files and teaching materials in these e-learning environments, there are e-assessment, learner–learner, and learner–instructor interactions. One of the most important features of Web-based e-learning environments is the keeping of interaction-based log records that provide important information about learners' learning experiences. These log records are used for the purpose of improving the learning process as well as shedding light on the learning process of the learners. Log records are derived from learners' interactions, such as learner–system, learner–content, learner–assessment, learner–learner, and so on.

The commonly accepted definition of the term interaction is mutual events that require two or more interrelated objects and actions (Wagner, 1994). Interaction occurs when these objects and actions influence each other. Therefore, interaction occurs not only among individuals but also among objects. Accordingly, Moore (1989) states that learning activities present three different interaction types, which are between (1) learning and content, (2) learner and teacher, and (3) learner and learner. Today, the learning environments are not only in the form of face-to-face classroom settings but also in the form of online platforms. During their experiences in the online learning environment, the users leave traces in relation to their interactions. Recently, researchers from different disciplines have developed methods to analyze and interpret these traces (Martin & Sherin, 2013).

Students' interaction with the learning environment and activities has a positive effect on completing learning tasks (Ma, Han, Yang, & Cheng, 2015). One of the methods to empower and increase that interaction is to recreate learning environments in accordance with individual characteristics and needs. Teaching content, methods, and media should be in consonance with learners' characteristics to get the best benefit from the learning environment (Rezaei & Katz, 2004). To put it another way, providing learners with instructional technology applications is not sufficient to ensure an efficient learning climate. The environments presented to learners must also be suited to individual characteristics. Numerous online learning and assessment environments are constructed to serve various purposes. Learners' navigation behaviors in this environment also vary according to various individual characteristics. Cognitive profiles (Altun, 2016; Chen, 2010; Chen & Ford, 1998; Ford & Chen, 2000), gender (Roy & Chi, 2003), ethnic groups (Lu, Yu, & Liu, 2003), experience (Roy & Chi, 2003), and prior knowledge (Rezende & de Souza Barros, 2008) can be given as examples of these individual characteristics. The differences observed in the navigational patterns not only affect learners' learning performance but also give important recommendations about what kind of personalization and adaptation should be made for more efficient and effective learning environments. Currently, educational data mining and learning analytics are frequently used and provide significant opportunities for researchers to make learning environments more effective and efficient. Baker and Inventado (2014) have taken this further and stated that all educational research will include analytics and data mining until 2022. At this point, in this research, the interactions of learners in an online learning environment are derived from log records and are expressed as navigation. We investigate navigational patterns of university students in a learning management system using system log records. Findings from this study, which are mainly based on the educational data mining, can guide designers and researchers in the design of next-generation digital learning environments. The remainder of the paper is structured as follows: Section 2 reviews learning analytics and educational data mining. In Sect. 3 we explain the research model. Section 4 presents the main findings. Finally, discussions are given in Sect. 5, and the paper is concluded in Sect. 6.

2 Learning Analytics and Educational Data Mining

Learning analytics refers to the analysis of interactions of learners in the online learning environment and the interpretations of these analyses to have a better understanding of the learning environment and to improve it, which includes measuring, gathering, and analyzing the data and reporting the findings (Ferguson, 2012; Siemens & Long, 2011). The aim of learning analytics is to organize existing information and explore meaningful knowledge in learning communities' and instruction processes. Educational data mining is defined as the development of methods for discovering unique types of data from educational contextual data (Romero, Ventura, Pechenizkiy, & Baker, 2010). When we summarize the definitions, educational data mining is pattern recognition and learning analytics is optimization of learning environments based on these patterns. Pattern recognition and the application of these patterns are based on the log data in e-learning environments. Log data is defined as information that is recorded while the computer systems are in operation (Kim, Han, Cui, & Lee, 2013). In e-learning environments, log data can be expressed as traces left by learners. The number of clicks on different contents, the amount of assessment, the length of time spent in assessment, the number of messages written in forums, the number of clicks on feedback, and the length of time spent on content are examples of log data in e-learning environments.

In e-learning environments, as well as navigation data, the individual characteristics of learners can also be used for learning analytics and educational data mining. Knowledge of individual characteristics of learners is important in designing adaptive learning environments and defining patterns in e-learning environments. Although distance education offers flexible and life-long learning opportunities, adults are known to dropout for a variety of reasons (Galusha, 1998; O'Connor, Sceiford, Wang, Foucar-Szocki, & Griffin, 2003). At this point, knowing learner characteristics and monitoring e-learning behaviors will help researchers and practitioners in both the prevention of dropout behaviors and determination of learners who have a tendency to quit. This can be accomplished in two stages: In the first stage, the learners are identified; in the second stage, improvements are made in the e-learning environment so that these learners interact with the environment, because these individual characteristics are important for improving e-learning environments. In order for learners' adaptations to be successful, the individual characteristics of learners and the log data must be used and the learner profiles must be dynamically updated on the basis of this data (Premlatha, Dharani, & Geetha, 2016).

In this context, learning analytics and educational data mining provide important opportunities for researchers. The literature reveals studies in which the learning patterns of the learners are determined and the dynamic profiling is done.

In the literature, there are many studies related to learners' interaction behaviors and navigation patterns. In Chen's (2010) study, a web-based learning system is offered to 105 undergraduate students. Navigational behaviors of the students are detected through log records in the system. The results of the study show that students who have different cognitive styles exhibit similar behaviors in the linear learning approach but students make use of different navigation tools in accordance with their cognitive styles. Rezende and de Souza Barros (2008) investigate navigational patterns in terms of learners' prior knowledge. Their study reveals that there are different navigational patterns for learners according to different prior knowledge. Those who have more prior knowledge have more systematic and organized behaviors, and those who have less prior knowledge display less organized behaviors; in other words, their navigation behaviors indicate that they lost their way in the system. In the study conducted by Puntambekar and Stylianou (2005), learners' navigation behaviors in a multimedia setting are examined to provide them different learning support. Students have four different types of navigation in the e-learning system. It has been proved that giving support according to their navigational behaviors has a positive impact on learners' achievement.

Puntambekar, Sullivan, and Hübscher (2013) developed a system called Compass that helps junior high school students navigate through a hypertext learning environment used in science classes. This system shows the relationships between concepts to learners and presents navigable concept maps. As a result of the analyses made on the basis of the log data, the learning behaviors of the learners were observed and the learners were divided into five classes according to their self-regulation behaviors. In printed learning materials, content is presented to learners in a sequential manner. However, along with evolving web technologies, learners can access learning content in a non-sequential manner. Owing to this non-sequential structure, learners may experience difficulties in establishing relationships between concepts while learning in these settings (Puntambekar et al., 2013). For this reason, self-regulating strategies that learners follow in this process have an important influence on learning. Likewise, how much it benefits from the possibilities offered in the e-learning environment beyond just the navigation of the course content will affect the learning process.

Premlatha et al. (2016) developed an adaptive e-learning environment to improve learning outcomes in e-learning environments, called dynamic learner profiling. Dynamic profiling is based on individual characteristics of learners and log data. "Bayesian Belief Network" and "Decision Trees" algorithms were used for classifying learners. As a result of the application, the satisfaction level of the students who use the dynamic learning profiling system was found to be higher. The study conducted by Şahin, Keskin, Özgür, and Yurdugül (2017) examined whether there is a relationship between individual characteristics of learners and their interaction levels. They found that students who have high-level regulation and explanatory cognitive strategy also have high-level interaction. Additionally, learners who have high test anxiety were also found to interact with the e-learning environment at a high level. This and similar studies that determine interaction profiles may lead to future research because, in these studies, the characteristics of learners who are interacting or not interacting are being identified. In addition to these studies, there are also feature selection studies that aim to select a subset of predictor variables. The subset selection is done by removing redundant or irrelevant features from the dataset. These studies intend to determine the variables that give the most information about student performance in e-learning environments (Osmanbegović, Suljić, & Agić, 2015; Şahin, Keskin, & Yurdugül, 2017). For example; Akçapınar, Altun, and Aşkar (2015) used feature selection to improve the predictive performance of a model that investigates students' academic performance based on their interactions in an online learning environment.

Most of the literature studies focus on profiling based on individual characteristics of learners using log data. In the educational context, sequential navigational pattern studies are limited. In addition, a preliminary part of the studies focus on learner–content interaction. Learners' e-learning interactions are composed of many components beyond content, such as self-assessment, discussion, and messaging. In this research, all interactions of learners are studied holistically beyond interaction with content only. Interactions of learners in an online learning environment are derived from log records, and they are expressed as navigation. The aim of the current study is to investigate navigational patterns of university students in a learning management system. After a close review of the literature, a research gap in the relation between online learners' navigational patterns and their learning performance was found. To fill the void, this study aims to examine whether there is a potential difference in navigational patterns of the learners in terms of their academic achievement (pass, fail). In the scope of the research, the navigational patterns of learners were examined using the sequential analysis method. This study tried to show the navigation profiles of passed and failed learners in the e-learning environment. This and similar research results will provide important information on designing adaptive and intelligent systems. Also, passed learners' navigation patterns in e-learning environments provide important information to researchers about how conceptual relationships are structured. The next section discusses the methodology in which research participants, online learning environments, data sources, and analyses are introduced.

3 Method

3.1 Participants

This study, aiming at investigating navigational patterns of learners in an LMS, draws on the data collected from 65 university students, who registered for a Computer Networks and Communication class in a state university. The students in the study group are in the sixth semester in the Department of Computer Education and Instructional Technology.

It is believed that the level of students' readiness for online learning is sufficient, and they have experience in using web 2.0 tools. However, a user's guide to the use of the learning environment was prepared and presented digitally to the learners. In this research, data were obtained from an achievement test and log records of LMS. The achievement test was created by subject matter experts and the psychometric properties (validity and reliability) of the test were evaluated. There are a total of 15 questions on the test. The test results were scored between 0 and 100. According to the test results, the students who score lower than 50 are considered to have failed, while the students with a score higher than 50 are considered to have passed the course. Another data source used in the research is log records. Detailed explanations about log records are given in the next section.

3.2 Online Learning Environment

An open source software, Moodle, is used as the online learning environment in this study. Moodle, which has a serial database, keeps a record of all users' interactions with the system. Moodle was arranged in accordance with the objectives of the class and weekly course content and assessment activities. Course contents, evaluation materials, and other activities were prepared by field experts and researchers. Within the context of the course, the functions of Moodle, such as providing learning content, discussion, messaging, assessment, feedback, profile, and schedule, were utilized. Learners used LMS for a class period and log records of this usage were kept in the database.

The navigational patterns of the learners while using these tools were categorized into eight themes by the researchers, namely homepage, content, discussion, messaging, profile, assessment, feedback, and ask the instructor.

Homepage: The first page that meets the students after username and password information is entered. Most of the links to the course are on this page. Course materials (learning content, discussion, assessment) are organized weekly on this page.

Content: Multimedia contents of the Computer Networks and Communication course were prepared with the help of researchers and field experts. Course contents are divided into weekly chapters and presented to the learners in written-visual texts. At the beginning of the weekly course content, achievements, and objectives are given. Each weekly course content chapter is divided into subchapters taking into account topic integrity. Students can navigate sequentially through the pages with the help of forward and back buttons. One can also navigate freely between contents using links in the table of contents section.

Discussion: Using the forum tool in Moodle LMS, discussion pages were created to provide learners–learners interactions. Students can participate in existing discussions on the discussion pages, as well as create new discussions. The discussion pages include the discussion starting time, the number of messages, the last message information, and the user information that initiated the discussions. Every week a new discussion environment is created, and more than one discussion has been added to it. Students are notified via e-mail when new messages arrive in their participated discussion.

Messaging: Students can send open messages to everyone on the discussion pages, as well as send private messages to friends using the messaging module. Multimedia files can also be sent alongside text messages using the Messaging module.

Profile: These are the students' own profile pages. By clicking on this link you can see the user name, password, user picture, etc. Learners can view and change their personal characteristics. In addition, usage statistics, registered lessons, and grades are displayed on this page.

Assessment: Self-assessment exams were prepared by researchers and field specialists. There are 15 questions for each topic. The questions were prepared in different question types, such as multiple-choice and pairing. Students can participate in assessment applications at any time and without any time limit. They can also take the self-assessment exams in the system over and over again. When the exam is completed, the students are given information on how many points they got from the exam. In addition, accuracy information is provided for each question they answer. After the exam is over, you can review the completed exams by making an exam preview.

Feedback: Feedback is included in the evaluation module. The feedback provides information for students to correctly answer each question in the self-assessment exams.

Ask the instructor: A messaging dialogue window has been added to the LMS course homepage. This dialog window is set to appear on all pages so that the learner can communicate with the instructor at any time. Hereby, an environment in which asynchronous learners–instructor interactions can be provided to the students is presented.

3.3 Data Preparation and Analysis

Moodle records data in the database sequentially based on user interaction. Navigational log records derived from the database were converted into sequential database format. Lag-sequential analysis (Bakeman & Gottman, 1997) or sequential pattern analysis in data mining is often used to determine learning behaviors of learners in LMS. However, in this study, since the LMS interaction themes are structured according to the interaction types proposed by Moore (1989), exploratory structural analysis based on frequency is used to bring these components to the foreground. In the following table (Fig. 7.1), information related to user login id, user name, date, time, the link of the visited page, and duration spent on the page are

Sira	ID	session	date	theme1	time1	theme2	time2	theme3	time3	theme4	time4	theme5	time5
32	23392	1RMDZ1j6c	4.03.14	HOMEPAGE	41	CONTENT	7	HOMEPAGI	14	CONTENT	4829	ASSESMEN	1890
3	517	0939N8Pap	15.03.14	HOMEPAGE	185	ASSESMEN	6	HOMEPAGI	5	CONTENT	326	ASSESMEN	948
667	34134	wtDQ8S75J	10.03.14	HOMEPAGE	8	FORUM	8	CONTENT	5	HOMEPAGI	6	CONTENT	934
318	21181	hMa3NMC	2.03.14	HOMEPAGE	13	DONUT	12	HOMEPAGI	13	PROFIL	21	CONTENT	847
181	31611	bIFvnQ3k6	9.03.14	HOMEPAGE	7	CONTENT	1103	ASSESMEN	652	CONTENT	10	ASSESMEN	792
247	29665	DxylaUe2JE	8.03.14	HOMEPAGE	65	CONTENT	127	PROFIL	26	HOMEPAGI	13	CONTENT	781
392	19206	KJaqVmHM	28.02.14	HOMEPAGE	18	CONTENT	2105	ASSESMEN	454	CONTENT	29	ASSESMEN	756
257	38290	Ekv3bfG9JC	12.03.14	HOMEPAGE	29	CONTENT	51	HOMEPAGI	56	CONTENT	352	ASSESMEN	706
310	39685	h0EYciovYu	13.03.14	HOMEPAGE	5	CONTENT	10	HOMEPAGI	7	FORUM	29	CONTENT	611
241	1520	dQKqCSum	16.03.14	HOMEPAGE	55	ASSESMEN	75	HOMEPAGI	16	CONTENT	194	ASSESMEN	581
496	20935	PVYDHgX6	2.03.14	HOMEPAGE	12	CONTENT	7	FORUM	213	CONTENT	848	ASSESMEN	517
209	34497	chJfvxnHVv	10.03.14	HOMEPAGE	64	CONTENT	2643	ASSESMEN	1596	HOMEPAGI	57	FORUM	474
250	15847	e71eZwjFal	26.02.14	HOMEPAGE	10	CONTENT	32	FORUM	212	HOMEPAGI	179	CONTENT	464
210	17311	CHqmd8Bn	27.02.14	HOMEPAGE	22	ASSESMEN	7	HOMEPAGI	6	CONTENT	267	ASSESMEN	427
365	22905	JICBW0OUh	3.03.14	HOMEPAGE	14	ASSESMEN	8	HOMEPAGI	16	CONTENT	320	ASSESMEN	365
703	20771	xvl9EYfC72	2.03.14	HOMEPAGE	44	CONTENT	165	HOMEPAGI	13	CONTENT	223	FORUM	271
601	3111	ttGLkWJ9z(	17.03.14	HOMEPAGE	23	CONTENT	146	HOMEPAGI	21	ASSESMEN	7	CONTENT	231
457	25880	nXo80Lc2vl	5.03.14	HOMEPAGE	24	CONTENT	258	HOMEPAGI	5	CONTENT	911	FORUM	209
527	15023	R7RXBcQzC	26.02.14	HOMEPAGE	40	EGITMENE_	8	FORUM	8	PROFIL	7	FORUM	150
661	30225	WLtzXuoTY	8.03.14	HOMEPAGE	18	CONTENT	1090	HOMEPAGI	5	ASSESMEN	601	CONTENT	127
740	17192	z4HtscePyL	27.02.14	HOMEPAGE	33	CONTENT	285	ASSESMEN	272	CONTENT	56	ASSESMEN	97
416	23911	IMK4wynBl	4.03.14	HOMEPAGE	39	CONTENT	698	ASSESMEN	286	CONTENT	24	ASSESMEN	88

Fig. 7.1 Sample data table

presented. According to students' achievement (pass, fail) at the end of the academic term, these data were divided into two tables. Afterwards, the tables were reorganized to show how long each user spent on which internet pages sequentially in a single login. With the available data, 437 alternate logins in relation to passed and 227 alternate logins with regard to failed students were found.

Page connections of the users were transformed into interaction themes, namely homepage, content, discussion, messaging, profile, assessment, feedback, and ask the instructor. After the processes mentioned above were carried out, the data, as presented in Fig. 7.1, were prepared for analysis. Users differed from each other in terms of the number of navigational steps and time they spent on the system in every unique login. The present study investigates the patterns users follow in the first four steps with regard to system interaction. Additionally, sequential navigations in the same theme were merged.

Data transformed into sequential patterns by the researchers were organized in navigational pattern graphics by taking frequency and ratio into consideration. To test the difference between obtained patterns, the ratio test was conducted by means of z statistics. The steps of the process are as follows: (a) in the first order analysis, frequencies related to which themes logged in students tend toward were detected and index values were obtained by dividing the frequencies into total number of logins in each system (passed–failed students). (b) Later on, students' tendency toward the second order navigations, after each theme in the first order, was computed using index values based on frequencies.

4 Findings

Within the scope of the research, navigational patterns of students who passed and failed the course were revealed. Patterns were examined in only the first order and second order navigations because, when considering the set "0.1" cut-off point, there are not enough observations to follow the next pattern steps and the students also often go back to the homepage after each theme. These patterns are presented with the ratios in Fig. 7.2.

First and second order navigational patterns of online students and index values based on login frequencies are displayed in Fig. 7.2. As shown in Fig. 7.2a, b, 41% of the passed group and 46% of the failed group interact with the content first. In the first order navigations, the second most preferred theme is the discussion. We can say that in both achievement groups the primary preference is to interact with the content and later interact with other students in the discussions. Therefore, within the scope of the current study, second order navigations are limited to merely navigations after content and discussion. After having content interaction (excluding those for the homepage and log out), passed students tended toward discussion or

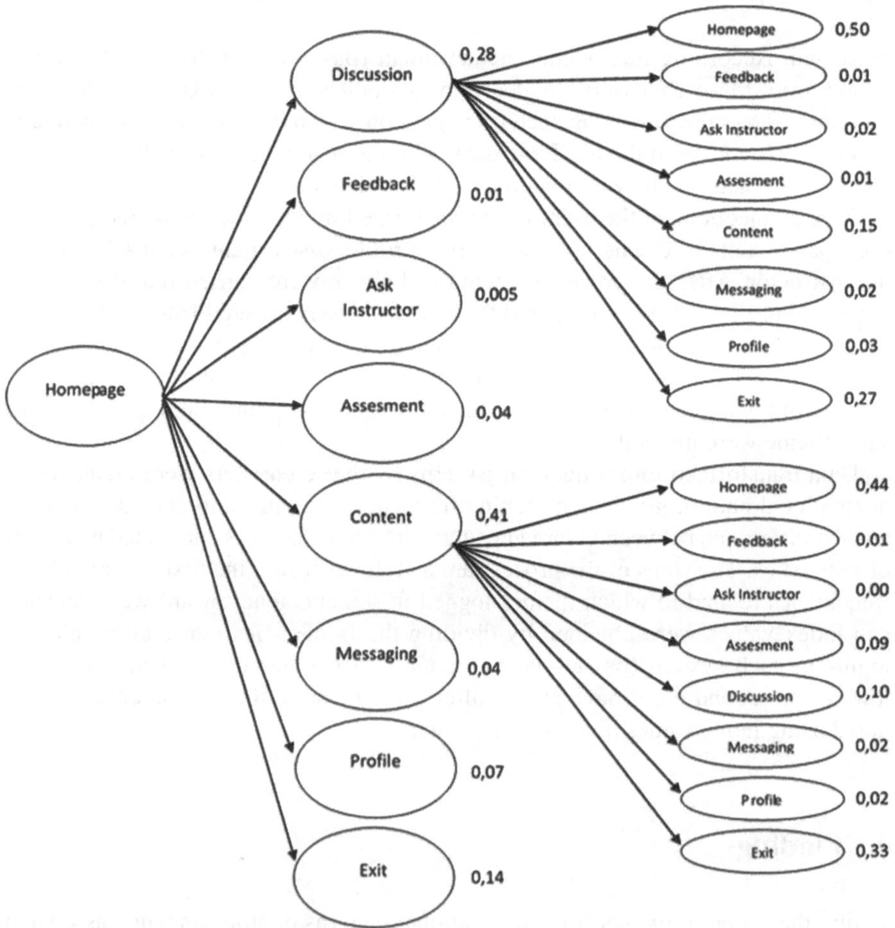

Fig. 7.2 (**a**) Online navigational patterns of passed students. (**b**) Online navigational patterns of failed students

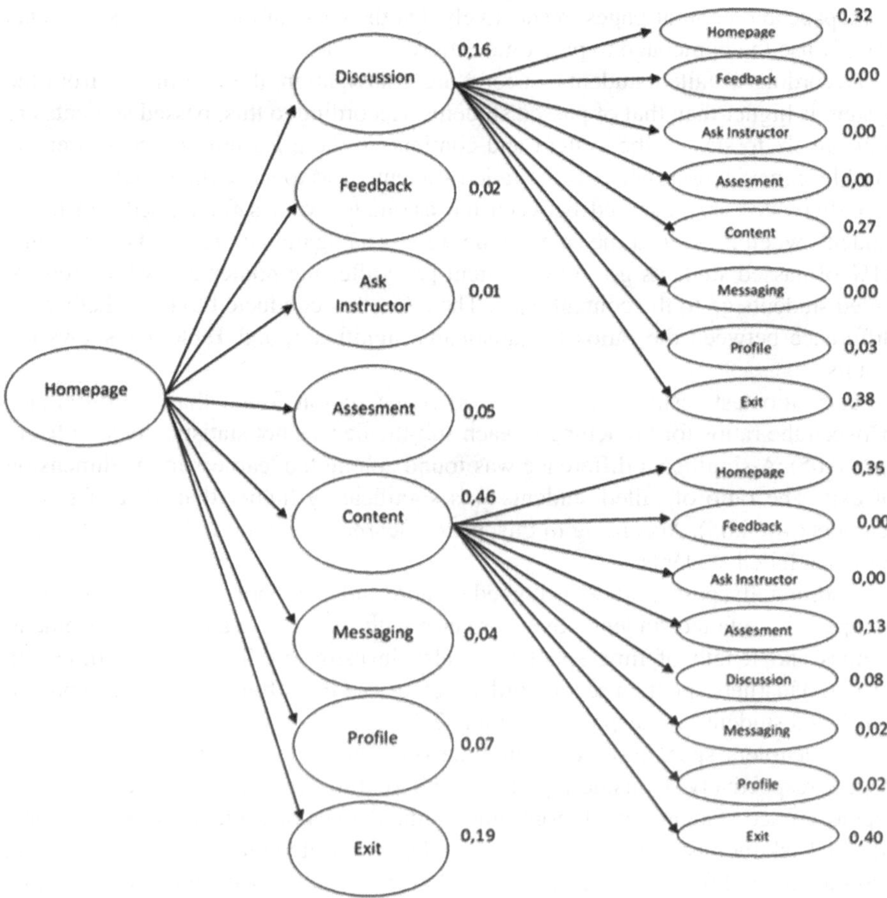

Fig. 7.2 (continued)

assessment in the second order navigations. Passed students preferring the discussion theme in the first order navigations opted for content interaction in the second order navigations. The researchers determined a ranking cut point of 10%.

The numbers in Fig. 7.2a, b represent percentages. For example, 28% of the passed students link from the homepage to the discussion page, and for the failed students this percentage is 16. The most visited themes for both groups are content, discussion, and exit from the system, respectively. When second order navigation is examined, it is seen that learners often return to the homepage in the next step. For example, a successful student who first goes to the homepage and then the discussion page, will likely return to the homepage again in the next step (rate = 50%). Another important possibility is the student's departure from the e-learning system (rate = 27%). On the other hand, a failed student is likely to logout, return to the homepage and content pages, respectively. On the basis of these findings, students usually use the homepage to pass onto different themes.

According to failed students' second order navigation, the rate of exit from the system is higher than that of passed students. According to this, passed students are more likely to stay in the system and continue to the e-learning process after the third level navigation, whereas the failed students tend to leave the system.

Differences are observed between the calculated values for passed and failed students when looking at the calculated rates for navigational themes. For example, 41% of passed students go to the content page after the homepage, while 46% of failed students go to the content page. The z test was conducted to test whether the difference between the ratios is statistically significant, and Table 7.1 shows the results.

The ratio test results for the first order navigation found that the difference between the ratios for branching to each sub-theme was not statistically significant ($p > 0.05$). A significant difference was found among the learners in the dimension of exit. The ratio of failed students was significantly higher than that of passed learners ($p < 0.05$). According to this, passed learners visit more themes in the system than failed students.

Additionally, passed students logged in more and had more content interaction in comparison to failed students. In accordance with students' academic achievement, themes and length of time spent were also investigated. The average times (in seconds) learners spent on second order themes and the differences between passed and failed students are displayed in Table 7.2.

The learners spent most of their time on content, evaluation, and discussion pages, respectively. Considering the length of time learners allocated for each theme, passed students spent more time on the themes of content, messaging, profile, and ask the instructor, while failed students allocated more time to discussion, assessment, and feedback themes. It is noteworthy that passed students spent more time communicating individually with both classmates and instructors. On the other hand, failed students spent a little more time than passed students on the discussion pages.

According to these findings, while passed students prefer individual communication channels in e-learning environments, failed students prefer to communicate in a community environment such as discussion pages. Another important finding is that failed students spend more time on the assessment and feedback pages. This finding may be interpreted in such a way that failed students might find the assessment activities demanding and challenging as more time was spent on them.

As can be seen from the navigational patterns in Fig. 7.2, there is not a navigational difference between passed and failed students, and in both achievement groups, content and discussion interactions are prioritized in the first order navigation. When these two types of interactions are considered, the contents are in the foreground. Passed students spend more intense time on content interaction in comparison to their counterparts.

Table 7.1 Comparison of passed and failed students' first order navigation ratios based on *z* test

Navigation theme	Passed	Failed	*z*	*p*
Content	0.41	0.46	−1.26	0.10
Discussion	0.28	0.16	3.45	0.99
Messaging	0.04	0.04	0.51	0.69
Profile	0.07	0.07	0.23	0.59
Assessment	0.004	0.005	−0.58	0.28
Feedback	0.01	0.02	−0.79	0.21
Ask instructor	0.005	0.01	−1.22	0.11
Exit	0.14	0.19	−1.73	0.04

Table 7.2 Times (seconds) learners spent on the second order page

	Cont.	Discuss.	Messag.	Profile	Assess.	Feedback	Ask Inst.
Passed	588.24	102.16	30.89	39.84	303.47	16.67	31
Failed	495.25	109.35	9.25	30.40	614	22.60	6.67
Differences	92.99	−7.19	21.64	9.44	−242.47	−5.93	24.33

5 Results

This research is a profiling study based on the navigation patterns of learners. Navigational patterns were handled as first order and second order, and whether there was a significant difference between these patterns according to students learning achievement was investigated. The results of the current study revealed the navigational patterns of learners in LMS. The most visited themes for both groups are content, discussion, and exit from the system, respectively. Second order navigation examination showed that learners often return to the homepage in the next step. Many of the students needed to return to the homepage again after the second theme, and many of the remaining students also exited the system. In other words, the students do not navigate directly among the navigation themes. In this context, it is necessary to give suggestions or direct links to the students as a recommendation system. Another important result is passed students are more likely to stay in the system and continue to the e-learning process after the third level navigation, whereas the failed students tend to leave the system. However, when looking at the inter-theme navigation rates, both groups are shown to follow similar routes. Both passed and failed students mostly visit content and discussion pages in the first order navigation. According to this, we can say if navigational patterns differ or not in terms of academic achievement of the learners.

Additionally, whether there was a difference between the times allocated for each login in terms of learners' academic achievement was examined. The findings showed that there were differences between the passed and failed students with regard to time spent on each login. The learners spent most of their time on content, evaluation, and discussion pages, respectively. Considering the length of time learners allocated for each theme, passed students spent more time on the themes of content, messaging, profile, and ask the instructor, while failed students allocated more time to discussion, assessment, and feedback themes.

The study yielded a general result that first and second order navigational patterns of passed and failed students in the online learning environment had similar features, but passed students allocated more time to each page in the learning environments. This study tried to show the navigation profiles of passed and failed learners in the e-learning environment. These and similar research results can provide a basis for further study and the optimization of e-learning environments.

6 Recommendations

The current study investigates the navigational patterns of online learners in terms of their achievement. The findings of the research may have potential for the design of intelligent tutorial systems. According to characteristics and navigations of the learners, intelligent tutoring systems would involve intervention and adaptive mechanisms. One of the most commonly used approaches in the study of learners' LMS log data is the data mining approach. Similarity search, classification, and clustering can be done by using log data. Particularly, the results of classification analysis based on learning characteristics are important inputs for recommender systems. Log data analysis can be used not only to design recommender systems but also to identify dropout students. The information obtained here may also guide the researcher to construct various interventions so that the students do not stay out of the system.

In the light of the study results, although learners differ in terms of their achievement, they draw upon similar processes in the online learning environments. Similarly, in a study conducted by Bagarinao (2015), the navigational patterns of the learners did not differ according to the course performances. Nevertheless, it was observed that students differ from each other when considering their system interaction durations. Accordingly, especially for those who perform poorly in school, the interactions of the learners with the system can be enriched with online learning agents and the interventional feedback suitable for the interaction period, so learners can be directed to deep learning.

Conducting studies that examine other important learner characteristics (cognitive style, motivation sources, cognitive strategies, etc.) and on the ordering of the important variables in the e-learning process are recommended. Findings from these research works can guide designers and researchers in the design of adaptive e-learning environments.

One of the most important learner characteristics influencing learning success in e-learning environments is self-regulated learning (Puntambekar et al., 2013) because the students are the managers of their own learning processes. In other words, they are learners who can take their own learning responsibilities, choose the necessary content, identify the methods, follow the learning processes, and make evaluations (Ribbe & Bezanilla, 2013). In this context, various directions, suggestions, feedbacks, and interventions are needed to support the autonomy of learners in e-learning environments. Passed learners' navigation patterns in e-learning environments provide important information to researchers about how conceptual relationships are structured. Suggestions, feedback, and interventions can be given to the learners in the light of this information. Therefore, this and similar research results will provide important information on self-regulated learning and metacognition scaffolding (Puntambekar et al., 2013). Findings from these studies can guide designers and researchers in the design of adaptive e-learning environments, which are also called next-generation digital learning environments. In this research, exploratory structural analysis based on navigational frequency was performed, with the aim of bringing the interaction components to the foreground. In addition to this analysis, it is also possible to use lag sequential analysis and sequential pattern analysis in data mining.

References

Akçapınar, G., Altun, A., & Aşkar, P. (2015). Modeling students' academic performance based on their interactions in an online learning environment. *Elementary Education Online, 14*(3), 815–824.

Ally, M. (2008). Foundations of educational theory for online learning. *Theory and Practice of Online Learning, 2*, 15–44.

Altun, A. (2016). Understanding cognitive profiles in designing personalized learning environments. In B. Gros, Kinshuk, & M. Maina (Eds.), *The future of ubiquitous learning* (pp. 259–271). Berlin, Germany: Springer.

Bagarinao, R. T. (2015). Students' navigational pattern and performance in an E-learning environment: A case from UP Open University, Philippines. *Turkish Online Journal of Distance Education, 16*(1), 101–111.

Bakeman, R., & Gottman, J. M. (1997). *Observing interaction: An introduction to sequential analysis*. Cambridge, UK: Cambridge University Press.

Baker, R. S., & Inventado, P. S. (2014). Educational data mining and learning analytics. In J. A. Larusson & B. White (Eds.), *Learning analytics: From research to practice* (Vol. 13, pp. 61–75). New York, NY: Springer.

Chen, L. H. (2010). Web-based learning programs: Use by learners with various cognitive styles. *Computers & Education, 54*, 1028–1035.

Chen, S. Y., & Ford, N. J. (1998). Modelling user navigation behaviours in a hyper-media-based learning system: An individual differences approach. *Knowledge Organization, 25*(3), 67–78.

Dagger, D., O'Connor, A., Lawless, S., Walsh, E., & Wade, V. P. (2007). Service-oriented e-learning platforms: From monolithic systems to flexible services. *IEEE Internet Computing, 11*(3), 28–35.

Ferguson, R. (2012). Learning analytics: Drivers, developments and challenges. *International Journal of Technology Enhanced Learning, 4*(5–6), 304–317.

Ford, N., & Chen, S. Y. (2000). Individual differences, hypermedia navigation, and learning: An empirical study. *Journal of Educational Multimedia and Hypermedia, 9*(4), 281–312.

Galusha, J. M. (1998). *Barriers to learning in distance education*. Hattiesburg, MS: University of Southern Mississippi.

Garrison, D. R. (2011). *E-learning in the 21st century: A framework for research and practice*. London, UK: Taylor & Francis.

Hwang, G. J. (2014). Definition, framework and research issues of smart learning environments-A context-aware ubiquitous learning perspective. *Smart Learning Environments, 1*(1), 4.

Kim, M., Han, S., Cui, Y., & Lee, H. (2013). Design and implementation of mongoDB-based unstructured log processing system over cloud computing environment. *Journal of Internet Computing and Services, 14*(6), 71–84.

Lu, J., Yu, C. S., & Liu, C. (2003). Learning style, learning patterns, and learning performance in a WebCT-based MIS course. *Information & Management, 40*(6), 497–507.

Ma, J., Han, X., Yang, J., & Cheng, J. (2015). Examining the necessary condition for engagement in an online learning environment based on learning analytics approach: The role of the instructor. *Internet and Higher Education, 24*, 26–34.

Malikowski, S. R., Thompson, M. E., & Theis, J. G. (2007). A model for research in to course management systems: Bridge technology & learning theory. *Journal of Educational Computing Research., 36*(2), 149–173.

Martin, T., & Sherin, B. (2013). Learning analytics and computational techniques for detecting and evaluating patterns in learning: An Introduction to the Special Issue. *Journal of the Learning Sciences, 22*(4), 511–520. https://doi.org/10.1080/10508406.2013.840466

Moore, M. G. (1989). Editorial: Three types of interaction. *American Journal of Distance Education, 3*(2), 1–7.

O'Connor, C., Sceiford, E., Wang, G., Foucar-Szocki, D., & Griffin, O. (2003). Departure, abandonment, and dropout of e-learning: Dilemma and solutions. In *TechLearn 2003 Conference*.

Osmanbegović, E., Suljić, M., & Agić, H. (2015). Determining dominant factor for students performance prediction by using data mining classification algorithms. *Tranzicija, 16*(34), 147–158.

Premlatha, K. R., Dharani, B., & Geetha, T. V. (2016). Dynamic learner profiling and automatic learner classification for adaptive e-learning environment. *Interactive Learning Environments, 24*(6), 1054–1075.

Puntambekar, S., & Stylianou, A. (2005). Designing navigation support in hypertext systems based on navigation patterns. *Instructional Science, 33*(5–6), 451–481.

Puntambekar, S., Sullivan, S. A., & Hübscher, R. (2013). Analyzing navigation patterns to scaffold metacognition in hypertext systems. In R. Azevedo & V. Aleven (Eds.), *International handbook of metacognition and learning technologies* (Vol. 26, pp. 261–275). New York, NY: Springer.

Rezaei, A. R., & Katz, L. (2004). Evaluation of the reliability and validity of the cognitive styles analysis. *Personality and Individual Differences, 36*, 1317–1327.

Rezende, F., & de Souza Barros, S. (2008). Students' navigation patterns in the interaction with a mechanics hypermedia program. *Computers & Education, 50*(4), 1370–1382.

Ribbe, E., & Bezanilla, M. J. (2013). Scaffolding learner autonomy in online university courses. *Digital Education Review, 24*, 98–112.

Richey, R. C., Silber, K. H., & Ely, D. P. (2008). Reflections on the 2008 AECT definitions of the field. *TechTrends, 52*(1), 24–25.

Romero, C., Ventura, S., Pechenizkiy, M., & Baker, R. S. (Eds.). (2010). *Handbook of educational data mining*. Boca Raton, FL: CRC Press.

Roy, M., & Chi, M. T. (2003). Gender differences in patterns of searching the web. *Journal of Educational Computing Research, 29*(3), 335–348.

Şahin, M., Keskin, S., Özgür, A., & Yurdugül, H. (2017). Determination of interaction profiles based on learner characteristics in e-learning environments. *Educational Technology Theory and Practice, 7*(2), 172–192.

Şahin, M., Keskin, S. & Yurdugül, H. (2017, May). *Determination of learner characteristics and interaction variables for e-learning design by feature selection algorithms 11*. International Computer and Instructional Technology Symposium (ICITS 2017), Malatya, Turkey. http://icits2017.inonu.edu.tr/dosya/1493369308092697100.pdf

Siemens, G., & Long, P. (2011). Penetrating the fog: Analytics in learning and education. *Educause Review, 46*(5), 30.

Wagner, E. D. (1994). In support of a functional definition of interaction. *American Journal of Distance Education, 8*(2), 6–26.

Sinan Keskin is a research assistant and Ph.D. student at Hacettepe University, Faculty of Education, Department of Computer Education and Instructional Technology. He completed his undergraduate education at Gazi University in 2010 and worked as a teacher for 1 year. He is planning to get his Ph.D. degree in 2019. His research interests relate to e-assessment, feedback design, adaptive e-learning, learning analytics, and educational data mining.

Muhittin Şahin is a research assistant for the Faculty of Education at Ege University. He completed his undergraduate education in the Department of Computer Education and Instructional Technology at Ege University in 2009. He get his Ph.D degree from Hacettepe University, Institute of Educational Sciences, Computer Education and Instructional Technology. His research interests relate to learning analytics, educational data mining, e-learning, decision theory, and statistics.

Halil Yurdugül has bachelor and master degrees from the Statistics Department at Hacettepe University. He completed his Ph.D. study at Hacettepe University Educational Sciences/Measurement and Evaluation Department. He works as a Professor at Hacettepe University Computer Education and Instructional Technology Department. His research interests relate to e-assessment, learning analytics, educational data mining, e-learning, decision theory, and statistics.

Chapter 8
Performance Analysis of a Serial Natural Language Processing Pipeline for Scaling Analytics of Academic Writing Process

David Boulanger, Clayton Clemens, Jeremie Seanosky, Shawn Fraser, and Vivekanandan Kumar

Abstract Capturing and analyzing just the final submission of a writing assignment ignores a substantial amount of information, providing only a partial view of the writer's effort and intent. Such a partial view of writing abilities limits opportunities for the generation of feedback to improve the final writing product as well as to aid in the development of effective writing techniques. Over-the-shoulder monitoring of the writing process for only a few individuals proves to be a challenge, while scaling specialized tutoring to as many writers as possible is simply impossible without leveraging technology. This research analyzes the computational requirements of a single-threaded writing analytics system for real-time monitoring and instructional intervention of writing processes. This chapter reports on the performance of this analytics system using the simulated writing processes of 391 compositions in higher education, a subset of the British Academic Written English (BAWE) corpus. It elaborates on computational requirements of analytics elements involving Natural Language Processing (NLP) and offers recommendations for building scalable big data NLP pipelines adapted to the analysis of academic writing process of learners.

1 Background

The quality of a product of writing is highly dependent on a writer's writing process and the writer's management of that process. However, writing is still assessed as a product and not as a process (Clemens, Kumar, Boulanger, Seanosky, & Kinshuk, 2018). Writing, as a process, can be measured in terms of the effort expended by

D. Boulanger · C. Clemens · J. Seanosky · S. Fraser · V. Kumar (✉)
Athabasca University, Edmonton, AB, Canada
e-mail: dboulanger@athabascau.ca; jseanosky@athabascau.ca; shawnf@athabascau.ca; vive@athabascau.ca

D. Sampson et al. (eds.), *Learning Technologies for Transforming Large-Scale Teaching, Learning, and Assessment*, https://doi.org/10.1007/978-3-030-15130-0_8

learners. It can also be measured in terms of portions of text displaced over the time of development of the composition. It can also measure various writing skills exhibited by the learner during writing episodes. One can also identify the contributions of such process-centric measures on the quality of the final composition, the writing product. Awareness of the writing process is a rich source of information that remains predominantly unexploited since observing and analyzing the writing process at large scale and at a fine-grained level is particularly computationally intensive. There exist very few (Yim & Warschauer, 2017) such systems that use sensor and analytics technology to assist writers manage their writing process by providing real-time feedback (Southavilay, Yacef, & Calvo, 2009). That is, there is a need for systems that do more than just shaping formative feedback over the current state of a composition, but that also track how the writing changes from state to state, recognizing writing patterns that define the writing behavior and writing profile of the writer. These time-sensitive metrics have not yet been included as predictive variables in automated writing evaluation systems except for a few cases (Southavilay et al., 2009; Torkildsen, Morken, Helland, & Helland, 2016).

Several studies (Alvarez-Fernandez & Garcia-Sanchez, 2015; Franklin & Hermsen, 2014; Freiman, 2015; Fuchs & Krivokapic, 2016; Garcia & Fidalgo, 2008; Ollagnier-Beldame, Brassac, & Mille, 2014; Southavilay et al., 2009; Torkildsen et al., 2016; Van Waes & Schellens, 2003; Yim & Warschauer, 2017) have targeted writing behaviors and writing profiles, but research in this area remains mainly underexplored (Yim & Warschauer, 2017). Analyzing the writing process requires intensive data collection, scaling, centralization, standardization, and special adaptation of contemporary natural language processing (NLP) software packages. This research investigates the performance of a single-threaded writing analytics system built upon a disparate NLP pipeline, and demonstrates the computational demands on the tracking and analyzing of the writing process. Further, this research recommends adaptations of NLP pipelines aimed at scaled analysis of the writing process. This study reports the results of a correlational analysis associating lexical, syntactic, and semantic aspects of a composition and the processing time required to process them. In addition, it explores relationships between the processing time and traits such as the length of the document, the substandard quality of writing during the development of the composition, and specific characteristics of texts that contribute to the overall composition.

2 Literature Review

This section looks into the extent at which scalable natural language processing or text mining software packages have been investigated in the literature, with an emphasis on whether they have already been explored with a focus on the writing process. It examines the areas in which these solutions were developed and discusses their implementation details and performance. An extensive search on the Web of Science, one of the biggest citation databases, was conducted using different combinations and forms of the following terms: "writing process," writing/essay/composition, analytics/track*/sensor/sensing/"learning traces"/metric/analysis/competenc*/"automated essay," natural language processing/text mining, big data/bigdata/scal*/distribut*. The sparsity of search results quickly revealed that (1) scaling big data natural language processing has been underinvestigated and never been explored in the setting of the writing process, and that (2) many, if not the majority, of the initiatives have been undertaken in the healthcare sector. Surprisingly, given the huge amount of research and literature available online on healthcare, such as the PubMed citation database that contains more than 27 million citations[1], much effort has been invested to automate knowledge extraction from this huge pool of clinical information to facilitate the discovery, implementation, and evaluation of new knowledge (Kaggal et al., 2016).

2.1 Research Applications

Generic big data architectures have been developed to support the integration and parallelization of disparate NLP software packages using technology such as Apache Storm (Agerri, Artola, Beloki, Rigau, & Soroa, 2015). In the domain of learning analytics, a Spark/Hadoop-based architecture has been proposed to measure the growth of writing competences over a writer's set of writing activities (Lewkow et al., 2016). Given the explosion in the generation of big data, whose size in 2020 is estimated to be 40 zettabytes (Turner, Gantz, Reinsel, & Minton, 2014), and that about 85% of the digital information on the Internet is unstructured (Monali & Sandip, 2014), researchers have also investigated the use of Hadoop technology for the extraction of keywords and key phrases from web documents retrieved by means of a web crawler. In the healthcare sector, large-scale NLP has been used in individualized care recommendation solutions for clinical care (Kaggal et al., 2016); to automate the extraction of data pertaining to cardiovascular structure and function from heterogeneous data sources (Nath, Albaghdadi, & Jonnalagadda, 2016); to classify journal articles per type of cancer (Ye, Tafti, He, Wang, & He, 2016); and for recognition and normalization of biomedical concepts (Wei, Leaman, & Lu, 2016). Automatic detection and tracking of events from social network streams (McCreadie, Macdonald, Ounis, Osborne, & Petrovic, 2013) and the identification of entities and their derivatives across corpora (also called coreference) (Singh, Subramanya, Pereira, & McCallum, 2011) have also contributed to the use of large-scale NLP.

[1]PubMed. Retrieved August 17, 2017, from https://www.ncbi.nlm.nih.gov/pubmed/

2.2 *Scalability Issues*

To achieve NLP scalability, several issues need to be addressed such as (1) real-time stream processing vs. batch processing, (2) integration of disparate technologies into a unified NLP pipeline, (3) availability of open source software packages for custom development, (4) the size of the dataset(s) to be processed, (5) high-performance computing resources, and (6) dynamically reconfigurable architecture to accommodate different NLP requirements. Agerri et al. (2015), Kaggal et al. (2016), and McCreadie et al. (2013) propose an architecture implemented through Apache Storm, which supports integration of disparate technologies (e.g., different programming languages, open source code versus proprietary software, third-party tools versus one's own solutions) and the parallelization of processing tasks for the formation of parallel pipelines made up of both domain-specific (e.g., healthcare) and generic (e.g., part-of-speech taggers) NLP solutions. In contrast, multinode Hadoop or Spark clusters (MapReduce paradigm) are ideal for less time-sensitive applications (batch processing).

2.3 *Implementations and Performance Analyses*

A number of studies have been conducted in NLP, particularly in the context of scaling up NLP's application. Goyal et al. (2016) report that many of the approximately 3.4 million PubMed articles are available in PDF format. They consequently developed a parallelized architecture to convert the PDF articles to XML format to facilitate the application of more advanced NLP. They compared the performance of a Kepler/Spark parallel architecture against its single-threaded Python counterpart and a single-threaded Kepler (a graphical workflow management tool) version, with a dataset of 200 documents. The dataset contained files that varied in terms of their number of pages, content, and size. The benchmarking occurred on a Lenovo Workstation machine, on which were installed a Spark server, Java Virtual Machine (JVM), and Kepler. To avoid network or I/O latencies, each version processed three times the 200-document dataset. Moreover, to avoid fast re-execution due to caching, the server's warm cache lines were refreshed between each re-execution. The average processing times (average of the three executions for each architecture) were then compared against each other. On average, the Kepler architecture took less than 12 h to process the 200-document dataset, a reduction of 17% compared to the 15 h of processing time for the single-threaded Python version, with most significant reductions occurring with larger file sizes (up to 26%). As for the parallel architecture, it reduced the total processing time by 75%, again in comparison with the Python version. A visualization was also created sorting the processing times of the individual documents and comparing the processing times of the Python and Kepler architectures for each document. The visualization showed that the processing time difference increased with documents that took longer time to process. Moreover, Goyal et al. also calculated the share of processing time taken by each of the architecture's four software packages, with one of the modules taking up to 60% of the total processing time.

Agerri et al. (2015) implemented two different NLP pipelines and measured their performance on an Apache Storm-based architecture. The first pipeline processed a dataset of 64,540 documents from a news collection describing events involving car companies, while the second pipeline processed a dataset containing 18,886 documents retrieved from the Wikinews website. The first NLP pipeline consisted of nine NLP modules, while the second pipeline consisted of these nine modules plus four others for a total of 13. The processing occurred parallelly on eight virtual machines, consuming 5 days to process the first dataset and 2 days to process the second. If the data were processed sequentially, it would have taken 34 days and 16 days, respectively. Agerri et al. also reported the amount of time taken per NLP module in order to detect tools that would need further parallelization. This underscores the fact that the granularity of parallelization is also a major issue when designing large-scale architectures.

Nesi, Pantaleo, and Sanesi (2015) constructed a Hadoop cluster to extract the keywords and key phrases from 20,000 web pages and documents. The processing was executed offline to eliminate any network latency. Different configurations were tested, ranging from two to five nodes. Each node was a Linux 8-core workstation. The dataset was processed several times for each configuration. The best processing time by configuration was then retained to minimize the number of attempts to reprocess aborted transactions. A single-node configuration took 115 h to extract nearly nine million keywords and key phrases. Nesi et al. also reported the speed-up factor for each extra node. The experiment showed that the speed-up factor grew linearly as the number of nodes increased, showing the scaling capabilities of their approach. It is, however, important to indicate that each node was allocated a distinct physical machine, implying that the granularity of the parallelization was rather low. Depending on the needs of the problem at hand, the usage of computing resources may not be maximized, and it may turn out to be a costlier approach.

Kaggal et al. (2016) benchmarked the performance of a NLP pipeline on a dataset of 20,000 clinical notes using a Storm architecture. The performance was measured for configurations of 1, 2, 4, 8, and 16 parallel instances. With only one instance, the system took about 20 min to process the 20,000 notes, while the 16-instance configuration accomplished the task in only 1.01 min! It is nevertheless important to mention that the speed-up factor increased more slowly as more instances were added to the architecture, suggesting that there exists a threshold number of instances beyond which there will be no significant gain in processing time. That threshold may depend on the dataset size. Kaggal et al. conducted another experiment using a 16-instance configuration, but this time doubling the number of clinical notes to be processed, that is, 20,000, 40,000, 80,000, and 160,000 clinical notes. It was found that the processing time approximately grew linearly as the number of clinical notes was increased. For instance, for the batch of 20,000 clinical notes, it took about 3 milliseconds (ms) to process a single note. On the other hand, on average, it took 3.28 ms per note for the 160,000-clinical note dataset. Kaggal et al. also piloted another experiment on a dataset of 1.6 million documents from

14,000 patients using the 16-instance architecture. Only 90 min were required to process the dataset (3.38 ms per document).

Ye et al. developed a text mining tool, called SparkText, to perform large-scale classification of medical literature. Their goal was to determine whether a journal article dealt with specific type(s) of cancer. They employed Apache Spark on a 20-node cluster platform, and each node was configured with 6 GB of memory, two CPUs (2.6 GHz), and 1 TB of hard disk space. They compared the performance of SparkText against the Weka Library and Tag Helper tool over three datasets. SparkText processed the first dataset in 3 min, while it took 138 and 201 min for the other two tools, respectively; the second dataset was processed in 4 min by SparkText compared to 309 and 571 min for Weka and Tag Helper. Finally, SparkText spent approximately 6 min (12 ms per document) to process a dataset of 29,437 full-text articles, while Weka and Tag Helper processed the dataset in more than 11 h. They reported a speed-up factor of 132 times. However, Ye et al. neither described the machine configuration on which Weka and Tag Helper were run nor if they were single- or multithreaded.

2.4 Summary

It appears from the literature reported above that the application of large-scale NLP in the analysis of the writing process has never been investigated before. In addition, only some limited literature directly addresses the domain of scalable automated writing evaluation systems (Kumar, Fraser, & Boulanger, 2017). Although the focus of this research is on developing a big data architecture to analyze the academic writing process, tracking and analyzing the writing process, whatever the field of application, will reveal new insights about (a) better assessment of writing competences, (b) addition of behavioral factors in the prediction of text quality, (c) detection of more advanced forms of plagiarism, (d) capture of authors' intents to resolve persisting mechanical and semantic errors, (e) measurement of the writer's effort, and (f) profiling of the writer's cognitive map. Obviously, the variety, amount, and accuracy of these insights depend on the capacity to scale natural language processing.

3 Research Questions

This study analyzes the performance of a writing analytics system that processed 744,848 text captures, constituting the simulated writing process of 391 academic compositions. The present research proposes to answer the following research questions in the context where the 744,848 text captures (also called writing events) were sorted by their processing time from the shortest to the longest (RQ1–RQ5); (RQ2, RQ4) half of the writing events that took the shortest processing times were grouped together (Group A_1), while the second half (the longest processing times) formed a second group (Group A_2) (A_1 and A_2 have the same size); (RQ3, RQ5) the set of writing events processed within the first half of the total processing time formed one group (Group B_1), while the set of writing events processed in the second half formed the second group (Group B_2) (B_1 and B_2 have different sizes, Group B_1 being larger than Group B_2).

- RQ1: How do structural elements of a text (e.g., lexical, syntactic, and semantic) impact processing time?
- RQ2: How do writing features differ between low (A_1) and high (A_2) processing times and how important are these differences?
- RQ3: How do writing features differ between low (B_1) and high (B_2) processing times and how important are theses differences?
- RQ4: How do NLP tools' shares of computational time differ between low (A_1) and high (A_2) processing times and how important are theses differences?
- RQ5: How do NLP tools' shares of computational time differ between low (B_1) and high (B_2) processing times and how important are theses differences?

The reader should note that the variability in length (e.g., number of words) and, hypothetically, the processing time per writing event (remember there are many writing events per assignment) is significantly greater for the corpus analyzed in this study than with a typical corpus where only the final writing products are analyzed (only the last writing event is actually evaluated). Hence, it is hypothesized that the number of characters, words, or sentences variable (and any other metric that takes into account text length) will be strongly correlated with the processing time. On the other hand, as the writing process progresses towards completion, the quality of the essay may tend to improve. Thus, this research proposes to perform a preliminary analysis on whether the quality of a text has some impact on the overall processing time of the NLP pipeline and also on the processing time per NLP tool within the pipeline. This chapter will conclude by providing recommendations on building large-scale parallel NLP pipelines adapted to the needs of the analysis of the writing process.

4 Methodology

4.1 Dataset

This research is based on a subset of the British Academic Written English (BAWE) corpus collected in the setting of a 2004–2007 project entitled "An investigation of genres of assessed writing in British Higher Education," which originally consisted of 2761 writing assignments written by 1039 students (Alsop & Nesi, 2009; Heuboeck, Holmes, & Nesi, 2010; Nesi, Sharpling, & Ganobcsik-Williams, 2004)[2]

[2] Sharpling, G. (2016). BAWE (British Academic Written English) and BAWE Plus Collections. Retrieved August 21, 2017, from http://www2.warwick.ac.uk/fac/soc/al/research/collections/bawe/

from four levels in undergraduate and master courses. The corpus was as diversified as possible, coming from 35 disciplines (e.g., History, English, Agriculture, Health, Computer Science, Engineering, Law, Economics), categorized in four broad disciplinary groupings (Arts and Humanities, Life Sciences, Physical Sciences, and Social Sciences), with 13 genre families (e.g., case study, critique, essay, literature review). The BAWE corpus consists of about 6.5 million words, and the numbers of assignments are approximately equally distributed in each category. Assignment and author data were also collected for every submitted assignment. For instance, the date of writing, the level of studies, the genre family, the discipline, the module title and code, the number of authors, and the grade obtained were collected for each assignment. The gender, year of birth, first language, native language, the number of years in United Kingdom's secondary education system, program of study, and the student ID were also provided about the authors. Several metrics about the assignments' text were also computed, including the number of words, s-units (sentences), and paragraphs/sections; the numbers of tables, figures, block quotes, formulas, lists, and the number of paragraphs formatted like lists; whether there is an abstract or not; and the average number of words per s-unit (sentence) and the average number of s-units per paragraph/section.

The present study analyzes the performance of a single-threaded NLP pipeline in parsing the simulated writing process of a subset of the BAWE corpus. As demonstrated by Table 8.1, the dataset used in this experiment consists of a one million-word corpus written in 390 assignments. Table 8.1 shows the distribution of assignments and the amounts of text over the four disciplinary groups and the four undergraduate and master's levels. From the disciplinary group perspective, the corpus is distributed roughly equally among every category in terms of the numbers of words and the numbers of assignments, while the first year of undergraduate programs is overrepresented when compared to other levels. Table 8.2 demonstrates the amount of assignments per discipline and per undergraduate and masters level. Interestingly, the dataset in this experiment covers a wide range of disciplines (over 30 disciplines), which will be an asset in generalizing this study's conclusions.

Table 8.1 Number of words and number of assignments per broad disciplinary grouping and per study level

Disciplinary group		Yr1	Yr2	Yr3	Masters	Total
Arts and humanities	Assignments	53	19	12	5	89
	Words	122,345	55,323	27,621	9149	214,438
Life sciences	Assignments	38	35	7	33	113
	Words	94,775	94,497	20,663	61,396	271,331
Physical sciences	Assignments	26	21	17	15	79
	Words	70,340	62,819	43,909	28,457	205,525
Social sciences	Assignments	66	17	19	7	109
	Words	178,625	33,338	32,446	15,020	259,429
Total assignments		183	92	55	60	390
Total words		466,085	245,977	124,369	114,022	950,723

Table 8.2 Number of assignments per discipline and per study level

Disciplinary group	Discipline	1	2	3	4	Total
Arts and humanities	Archaeology	2	4	1	3	10
	Classics	13	0	0	2	15
	Comparative American studies	0	1	1	0	2
	English	5	3	4	0	12
	History	3	0	1	0	4
	Linguistics	12	3	1	0	16
	Other	4	3	2	0	9
	Philosophy	14	5	2	0	21
	Total	53	19	12	5	89
Life sciences	Agriculture	1	17	2	6	26
	Biological sciences	7	4	1	8	20
	Food sciences	2	6	3	2	13
	Health	4	7	1	0	12
	Medicine	0	0	14	0	14
	Psychology	24	1	0	3	28
	Total	38	35	7	33	113
Physical sciences	Architecture	2	1	0	0	3
	Chemistry	0	2	3	1	6
	Computer science	3	3	4	3	13
	Cybernetics and electronics	1	1	2	1	5
	Engineering	12	9	5	4	30
	Mathematics	2	0	1	1	4
	Meteorology	2	3	0	4	9
	Other	0	0	0	0	0
	Physics	2	0	1	1	4
	Planning	2	2	1	0	5
	Total	26	21	17	15	79
Social sciences	Anthropology	4	2	0	0	6
	Business	10	4	7	1	22
	Economics	5	1	5	2	13
	HLTM	3	2	4	0	9
	Law	12	0	0	0	12
	Other	0	0	0	0	0
	Politics	7	8	0	0	15
	Publishing	2	0	0	0	2
	Sociology	23	0	3	4	30
	Total	66	17	19	7	109
Total		183	92	55	60	390

1=Yr1, 2=Yr2, 3=Yr3, 4=Masters

Finally, Table 8.3 lists the number of assignments per family genre, with the essay genre being the most prominent one followed by the critique and methodology recount genres.

Table 8.3 Number of assignments per family genre and per broad disciplinary grouping

	Arts and humanities	Life sciences	Physical sciences	Social sciences	Total
Case study	0	9	3	4	16
Critique	7	21	8	18	54
Design specification	1	0	9	0	10
Empathy writing	0	2	1	1	4
Essay	69	27	12	70	178
Exercise	1	3	11	2	17
Explanation	0	20	6	2	28
Literature review	2	0	0	2	4
Methodology recount	7	18	24	3	52
Narrative recount	0	4	2	2	8
Problem question	0	0	0	4	4
Proposal	1	8	2	1	12
Research report	1	1	1	0	3
Total	89	113	79	109	390

4.2 *WriteSim*

For the purpose of demonstrating the challenge of tracking and analyzing the writing process underlying every writing assignment, a tool called WriteSim was developed (Clemens, 2017) to simulate the writing process and generate a sequence of writing events for each assignment.

A writing event is the capture of the student's text at a specific time in the writing process, which encloses the student ID, the course ID, and the assignment ID along with the timestamp at which the capture is made. On average, WriteSim produced 1905 writing events per writing assignment.

The simulation was based on the results of a study conducted by Van Waes and Schellens (2003), in which the writing profiles of 40 experienced writers (faculty and graduate students) were derived by analyzing their writing process in a word processor environment. Each participant was assigned two writing tasks and was allocated 2–3 h to complete each task. Basically, the objective of the study was to quantify the writing process for each writing task along the following metrics: the average number of pauses, average pause time, average number of revisions, average length of compositions, average numbers of sentences and paragraphs, and keystroking speed.

Each metric was also measured for multiple categories. For instance, pauses were classified as being either a formulation pause or a revision pause. In addition, the linguistic area where the pause occurred was also noted and recorded (e.g., within a sentence, at a sentence boundary, or a paragraph boundary).

Waes and Schellens derived the following writing profiles based on the metrics collected during the experiment: the initial planner, the average writer, the fragmentary Stage I writer, the Stage II writer, and the nonstop writer (Stage I refers to the phase from initiation to the completion of the first draft, while Stage II refers to the phase from the completion of the first draft to the completion of the final version).

During the simulation, WriteSim (a) simulated formulation and revision pauses as well as the duration of these pauses, (b) simulated spelling errors by randomizing the sequence of the characters in a word, and (c) introduced deviations by substituting tokens in the text for synonyms coming from WordNet, which were corrected back to their original forms after revision.

It is important to note that the simulation process is not fully representative of the real writing process. For example, the modifications are done only at the word level and do not include, for instance, reordering sections of the text to improve flow and coherence. A separate study is warranted to determine similarities between WriteSim's simulated writing and students' writing traits.

4.3 NLP Pipeline

Figure 8.1 displays the architecture of the writing analytics system and its underlying NLP pipeline that analyzed writing products and their corresponding writing processes. The writing process of each of the 390 writing assignments from the BAWE corpus (input) was simulated by WriteSim, which generated a set of writing events (average of 1905) per assignment, for a total of 744,848 writing events. These events were then serially fed into the NLP pipeline in chronological order.

The NLP pipeline consisted of four major NLP software packages: Apache OpenNLP 1.6.0, Stanford CoreNLP 3.6.0, Text Mining Library (TML) 3.2, and the

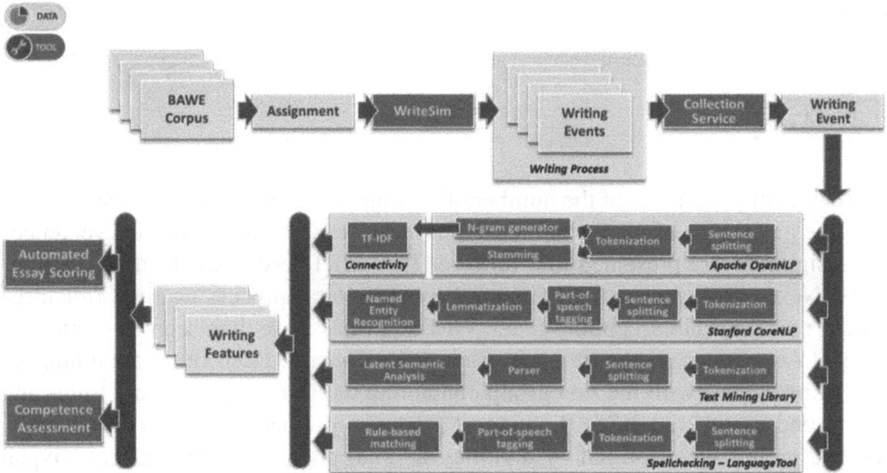

Fig. 8.1 Architecture of writing analytics system

spellchecker LanguageTool 3.4 (enhanced by the Google *n*-gram corpus). Although these four NLP solutions appear parallel in the diagram, their execution was rather serial.

Eighty-six writing features were produced out of this NLP pipeline. For more information about the writing features extracted using this architecture, the reader is invited to consult Kumar et al. (2017). Among the most important metrics are the (1) ratios of each of the parts of speech over the total number of words; (2) the numbers of characters, words, and sentences; (3) average number of characters per word and the average number of words per sentence; (4) number of connectors and a TF-IDF-based connectivity measure; (5) the ratios of content (noun, verb, adjective, adverb) and function words (e.g., determiners, articles, prepositions, conjunctions) over the total number of words; (6) ratios of grammatical and spelling errors; (7) lexical diversity and number of unique words; (8) number and ratio of unknown words; (9) ratios of words with 5, 6, 7, or 8 characters or more; and (10) semantic similarity. These writing features served to automatically score and provide a holistic and rubric-based scores to each writing assignment based on trained regression models and to assess the writing competences of the student cumulatively over all his/her writing assignments (Boulanger, Seanosky, Clemens, Kumar, & Kinshuk, 2016).

The architecture consists of three processing phases: (1) parsing where writing features are extracted, (2) automated writing scoring where holistic and rubric scores are assigned to a writing assignment, and (3) competence assessment where evidences underlying specific writing competences are cumulated throughout all writing assignments of students. The time used to execute each phase for each writing event was measured for all 744,848 writing events. Moreover, the processing time for each major NLP software package was also measured for every writing event. Hence, for every processed writing event, there is a corresponding set of writing features and processing times. The next section offers an analysis of writing events and the corresponding features to determine how they correlate with each other.

4.4 Analysis

The descriptive statistics of the number of writing events generated and the processing time and length of the assignments in terms of characters, words, and sentences per assignment are presented first followed by a brief description of their distributions. Next, writing events were sorted by their total processing time (all three phases combined) in ascending order. Writing events were then separated into two pairs of two groups. In the first pair, each group contained half of the total number of writing events, with the first group containing the shortest processing times and the second group containing the longest processing times. As for the second pair, the two groups were formed by dividing the total processing time into two equal periods. Hence, the first group contained all those writing events processed in the first period, while the second group included the writing events processed during the second half of the overall processing. Naturally, the size of the first group was much larger than the size of the second group.

In order to investigate whether there is a correlation among certain lexical, syntactic, and semantic aspects of the text with the overall processing time, the Kendall's tau-b rank correlation coefficient was used to avoid assumptions on this study's variable distributions and to assess the monotonic relationships between the extracted writing features and processing time. Kendall's tau-b was selected instead of Spearman's rho since the variables within this study's dataset had a large number of ties. However, given that the number of observations per variable was very large (744,848), applying Kendall's tau-b on all observations was computationally prohibitive. Hence, a sample of 20,000 observations was randomly selected from the original dataset. Kendall's tau-b was, therefore, calculated on this sample dataset.

The Wilcoxon rank sum test determined whether there was a significant difference in medians for each of the writing features listed in Sect. 4.3 between both pairs of groups. In addition, the difference in median processing time percentages was also assessed for the four NLP software packages (Stanford CoreNLP, Apache OpenNLP, TML, LanguageTool) for each pair of groups using the Wilcoxon rank sum test. The rank biserial correlation coefficient measured the effect sizes. This nonparametric effect size estimator is particularly useful when dealing with one continuous/discrete variable (e.g., writing feature) and one dichotomous variable (e.g., higher (1) versus lower processing time (0)). The reader may consult Cureton (1968) and Glass (1966) for more details. The results revealed new information on scaling of natural language processing and also on adapting the NLP pipeline especially in the context of tracking and analyzing the writing process.

5 Results

The subset dataset from the BAWE corpus analyzed in this study consisted of 390 writing assignments written by 390 distinct students. Only one student had one assignment with two parts for a total of 391 compositions. From Table 8.4, it can be seen that on average 1905 writing events were generated per composition. In most cases, a writing event is generated every time a new word is input, that is, more

Table 8.4 Descriptive statistics of the distributions of numbers of words, sentences, characters, and writing events and processing time per composition (Clemens et al., 2018)

	Min	Max	Q1	Q3	Median	Mean	SD
Writing events	1000	2229	1789	2020	1905	1904.98	143.70
Words[a]	51	2162	1695	1926	1799	1785.55	219.24
Sentences	4	124	58	77	67	67.76	15.80
Characters[a]	248	10,120	7818	8964	8408	8270.22	1053.43
Processing time (h)[a]	0.53	49.12	1.66	3.24	2.17	3.34	3.79

[a]Significantly departed from normality (tested using QQ-plots, histograms, and Shapiro-Wilk tests)

precisely whenever a blank character is entered. Moreover, it took roughly 3 h and a half to analyze the whole writing process of a single composition on average. The final submission of each composition had a mean of 1786 words, 68 sentences, and 8271 characters. In all, 744,848 writing events were generated from the 391 compositions.

Processing all these writing events took about 1304 h (54.3 days). Tables 8.5 and 8.6 examine the distributions of the writing features extracted by the NLP pipeline and the processing times for every phase in the overall architecture and every NLP tool in the pipeline. As it can be seen, almost all distributions (including distributions from Table 8.4) depart significantly from normality (several had shapes similar to *F*, chi-squared, and uniform distributions). Given this disparity in distributions, only nonparametric tests were used in this analysis. The normality of distributions was tested by examining QQ-plots and histograms of samples of 50,000 writing events, randomly selected out of the 744,848 writing events, and by performing the Shapiro-Wilk normality test on samples of 5000 randomly selected writing events. These results in terms of nonnormality are expected given the nature of the simulation and generation of the writing events. For instance, it can be seen from Table 8.4 that 25% of the compositions (at submission) had between 1694 and 1799 words and 50% had more than 1799 words. According to the simulation process as described in Sect. 4.2, many more writing events were generated having between 1694 and 1799 words than there were compositions with these final numbers of

Table 8.5 Descriptive statistics of the writing features of the writing event distribution

	Min	Max	Q1	Q3	Median	Mean	SD
Avg. # of characters/word	1.00	14.00	4.46	4.84	4.65	4.66	0.34
Avg. # of words/sentence[a]	1.00	137.00	22.46	30.33	25.71	26.64	6.60
Characters[a]	1.00	10,123.00	2146.00	6376.00	4257.00	4286.93	2489.82
Connectivity index[a]	0.00	2.33	1.33	1.72	1.55	1.48	0.37
Connectors[a]	0.00	398.00	72.00	218.00	144.00	147.89	89.55
Content word ratio	0.00	1.00	0.51	0.56	0.54	0.54	0.04
Function word ratio	0.00	1.00	0.44	0.49	0.46	0.46	0.04
Grammatical errors[a]	0.00	119.00	2.00	10.00	5.00	7.96	10.44
Grammatical error ratio[a]	0.00	1.00	0.00	0.01	0.01	0.01	0.01
Lexical diversity[a]	0.00	1.00	0.29	0.41	0.33	0.37	0.13
Sentences[a]	1.00	124.00	17.00	52.00	34.00	35.65	21.95
Spelling errors[a]	0.00	192.00	4.00	17.00	9.00	13.22	15.33
Spelling error ratio[a]	0.00	1.00	0.01	0.02	0.01	0.01	0.01
Topic flow index[a]	0.00	0.95	0.61	0.87	0.79	0.70	0.25
Unique words[a]	0.00	685.00	184.00	390.00	293.00	286.83	135.08
Unknown words[a]	0.00	408.00	13.00	75.00	39.00	48.56	42.59
Unknown word ratio[a]	0.00	1.00	0.03	0.06	0.05	0.05	0.03
Words[a]	1.00	2162.00	462.00	1382.25	922.00	926.78	539.01

[a]Significantly departed from normality (tested using QQ-plots, histograms, and Shapiro-Wilk tests)

Table 8.6 Descriptive statistics of processing time for each phase and tool for the distribution of writing events

Time in ms	Min	Max	Q1	Q3	Median	Mean	SD
Processing time[a]	250	668,003	2003	6228	4004	6303	11,283
Parsing time[a]	73	439,356	1263	4487	2697	4271	7437
Grading time[a]	123	77,386	151	262	168	692	2141
Competence assessment time[a]	12	8851	33	59	46	59	206
Stanford CoreNLP[a]	0	87,221	202	658	433	846	1741
Apache OpenNLP[a]	0	7443	5	12	8	13	109
TML[a]	8	81,672	43	147	81	428	1520
LanguageTool[a]	1	209,546	429	1407	861	1545	3273

[a]Significantly departed from normality (tested using QQ-plots, histograms, and Shapiro-Wilk tests)

Table 8.7 Writing events sorted from shortest to longest processing time

Rank	Processing time (ms)	Cum. processing time	% (total processing time)
1	250	250	0
2	251	501	0
3	256	757	0
⋮	⋮	⋮	⋮
372,423	4004	768,536,891	16
372,424	4004	768,540,895	16
372,425	4004	768,544,899	16
⋮	⋮	⋮	⋮
639,527	9393	2,323,803,982	49
639,528	9393	2,323,813,375	50
639,529	9393	2,323,822,768	50
⋮	⋮	⋮	⋮
744,846	656,940	4,693,220,944	100
744,847	667,848	4,693,888,792	100
744,848	668,003	4,694,556,795	100
Total	4,694,556,795		

words since half of the compositions at some time had these numbers of words during their writing process.

In order to answer the research questions RQ2, RQ3, RQ4, and RQ5, the data were further preprocessed. The 744,848 writing events were sorted by their processing time in ascending order (from the shortest to the longest). To answer RQ2 and RQ4, writing events were divided into two equal-size groups, A_1 and A_2. A_1 included all the writing events with the shortest processing times and A_2 included those writing events having the longest processing times. Similarly, to answer RQ3 and RQ5, the 744,848 writing events were separated in two groups, B_1 and B_2, by assigning to B_1 all the shortest (in term of processing time) writing events making up 50% of the

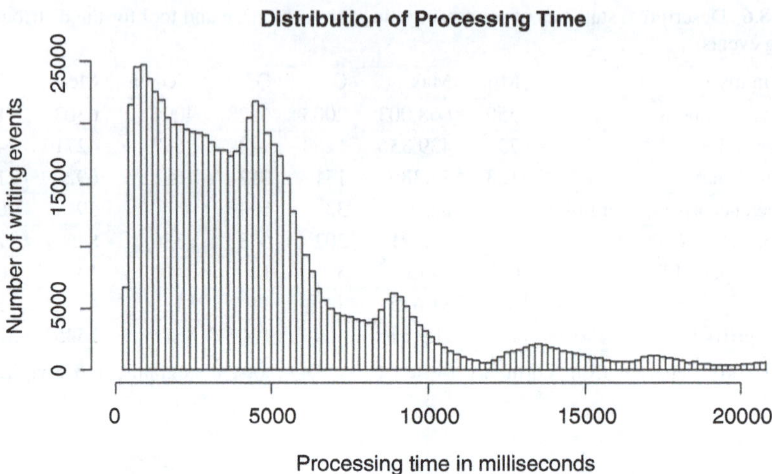

Fig. 8.2 Distribution of processing time per writing event

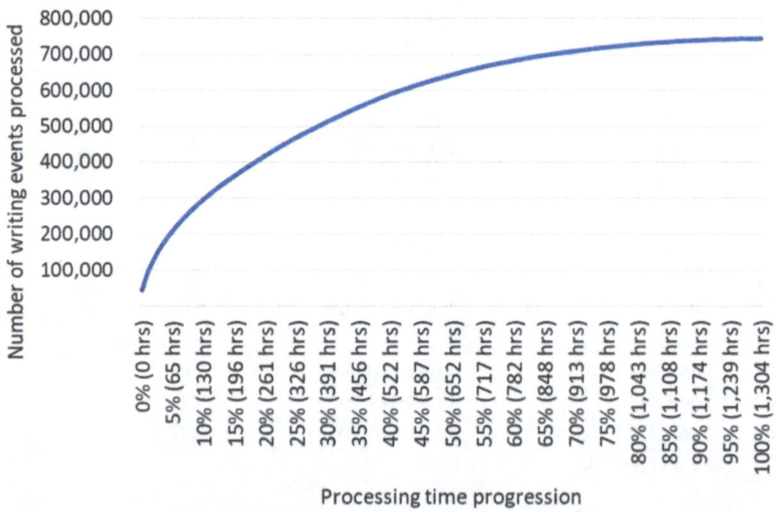

Fig. 8.3 Progression of the number of writing events as they are processed from shortest to longest processing time

total processing time (652 h) and assigning to B_2 the longest writing events making up the other 50%. In summary, A_1 contained the 372,424 shortest writing events, A_2 contained the 372,424 longest writing events, B_1 the 639,528 shortest events, and B_2 the remaining 105,320 events as displayed in Table 8.7. The histogram of the distribution of processing time for all writing events is also displayed in Fig. 8.2, while Fig. 8.3 demonstrates visually the progression and the number of writing events processed as if they were processed from the shortest to the longest processing time. Hence, it can be seen that half (372,424) of the writing events could have been processed within only 16% of the total processing time, that is, within 8.7 days. In addition, after half of the total processing time (27.15 days), 85.9% of the writing events (639,528) were processed.

5.1 RQ1

To assess whether there exists a monotonic relationship between the extracted writing features and the processing time, the nonparametric rank correlation coefficient Kendall's tau-b (τ_b) was selected over the nonparametric Spearman's rho (ρ) given that Kendall's tau-b was better suited to deal with large numbers of ties due to the large number of observations in the dataset. Table 8.8 lists the percentages of unique values over the total number of observations per variable. For instance, the number of words variable had 2162 unique values over a set of 744,848 observations, resulting in a percentage of uniqueness equal to 0.3%.

Since calculating Kendall's tau-b (τ_b) using all the observations for each variable is computationally prohibitive, it was calculated over subsamples of 20,000 random observations as reported in Table 8.9. The Spearman's rho values (ρ) are also provided for comparison. The scatterplots between each writing feature variable and the processing time variable were manually verified and confirm the results in Table 8.9.

In order to see whether the architecture scaled well as more and more writing events were processed, the original dataset was filtered to recover only those writing events whose text had exactly 1000 words, that is, 401 observations. The processing time values were ranked and correlated to their order of processing (ranks). The computed Kendall's tau-b was 0.37, while Spearman's rho was 0.51. There were only 25 ties. The correlation linked to the single-threaded architecture's scalability

Table 8.8 Percentages of unique values over total number of observations per variable

Variable	%	Variable	%	Variable	%
Processing time	5.6%	Avg. # of characters/ word	51.8%	Lexical diversity	23.3%
Parsing time	4.3%	Avg. # of words/ sentence	6.6%	Sentences	0.02%
Grading time	1.5%	Characters	1.3%	Spelling errors	0.03%
Competence assessment time	0.2%	Connectivity index	14.9%	Spelling error ratio	7.9%
Stanford CoreNLP	1.4%	Connectors	0.1%	Topic flow index	40.8%
Apache OpenNLP	0.1%	Content word ratio	17.7%	Unique words	0.1%
TML	1.2%	Function word ratio	17.7%	Unknown words	0.1%
LanguageTool	2.3%	Grammatical errors	0.02%	Unknown word ratio	14.8%
		Grammatical error ratio	5.9%	Words	0.3%

Table 8.9 Kendall's τ_b (top-right) and Spearman's ρ (bottom-left) rank correlation coefficients between the study variables (processing time and writing features)

Variable	1	2	3	4	5	6	7	8	9	10
1. Processing time	–	−0.11**	0.06**	0.62**	0.41**	0.59**	−0.01	0.01	0.32**	0.02**
2. Avg. # of characters/word	−0.16**	–	0.05**	−0.04**	−0.16**	−0.12**	0.36**	−0.36**	−0.12**	−0.09**
3. Avg. # of words/sentences	0.09**	0.07**	–	0.12**	−0.13**	0.13**	−0.12**	0.12**	0.06**	−0.01
4. Characters	0.79**	−0.06**	0.17**	–	0.45**	0.83**	0.00	0.00	0.43**	0.06**
5. Connectivity index	0.58**	−0.23**	−0.18**	0.63**	–	0.45**	−0.01	0.01	0.30**	0.06**
6. Connectors	0.76**	−0.17**	0.19**	0.95**	0.62**	–	−0.04**	0.04**	0.43**	0.05**
7. Content word ratio	−0.01	0.51**	−0.17**	0.00	−0.01**	−0.06**	–	−1.00**	−0.11**	−0.13**
8. Function word ratio	0.01	−0.51**	0.17**	0.00	0.01*	0.06**	−1.00**	–	0.11**	0.13**
9. Grammatical errors	0.45**	−0.17**	0.08**	0.59**	0.42**	0.59**	−0.16**	0.16**	–	−0.65**
10. Grammatical error ratio	0.04**	−0.12**	−0.01**	0.09**	0.09**	0.10**	−0.19**	0.19**	0.79**	–
11. Lexical diversity	−0.73**	0.25**	−0.09**	−0.84**	−0.60**	−0.83**	0.06**	−0.06**	−0.51**	−0.06**
12. Sentences	0.78**	−0.18**	−0.13**	0.93**	0.72**	0.90**	0.00	0.00	0.59**	0.12**
13. Spelling errors	0.56**	0.07**	0.15**	0.69**	0.43**	0.61**	0.07**	−0.7**	0.38**	0.03**
14. Spelling error ratio	0.08**	0.24**	0.06**	0.09**	0.01	0.02*	0.15**	−0.15**	−0.02*	−0.06**
15. Topic flow index	0.47**	−0.17**	−0.21**	0.60**	0.50**	0.59**	−0.07**	0.07**	0.42**	0.13**
16. Unique words	0.74**	−0.07**	0.19**	0.95**	0.61**	0.93**	−0.04**	0.04**	0.61**	0.13**
17. Unknown words	0.70**	−0.17**	0.06**	0.82**	0.60**	0.77**	−0.06**	0.06**	0.55**	0.13**
18. Unknown word ratio	0.33**	−0.13**	−0.10**	0.32**	0.31**	0.27**	−0.05**	0.05**	0.27**	0.11**
19. Words	0.79**	−0.15**	0.16**	0.99**	0.64**	0.97**	−0.04**	0.04**	0.60**	0.10**
Variable	**11**	**12**	**13**	**14**	**15**	**16**	**17**	**18**	**19**	
1. Processing time	−0.55**	0.61**	0.40**	0.05**	0.33**	0.57**	0.52**	0.22**	0.63**	
2. Avg. # of characters/word	0.17**	−0.12**	0.05**	0.17**	−0.12**	−0.05**	−0.12**	−0.09**	−0.10**	
3. Avg. # of words/sentence	−0.06**	−0.10**	0.10**	0.04**	−0.14**	0.13**	0.03**	−0.07**	0.11**	
4. Characters	−0.66**	0.78**	0.51**	0.06**	0.43**	0.82**	0.63**	0.22**	0.94**	

5. Connectivity index	−0.43**	0.54**	0.30**	0.00	0.35**	0.44**	0.43**	0.22**	0.46**	
6. Connectors	−0.65**	0.74**	0.44**	0.01	0.43**	0.78**	0.58**	0.19**	0.85**	
7. Content word ratio	0.04**	0.00	0.05**	0.11**	−0.04**	−0.02**	−0.04**	−0.03**	−0.03**	
8. Function word ratio	−0.04**	0.00	−0.05**	−0.11**	0.04**	0.02**	0.04**	0.03**	0.03**	
9. Grammatical errors	−0.36**	0.43**	0.27**	−0.01**	0.30**	0.44**	0.40**	0.19**	0.44**	
10. Grammatical error ratio	−0.04**	0.08**	0.02**	−0.04**	0.09**	0.08**	0.09**	0.08**	0.06**	
11. Lexical diversity	–	−0.67**	−0.43**	−0.05**	−0.34**	−0.50**	−0.57**	−0.25**	−0.68**	
12. Sentences	−0.85**	–	0.46**	0.04**	0.51**	0.71**	0.64**	0.27**	0.80**	
13. Spelling errors	−0.60**	0.63**	–	0.57**	0.26**	0.47**	0.46**	0.25**	0.49**	
14. Spelling error ratio	−0.07**	0.06**	0.72**	–	0.00	0.04**	0.10**	0.14**	0.04**	
15. Topic flow index	−0.48**	0.68**	0.38**	0.00	–	0.45**	0.37**	0.17**	0.44**	
16. Unique words	−0.69**	0.88**	0.65**	0.07**	0.61**	–	0.58**	0.19**	0.82**	
17. Unknown words	−0.76**	0.82**	0.63**	0.15**	0.53**	0.77**	–	0.59**	0.64**	
18. Unknown word ratio	−0.36**	0.38**	0.36**	0.20**	0.25**	0.28**	0.77**	–	0.23**	
19. Words	−0.86**	0.94**	0.67**	0.07**	0.61**	0.95**	0.83**	0.33**	–	

*$p \leq 0.05$, **$p \leq 0.01$

is moderate and, hence, may have a relatively confounding effect on the correlation coefficients calculated in Table 8.9.

5.2 *RQ2 and RQ3*

The next step in this analysis is to test whether the two sample medians between A_1 and A_2 and between B_1 and B_2 are significantly different. The goal is to verify whether the structure elements of a text (e.g., lexical, syntactic, semantic) may have some impact on processing time. Because most of the original distributions of the 26 variables was shown to depart significantly from normality, a nonparametric two-sided Wilcoxon rank sum test was selected to test whether the samples come from different populations, hypothesizing that (1) the A_1 and A_2 distributions for a specific writing feature are identical and (2) the B_1 and B_2 distributions for a specific writing feature are identical. In both cases, it tests whether the medians of A_2 and B_2 are significantly different from the medians of A_1 and B_1. Furthermore, the effect sizes are measured by rank biserial correlation coefficients (Glass, 1966):

$$r = \frac{2(M_1 - M_2)}{n_1 + n_2},$$

where M_1 and M_2 are the mean ranks for either groups A_1 and A_2 or B_1 and B_2, while n_1 and n_2 are the number of observations per group. The value ranges between −1 and 1 and is interpreted similarly to the Spearman's rho rank coefficient. Table 8.10 exhibits the median of each writing feature for the four groups along with their corresponding effect size and significance level. It should be noted that all processing time values and writing features are independent from one writing event to the other even though many writing events have been generated from the same composition.

Furthermore, the numbers of distinct compositions represented by A_1, A_2, B_1, and B_2 were calculated to ensure that some small subset of compositions (e.g., with many words from foreign languages) in the second group (longest processing times) of each pair was not the cause of these longer processing times. It is important to mention that all of these compositions reflect a sincere endeavor from students. All have received a Distinction (70–100) or a Merit (60–69) mark. Both A_1 and A_2 had writing events from the 391 compositions. However, B_2 had writing events from 264 compositions (still a large number), while B_1 had writing events from all 391 compositions.

5.3 *RQ4 and RQ5*

The same process described under Sect. 5.2 was repeated to analyze whether there is a difference between the median shares of processing time of the NLP solutions in this study's NLP pipeline. First, Table 8.11 shows that the parsing phase of the

Table 8.10 A_1, A_2, B_1, and B_2 medians of writing features along with the effect sizes and significance levels of the differences in medians

	A_1	A_2	r	B_1	B_2	r
Avg. # of characters/word	4.69	4.62	−0.14**	4.66	4.60	−0.09**
Avg. # of words/sentence	25.43	25.90	0.06**	25.73	25.66	0.00
Characters	2333	6348	0.81**	3799	6545	0.54**
Connectivity index	1.39	1.66	0.54**	1.52	1.67	0.37**
Connectors	79	215	0.78**	129	218	0.50**
Content word ratio	0.53	0.54	0.01**	0.53	0.54	0.00**
Function word ratio	0.47	0.46	−0.01**	0.47	0.46	0.00**
Grammatical errors	3	7	0.44**	5	7	0.25**
Grammatical error ratio	0.006	0.006	0.03**	0.006	0.005	−0.05**
Lexical diversity	0.40	0.29	−0.72**	0.35	0.29	−0.48**
Sentences	19	51	0.79**	31	54	0.53**
Spelling errors	5	14	0.54**	8	15	0.38**
Spelling error ratio	0.010	0.011	0.06**	0.010	0.011	0.08**
Topic flow index	0.68	0.84	0.49**	0.78	0.84	0.26**
Unique words	196	380	0.75**	273	389	0.49**
Unknown words	16	70	0.70**	33	78	0.51**
Unknown word ratio	0.04	0.05	0.32**	0.05	0.06	0.28**
Words	502	1380	0.82**	821	1419	0.54**

$^{*}p \leq 0.05$, $^{**}p \leq 0.01$

Table 8.11 Percentages of total processing time accounted for by the three phases of the writing analytics system and the percentages of processing time taken by each of the four NLP tools over the total parsing time

	A_1	A_2	B_1	B_2	Total
Phases					
Parsing	66.9%	67.9%	68.4%	67.1%	67.8%
Grading	9.0%	11.4%	8.0%	14.0%	11.0%
Competence assessment	1.7%	0.8%	1.3%	0.6%	0.9%
Other	22.3%	19.9%	22.4%	18.3%	20.3%
Tools					
Stanford CoreNLP	16.8%	20.4%	17.8%	21.8%	19.8%
Apache OpenNLP	0.7%	0.2%	0.4%	0.2%	0.3%
TML	3.7%	11.2%	5.4%	14.6%	10.0%
LanguageTool	35.2%	36.4%	33.3%	39.1%	36.2%
Other	43.6%	31.8%	43.1%	24.3%	33.7%

writing analytics system proposed in this study accounts for 68% of the total processing time, implying that the scalability of the system depends mostly on the scalability of natural language processing. Table 8.11 also highlights the share of processing taken by each NLP tool on the total parsing time for each group. It can be observed that Stanford CoreNLP and LanguageTool are the most intense

Table 8.12 A_1, A_2, B_1, and B_2 in medians of NLP tools' processing time ratios along with the effect sizes and significance levels of the differences in medians

	A_1	A_2	r	B_1	B_2	r
Stanford CoreNLP	16.3%	16.6%	0.03**	16.4%	18.5%	0.02**
Apache OpenNLP	0.6%	0.2%	−0.13**	0.4%	0.1%	−0.13**
TML	3.9%	3.1%	−0.04**	3.6%	3.4%	−0.06**
LanguageTool	34.7%	35.2%	0.04**	34.7%	38.6%	0.04**
Parsing	66.3%	71.0%	0.08**	68.9%	68.5%	0.08**

$*p \leq 0.05$, $**p \leq 0.01$

consumers of computational power and that their share of the parsing time increases in A_2 and B_2, that is, with the writing events having the longest processing times.

Table 8.12 displays the median shares of parsing time by each NLP tool within each group. It also calculates the median share of the total processing time by the parsing phase. The nonparametric Wilcoxon rank sum test was again employed to evaluate whether the underlying populations of processing time are identical or not. The effect sizes are also reported as rank biserial correlation coefficients, and the values are provided to indicate whether the differences in medians are statistically significant.

6 Discussion

Based on the moderate-strong positive correlations ($0.61 \leq \tau_b \leq 0.63$) that exist between the number of words, the number of sentences, and the number of characters variables and processing time, there is significant evidence that the length of a text influences the duration of processing time. These three variables have the strongest correlation coefficients among all the variables analyzed in this study. It is important to note, when interpreting the Kendall's tau-b and Spearman's rho correlation coefficients, that Kendall's correlations usually generate smaller values than Spearman's correlations. They are, however, measured on the same scale and have the same meaning.

The number of connectors (transition words/phrases), the lexical diversity (number of unique words over total number of words), the number of unique words in the text, and the number of unknown words have all a moderate-strong correlation ($0.53 \leq |\tau_b| \leq 0.59$) with processing time. It is relevant to underscore, nevertheless, that these variables are highly correlated with the number of words that a text has. For example, having a greater number of connecting phrases may result, in many cases, in a higher number of words.

As for the syntactic complexity, measured in this study by the average number of words per sentence, it is interesting to note that there is no evidence at all of a correlation with processing time.

There is a weak-moderate positive relationship ($0.34 \leq \tau_b \leq 0.53$) between the numbers of grammatical and spelling errors (including unknown words) and processing time, interestingly implying that a no-fault text may be quicker to parse.

At the lexical level, it is worth noting a higher density of nouns, verbs, adjectives, and adverbs has no relationship with the duration of the processing time, and that the average number of characters per word is only very weakly correlated with processing time.

The higher presence of cohesive devices, as measured by the connectivity and topic flow (semantic similarity) indexes, is weakly moderately correlated ($0.33 \leq \tau_b \leq 0.41$) with the duration of processing time.

In summary, the correlational analysis performed in this study, provides evidence that the structural elements of a text have some impact on the time required to process it.

In Table 8.10, it can be seen that all differences in medians are statistically significant except for one case, and that, more importantly, the effect sizes corroborate the results of the correlational analysis. The difference in median average numbers of words per sentence between B_1 and B_2 is very small, providing further evidence that the length of sentences (a measure of syntactical complexity) does not seem to incur extra processing time. The Wilcoxon rank sum tests demonstrate that (1) the length of a text is directly related to the processing time and (2) there are significant disparities at the lexical, syntactic, and semantic levels between the groups. This supports the hypothesis that the quality and length of a composition may have an impact and, hence, help to predict the computational time that will be required to process it.

Tables 8.11 and 8.12 demonstrate that the share of parsing time on the total processing time increases slightly in A_2 and B_2 (the longest-to-process writing events), potentially suggesting some scalability issue. For example, Stanford CoreNLP increases its share of parsing time of 3.6% from A_1 to A_2 and 4.0% from B_1 to B_2. As for LanguageTool, the percentages of parsing time increase 1.2% and 5.8% from A_1 to A_2 and from B_1 to B_2, respectively. In other words, not only the processing time taken by Stanford CoreNLP and LanguageTool increases as the length and complexity of writing events increase, but it may increase more sharply than other tools. Nevertheless, the effect sizes are quite small and may suggest investigating other unidentified factors underlying this small degradation.

Through a relatively small set of 391 compositions, this study underscores the reality that capturing and analyzing the writing process of English academic writing is computationally intensive. For instance, the writing process of a 1786-word composition will on average be processed within less than 3 h and a half on a Linux server instance (Ubuntu 14.04) with 16 GB of RAM and a 4-core Intel Xeon CPU E5-2650 @ 2.00 GHz with 20 MB of cache memory. Additionally, this study demonstrates the need for more scalable solutions adapted to the analysis of the writing process instead of scaling solutions to the analysis of the final writing product. For example, many parts of the compositions were unnecessarily and redundantly processed in analyzing the writing process.

The provision of real-time feedback and suggestions of writing strategies may prove central to enhance significantly writers' success. For example, students who are lagging behind in writing their first draft, while maintaining a high level of writing quality, may receive a recommendation to accelerate their drafting stage by undertaking short brainstorming sessions for the remaining paragraphs. Conversely, the system may evaluate the coherence and cohesion in the writings of students who quickly produced their first draft, and forewarn them to put aside more time to improve the consistency and organization of their writings. Moreover, by regularly supplying students with holistic and rubric-based scores all along the writing process, students will know what outcomes (e.g., grades) to expect and where their weaknesses are in relation to the scoring rubrics. This will give them opportunities to improve and target higher performance levels. To sum up, the writing analytics system will discover the writing behaviors that are highly correlated with or even that have been proved to be causing successful writings and will shape feedback to aid writers pass from a suboptimal performance to a more optimal one.

6.1 Limitations

This section acknowledges the main limitations of this study. First, although the server instance on which the writing analytics system ran was totally allocated for that processing, the monitoring of the server activity level has not been recorded to see whether any other activity on the server could have interfered with the writing analytics system's processing (although nothing is expected to have interfered). Second, the system required a restart almost daily to counter a memory leak found in the system. This incurred some significant extra initialization time for the NLP software packages and the grading component, which was calculated in the processing time of the writing event processed after the start-up. Third, the memory leak also degraded a bit the speed at which writing events were processed. However, given that all writing events were subject to the same condition, this should reduce the bias inflicted by the memory leak. Fourth, this study has not investigated in detail the performance of the NoSQL MongoDB database, though there was no major apparent issue. Fifth, the writing features evaluated in the present research do not accurately capture the complexity of higher education writing, such as the rhetorical effectiveness and the strength of argumentation (Kumar et al., 2017). Sixth, lower processing time in many cases is associated with lower-quality text since these texts were part of the development process, which may add some bias when interpreting the results in this study. The reduced effect sizes as displayed for B_1 and B_2 (where B_2 contains many outlier processing times) in Table 8.10 serve as evidence of the potential impact of these limitations. Nevertheless, this research provided a diversified dataset, limiting the bias that would be introduced by a particular type of writing.

6.2 Recommendations for Scalability

To adapt and scale natural language processing to the writing process, this research proposes to apply the Map-Reduce paradigm at the sentence level since sentences are the smallest units that NLP usually works with. This would provide the advantage of distributing the processing across a cluster of computing resources, while avoiding reprocessing all the sentences that have not changed since the last edit. In most cases, the difference between two writing events is tiny and consists of the addition of a new word. The Map functions could split the text into its constituent sentences to be then analyzed by a part-of-speech tagger, named entity recognizer, lemmatizer, stemmer, spellchecker, etc., to derive and compute the desired set of writing metrics. On the other side, the Reduce functions could aggregate together the various writing metrics to describe higher-level composition parts, such as pairs of consecutive sentences, paragraphs, the whole composition, and finally the set of all compositions pertaining to a student. It means that every sentence or text constituent, no matter the level, will ultimately be associated with a set of writing metrics as well as data describing (1) the assignment to which it pertains, (2) the writing event from which it was calculated (e.g., the 300th writing event), and (3) its position within a higher-level text part (i.e., second sentence within first paragraph). For example, an essay could consist of ten sentences and three paragraphs. A student might want to add an adverb in Sentence 2 from Paragraph 1 to enhance the meaning of an action verb. With the proposed architecture, the updated essay text will again be sentence-split. Every sentence will then be compared against the sentences of the previous writing event to identify which sentences have changed. In this case, only Sentence 2 will be required to be parsed again by the suite of NLP solutions (instead of re-parsing all ten sentences), only the metrics of Paragraph 1 will have to be updated, and finally the metrics of the encompassing essay will be recalculated. It is important to note that the Map functions would be significantly more computationally expensive than the Reduce functions, which would merely be aggregating functions (Clemens et al., 2018).

Another measure of optimization that this research proposes is to unify the various disparate NLP solutions that often redo what other solutions have already performed. For instance, the NLP pipeline in this study's writing analytics system consists of a conglomerate of NLP tools such as Stanford CoreNLP, Apache OpenNLP, Text Mining Library, and LanguageTool, which all need to perform sentence splitting and tokenization and some of them part-of-speech tagging separately to feed their functionalities that are unique to them. For instance, Stanford CoreNLP is the only tool that provides the lemma of every word, while Apache OpenNLP, although less powerful than Stanford CoreNLP, gives the possibility to extract the *n*-grams of a text. Given that most of these software packages are open source, centralizing and reconciling certain NLP tasks become priority to improve the efficiency of writing analytics systems.

In summary, this research recommends (1) unifying disparate open source NLP solutions into a unified pipeline, (2) parallelizing NLP tasks using a Storm topology or the Spark/Hadoop MapReduce paradigm, and (3) breaking NLP tasks down at the sentence level to avoid re-parsing unchanged sections of the text. By incorporating these suggested changes in a big data NLP architecture, the processing time gain expected in the context of the analysis of the writing process would range between several orders of magnitude (100–1000). The dataset in this study could then be processed in 13.04 h or even 1.3 h instead of 54.3 days! Such an architecture would allow to unleash a rich source of potential new insights never captured before, such as new predictive variables based on the writing behavior for automated writing evaluation, large-scale and early detection of ADHD students, and very fine-grained provision of feedback and self-regulatory strategies along the writing process.

7 Conclusions

The present research analyzed the performance of a single-threaded writing analytics system, which included a serial NLP pipeline of four different NLP solutions. The writing process of a subset of 390 writing assignments (391 actual compositions) from the BAWE corpus was simulated, generating over 700,000 texts to be processed by the writing analytics systems. These assignments were representative of many disciplines in four broad disciplinary groupings in higher education. More than 54 days were necessary to process the writing process of these 391 compositions. This study reveals that the length of text has a moderate-strong positive correlation with the duration of processing time; that there is evidence of the impact of lexical, syntactic, and semantic structural elements on the performance of NLP software packages; and that the processing time ratios of Stanford CoreNLP and LanguageTool increase with texts requiring longer processing time. This research proposes a methodology to analyze performance data to get insight into the scaling of natural language processing at the big data level. It concludes by recommending reconciling and centralizing NLP software packages and parallelizing NLP tasks at the sentence level, expecting gains up to several orders of magnitude.

As a result of this research, it will be possible to analyze the processing times of the various states of a student's writing, which will allow to measure in real time the student's level of writing engagement. Furthermore, fine-grained formative feedback could be provided not only at the end of the writing episode, but also all along the writing process to scaffold the student's writing effort (e.g., helping him/her to overcome the blank page syndrome). This will lay the foundation for the implementation of a real-time pedagogical agent that would balance timely pedagogical interventions and opportunities for practice. In addition, a smart automated writing scoring module built using deep learning techniques (e.g., long short-term memory neural networks) could be integrated to empower the pedagogical agent to assign both holistic and rubric scores (e.g., ideas and content, organization, voice, vocabulary, sentence fluency, conventions) at important milestones in the student's writing process. This way, students will be able to reflect on their current level of writing proficiency and assess how they are going to meet the learning outcomes. Finally, by improving the efficiency of NLP pipelines, feedback over writing performance could be extended to areas where writing is a prerequisite skill but not a core component of the targeted learning outcomes (e.g., writing a scientific report in a physics course). This will contribute both to the short-term and long-term development of the writing skill.

Acknowledgements The authors gratefully acknowledge NSERC funding for this research.

References

Agerri, R., Artola, X., Beloki, Z., Rigau, G., & Soroa, A. (2015). Big data for natural language processing: A streaming approach. *Knowledge-Based Systems, 79*, 36–42. https://doi.org/10.1016/j.knosys.2014.11.007

Alsop, S., & Nesi, H. (2009). Issues in the development of the British Academic Written English (BAWE) corpus. *Corpora, 4*(1), 71–83.

Alvarez-Fernandez, M.-L., & Garcia-Sanchez, J.-N. (2015). The orchestration of processes in relation to the product, and the role of psychological variables in written composition. *Anales de Psicologia, 31*(1), 96–108. https://doi.org/10.6018/analesps.31.1.169621

Boulanger, D., Seanosky, J., Clemens, C., Kumar, V., & Kinshuk. (2016). SCALE: A smart competence analytics solution for English writing. In *Proceedings of the 2016 IEEE 16th International Conference on Advanced Learning Technologies (ICALT)* (pp. 468–472). Washington, DC: IEEE. https://doi.org/10.1109/ICALT.2016.108

Clemens, C. (2017). *A causal model of writing competence* (Doctoral dissertation, Athabasca University, 2017). Retrieved from https://dt.athabascau.ca/jspui/handle/10791/233

Clemens, C., Kumar, V., Boulanger, D., Seanosky, J., & Kinshuk. (2018). Learning traces, competence assessment, and causal inference for English composition. In *Frontiers of cyberlearning* (pp. 49–67). Singapore: Springer.

Cureton, E. E. (1968). Rank-biserial correlation when ties are present. *Educational and Psychological Measurement, 28*(1), 77–79.

Franklin, S. V., & Hermsen, L. M. (2014). Real-time capture of student reasoning while writing. *Physical Review Special Topics-Physics Education Research, 10*(2), 020121. https://doi.org/10.1103/PhysRevSTPER.10.020121

Freiman, M. (2015). The art of drafting and revision: Extended mind in creative writing. *New Writing – The International Journal for the Practice and Theory of Creative Writing, 12*(1), 48–66. https://doi.org/10.1080/14790726.2014.977797

Fuchs, S., & Krivokapic, J. (2016). Prosodic boundaries in writing: Evidence from a keystroke analysis. *Frontiers in Psychology, 7*, 1678. https://doi.org/10.3389/fpsyg.2016.01678

Garcia, J.-N., & Fidalgo, R. (2008). Orchestration of writing processes and writing products: A comparison of sixth-grade students with and without learning disabilities. *Learning Disabilities: A Contemporary Journal, 6*(2), 77–98.

Glass, G. V. (1966). Note on rank biserial correlation. *Educational and Psychological Measurement, 26*(3), 623–631. https://doi.org/10.1177/001316446602600307

Goyal, A., Singh, A., Bhargava, S., Crawl, D., Altintas, I., & Hsu, C.-N. (2016). Natural language processing using Kepler workflow system: First steps. *Procedia Computer Science, 80*, 712–721. https://doi.org/10.1016/j.procs.2016.05.358

Heuboeck, A., Holmes, J., & Nesi, H. (2010). *The BAWE corpus manual*. Reading: University of Reading.

Kaggal, V. C., Elayavilli, R. K., Mehrabi, S., Pankratz, J. J., Sohn, S., Wang, Y., … Liu, H. (2016). Toward a learning health-care system – Knowledge delivery at the point of care empowered by big data and NLP. *Biomedical Informatics Insights, 8*(Suppl. 1), 13–22. https://doi.org/10.4137/BII.S37977

Kumar, V., Fraser, S. N., & Boulanger, D. (2017). Discovering the predictive power of five baseline writing competences. *Journal of Writing Analytics, 1*(1), 176–226.

Lewkow, N., Feild, J., Zimmerman, N., Riedesel, M., Essa, A., Boulanger, D., … Kode, S. (2016). A scalable learning analytics platform for automated writing feedback. In *Proceedings of the Third (2016) ACM Conference on Learning @ Scale* (pp. 109–112). New York, NY: ACM. https://doi.org/10.1145/2876034.2893380

McCreadie, R., Macdonald, C., Ounis, I., Osborne, M., & Petrovic, S. (2013). Scalable distributed event detection for Twitter. In *2013 IEEE International Conference on Big Data* (pp. 543–549). Washington, DC: IEEE. https://doi.org/10.1109/BigData.2013.6691620

Monali, P., & Sandip, K. (2014). A concise survey on text data mining. *International Journal of Advanced Research in Computer and Communication Engineering, 3*(9), 8040–8043.

Nath, C., Albaghdadi, M. S., & Jonnalagadda, S. R. (2016). A natural language processing tool for large-scale data extraction from echocardiography reports. *PLoS One, 11*(4), e0153749. https://doi.org/10.1371/journal.pone.0153749

Nesi, H., Sharpling, G., & Ganobcsik-Williams, L. (2004). Student papers across the curriculum: Designing and developing a corpus of British student writing. *Computers and Composition, 21*(4), 439–450. https://doi.org/10.1016/j.compcom.2004.08.003

Nesi, P., Pantaleo, G., & Sanesi, G. (2015). A Hadoop-based platform for natural language processing of web pages and documents. *Journal of Visual Languages & Computing, 31*, 130–138. https://doi.org/10.1016/j.jvlc.2015.10.017

Ollagnier-Beldame, M., Brassac, C., & Mille, A. (2014). Traces and activity: A case study of a joint writing process mediated by a digital environment. *Behaviour & Information Technology, 33*(9, SI), 954–967. https://doi.org/10.1080/0144929X.2013.819528

Singh, S., Subramanya, A., Pereira, F., & McCallum, A. (2011). Large-scale cross-document coreference using distributed inference and hierarchical models. In *Proceedings of the 49th Annual Meeting of the Association for Computational Linguistics: Human Language Technologies - Volume 1* (pp. 793–803). Stroudsburg, PA: Association for Computational Linguistics. Retrieved from http://dl.acm.org/citation.cfm?id=2002472.2002573

Southavilay, V., Yacef, K., & Calvo, R. A. (2009). WriteProc: A framework for exploring collaborative writing processes. In *ADCS 2009 - Proceedings of the Fourteenth Australasian Document Computing Symposium* (pp. 129–136). Retrieved from https://www.scopus.com/inward/record.uri?eid=2-s2.0-84864874796&partnerID=40&md5=48c193aa1c55dd7706e33a903f9914c6

Torkildsen, J. v. K., Morken, F., Helland, W. A., & Helland, T. (2016). The dynamics of narrative writing in primary grade children: Writing process factors predict story quality. *Reading and Writing, 29*(3), 529–554. https://doi.org/10.1007/s11145-015-9618-4

Turner, V., Gantz, J. F., Reinsel, D., & Minton, S. (2014). The digital universe of opportunities: Rich data and the increasing value of the Internet of Things. In *IDC Analyze the future*.

Van Waes, L., & Schellens, P. J. (2003). Writing profiles: The effect of the writing mode on pausing and revision patterns of experienced writers. *Journal of Pragmatics, 35*(6), 829–853. https://doi.org/10.1016/S0378-2166(02)00121-2

Wei, C.-H., Leaman, R., & Lu, Z. (2016). Beyond accuracy: Creating interoperable and scalable text-mining web services. *Bioinformatics, 32*(12), 1907–1910. https://doi.org/10.1093/bioinformatics/btv760

Ye, Z., Tafti, A. P., He, K. Y., Wang, K., & He, M. M. (2016). SparkText: Biomedical text mining on big data framework. *PLoS One, 11*(9), e0162721. https://doi.org/10.1371/journal.pone.0162721

Yim, S., & Warschauer, M. (2017). Web-based collaborative writing in L2 contexts: Methodological insights from text mining. *Language Learning and Technology, 21*(1), 146–165. Retrieved from https://www.scopus.com/inward/record.uri?eid=2-s2.0-85013173145&partnerID=40&md5=0cbf14349550945a59a8fbc50f28677e

David Boulanger is an undergraduate student in Computing and Information Systems, and data scientist involved in the learning analytics research group at Athabasca University. His primary research focus is on observational study designs and the application of computational tools and machine learning algorithms in learning analytics including writing analytics.

Clayton Clemens holds a Master of Science in Information Systems, with a specialization in natural language processing, learning analytics, and causal inference. Clayton works full-time as a business analyst for the City of Edmonton, Alberta, where he leverages his knowledge of computational techniques to support continuously improving recreation opportunities for citizens.

Jeremie Seanosky is an undergraduate student in Computing and Information Systems, and research assistant at Athabasca University. His areas of research interests include bigdata analytics; learning analytics sensors; failsafe data collection, retrieval, analysis; virtual reality; augmented reality; and automated assessment.

Shawn Fraser earned his bachelor's degree in Mathematics from the University of Regina in 1995. He completed a Master's degree in Kinesiology at the University of Saskatchewan in 1999. He obtained his PhD in Physical Education and Recreation from the University of Alberta in 2006. He is currently Associate Professor at Athabasca University and an Adjunct Assistant Professor in Physical Education and Recreation at the University of Alberta. His research interests include understanding how stress can impact upon rehabilitation success for heart patients. He teaches research methods courses in the Faculty of Health Disciplines and is interested in interdisciplinary approaches to studying and teaching research methods and data analysis.

Vivekanandan Kumar completed his bachelor's degree (BSc) in Physics with a minor in Mathematics (1987) as well as a Master's degree in Computer Science Applications (1990) at Bharathiar University, India. He earned his doctoral degree in Computer Science (PhD) from the University of Saskatchewan, Canada, as the best graduating student in 2001. He is currently Full Professor in the School of Computing and Information Systems at Athabasca University, Canada. He holds the Natural Sciences and Engineering Research Council of Canada's (NSERC) Discovery Grant on Anthropomorphic Pedagogical Agents, funded by the Government of Canada. His research focuses on developing anthropomorphic agents, which mimic and optimize human-like traits to better assist learners in their regulatory and domain tasks. His research includes technology-enhanced erudition methods that employ Big Data Learning Analytics, Self-Regulated Learning, Co-regulated Learning, Authentic Learning, Causal Modelling, and Machine Learning, to facilitate deep learning. He is an IEEE senior member.

Part III
Analytics for Personalizing Teaching and Assessment

Chapter 9
An Analysis of Open Learner Models for Supporting Learning Analytics

Stylianos Sergis and Demetrios Sampson

Abstract Teaching and learning are increasingly being offered in distributed, online digital environments, often openly and at large-scale, traversing spatial and temporal boundaries. Within such environments, Learning Analytics technologies aim to provide the means for tracking and making sense of the multitude of educational data that is being generated, in order to inform educational and pedagogical decision making of different actors, such as learners, teachers, school leaders and parents. However, at the heart of Learning Analytics technologies in such distributed and open learning environments lies the Open Learner Model (OLM), that informs the data collection, processing and sense-making capabilities of the analytics technology. In this context the contribution of this chapter is to present a generic educational data-driven layered Open Learner Modelling framework, which can be used as a blueprint for the analysis (and design) of OLM instances. Furthermore, capitalizing on this framework, the chapter also performs a critical analysis of existing research in OLM works, in order to draw conclusions on the current status of this emerging field.

1 Introduction

Teaching and learning are increasingly being offered in distributed and digital environments, traversing former spatial and temporal boundaries (Chatti, Muslim, & Schroeder, 2017). Within such environments, educational data are continuously generated as a result of the interactions between the various actors (learners, peers, teachers, parents) within a given learning environment. Evidence has shown that

S. Sergis (✉)
Department of Digital Systems, University of Piraeus, Piraeus, Greece

D. Sampson
Department of Digital Systems, University of Piraeus, Piraeus, Greece

School of Education, Curtin University, Perth, WA, Australia
e-mail: sampson@unipi.gr; demetrios.sampson@curtin.edu.au

D. Sampson et al. (eds.), *Learning Technologies for Transforming Large-Scale Teaching, Learning, and Assessment*, https://doi.org/10.1007/978-3-030-15130-0_9

these data can be beneficial to inform and personalize teaching and learning, especially when educational data analytics technologies are employed to support their collection, processing and sense-making.

Educational Data Analytics, in particular Learning Analytics, aim to provide the means for tracking and making sense of the multitude of educational data, generated in online and blended environments where physical interaction is limited. Capitalizing on Learning Analytics technologies, different stakeholders can inform their decision making, spanning from self-assessment of learners (Verbert, Duval, Klerkx, Govaerts, & Santos, 2013), personalized feedback and scaffolding by tutors (Ali, Hatala, Gašević, & Jovanović, 2012) to systematic evaluation of teaching and learning designs for teachers and instructional designers (Sergis & Sampson, 2017).

Regardless of the particular purpose of using Learning Analytics, however, these systems share a core element, which is the *learner model*. The learner model is the systems' representation of the learner, which is used for example to provide personalized services by the system or inform the decision making of other actors (Brusilovsky & Millan, 2007).

In the specific context of technology-enhanced teaching and learning design and delivery, learner models have been extensively used in the field of Intelligent Tutoring Systems (ITS) and Adaptive Hypermedia (AH) (Woolf, 2010). To a large extent, learner models in ITSs are 'closed', namely they are accessed and edited strictly by the system, without any of this information reaching directly the learner (Brusilovsky et al., 2016). However, as Learning Analytics approaches evolve to support the paradigm shifts to more 'open', self-regulated blended and online environments, so does the field of learner modelling, introducing *Open Learner Models* (OLM). OLM are a sub-class of learner models that allow various actors (e.g., learners, peers, teachers, parents) to view the content of the model, in a human understandable form (Bull & Kay, 2016). The main purpose for the 'openness' of the learner model is to inform the educational and pedagogical decision making of different actors in the teaching and learning process. For example, learners can inform their self-reflection on their performance (Bull, Johnson, Masci, & Biel, 2015); teachers can monitor learners' progress and performance (Pohl, Bry, Schwarz, & Gottstein, 2012); and parents can be included in their children's learning process, by gaining direct access to their outcomes and progress (Bull & Kay, 2010).

As OLM have largely evolved inline to the recent advancements of Learning Analytics and (large-scale) self-regulated learning, such as in Massive Open Online Courses (MOOCs), there is still a strong interest in this field. Thus, the contribution of this chapter is twofold. First, it presents an educational data-driven layered Open Learner Model framework which, extending existing works, provides the means to present the different layers of the learner modelling process and can be used as a blueprint for analyzing (and designing) OLM. Second, capitalizing on this framework, the chapter reports on a critical analysis of existing OLM research, in order to draw conclusions on the current status of the OLM research and potentially inform future works.

The remainder of the chapter is structured as follows. Section 2 presents the background of this work, namely the concept and purposes of Open Learner Models.

Furthermore, it outlines the prevalent method for describing OLM that this work has built on to formulate the educational data-driven layered Open Learner Modelling Framework presented in Sect. 3. Section 4 discusses the methodology and results of the review of research OLM, using this framework as an analysis benchmark. Finally, Sect. 5 summarizes the conclusions drawn as a result of the review reported in this chapter.

2 Background: Open Learner Models

2.1 *Open Learner Models: Definition and Relevant Concepts*

Prior to discussing Open Learner Models, it is important to first describe a set of relevant concepts that are directly related to OLM and inform their definition. To begin with, a *Learner (or student) Model* is a representation of specific characteristics of learners, relevant to the educational practice (Giannandrea & Sansoni, 2013). Learner models aim to codify the individual learner based on a specific set of dimensions (Nakic, Granic, & Glavinic, 2015). Depending on the specific area of application, these dimensions can include among others, competences, misconceptions, affective states or interests (Chrysafiadi & Virvou, 2013). Typically, such models aim to inform the provision of personalized experiences to learners, such as adaptive sequencing of learning activities (Hosseini, Hsiao, Guerra, & Brusilovsky, 2015), or recommendations of educational resources (Chrysafiadi & Virvou, 2013).

A *Learner (or student) Profile* is the instantiation of the learner model for a given time, using *educational data* (Martins, Faria, De Carvalho, & Carrapatoso, 2008). Examples of such data include, for example, personal details, scores in assessment activities, educational resource access/usage patterns and learning activity access/completion patterns during the delivery of the learning process. These data can be either automatically captured by a system implicitly (such as Learning Management Systems or Intelligent Tutoring Systems) or provided in a manual manner (Al-Shamri & Bharadwaj, 2008).

Open Learner Models refer to learner models that are explicitly communicated to the learner or other actors in the teaching and learning process (e.g. peers teachers, parents) through allowing visualization and/or editing of the relevant profiles (Bull & Kay, 2010). According to Bull and Kay (2016), OLM can be either inspectable, negotiated or editable. *Inspectable* open learner models do not allow editing of the profile, and simply visualize the profile as defined and populated by the system (e.g., an LMS). *Negotiated* open learner models allow various actors to alter the values of the profile; however, they typically require evidence that supports the updated value in order to accept it (e.g., require the learner to take a test to demonstrate his new competence level). *Editable* models allow the various actors to freely update the values of the profiles.

Furthermore, most OLM are embedded within digital learning environments, but there is increasing interest in *Independent* OLM, namely OLM that are not part of a specific system and may collect and exploit educational data from diverse sources (Bull, Gakhal, et al., 2010; Bull, Jackson, & Lancaster, 2010). This trend is aligned to the overarching shift of Learning Analytics within open, distributed and large-scale learning environments (such as MOOCs). In such environments, useful educational data are generated from diverse sources and thus, OLM needs to capture and process them. Additionally, in such environments, the task of personalizing the learning experiences can also be partly assigned to the learner independently of a specific system (Bull & Kay, 2010), therefore Independent OLM have gained attention due to their capacity to deliver this capability.

2.2 Purpose of Open Learner Models

The overarching and core need and use of (open) learner models is the codification of the learner and his characteristics so as to adapt accordingly the teaching and learning process (design and delivery) towards offering personalized learning experiences (Desmarais & Baker, 2012). Therefore, Learner Models are directly related to the *Analysis* phase of teaching and learning design, following the well-known Analysis-Design-Develop-Implementation-Evaluation (ADDIE), model (Branch, 2010), in which the learner characteristics (e.g., their prior competences) are explicitly defined. This requires an initial population of the learner profile which is commonly performed via explicit input from the teacher or learners, using assessment tests (Schiaffino & Amandi, 2009).

Furthermore, (open) learner models are also closely related with the *Implementation* and *Evaluation* Phases of the ADDIE model, since the profiles can be dynamically re-populated during the teaching and learning process and remain up-to-date, based on both implicit and explicit educational data (collected manually or within a system) (Chrysafiadi & Virvou, 2015). In this way, relevant actors (e.g., learner, teacher) or even a system, can exploit the learner profiles at any time to track learners' progress and engage in both formative (during the delivery of the learning process) and summative (self-) assessment and provide targeted feedback and scaffolding provision.

As aforementioned, the global shift to more open and large-scale learning paradigms pushes learners to become more responsible for their own learning, in terms of self-regulation, self-assessment and self-reflection (Chatti et al., 2017). In this context, *open learner models* are being increasingly exploited, given their reported added value compared to 'closed' learner models. More specifically, as it will be discussed in detail in Sect. 3, open learner models allow learners and other actors engaged in the teaching and learning process to have access to the model and the profiles so as to inform their actions. Therefore, given the potential of (open) learner models to provide added value to the learners and other actors for informing personalized learning experiences, the relevant research field is expanding. Following this increased attention, there have been efforts to propose generic frameworks for describing the elements of OLM in order to provide 'interoperable' instruments to both design and analyze OLM. The following section presents a prominent such framework.

Table 9.1 Overview of the SMILI (student models that invite the learner in) framework

How does the OLM fit into the overall interaction with an adaptive system	This aspect defines the way in which the OLM being described is integrated within an adaptive system
How will it be or was it evaluated	This aspect is related to the description of the evaluation methodology and types of evidence collected for the OLM in hand
What is the purpose of the OLM	This aspect is related to the intended purpose of the OLM, i.e., the reasons for utilizing it. However, in SMILI there is no distinction between the intended role for each option (e.g., students, teachers)
What dimensions of the learner model are open	This aspect refers to identifying which elements of the OLM are open to the various actors and in what way
How are these components of the learner model visualized.	This aspect aims to capture the visualization methods used in the OLM (e.g., graphical, textual) as well as the overall 'access rights' to the OLM (i.e., whether the OLM is inspectable, editable, negotiated)
Who controls access to the OLM	This aspect defines which stakeholders have access to the OLM, for example, learners, teachers, the system or other
Who is the intended user of the OLM	This aspect defines the stakeholders who are intended to use the OLM, such as learners, the learners' peers and teachers

2.3 Frameworks for Open Learner Modelling

In the context of OLM, Bull and Kay (2010) have proposed the SMILI (Student Models that Invite the Learner In) framework as a systematic way to describe open learner models, based on a set of seven indicators, as captured in Table 9.1.

Overall, the SMILI framework mainly addresses the *'openness' aspects* of the modelling process; however, it offers limited support in describing other layers of the learner modelling process related to the data collection, data processing and data exploitation (e.g., Brusilovsky & Millan, 2007). This generic process, and its decomposition to layers, is fundamental for all modelling systems including open learner models (OLM) (Bull & Kay, 2016).

Therefore, this chapter capitalizes on the pioneering SMILI framework as well as the generic works on learner modelling processes to present a generic educational data-driven Open Learner Modelling framework that addresses the full set of the interrelated layers of the learner modelling process. Following that, this framework is used as a benchmark to analyse existing OLM research and offer critical overview of this field.

3 A Generic Educational Data-Driven Open Learner Modelling Framework

A generic learner modelling process and its constituting layers are captured in Fig. 9.1. The modelling process is typically initiated in Layer 3, namely by selecting the learner model dimensions and the instantiation means. Then, the conceptual

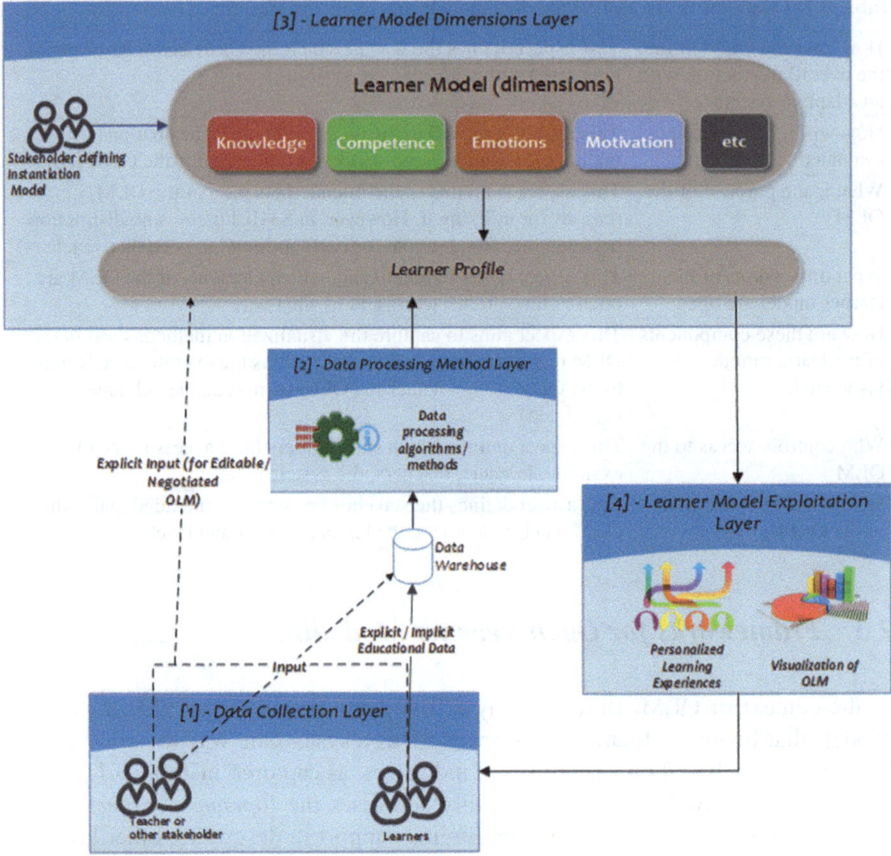

Fig. 9.1 Overview of learner modelling process layers

flow commonly follows the sequence: Data Collection → Data Processing → Learner Profiling (create an instance of the model) → Learner Model Exploitation (based on the current profile). Each layer is briefly described in the following sections.

3.1 The Data Collection Layer

This layer is related to the types of explicit/implicit educational data that can be collected regarding the learner as well as the way that they are collected, i.e., implicitly by a system (such as a course management system) or explicitly by a given actor (e.g., learner or teacher). The specific types of educational data to be collected are an important aspect of any OLM, since they are the primary means for creating the learner profile, using the selected data processing method(s).

Examples of *explicit* educational data can include learners' activity access patterns (Mazzola & Mazza, 2010; Kump, Seifert, Beham, Lindstaedt, & Ley, 2012), educational resources access frequency (Gaudioso, Montero, & Hernandez-Del-Olmo, 2012; Papanikolaou, 2015), level of social collaboration (Pohl et al., 2012), assessment scores (Gakhal & Bull, 2008) or background information (e.g., demographics or prior academic performance) (Gaudioso, Montero, Talavera, & Hernandez-del-Olmo, 2009; Clemente, Ramírez, & De Antonio, 2011). Furthermore, recent advances (focusing on independent open learner models) posit the notion that educational data of the learners can be collected from diverse digital sources. For example, in the context of MOOCs, learner data can be retrieved from the MOOC platform (e.g., Cook, Kay, & Kummerfeld, 2015) as well as from external sources such as social networks, blogs or websites and be processed in combination (e.g., Cruz-Benito, Borrás-Gené, García-Peñalvo, Blanco, & Therón, 2015).

Regarding *implicit* data, it can relate to two options. First, stakeholders (e.g., learner or teacher) may directly input educational data to the data warehouse. For example, a teacher may input and/or update assessment scores based on their own observations. Second, (for editable/negotiated OLM) stakeholders are also allowed to directly process the *learner profile* (i.e., the instance of the learner model) (Bull & Kay, 2010). For example, they could increase the level of competence of a learner. In the case of editable OLM, this process is openly available, whereas in negotiated OLM, different actors should provide evidence to support their input. For example, learners might need to take a well-planned assessment to demonstrate their new level of competence (Bull, Johnson, Alotaibi, Byrne, & Cierniak, 2013).

3.2 The Data Processing Method Layer

The purpose of this layer is to process the educational data so as to infer the learner profile. This layer can have an important effect on the granularity of the learner model and profile, depending on the method used for processing the learner profile related educational data. The selection of a specific data processing method is influenced by the context of application of the learner model and the needs of the various actors in the teaching and learning process. The most prevalent methods used to process data to populate the learner profile are as follows (Woolf, 2010; Chrysafiadi & Virvou, 2013):

- *Machine Learning*: Machine learning approaches are used in order to translate observations of the user's behaviour an educational data, in order to exploit them to populate the learner profile. Examples of such techniques include data fusion techniques, probabilistic weighted multi-criterion algorithms or constraint-based reasoning methods (Bull et al., 2015).
- *Fuzzy Model*: The fuzzy model presents a more accurate method of depicting learner dimensions captured in a learner model (structured with any type), by

processing the educational data over fuzzy scales instead of binary classifications (Al-Shamri & Bharadwaj, 2008).
- *Bayesian Network Model*: This model exploits Bayesian networks for representing and reasoning about uncertainty in learner models (Millan, Loboda, & Pırez-de-la-Cruz, 2010).
- *Ontology-based Model*: This model exploits ontologies and the interconnections between the ontology concepts are utilized for inferring and updating the values of the learner model (Clemente et al., 2011).

3.3 The Learner Model Dimensions Layer

This layer is related to (a) the definition of the specific learner *dimensions* which will be used for codifying the learner in the particular case (e.g., knowledge, competences, affective status) (b) the *instantiation means*, namely the specific means for representing each learner model dimension (e.g., existing competence qualification frameworks, ad hoc competences, subject domain ontologies for knowledge representation, specific emotion taxonomies) and (c) the *structuring method* used for structuring the instantiation means (e.g., as an overlay of the individual learner model, as an ontology or as a taxonomy).

Regarding the *learner model dimensions*, their selection for each learner model depends on the context in which it is being designed for. The most prevalent learner dimensions identified in the literature are as follows:

- *Knowledge*. This dimension is related to learners' (prior and) current level of knowledge on the topic of the learning process (e.g., (Bull, Gakhal, et al., 2010; Bull, Jackson, & Lancaster, 2010); Gaudioso et al., 2012). This mainly addresses the level of attainment of the defined educational objectives by each learner, in terms of knowledge and understanding of the topics being delivered in the learning process. Knowledge is defined as a separate category from competence since it is very common for learner models to strictly focus on this aspect and do not accommodate other competence aspects (such as skills and attitudes).
- *Competence*. This dimension is related to learners' (prior and) current level of skills and/or attitudes on the topic of the learning process. It is related to the level of attainment of the defined educational objectives by each learner, in terms of skills and/or attitudes. It differs from knowledge in the sense that it aims to capture not just the learners' understanding of the concepts being taught but also their capacity to apply them and, possibly, their predisposition towards them (e.g., Ting & Phon-Amnuaisuk, 2012).
- *Emotions*. This dimension is related to learners' emotional states during the learning process (and possibly prior to it). This mainly addresses how learners' emotions progressively unravel during the learning process and can be used to identify patterns that can feed personalized scaffolding to promote positive emotions (D'Mello, Blanchard, Baker, Ocumpaugh, & Brawner, 2014). This is an important

aspect since it is evident that emotions can be a very significant 'personalization' factor in the learning process, namely not only can they affect the learners' performance (LeBlanc, McConnell, & Monteiro, 2015) but also that each learners' performance might be affected in a unique manner (D'Mello & Graesser, 2012; D'Mello, Lehman, Pekrun, & Graesser, 2014).

– *Disabilities*. This dimension is related to learners' potential disabilities that might affect their performance in the learning process and therefore should be considered so as to provide personalized learning experiences (e.g., Woolf et al., 2010). Examples include language impairment e.g., (Georgopoulos, Malandraki, & Stylios, 2003), autism (e.g., Arthi & Tamilarasi, 2008), dyslexia (e.g., Kohli & Prasad, 2010) or dyscalculia (Jain, Manghirmalani, Dongardive, & Abraham, 2009). Furthermore, modelling learners' disabilities might also be the core focal point of a learning process in cases of special needs education. In these cases, the learner model of disabilities could be linked to the educational objectives of the learning process and be used for diagnostic purposes (e.g., Kohli & Prasad, 2010) as well as customizing teaching support
– *Preferences*. This dimension is related to learners' preferences in terms of different aspects of the learning process, such as preferred types of educational resources (Brusilovsky & Millan, 2007), visualization methods (Bull, Gakhal, et al., 2010; Bull, Jackson, & Lancaster, 2010) or preferred access patterns to learning activities and resources (e.g., Glushkova, 2008). Modelling learners' preferences can allow the provision of personalized experiences (e.g., activity navigational support) that may lead to enhanced learning performance and satisfaction from the learners (e.g., Chrysafiadi & Virvou, 2012).
– *Motivation*. This dimension is related to learners' level of motivation during the learning process. Motivation is commonly defined as the predisposition to a learners' behaviour which leads to the actual actions they do during the learning process (Darr, 2012). Given that learners' level of motivation can significantly affect their performance (e.g., Kusurkar, Ten Cate, Vos, Westers, & Croiset, 2013), keeping track of learners' motivation prior and during a learning process can be useful for providing personalized feedback and scaffolding. This is important for all educational contexts, but even more so in the context of online education (e.g., MOOCs) where learners' motivation when enrolling has been shown to provide a useful indicator of their final performance (e.g., Chang, Hung, & Lin, 2015).
– *Engagement*. This dimension is related to learners' level of engagement during the learning process. Engagement is commonly defined as the observable display in learning process which may lead to measurable outcomes (Reeve, 2012). Learner engagement is commonly used as an assessment method both in face-to-face or blended learning (Carini, Kuh, & Klein, 2006; Trowler, 2010; Henrie, Halverson, & Graham, 2015) as well as in the context of online education and MOOCs (e.g., Hew, 2015). Furthermore, (as with the rest of the learner dimensions) other actors involved in the teaching and learning process may also benefit from aggregated analysis of learners' engagement models so as to evaluate the learning process itself (i.e., the teaching and learning design) and possibly

perform reflective amendments for parts of it that correlated with low learners' engagement (e.g., Haya, Daems, Malzahn, Castellanos, & Hoppe, 2015).

- *Metacognitive and other generic skills*. This dimension is related to modelling learners' generic skills, for example problem-solving (e.g., Wedelin, Adawi, Jahan, & Andersson, 2015), creativity (Muldner & Burleson, 2015), abstract reasoning (Clemente et al., 2011) or self-regulation (e.g., Cho & Kim, 2013). These learner dimensions are commonly modelled in order to allow other actors involved in the teaching and learning process to assess the learners against them and, therefore, identify learners in need of further support and scaffolding.
- *Cultural Aspects*. This dimension is related to a diverse set of learners' characteristics related to their cultural background. Cultural issues in teaching and learning design are difficult to be explicitly defined; however, it is evident that it transcends mere "national differences" between learners (e.g., country of origin or language) and can include the total of values, beliefs, aesthetic standards, linguistic expression, patterns of thinking, behavioural norms, and styles of communication (Powell, 1997). Cultural aspects have been shown to influence learners' performance in the learning process (e.g., Lam et al., 2016). Therefore, modelling learners' cultural aspects is an important aspect of providing personalized learning experiences, especially in the context of MOOCs where vast numbers of culturally diverse learners participate (Literat, 2015).

Regarding the *instantiation means*, they are used for instantiating the generic learner dimensions in each learner model. For example, if the selected learner dimension is 'Competence', the instantiation means would need to be a specific competence set (or framework) which will define the specific competences to be maintained in the model. Another example is if the learner dimension is emotions¸ the instantiation means would need to define a specific emotion taxonomy (e.g., D'Mello & Graesser, 2012) that the learner model will store. The most common methods to define the instantiation means are (Bull et al., 2015):

- the use of *pre-defined instantiation* sets (frameworks) (e.g., Kump et al., 2012). The specific instantiation sets used are dependent on which learner dimensions are being modelled. For example, if the learner dimensions are knowledge or competence, then potential instantiation means may include educational competence sets (e.g., van Labeke, 2007), professional competence qualification frameworks (Gakhal & Bull, 2008) or professional taxonomies of competences (Lazarinis & Retalis, 2007; Cook et al., 2015). Another example is the use of pre-existing emotion taxonomies for instantiating emotional learner dimensions (e.g., Girard & Johnson, 2010). Potential benefits of this approach include the interoperable validation of learners' outcomes since these will be aligned to externally defined and acknowledged frameworks.
- the *ad hoc* definition of instantiation sets by a certain role (usually a teacher or instructional designer). For example, this could include the definition of ad hoc competences for addressing a specific learning process (e.g., Vélez, Fabregat, Bull, & Hueva, 2009) or the definition of ad hoc motivation performance indicators for measuring learners' motivation levels (e.g., Devedzic & Jovanović, 2015).

Potential benefits of this approach include the capacity of the interested stakeholder to define a very specific instantiation set for the learner dimensions relevant to their educational context. This method might also be relevant for the cases where no existing framework is available for instantiating the learner dimensions or when an adaptation of an existing framework might be needed.

Regarding the *structuring method*, it refers to the manner in which the individual learner data will populate the learner model. More specifically, common structuring methods include:

- *Overlay Method*: According to the overlay model, the learner model is a subset of the selected instantiation means (Chrysafiadi & Virvou, 2015). More specifically, a learner model structured using the overlay method will accommodate the full contents of the instantiation means defined as a set of topics (e.g., the full range of competences defined in a professional qualification framework) and it will highlight the individual learners' current level of attainment (and potentially misconceptions). The overlay model has been utilized for structuring learner models using dimensions such as knowledge (e.g., Gaudioso et al., 2012) and competence (e.g., Zapata-Rivera, Hansen, Shute, Underwood, & Bauer, 2007).
- *Perturbation Method*: A perturbation learner model is an extension of the overlay model that represents the learner's knowledge as a subset of the expert's knowledge, but can also define possible misconceptions. The perturbation model has been utilized for structuring learner models using learner dimensions similar to the overlay method, including knowledge (e.g., Hsiao, Bakalov, Brusilovsky, & König-Ries, 2013) and competence (e.g., Baschera & Gross, 2010).
- *Constraint-based Method*: This method is rule-based and structures the learner model in terms of specific constraints that the learners either fulfil based on their performance (in which case he has successfully attained it) or do not (in which case the constraint is violated and the learners do not attain it). The constraint-based model has been utilized for structuring learner dimensions, including knowledge (e.g., Mitrovic & Martin, 2007) and competence (e.g., Ohlsson, 2015).
- *Ontology*: The ontology method is similar to the overlay method, in the sense that it defines the instantiation means in a set of topics. However, it also defines links between these topics (which are structured as an ontology) and therefore can be used for inferring the learners' level of attainment of specific topics based on the level of other topics and the nature of their interrelation within the ontology (Clemente et al., 2011). Ontologies have been utilized for structuring learner models using a diverse set of learner dimensions including knowledge (e.g., Nguyen, Vo, Bui, & Nguyen, 2011), competence (e.g., Bremgartner, Netto, & Menezes, 2014), reasoning skills (e.g., Clemente et al., 2011) and disabilities (e.g., Panagiotopoulos, Kalou, Pierrakeas, & Kameas, 2012).
- *Stereotype Method*. This method requires the a priori manual definition of general rules (e.g., by the teacher or instructional designer) which will be used for modelling the learners (Kay, 2000). More specifically, the stereotypes are clusters to which learners are assigned based on the general rules (usually focusing on

learner attributes or performance). Therefore, the stereotype method does not create individual learner models, but simply assigns learners across a set of pre-existing, general clusters (e.g., Grubisic, Stankov, & Žitko, 2013). Furthermore, the rules that control the assignment of learners to clusters are not revised automatically but manually, leading to lack of flexibility of stereotype-based systems (Chrysafiadi & Virvou, 2013).

- *Taxonomy*: A learner model using this method does not accommodate the *progress* of the learner in a set of topics (e.g., competence development), but it is focused on populating the learner model based on taxonomy-based instantiation means in different points in time (potentially disregarding the prior population of the model). For example, for *learner emotions*, the learner model does not accommodate the progress of the learner's attained emotions through time, but it is focused on capturing which emotions the learner experiences in different points in time (e.g., Muldner, Burleson, & VanLehn, 2010). Therefore, this structuring method can be used for keeping track of learner's dimensions that are not progressively attained or developed, but are manifested differently as time unfolds, for example, emotions (e.g., Calvo & D'Mello, 2010), personal goal attainment for specific time intervals (e.g., Barua, Kay, Kummerfeld, & Paris, 2014), engagement (e.g., Galan & Beal, 2012) and motivation (e.g., Carmona & Conejo, 2004).

3.4 The Learner Model Exploitation Layer

This layer is related to the way that the learner model is exploited by the different actors in the teaching and learning process. Depending on the actor's role, the purpose of exploiting the learner model (and the profile) can differ, as follows:

- *Learner (and peers)*. Learners can primarily engage in reflection (Bull et al., 2015) on their performance and improving their (self-)regulation (Long & Aleven, 2013), especially in independent open learner models. Furthermore, they can perform formative self-assessment (Mitrovic & Martin, 2007; Bull et al., 2015) and, therefore, identify potential shortcomings in their performance, e.g., identify learning material not accessed or competences not yet adequately attained (Kay & Bull, 2015). Additionally, learners can utilize open learner models to compare their progress to that of their peers' (Upton & Kay, 2009), therefore pinpointing areas where additional effort is perhaps required to meet their peers' performance. Finally, they can receive personalized navigational support to learning activities and/or educational resources (Brusilovsky et al., 2016).
- *Teacher (and Educational Leader)* can have additional means to monitor the learners' progress and performance, both on an individual basis as well as in an aggregated manner (e.g., for the entire class) (Pohl et al., 2012). This can offer higher levels of granularity in terms of formative and summative assessment (Gaudioso et al., 2009). Additionally, the capacity of open learner models to allow direct editing can lead to more accurate depictions of learners, since

teachers (and possibly learners themselves) can adjust the values of specific dimensions of the model to better meet the actual characteristics of the learner.

- *Parents* can be effectively included in the learning process, by having more granulated access to their children's outcomes and progress, informing the provision of feedback (Lee & Bull, 2008; Bull & Kay, 2010).

Another important aspect of this layer (applicable to OLM) is the *visualization methods* that will be used for presenting the learner model (and the profile) to the various actors in the teaching and learning process. The selection of the visualization method for an OLM (and the created profiles) is important, given the potentially diverse preferences and needs of the different roles of the various actors who will have access to the visualized data (Bull, Gakhal, et al., 2010; Bull, Jackson, & Lancaster, 2010). Different visualization methods have been employed, including skill meters (Papanikolaou, 2015), concept maps (e.g., Van Labeke, Brna, & Morales, 2007), treemaps (Brusilovsky, Hsaio, & Folajimi, 2011), word or tag clouds (Mathews, Mitrovic, Lin, Holland, & Churcher, 2012), tabular and textual descriptions (Gaudioso et al., 2009), histograms (Bull et al., 2013) or combinations of the previous.

Overall, it is evident that the process of creating and utilizing (open) learner models is a composition of different interrelated layers, each affecting the potential of the resulting model to address the needs of the various actors in the teaching and learning process. This generic educational data-driven Open Learning Modelling framework aims to provide a structured way to outline these layers and also act as a blueprint for designing and analysing OLM. Therefore, using this framework as an analysis instrument, 38 existing research OLM were processed to get an insight of potential trends in the way that this field has evolved. The next section presents the methodology and results of the review of OLM research literature.

4 Review of Open Learner Models: Methodology and Results

4.1 Review Methodology

The aim of the review methodology is to provide a structured way to identify, process and analyze the research works of the literature. The first essential step is to define the keywords and databases for identifying the relevant works. In this chapter, the main keywords included 'student model', 'learner model', 'open learner model', 'open student model'. Additionally, the use of Boolean operators (OR, AND) among the keywords was also performed in order to extend the search results. Regarding digital databases, well-established repositories of scientific journals and international conference proceedings were exploited, as follows:

- Taylor & Francis Online (http://www.tandfonline.com)
- Science Direct (http://www.sciencedirect.com)
- Sage Publications (http://online.sagepub.com)

- SpringerLink (http://link.springer.com)
- Google Scholar (https://scholar.google.gr) (for more general searches)

Furthermore, a set of inclusion and exclusion criteria was defined as a filter to select the most appropriate works for this review. The inclusion criterion was that publications should describe an Open Learner Model and provide information on the aspects of the analysis framework (see Sect. 3). The exclusion criteria included: (a) publications not presenting *Open* Learner Models, (b) publications not written in English, (c) abstract-only and poster publications were excluded, and (d) duplicate publications and outdated versions of the same publications.

Finally, the final set of 38 works that were identified were analysed against the layered Educational Data-Driven Open Learner Modelling framework, presented in Sect. 3, as well as against an additional indicator; whether they were Independent OLM or not. The results of this analysis are discussed in the following section. A fully detailed depiction of the analysis results is provided in the Appendix 1 section.

4.2 Review Results

4.2.1 Data Collection Layer

Figure 9.2 presents the findings regarding the *data types* that OLM utilize in the Data Collection layer.[1]

As Fig. 9.2 depicts, the majority of OLM ($N = 34$, $x = 89\%$) utilizes learners' explicit assessment score data (mostly related to quizzes), whereas a smaller portion

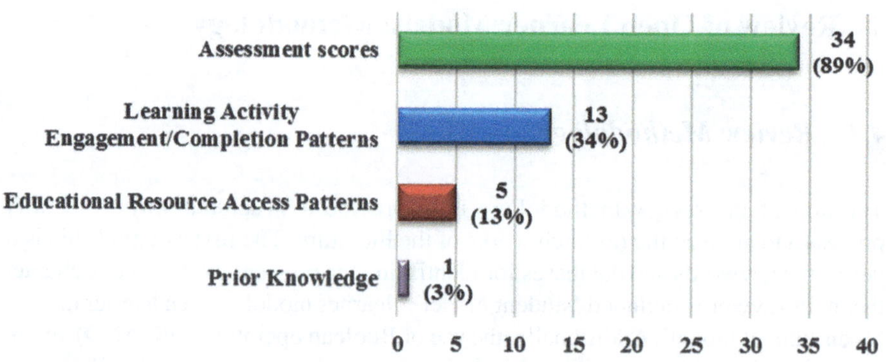

Fig. 9.2 Overview of data types used in the data collection layer

[1] It is mentioned that percentages in the Figures throughout this section might not always add to 100%, since in some cases there were overlaps in the characterization of OLM based on the analysis framework.

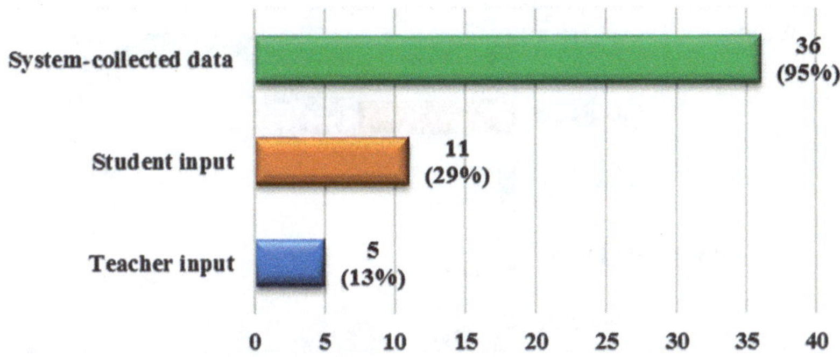

Fig. 9.3 Overview of data collection methods used in the data collection layer

(N = 13, x = 34%) exploits learners' learning activity engagement and completion patterns (mostly related to which learning activities were performed and the relevant timeframe). Finally, educational resources access patterns (N = 5, x = 13%) and learners' background in terms of prior knowledge (N = 1, x = 3%) are less frequently utilized.

Furthermore, Fig. 9.3 depicts the analysis results regarding the *data collection methods* to feed the OLM.

As Fig. 9.3 depicts, the most prevalent method of collecting data is through the logs of the systems that host the OLM (N = 36, x = 95%). However, since a portion of OLM are negotiable or editable, other data input methods were identified, including student input (N = 11, x = 29%) and teacher input (N = 5, x = 13%).

Overall, from a Learning Analytics perspective, these findings are only partially consistent with the state-of-the-art developments in the Learning Analytics field (e.g., Sergis & Sampson, 2016). In particular, these developments argue that in order to create accurate learner profiles and effectively inform pedagogical decision making, it is important to not only make effective use of different sources of educational data but also to jointly exploit these data to formulate more holistic profiles (Blikstein & Worsley, 2016). Therefore, current OLM approaches appear to only partially accommodate this standpoint, since they tend to place their focus on individual data sources and also, they heavily capitalize on particular types (e.g., assessment scores).

4.2.2 Data Processing Method Layer

Figure 9.4 outlines the findings regarding the *methods for processing* the educational data from the previous layer.

As Fig. 9.4 depicts, the most frequently (N = 23, x = 61%) used method for processing data refers to algorithms that calculate a weighted total from different data sources, so as to infer a consolidated summary of the learners' dimension (e.g., calculate competence level from different assessment activities). Furthermore, a significant portion of OLM utilize rule-based methods (N = 9, x = 24%) which apply

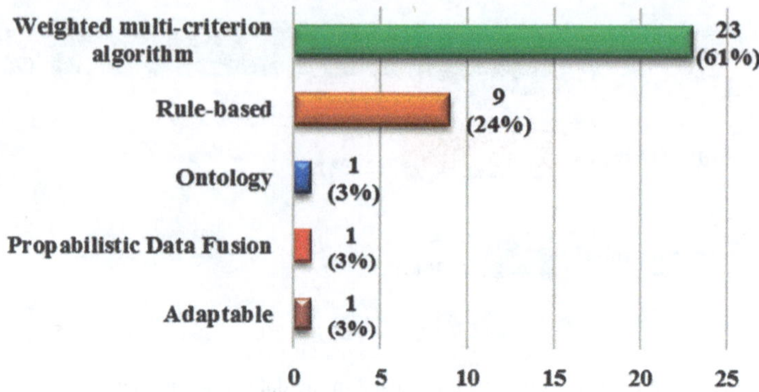

Fig. 9.4 Overview of data processing methods used in the data processing layer

pre-defined rules on data so as to interpret and process them. Finally, less frequent methods ($N = 1$, $x = 3\%$) are ontologies, probabilistic data fusion techniques and adaptable methods. The latter refers to the capacity of OLM to accommodate more than one data processing method. These findings are partly consistent with the current research in Learning Analytics (Nunn, Avella, Kanai, & Kebritchi, 2016). More specifically, it appears that the OLM research is not fully exploiting emerging approaches in data processing such as (un)supervised machine learning methods that could be used to both streamline and improve the accuracy of profiling. As the educational data generated within learning environments become more diverse (from various and multimodal sources of data) and 'bigger' (larger volumes and increased generation frequency), it is expected that such data processing methods will become more prominent. Indeed, Learning Analytics research has placed significant attention to investigate such methods, especially in the domain of online education (Papamitsiou & Economides, 2014).

4.2.3 Learner Model Dimensions Layer

Figure 9.5 presents the results of the review in terms of the *dimensions* that OLM adopt for modelling learners.

As it can be derived from Fig. 9.5, the vast majority of OLM models learners' level of knowledge ($N = 31$, $x = 82\%$), while a significant portion also captures relevant misconceptions ($N = 20$, $x = 53\%$). This is consistent with the insights from the analysis of data types used in OLM, where the majority focused on assessment scores (a well-established way to infer learners' knowledge). Furthermore, a smaller fraction of OLM focused on modelling learners' competences, namely, extend knowledge to also include skills—however not attitudes ($N = 6$, $x = 16\%$). Lastly, learners' engagement in the learning process ($N = 2$, $x = 5\%$), motivation ($N = 1$, $x = 3\%$) and affective states ($N = 1$, $x = 3\%$) were rarely accommodated. Again, from a Learning Analytics perspective, this finding suggests a narrow perspective as important learner dimensions

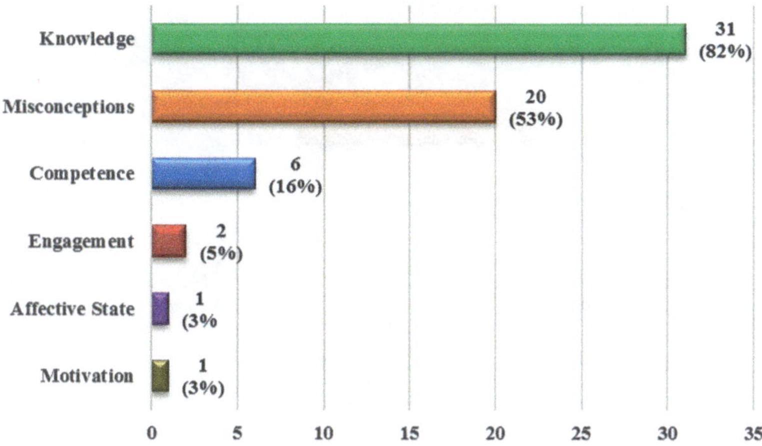

Fig. 9.5 Overview of dimensions used in the learner model dimensions layer

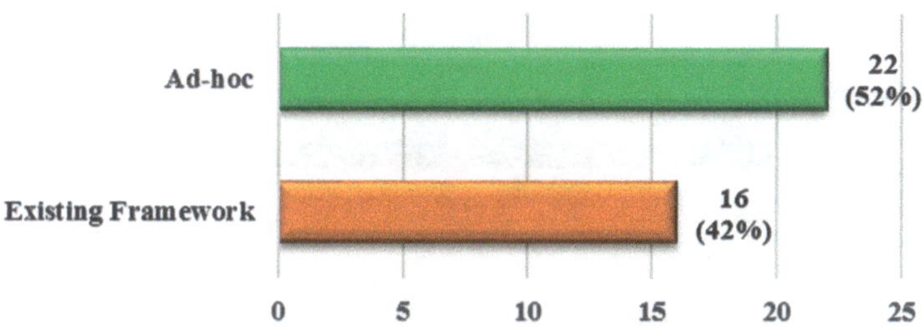

Fig. 9.6 Overview of instantiation means used in the learner model dimensions layer

related to engagement (Tempelaar, Rienties, & Giesbers, 2015) and affective and motivational dimensions (D'Mello & Kory, 2015) are not widely accommodated in current OLM literature. These advancements have partly emerged as the means to address key challenges in technology-enhanced education, including emotion regulation in online contexts as well as informing teacher decision making through diverse educational data (Eberle, Lund, Tchounikine, & Fischer, 2016).

In terms of *instantiation means*, Fig. 9.6 depicts that the distribution between adopting existing frameworks for instantiating the model dimensions or allowing ad hoc definitions is almost even ($N = 16$, $x = 42\%$ and $N = 22$, $x = 52\%$ respectively). It is interesting to observe that although there is a global trend to exploit standard commonly agreed competence frameworks, still this has only party informed current OLM.

Finally, regarding the *structuring method* of learner dimensions, Fig. 9.7 shows that the perturbation ($N = 20$, $x = 53\%$) and the overlay ($N = 13$, $x = 34\%$) methods are the most widely used. Furthermore, less often utilized methods include the constraint-based approach ($N = 2$, $x = 5\%$), ontologies ($N = 1$, $x = 3\%$) and taxonomies ($N = 1$, $x = 3\%$).

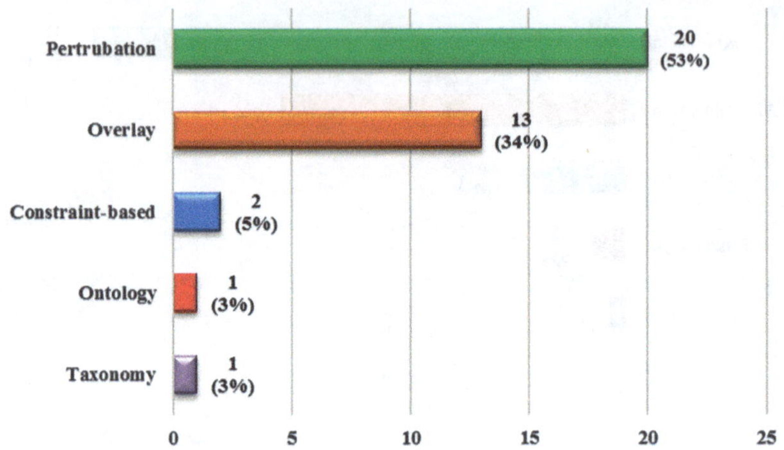

Fig. 9.7 Overview of structuring methods used in the learner model dimensions layer

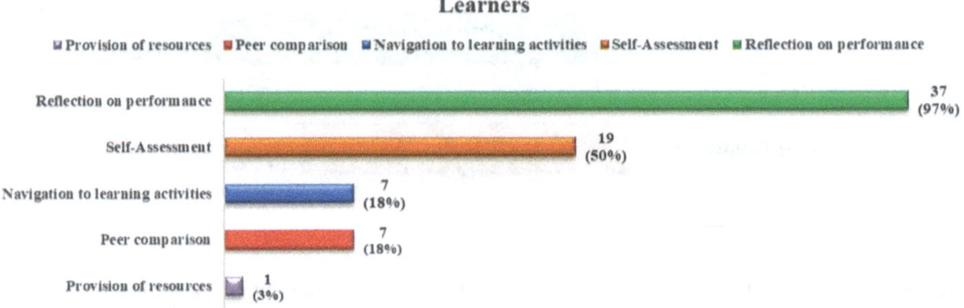

Fig. 9.8 Overview of exploitation purpose for OLM

4.2.4 Learner Model Exploitation Layer

Figure 9.8 depicts the findings regarding the purpose that OLM are utilized for.

The analysis of works indicated that:

- for *learners* (Fig. 9.8), the most common purpose for using the OLM was reflection on progress and performance ($N = 37$, $x = 97\%$). Other purposes included formative self-assessment ($N = 19$, $x = 50\%$), performance comparison with peers ($N = 7$, $x = 18\%$) and navigation support to learning activities ($N = 7$, $x = 18\%$). Educational resource provision ($N = 1$, $x = 3\%$) was less common. These findings suggest that existing OLM approaches have largely adopted a standpoint for informing learners on their past actions, expecting them to make sense of how to use this knowledge on their own. Although this is consistent with the majority of current Learning Analytics technologies which, indeed fall into this predictive perspective, the real challenge today is prescriptive learning analytics, that is, generating recommendations for further teaching and learning actions based on the past data analysis (Sampson, 2017).

- For other actors, namely, teachers and parents, a total of 22 (x = 58%) and 3 (x = 8%) OLM were identified respectively. The core purpose mentioned for teachers was the assessment of learner performance (N = 20, x = 100%) and for parents, reflection on the learner performance for the provision of feedback and support (N = 3, x = 100%). Again, from a Learning Analytics perspective, these findings suggest a significant level of consistency. Providing teachers with an overview of students' profile, and even further how this profile is associated with elements of the teaching design, has been highlighted as a core challenge in (Teaching and) Learning Analytics (Sergis & Sampson, 2017). Therefore, OLM that can deliver such insights could support teachers to make more informed decisions on how to improve their practice and deliver better learning experiences to their learners.

Finally, an analysis of the *visualization methods* was also performed. Figure 9.9 depicts that the most frequently used visualization methods include skill meters (N = 26, x = 68%). These skill meters can be operationalized through different types of charts, such as bar charts or pie charts. Furthermore, text descriptions were also a very frequent method for feeding back the learner profiles (N = 24, x = 63%). These descriptions commonly offer consolidated overviews of the profile and facilitate the learners (or other actors in the teaching and learning process) to make better sense of it. Beyond these visualization types, there is a range of other approaches that were identified in a less frequent manner, as presented in Fig. 9.9.

The identified distribution in terms of the purpose of use as well as visualization methods is consistent with the findings of relevant reviews focusing on the domain of Learning Analytics (Schwendimann et al., 2017). However, even though this

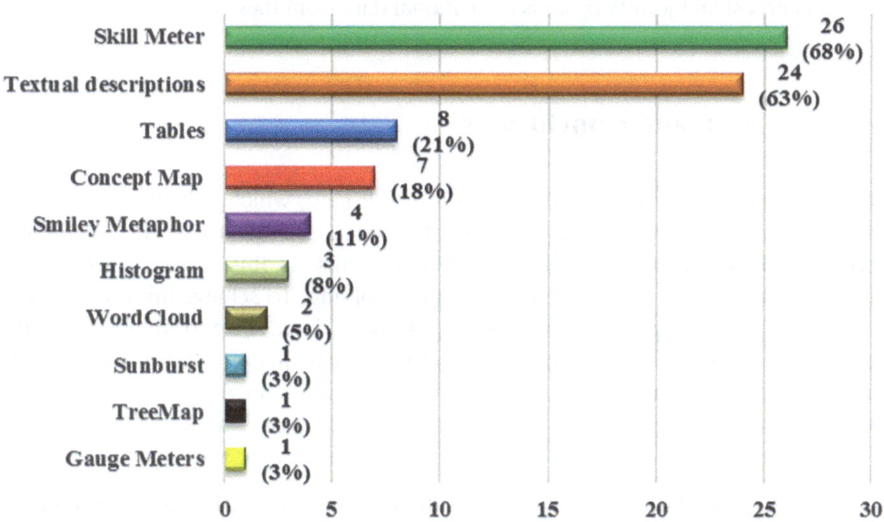

Fig. 9.9 Overview of visualization methods

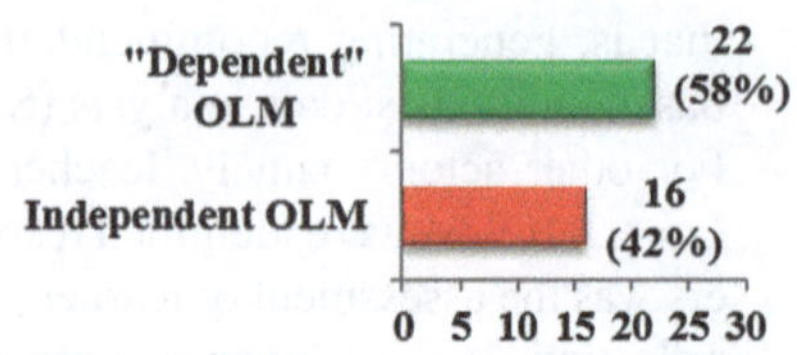

Fig. 9.10 Occurrence of independent OLM

aspect is beyond the scope of this work, it is important to note that apart from the type of visualization that is being used, an important (and emerging) research strand is related to the type and amount of *information* that should be visualized to the various actors so as to maximize their decision making and minimize their cognitive load for interpreting the visualized data (e.g., Guerra-Hollstein, Barria-Pineda, Schunn, Bull, & Brusilovsky, 2017).

4.2.5 Independent Open Learner Models

Figure 9.10 depicts the findings regarding the frequency of independent OLM in the research literature.

As Fig. 9.10 depicts, the majority of OLM are dependent OLM ($N = 22$, $x = 58\%$), therefore, they are embedded within existing systems and utilize data from specific sources within these systems. In this way, their modelling process is aligned to (and restricted by) with the functionalities and scope of the hosting system. On the other hand, independent OLM seem to still be under-explored ($N = 16$, $x = 42\%$) and only recently to have received more focused research attention. Again, this shift can be attributed to the expansion of open and online learning environments, in which multiple tools and systems are used in the learning process, generating the need for OLM that can harvest and jointly process educational data from these diverse sources.

5 Discussion and Conclusions

Open Learner Modelling is an emerging research field, which is becoming increasingly important as the global educational landscape shifts to more technology-supported, blended/online and large-scale paradigms. In this context, this chapter aimed to take stock of how this field has been evolving. To achieve this aim, an educational data-driven open learner modelling framework was discussed, aligned to the generic learner modelling process and informed by existing works in the OLM field to support learning analytics. Furthermore, the chapter presented an overview of OLM literature, classified against this framework, providing a transparent analysis.

Based on this analysis, a set of conclusions can be drawn, as follows:

- Regarding the *Data Collection Layer*, the majority of OLM utilize *explicit* educational data, mostly related to assessment scores. On the other hand, implicit data, such as learning activity and educational resource access patterns, are less frequently used. Overall, this trend is consistent with the most common educational data types used in the Learning Analytics domain too (Verbert et al., 2013; Tempelaar et al., 2015; Sergis & Sampson, 2017), even though such systems are increasingly adopting more implicit data in their mechanisms as they expand their reach in the online/blended large-scale learning environment (e.g., De Barba, Kennedy, & Ainley, 2016). This trend is also inline with the emerging focus on *multimodal Learning Analytics* approaches, which argues for using educational data from diverse sources in order to build a more holistic and accurate profile for learners (Blikstein & Worsley, 2016). Therefore, it is reasonable to expect that research in OLM will mirror this trend and investigate ways to exploit implicitly collected educational data as well as explicit ones.

- Regarding the *Data Processing Method Layer*, the majority of OLM systems adopt weighted multi-criteria algorithms to process data and populate learners' profiles. This is partly consistent with the methods utilized in Learning Analytics approaches (Papamitsiou & Economides, 2014) and it appears that the aspect of introducing new computational techniques for processing data has not attracted significant research attention in the OLM domain. However, as both OLM and Learning Analytics expand to new areas of student dimensions (e.g., sentiment analysis) and larger volumes of educational data (e.g., within MOOCs) it is expected that novel algorithmic solutions will need to be introduced to effectively and meaningfully process such 'unconventional' data. For example, (un) supervised machine learning approaches, which are emerging as a promising processing method in (large-scale) Learning Analytics (Agudo-Peregrina, Iglesias-Pradas, Conde-González, & Hernández-García, 2014), could provide new ways to create more accurate profiles based on diverse data sources, as well as use these profiles to predict learners' future progress trends and recommend teaching and learning actions.
- Regarding the *Learner Model Dimension Layer*, there is an evident trend in the existing OLM literature. In particular, the majority of OLM focuses on learner knowledge (or competence) and relevant misconceptions. This can be largely attributed to the similar focus of Learning Analytics approaches that had a predominant focus towards monitoring learners' performance progress and level (mostly related to assessment scores). However, important aspects such as motivation, affective state and engagement level are rarely accommodated. This is a weakness that can highlight a potential area of future research. As the field of Affective Computing and relevant educational data analytics continues to emerge (D'Mello & Kory, 2015), it is reasonable to expect that OLM will need to extend their scope to include such learner dimensions too. This need has already been stressed in the area of MOOCs (Sergis, Sampson, & Pelliccione, 2017), which face the challenge of effectively supporting learners' motivation and engagement. Finally, it can also be argued that apart from introducing new dimensions in OLM approaches, future developments will also adopt more complex ways to populate existing dimensions. In particular, capitalizing on advancements in multimodal Learning Analytics, learners could be profiled in a more holistic way using a spectrum of educational data, including for example system log data,

self-reported data through surveys, demographics and prior instances of their profiles, or data provided by their teachers. Such a diversified profiling approach can also prove beneficial for researchers, since it can provide them with richer pools of information to conduct exploratory studies and unravel underlying knowledge on (online) learning, for example, factors that support or impede it for different groups of learners.

- Regarding the *Learner Model Exploitation Layer*, for learners, the most common purpose for using the OLM was reflection on progress, self-assessment as well as performance comparison with peers. However, 'smarter' functionalities related to navigational support and educational resource provision were more infrequently described. These findings are also consistent with the current status of the majority of existing learning analytics systems which are descriptive or predictive (namely depict what has already happened or what will happen in the future based on the analysis of past history), rather than providing actionable insights to the various actors on what to do in response to this information (prescriptive analytics). Despite the fact that advances in the field of Recommender Systems have been adopted as a means to drive such prescriptive analytics approaches, this research (and innovation) field is still in its infancy. Indeed, designing such prescriptive analytics systems is regarded as a significant challenge in technology-enhanced learning, especially in the field of (large-scale) online learning, where there is a greater need to inform and support learners' autonomous decision making.
- In terms of supporting the decision making of other stakeholders, namely, teachers and parents, existing OLM have placed less attention compared to learners, mainly aiming to support assessment or reflection on student performance. However, especially for parents, few systems were explicitly designed to provide insights particularly designed for them. This finding suggests an inconsistency between the fields of OLM and Learning Analytics, since the latter has incorporated those actors as a common targeted end-user, both in terms of supporting on-the-fly scaffolding of students, as well as providing the means for systematic reflection on the teaching practice (Sergis & Sampson, 2017). Furthermore, recent developments in the field of Teaching and Learning Analytics have also been focused on collecting, processing and sense-making educational data regarding the teacher and how they deliver their own practice (e.g., Rodríguez-Triana, Martínez-Monés, Asensio-Pérez, & Dimitriadis, 2015). The aim of such approaches is to inform self-reflection and exchange of good practices among teaching professionals and their mentors. Therefore, even though this aspect is not currently addressed in OLM research, it is expected to attract research attention in the future, especially considering the increasing need for teachers to meet accountability criteria and effectively improve their practice through their participation in communities.
- Finally, the majority of OLM are dependent, meaning they are embedded within existing systems. Therefore, their modelling process is very much aligned with the functionalities and scope of the hosting system, restricting potential alterations

that the stakeholders might wish to do so as to address their specific needs. On the other hand, Independent OLM appear to be emerging, yet still under-explored. The existing independent OLM, even though they are external to specific systems, still support a limited range of adjustment capabilities, largely restricted to the provision of more than one visualization methods for the learner model (Cook et al., 2015), placing the focus on visualization to specific parts of the learner model (e.g., Conejo, Trella, Cruces, & Garcia, 2011) and allowing the capacity of stakeholders (usually teachers) to define specific instantiation means to describe the learner model dimensions (e.g., define specific competences to describe the 'competence' learner dimension). However, still, there is no capacity of the stakeholders to adjust other aspects of the modelling process, such as the learner dimensions to be modelled or the types of educational data being collected. As OLM will continue to evolve and meet the self-awareness needs of learners in online large-scale learning environments, Independent OLM are expected to become more prominent and allow additional functionalities for personalizing the monitoring and reflection capacity of learners.

Regarding the limitations of this study, they are primarily related to the search strategy employed to build the literature pool for the analysis of OLM literature. Future studies should take this into account and extend their scope of search and analysis. Furthermore, it is envisaged that future works for OLM systems can benefit from the research overview provided in this chapter, as well as from the proposed generic Educational Data-Driven Open Learner Modelling framework. Using this framework as a blueprint for designing OLM for each step of the modelling process, as well as taking into account the patterns of how other OLM have been created, researchers and practitioners could be facilitated in constructing and using OLM that will be better calibrated to meet the awareness and decision support needs of their own, as well as of their students.

Acknowledgements The work presented in this paper has been partially funded by (a) the European Commission in the context of the OSOS project (Grant Agreement no. 741572) under the Horizon 2020 Framework Programme, Science with and for Society: Open Schooling and Collaboration on Science Education (H2020-SwafS-15-2016), and (b) the Greek General Secretariat for Research and Technology, under the Matching Funds 2014–2016 for the EU project "Inspiring Science: Large Scale Experimentation Scenarios to Mainstream eLearning in Science, Mathematics and Technology in Primary and Secondary Schools" (Project Number: 325123). This document does not represent the opinion of neither the European Commission nor the Greek General Secretariat for Research and Technology, and the European Commission and the Greek General Secretariat for Research and Technology are not responsible for any use that might be made of its content.

Appendix 1

Table 9.2 presents the detailed analysis of the OLM literature reported in Sect. 4.2.

Table 9.2 Analysis of OLM literature works

#	Reference	OLM	Types of raw educational data collected	Learner dimensions	Instantiation means from	Data collection method	Methods for structuring learner dimensions	Data processing method	Access to the model	Purpose of model (learner)	Purpose of model (other stakeholder)	Visualization method(s)	Type of model	Independent OLM	Adaptation of modelling process permitted
1	Bull, Pain, and Brna (1995)	Mr. Collins	Explicit assessment scores	Knowledge–misconceptions	Existing framework	System data–student input	Perturbation	Rule-based	Student	Reflection–assessment	–	Textual descriptions	Editable visualization–negotiable model (based on evidence)	✘	Select visualization method
2	Weber and Brusilovsky (2001)	ELM-ART OLM	Explicit assessment scores–learning activity patterns	Knowledge–misconceptions	Ad hoc	System data–student input	Perturbation	Weighted algorithm	Student	Reflection–assessment–resource navigation support–learning activity navigation support	–	Skill meter–textual descriptions	Editable visualization–negotiable model (based on evidence)	✘	Select visualization method
3	Dimitrova (2003)	STyLE-OLM	Explicit assessment scores	Knowledge–misconceptions	Existing framework	System data–student altering	Perturbation	Rule-based	Student–teacher	Reflection	Assessment	Concept map	Negotiable model	✘	Select visualization method
4	Bull and McKay (2004)	Subtraction master OLM	Explicit assessment scores	Knowledge–misconceptions	Ad hoc	System data	Perturbation	Weighted algorithm	Student–peers–teacher	Reflection	Assessment	Smiley metaphor–textual descriptions–histogram	Editable visualization–inspectable	✘	Select educational data to be used–select visualization method
5	Yacef (2005)	Logic-ITA OLM	Explicit assessment scores	Knowledge–misconceptions	Ad hoc	System data	Perturbation	Weighted algorithm	Student–teacher	Reflection	Assessment	Table–textual descriptions	Editable visualization–inspectable	✘	–
6	Zakharov, Mitrovic, and Ohlsson (2005)	EER-Tutor	Explicit assessment scores	Knowledge	Existing framework	System data	Constraint-based	Rule-based	Student	Reflection	–	Concept map–textual descriptions	Inspectable	✘	–
7	Mabbott and Bull (2006)	Flexi-OLM	Explicit assessment scores	Knowledge–misconceptions	Ad hoc	System data–student input	Perturbation	Ontology	Student–peers–teacher	Reflection–assessment	Assessment	Concept map	Editable visualization–negotiable model (based on evidence)	✘	Select visualization method

8	Bull, Mabbott, and Abu Issa (2007)	UMPTEEN	Explicit assessment scores	Knowledge–misconceptions	Ad hoc	System data–teacher input–student input	Perturbation	Weighted Algorithm	Student–peers–teacher	Feedback–peer comparison	Assessment	Skill meter–textual descriptions	Editable visualization–negotiable model (based on evidence)	✓	Select visualization method
9	Van Labeke et al. (2007)	xOLM	Explicit assessment scores–explicit evaluation reports–learning activity patterns	Knowledge–misconceptions–motivation–affect	Ad hoc	System data–student input	Perturbation–taxonomy	Probabilistic Data Fusion	Student–teacher	Reflection–assessment	Assessment	Skill meter–textual descriptions–concept map	Editable visualization–negotiable model (based on evidence)	✓	Select visualization method–visualize specific part of student model
10	Lazarinis and Retalis (2007)	AnalyzeMe	Explicit assessment scores	Knowledge–misconceptions	Existing framework	System data	Perturbation	Weighted Algorithm	Student–peers–teacher	Reflection–assessment	Assessment–adaptive assessment activities	Skill meter–textual descriptions–concept map	Editable visualization–inspectable	×	Select visualization method
11	Kerly, Ellis, and Bull (2007)	CALMsystem	Explicit assessment scores	Knowledge	Existing framework	System data–student input	Overlay	Weighted Algorithm	Student	Reflection	–	Smiley metaphor–textual descriptions	Editable visualization–negotiable model (based on evidence)	×	Select visualization method
12	Zapata-Rivera et al. (2007)	EI-OSM	Explicit assessment scores	Competence	Ad hoc	Teacher input–system data	Overlay	Rule-based	Student–peers–teacher–parents	Reflection–assessment	Assessment	Skill meter–textual descriptions–concept map	Editable visualization–negotiable model (based on evidence)	✓	Select visualization method
13	Mitrovic & Martin (2007)	SQL-Tutor	Explicit assessment scores	Knowledge	Existing framework	System data	Constraint-based	Rule-based	Student	Reflection	–	Skill meter–textual descriptions	Inspectable	×	–
14	Gakhal and Bull (2008)	Flight Club OLM	Explicit assessment scores	Knowledge–misconceptions	Existing framework	System data	Perturbation	Weighted algorithm	Student	Reflection–assessment	–	Skill meter–textual descriptions	Editable visualization–inspectable	×	Select visualization method
15	Lee and Bull (2008)	Fraction Helper OLM	Explicit assessment scores	Knowledge–misconceptions	Existing framework	System data	Perturbation	Weighted algorithm	Student–parent	Reflection–assessment–resource navigation support	Assessment	Skill meter–textual descriptions	Inspectable	×	–

(continued)

Table 9.2 (continued)

#	Reference	OLM	Types of raw educational data collected	Learner dimensions	Instantiation means from	Data collection method	Methods for structuring learner dimensions	Data processing method	Access to the model	Purpose of model (learner)	Purpose of model (other stakeholder)	Visualization method(s)	Type of model	Independent OLM	Adaptation of modelling process permitted
16	Vélez et al. (2009)	SAVEMA	Explicit assessment scores	Competence	Existing framework	System data	Overlay	Rule-based	Student	Reflection–adaptive navigation	–	Skill meter	Editable visualization–inspectable	×	Select visualization method
17	Upton and Kay (2009)	Narcissus	Learning activity pattern	Engagement	Ad hoc	System data	–	Weighted algorithm	Student–peers–teacher	Reflection–navigation support–peer comparison	Assessment	Skill meter	Editable visualization–inspectable	✓	Select visualization method
18	Ahmad and Bull (2009)	t-OLM	–	Knowledge–misconceptions	Ad hoc	–	–	–	Student	Reflection	–	Skill meter	Editable visualization–inspectable	✓	Select visualization method
19	Gaudioso et al. (2009)	Pdinamet OLM	Explicit assessment scores–learning activity pattern–educational resources access patterns–background data	Knowledge	Existing framework	Teacher input–system data	Overlay	Weighted algorithm	Student–teacher	Reflection–resource recommendation	Assessment	Skill meter–textual descriptions–table	Editable visualization–inspectable	×	Select educational data to be used–select visualization method
20	Johnson and Bull (2009)	MusicaLM	Explicit assessment scores	Knowledge–misconceptions	Existing framework	System data	Perturbation	Rule-based	Student	Reflection–assessment	–	Skill meter–textual descriptions	Editable visualization–inspectable	×	Select visualization method
21	Kump et al. (2012)	MyExperiences	Learning activity pattern	Knowledge	Existing framework	System data–student input	Perturbation	Rule-based	Student–peers	Reflection	–	TreeMap	Editable visualization–negotiable model	✓	Select visualization method–visualize specific part of student model
22	Mazzola and Mazza (2010)	GVIS	Explicit assessment scores–learning activity patterns	Knowledge–misconceptions	Ad hoc	System data	Overlay	Adaptable	Student–peers–teacher	Reflection	Assessment	Skill meter	Editable visualization–inspectable	✓	Select visualization method for diverse types of data

23	Bull, Gakhal, et al. (2010), Bull, Jackson, and Lancaster (2010)	OLMlets	Explicit assessment scores	Knowledge–misconceptions	Ad hoc	System data–student input	Perturbation	Weighted algorithm	Student	Reflection–assessment	–	Skill meter–table–textual descriptions	Editable visualization–negotiable model	✓	Select visualization method
24	Xu and Bull (2010)	OLMLA	Explicit assessment scores	Knowledge–misconceptions	Ad hoc	System data	Perturbation	Rule-based	Student	Reflection–assessment–educational resources provision	–	Skill meter–textual descriptions	Editable visualization–inspectable	✓	Select visualization method–visualize specific part of student model
25	Conejo et al. (2011)	INGRID	–	–	Ad hoc	–	Ontology	–	Student–peers–teacher	Reflection–feedback	Assessment	Concept map–sunburst–table	Editable visualization–inspectable	✓	Select visualization method–visualize specific part of student model
26	Verginis, Gouli, Gogoulou, and Grigoriadou (2011)	OLM_SCALE	Explicit assessment scores–learning activity patterns	Knowledge–misconceptions	Existing framework	System data	Perturbation	Weighted algorithm	Student–peers–teacher	Reflection–peer comparison	Assessment	Skill meter	Editable visualization–inspectable	×	Select visualization method–visualize specific part of student model
27	Epp and McCalla (2011)	ProTutor OLM	Explicit assessment scores	Competence	Ad hoc	System data	Overlay	–	Student	Reflection	–	Skill meter–textual descriptions	Inspectable	×	–
28	Bull et al. (2013)	NEXT-TELL OLM	Explicit assessment scores–learning activity pattern	Competence–knowledge–misconceptions	Ad hoc	Teacher input–system data–student altering	Perturbation	Weighted Algorithm	Student–peers–teacher	Reflection–peer comparison	Assessment	Smiley metaphor–skill meter–table–histogram–tree map–word clouds	Editable visualization–negotiable model	✓	Select educational data to be used–select visualization method

(continued)

Table 9.2 (continued)

#	Reference	OLM	Types of raw educational data collected	Learner dimensions	Instantiation means from	Data collection method	Methods for structuring learner dimensions	Data processing method	Access to the model	Purpose of model (learner)	Purpose of model (other stakeholder)	Visualization method(s)	Type of model	Independent OLM	Adaptation of modelling process permitted
29	Hsiao et al. (2013)	Progressor	Explicit assessment scores	Knowledge–misconceptions	Ad hoc	System data	Perturbation	Weighted algorithm	Student–peers–teacher	Reflection–resource navigation–peer comparison	Assessment	Colored sector gauge meter	Editable visualization–inspectable	✓	Select visualization method–visualize specific part of student model
30	Bull and Al-Shanfari (2015)	LEA's Box OLM	Explicit assessment scores–learning activity pattern–peer assessment scores	Competence	Ad hoc	Teacher input–system data–student altering	Overlay	Weighted algorithm	Student–peers–teacher	Reflection–peer comparison	Assessment	Smiley metaphor–skill meter–table–histogram–tree map–word clouds	Editable visualization–negotiable model (based on evidence)	✓	Select educational data to be used–select visualization method
31	Papanikolaou (2015)	INSPIREus OLM	Explicit assessment scores–learning activity access patterns–educational resources access patterns	Knowledge–misconceptions	Existing framework	System data	Perturbation	Weighted algorithm	Student–peers–teacher	Reflection–assessment	Assessment	Skill meter–textual descriptions	Editable visualization–inspectable	×	Select visualization method–visualize specific part of student model
32	Cook et al. (2015)	MOOC-LM	Explicit assessment scores–learning activity pattern–educational Resources access patterns	Knowledge	Existing framework	System data	Overlay	Weighted algorithm	Student–teacher	Reflection–assessment	Assessment	Skill meter	Editable visualization–inspectable	×	Select visualization method

33	Brusilovsky et al. (2016)	MasteryGrids OLM	Explicit assessment scores	Knowledge	Ad hoc	System data	Overlay	Weighted algorithm	Student–peers–teacher	Reflection–assessment–peer comparison–resource navigation	Assessment	Skill meter	Editable visualization–inspectable	✓	Select visualization method–visualize specific part of student model
34	Tongchai (2016)	Moodle-based OLM	Explicit assessment scores–learning activity pattern–educational Resources access patterns	Knowledge	Ad hoc	System data	Overlay	Weighted algorithm	Student–teacher	Reflection–assessment	Assessment	Textual descriptions	Inspectable	✓	
35	Wetzel et al. (2017)	Dragoon	Explicit assessment scores	Knowledge	Ad hoc	System data	Overlay	Weighted algorithm	Student–teacher	Reflection–assessment	Assessment	Table–textual descriptions	Inspectable	×	–
36	Davis et al. (2017)	Social Comparison OLM	Explicit assessment scores–learning activity pattern–educational resources access patterns	Knowledge–engagement	Ad hoc	System data	Overlay	Weighted algorithm	Student	Reflection–assessment	–	Skill meter–textual descriptions	Inspectable	✓	–
37	Long and Aleven (2017)	Lynnette	Explicit assessment scores	Competence	Ad hoc	System data	Overlay	Weighted algorithm	Student	Reflection–assessment	–	Skill meter–textual descriptions	Inspectable	×	
38	Abu Issa et al. (2017)	OLM	Explicit assessment scores	Knowledge	Existing framework	System data	Perturbation	Weighted algorithm	Student–peers–teacher–parent	Reflection–assessment	Assessment	Skill meter–table–textual descriptions	Negotiable Model (based on evidence)	×	

References

Abu Issa, A., Al-Jadaa, A., Ghanem, W., & Hussein, M. (2017). Enhancing the intelligence of web tutoring systems using a multi-entry based open learner model. In *Proceedings of the ICC'2017.*

Agudo-Peregrina, Á. F., Iglesias-Pradas, S., Conde-González, M. Á., & Hernández-García, Á. (2014). Can we predict success from log data in VLEs? Classification of interactions for learning analytics and their relation with performance in VLE-supported F2F and online learning. *Computers in Human Behavior, 31*, 542–550.

Ahmad, N., & Bull, S. (2009). Learner trust in learner model externalisations. In *Proceedings of the 2009 Conference on Artificial Intelligence in Education* (pp. 617–619). Amsterdam: IOS Press.

Ali, L., Hatala, M., Gašević, D., & Jovanović, J. (2012). A qualitative evaluation of evolution of a learning analytics tool. *Computers & Education, 58*(1), 470–489.

Al-Shamri, M. Y. H., & Bharadwaj, K. K. (2008). Fuzzy-genetic approach to recommender systems based on a novel hybrid user model. *Expert Systems with Applications, 35*(3), 1386–1399.

Arthi, K., & Tamilarasi, A. (2008). Prediction of autistic disorder using neuro fuzzy system by applying ANN technique. *International Journal of Developmental Neuroscience, 26*, 699–704.

Barua, D., Kay, J., Kummerfeld, B., & Paris, C. (2014). Modelling long term goals. In V. Dimitrova, T. Kuflik, D. Chin, F. Ricci, P. Dolog, & G. J. Houben (Eds.), *User modeling, adaptation, and personalization* (pp. 1–12). Cham: Springer International Publishing.

Baschera, G. M., & Gross, M. (2010). Poisson-based inference for perturbation models in adaptive spelling training. *International Journal of Artificial Intelligence in Education, 20*(4), 333–360.

Blikstein, P., & Worsley, M. (2016). Multimodal learning analytics and education data mining: Using computational technologies to measure complex learning tasks. *Journal of Learning Analytics, 3*(2), 220–238.

Branch, R. M. (2010). *Instructional design: The ADDIE approach*. New York, NY: Springer.

Bremgartner, V., Netto, J. M., & Menezes, C. (2014). Using agents and open learner model ontology for providing constructive adaptive techniques in virtual learning environments. In A. Bazzan & K. Pichara (Eds.), *Advances in artificial intelligence* (pp. 625–636). Cham: Springer International Publishing.

Brusilovsky, P., Hsaio, I.-H., & Folajimi, Y. (2011). QuizMap: Open social student modeling and adaptive navigation support with treemaps. In C. D. Kloos, D. Gillet, R. M. Crespo Garcia, F. Wild, & M. Wolpers (Eds.), *Proceedings of the 2011 EC-TEL* (pp. 71–82). Berlin: Springer.

Brusilovsky, P., & Millan, E. (2007). User models for adaptive hypermedia and adaptive educational systems. In *The adaptive web* (pp. 3–53). Berlin: Springer.

Brusilovsky, P., Somyurek, S., Guerra, J., Hosseini, R., Zadorozhny, V., & Durlach, P. (2016). Open social student modeling for personalized learning. *IEEE Transactions on Emerging Topics in Computing, 4*, 450.

Bull, S., & Al-Shanfari, L. (2015). Negotiating individual learner models in contexts of peer assessment and group learning. In *Proceedings of Workshop on Intelligent Support for Learning in Groups, AIED.*

Bull, S., Gakhal, I., Grundy, D., Johnson, M., Mabbott, A., & Xu, J. (2010). Preferences in multiple-view open learner models. In *Sustaining TEL: From innovation to learning and practice* (pp. 476–481). Berlin: Springer.

Bull, S., Jackson, T. J., & Lancaster, M. J. (2010). Students' interest in their misconceptions in first-year electrical circuits and mathematics courses. *International Journal of Electrical Engineering Education, 47*(3), 307–318.

Bull, S., Johnson, M., Masci, D., & Biel, C. (2015). Integrating and visualising diagnostic information for the benefit of learning. In P. Reimann, S. Bull, M. Kickmeier-Rust, R. K. Vatrapu, & B. Wasson (Eds.), *Measuring and visualizing learning in the information-rich classroom.* Routledge: Taylor & Francis. (Chapter 12).

Bull, S., Johnson, M. D., Alotaibi, M., Byrne, W., & Cierniak, G. (2013). Visualising multiple data sources in an independent open learner model. In *Artificial intelligence in education* (pp. 199–208). Berlin: Springer.

Bull, S., & Kay, J. (2010). Open learner models. In R. Nkambou, R. Mizoguchi, & J. Bourdeau (Eds.), *Advances in intelligent tutoring systems* (pp. 301–322). Berlin: Springer.

Bull, S., & Kay, J. (2016). SMILI☺: A framework for interfaces to learning data in open learner models, learning analytics and related fields. *International Journal of Artificial Intelligence in Education, 26*, 293–331.

Bull, S., Mabbott, A., & Abu Issa, A. S. (2007). UMPTEEN: Named and anonymous learner model access for instructors and peers. *International Journal of Artificial Intelligence in Education, 17*(3), 227–253.

Bull, S., & McKay, M. (2004). An open learner model for children and teachers: Inspecting knowledge level of individuals and peers. In J. C. Lester, R. M. Vicari, & F. Paraguaçu (Eds.), *Intelligent tutoring systems* (pp. 646–655). Berlin: Springer.

Bull, S., Pain, H., & Brna, P. (1995). Mr. Collins: A collaboratively constructed, inspectable student model for intelligent computer assisted language learning. *Instructional Science, 23*(1-3), 65–87.

Calvo, R., & D'Mello, S. (2010). Affect detection: An interdisciplinary review of models, methods, and their applications. *IEEE Transactions on Affective Computing, 1*(1), 18–37.

Carini, R. M., Kuh, G. D., & Klein, S. P. (2006). Student engagement and student learning: Testing the linkages. *Research in Higher Education, 47*(1), 1–32.

Carmona, C., & Conejo, R. (2004). A learner model in a distributed environment. In N. Wolfgang & P. De Bra (Eds.), *Adaptive hypermedia and adaptive web-based systems* (pp. 353–359). Berlin: Springer.

Chang, R. I., Hung, Y. H., & Lin, C. F. (2015). Survey of learning experiences and influence of learning style preferences on user intentions regarding MOOCs. *British Journal of Educational Technology, 46*(3), 528–541.

Chatti, M. A., Muslim, A., & Schroeder, U. (2017). Toward an open learning analytics ecosystem. In B. Daniel (Ed.), *Big data and learning analytics in higher education* (pp. 195–219). Cham: Springer International Publishing.

Cho, M.-H., & Kim, B. J. (2013). Students' self-regulation for interaction with others in online learning environments. *Internet and Higher Education, 17*, 69–75.

Chrysafiadi, K., & Virvou, M. (2012). Evaluating the integration of fuzzy logic into the student model of a web-based learning environment. *Expert Systems with Applications, 39*(18), 13127–13134.

Chrysafiadi, K., & Virvou, M. (2013). Student modeling approaches: A literature review for the last decade. *Expert Systems with Applications, 40*(11), 4715–4729.

Chrysafiadi, K., & Virvou, M. (2015). Student modeling for personalized education: A review of the literature. In K. Chrysafiadi & M. Virvou (Eds.), *Advances in personalized web-based education* (pp. 1–24). Cham: Springer International Publishing.

Clemente, J., Ramírez, J., & De Antonio, A. (2011). A proposal for student modeling based on ontologies and diagnosis rules. *Expert Systems with Applications, 38*(7), 8066–8078.

Conejo, R., Trella, M., Cruces, I., & Garcia, R. (2011). INGRID: A web service tool for hierarchical open learner model visualization. In L. Ardissono & T. Kuflik (Eds.), *Advances in user modeling* (pp. 406–409). Berlin: Springer.

Cook, R., Kay, J., & Kummerfeld, B. (2015). MOOClm: User modelling for MOOCs. In S. Carberry, S. Weibelzahl, A. Micarelli, & G. Semeraro (Eds.), *User modeling, adaptation and personalization* (pp. 80–91). Cham: Springer International Publishing.

Cruz-Benito, J., Borrás-Gené, O., García-Peñalvo, F. J., Blanco, Á. F., & Therón, R. (2015). Extending MOOC ecosystems using web services and software architectures. In *Proceedings of the XVI International Conference on Human Computer Interaction* (pp. 438–444). New York, NY: ACM.

D'Mello, S., & Graesser, A. (2012). Dynamics of affective states during complex learning. *Learning and Instruction, 22*(2), 145–157.

D'Mello, S., Lehman, B., Pekrun, R., & Graesser, A. (2014). Confusion can be beneficial for learning. *Learning and Instruction, 29*, 153–170.

D'Mello, S. K., Blanchard, N., Baker, R., Ocumpaugh, J., & Brawner, K. (2014). I feel your pain: A selective review of affect-sensitive instructional strategies. In R. Sottilare, A. Graesser, X. Hu, & B. Goldberg (Eds.), *Design recommendations for adaptive intelligent tutoring systems: Volume 2 – Instructional management* (pp. 35–48). Orlando, FL: U.S. Army Research Laboratory.

D'mello, S. K., & Kory, J. (2015). A review and meta-analysis of multimodal affect detection systems. *ACM Computing Surveys, 47*(3), 43-1–43-36.

Darr, C. W. (2012). Measuring student engagement: The development of a scale for formative use. In S. L. Christenson, A. L. Reschly, & C. Wylie (Eds.), *Handbook of research on student engagement* (pp. 149–172). New York, NY: Springer.

Davis, D., Jivet, I., Kizilcec, R. F., Chen, G., Hauff, C., & Houben, G. J. (2017). Follow the successful crowd: Raising MOOC completion rates through social comparison at scale. In *Proceedings of the 7th International Conference on Learning Analytics and Knowledge* (pp. 454–463). New York, NY: ACM.

De Barba, P., Kennedy, G. E., & Ainley, M. D. (2016). The role of students' motivation and participation in predicting performance in a MOOC. *Journal of Computer Assisted Learning, 32*(3), 218–231.

Desmarais, M. C., & Baker, R. S. J. D. (2012). A review of recent advances in learner and skill modeling in intelligent learning environments. *User Modeling and User-Adapted Interaction, 22*(1-2), 9–38.

Devedzic, V., & Jovanović, J. (2015). Developing open badges: A comprehensive approach. *Educational Technology Research and Development, 63*(4), 603–620.

Dimitrova, V. (2003). STyLE-OLM: Interactive open learner modelling. *International Journal of Artificial Intelligence in Education, 13*(1), 35–78.

Eberle, J., Lund, K., Tchounikine, P., & Fischer, F. (Eds.). (2016). *Grand challenge problems in technology-enhanced learning II: MOOCs and beyond: Perspectives for research, practice, and policy making*. Cham: Springer International Publishing.

Epp, C. D., & McCalla, G. (2011). ProTutor: Historic open learner models for pronunciation tutoring. In G. Biswas, S. Bull, J. Kay, & A. Mitrovic (Eds.), *Artificial intelligence in education* (pp. 441–443). Berlin: Springer.

Gakhal, I., & Bull, S. (2008). An open learner model for trainee pilots. *Research in Learning Technology, 16*(2), 123–135.

Galan, F. C., & Beal, C. R. (2012). EEG estimates of engagement and cognitive workload predict math problem solving outcomes. In J. Masthoff, B. Mobasher, M. Desmarais, & R. Nkambou (Eds.), *User modeling, adaptation, and personalization* (pp. 51–62). Berlin: Springer.

Gaudioso, E., Montero, M., & Hernandez-Del-Olmo, F. (2012). Supporting teachers in adaptive educational systems through predictive models: A proof of concept. *Expert Systems with Applications, 39*(1), 621–625.

Gaudioso, E., Montero, M., Talavera, L., & Hernandez-del-Olmo, F. (2009). Supporting teachers in collaborative student modeling: A framework and an implementation. *Expert Systems with Applications, 36*(2), 2260–2265.

Georgopoulos, V. C., Malandraki, G. A., & Stylios, C. D. (2003). A fuzzy cognitive map approach to differential diagnosis of specific language impairment. *Artificial Intelligence in Medicine, 29*, 261–278.

Giannandrea, L., & Sansoni, M. (2013). A literature review on intelligent tutoring systems and on student profiling. *Learning & Teaching with Media & Technology, 287*.

Girard, S., & Johnson, H. (2010). Designing affective computing learning companions with teachers as design partners. In *Proceedings of the 3rd International Workshop on Affective Interaction in Natural Environments* (pp. 49–54). New York, NY: ACM.

Glushkova, T. (2008). Adaptive model for user knowledge in the e-learning system. In *Proceedings of the International Conference on Computer Systems and Technologies* (pp. 16-1–16-6). New York, NY: ACM.

Grubisic, A., Stankov, S., & Žitko, B. (2013). Stereotype student model for an adaptive e-learning system. *World Academy of Science, Engineering and Technology, 7*, 16–23.

Guerra-Hollstein, J., Barria-Pineda, J., Schunn, C., Bull, S., & Brusilovsky, P. (2017). Fine-grained open learner models: Complexity versus support. In *Proceedings of the 25th Conference on User Modeling, Adaptation and Personalization* (pp. 41–49). New York, NY: ACM.

Haya, P. A., Daems, O., Malzahn, N., Castellanos, J., & Hoppe, H. U. (2015). Analysing content and patterns of interaction for improving the learning design of networked learning environments. *British Journal of Educational Technology, 46*(2), 300–316.

Henrie, C. R., Halverson, L. R., & Graham, C. R. (2015). Measuring student engagement in technology-mediated learning: A review. *Computers & Education, 90*, 36–53.

Hew, K. F. (2015). Promoting engagement in online courses: What strategies can we learn from three highly rated MOOCS. *British Journal of Educational Technology, 47*(2), 320–341.

Hosseini, R., Hsiao, I. H., Guerra, J., & Brusilovsky, P. (2015). Off the beaten path: The impact of adaptive content sequencing on student navigation in an open social student modeling interface. In *Artificial intelligence in education* (pp. 624–628). Cham: Springer International Publishing.

Hsiao, I. H., Bakalov, F., Brusilovsky, P., & König-Ries, B. (2013). Progressor: Social navigation support through open social student modeling. *New Review of Hypermedia and Multimedia, 19*(2), 112–131.

Jain, K., Manghirmalani, P., Dongardive, J., & Abraham, S. (2009). Computational diagnosis of learning disability. *International Journal of Recent Trends in Engineering, 2*(3), 64–66.

Johnson, M., & Bull, S. (2009). Belief exploration in a multiple-media open learner model for basic harmony. In *Artificial intelligence in education: Building learning systems that care: From knowledge representation to affective modelling* (pp. 299–306). New York, NY: ACM.

Kay, J. (2000). Stereotypes, student models and scrutability. In G. Gauthier, C. Frasson, & K. Van Lehn (Eds.), *Intelligent tutoring systems* (pp. 19–30). Berlin: Springer.

Kay, J., & Bull, S. (2015). New opportunities with open learner models and visual learning analytics. In C. Conati, N. Heffernan, A. Mitrovic, & M. F. Verdejo (Eds.), *Artificial intelligence in education* (pp. 666–669). Cham: Springer International Publishing.

Kerly, A., Ellis, R., & Bull, S. (2007). CALMsystem: A conversational agent for learner modelling. In R. Ellis, T. Allen, & M. Petridis (Eds.), *Applications and innovations in intelligent systems* (Vol. XV, pp. 89–102). Berlin: Springer.

Kohli, M., & Prasad, T. V. (2010). Identifying dyslexic students by using artificial neural networks. In *Proceedings of the World Congress on Engineering* (pp. 118–121).

Kump, B., Seifert, C., Beham, G., Lindstaedt, S. N., & Ley, T. (2012). Seeing what the system thinks you know: Visualizing evidence in an open learner model. In *Proceedings of the 2nd International Conference on Learning Analytics and Knowledge* (pp. 153–157).

Kusurkar, R. A., Ten Cate, T. J., Vos, C. M. P., Westers, P., & Croiset, G. (2013). How motivation affects academic performance: A structural equation modelling analysis. *Advances in Health Sciences Education, 18*(1), 57–69.

Lam, S. F., Jimerson, S., Shin, H., Cefai, C., Veiga, F. H., Hatzichristou, C., … Basnett, J. (2016). Cultural universality and specificity of student engagement in school: The results of an international study from 12 countries. *British Journal of Educational Psychology, 86*, 137–153.

Lazarinis, F., & Retalis, S. (2007). Analyze me: Open learner model in an adaptive web testing system. *International Journal of Artificial Intelligence in Education, 17*(3), 255–271.

LeBlanc, V. R., McConnell, M. M., & Monteiro, S. D. (2015). Predictable chaos: A review of the effects of emotions on attention, memory and decision making. *Advances in Health Sciences Education, 20*(1), 265–282.

Lee, S. J., & Bull, S. (2008). An open learner model to help parents help their children. *Technology Instruction Cognition and Learning, 6*(1), 29–51.

Literat, I. (2015). Implications of massive open online courses for higher education: Mitigating or reifying educational inequities? *Higher Education Research & Development, 34*(6), 1164–1177.

Long, Y., & Aleven, V. (2013). Supporting students' self-regulated learning with an open learner model in a linear equation tutor. In H. C. Lane, K. Yacef, J. Mostow, & P. Pavlik (Eds.), *Artificial intelligence in education* (pp. 219–228). Berlin: Springer.

Long, Y., & Aleven, V. (2017). Enhancing learning outcomes through self-regulated learning support with an open learner model. *User Modeling and User-Adapted Interaction, 27*, 55–88.

Mabbott, A., & Bull, S. (2006). Student preferences for editing, persuading, and negotiating the open learner model. In M. Ikeda, K. D. Ashley, & T.-W. Chan (Eds.), *Intelligent tutoring systems* (pp. 481–490). Berlin: Springer.

Martins, C., Faria, L., De Carvalho, C. V., & Carrapatoso, E. (2008). User modeling in adaptive hypermedia educational systems. *Educational Technology & Society, 11*(1), 194–207.

Mathews, M., Mitrovic, A., Lin, B., Holland, J., & Churcher, N. (2012). Do your eyes give it away? Using eye-tracking data to understand students' attitudes towards open student model representations. In S. A. Cerri, W. J. Clancey, G. Papadourakis, & K. Panourgia (Eds.), *Intelligent tutoring systems* (pp. 422–427). Berlin: Springer.

Mazzola, L., & Mazza, R. (2010). GVIS: A facility for adaptively mashing up and representing open learner models. In M. Wolpers, P. A. Kirschner, M. Scheffel, S. Lindstaedt, & V. Dimitrova (Eds.), *Sustaining TEL: From innovation to learning and practice* (pp. 554–559). Berlin: Springer.

Millan, E., Loboda, T., & Pırez-de-la-Cruz, J. L. (2010). Bayesian networks for student model engineering. *Computers and Education, 55*(4), 1663–1683.

Mitrovic, A., & Martin, B. (2007). Evaluating the effect of open student models on self-assessment. *International Journal of Artificial Intelligence in Education, 17*(2), 121–144.

Muldner, K., & Burleson, W. (2015). Utilizing sensor data to model students' creativity in a digital environment. *Computers in Human Behavior, 42*, 127–137.

Muldner, K., Burleson, W., & VanLehn, K. (2010). "Yes!": Using tutor and sensor data to predict moments of delight during instructional activities. In P. De Bra, A. Kobsa, & D. Chin (Eds.), *User modeling, adaptation, and personalization* (pp. 159–170). Berlin: Springer.

Nakic, J., Granic, A., & Glavinic, V. (2015). Anatomy of student models in adaptive learning systems: A systematic literature review of individual differences from 2001 to 2013. *Journal of Educational Computing Research, 51*(4), 459–489.

Nguyen, C. D., Vo, K. D., Bui, D. B., & Nguyen, D. T. (2011). An ontology-based IT student model in an educational social network. In *Proceedings of the 13th International Conference on Information Integration and Web-based Applications and Services* (pp. 379–382). New York, NY: ACM.

Nunn, S., Avella, J. T., Kanai, T., & Kebritchi, M. (2016). Learning analytics methods, benefits, and challenges in higher education: A systematic literature review. *Online Learning, 20*(2), 13.

Ohlsson, S. (2015). Constraint-based modeling: From cognitive theory to computer tutoring–And back again. *International Journal of Artificial Intelligence in Education, 26*, 1–17.

Panagiotopoulos, I., Kalou, A., Pierrakeas, C., & Kameas, A. (2012). An ontology-based model for student representation in intelligent tutoring systems for distance learning. In L. Iliadis, I. Maglogiannis, & H. Papadopoulos (Eds.), *Artificial intelligence applications and innovations* (pp. 296–305). Berlin: Springer.

Papamitsiou, Z. K., & Economides, A. A. (2014). Learning analytics and educational data mining in practice: A systematic literature review of empirical evidence. *Educational Technology & Society, 17*(4), 49–64.

Papanikolaou, K. A. (2015). Constructing interpretative views of learners' interaction behavior in an open learner model. *IEEE Transactions on Learning Technologies, 8*(2), 201–214.

Pohl, A., Bry, F., Schwarz, J., & Gottstein, M. (2012). Sensing the classroom: Improving awareness and self-awareness of students in Backstage. In *15th International Conference on Interactive Collaborative Learning* (pp. 1–8). Washington, DC: IEEE.

Powell, G. (1997). On being a culturally sensitive instructional designer and educator. *Educational Technology, 37*(2), 6–14.

Reeve, J. (2012). A self-determination theory perspective on student engagement. In S. L. Christenson, A. L. Reschly, & C. Wylie (Eds.), *Handbook of research on student engagement* (pp. 149–172). New York, NY: Springer.

Rodríguez-Triana, M. J., Martínez-Monés, A., Asensio-Pérez, J. I., & Dimitriadis, Y. (2015). Scripting and monitoring meet each other: Aligning learning analytics and learning design to support teachers in orchestrating CSCL situations. *British Journal of Educational Technology, 46*(2), 330–343.

Sampson, D. (2017). Teaching and learning analytics to support teacher inquiry. In *IEEE Global Engineering Education Conference (EDUCON2017)*. Washington, DC: IEEE.

Schiaffino, S., & Amandi, A. (2009). Intelligent user profiling. In M. Bramer (Ed.), *Artificial intelligence an international perspective* (pp. 193–216). Berlin: Springer.

Schwendimann, B. A., Rodriguez-Triana, M. J., Vozniuk, A., Prieto, L. P., Boroujeni, M. S., Holzer, A., … Dillenbourg, P. (2017). Perceiving learning at a glance: A systematic literature review of learning dashboard research. *IEEE Transactions on Learning Technologies, 10*(1), 30–41.

Sergis, S., & Sampson, D. (2016). School analytics: A framework for supporting systemic school leadership. In J. M. Spector, D. Ifenthaler, D. Sampson, & P. Isaias (Eds.), *Competencies in teaching, learning and educational leadership in the digital age* (pp. 79–122). New York, NY: Springer.

Sergis, S., & Sampson, D. (2017). Teaching and learning analytics to support teacher inquiry: A systematic literature review. In A. Ayala (Ed.), *Learning analytics: Fundaments, applications, and trends: A view of the current state of the art* (pp. 25–63). Cham: Springer International Publishing.

Sergis, S., Sampson, D. G., & Pelliccione, L. (2017). Educational design for MOOCs: Design considerations for technology-supported learning at large scale. In *Open education: From OERs to MOOCs* (pp. 39–71). Berlin: Springer.

Tempelaar, D. T., Rienties, B., & Giesbers, B. (2015). In search for the most informative data for feedback generation: Learning analytics in a data-rich context. *Computers in Human Behavior, 47*, 157–167.

Ting, C. Y., & Phon-Amnuaisuk, S. (2012). Properties of Bayesian student model for INQPRO. *Applied Intelligence, 36*(2), 391–406.

Tongchai, N. (2016). Impact of self-regulation and open learner model on learning achievement in blended learning environment. *International Journal of Information and Education Technology, 6*(5), 343.

Trowler, V. (2010). Student engagement literature review. Report for the Higher Education Academy. Retrieved from http://tinyurl.com/ztz2q2e

Upton, K., & Kay, J. (2009). Narcissus: Group and individual models to support small group work. In *User modeling, adaptation, and personalization* (pp. 54–65). Berlin: Springer.

Van Labeke, N., Brna, P., & Morales, R. (2007). Opening up the interpretation process in an open learner model. *International Journal of Artificial Intelligence in Education, 17*(3), 305–338.

Vélez, J., Fabregat, R., Bull, S., & Hueva, D. (2009). The potential for open learner models in adaptive virtual learning environments. In *AIED 2009: 14th International Conference on Artificial Intelligence in Education Workshops Proceedings* (p. 11).

Verbert, K., Duval, E., Klerkx, J., Govaerts, S., & Santos, J. L. (2013). Learning analytics dashboard applications. *American Behavioral Scientist, 57*(10), 1500–1509.

Verginis, I., Gouli, E., Gogoulou, A., & Grigoriadou, M. (2011). Guiding learners into reengagement through the SCALE environment: An empirical study. *IEEE Transactions on Learning Technologies, 4*(3), 275–290.

Weber, G., & Brusilovsky, P. (2001). ELM-ART: An adaptive versatile system for web-based instruction. *International Journal of Artificial Intelligence in Education (IJAIED), 12*, 351–384.

Wedelin, D., Adawi, T., Jahan, T., & Andersson, S. (2015). Investigating and developing engineering students' mathematical modelling and problem-solving skills. *European Journal of Engineering Education, 40*(5), 557–572.

Wetzel, J., VanLehn, K., Butler, D., Chaudhari, P., Desai, A., Feng, J., … Samala, R. (2017). The design and development of the Dragoon intelligent tutoring system for model construction: Lessons learned. *Interactive Learning Environments, 25*(3), 361–381.

Woolf, B. P. (2010). Student modeling. In R. Nkambou, R. Mizoguchi, & J. Bourdeau (Eds.), *Advances in intelligent tutoring systems* (pp. 267–279). Berlin: Springer.

Woolf, B. P., Arroyo, I., Muldner, K., Burleson, W., Cooper, D. G., Dolan, R., & Christopherson, R. M. (2010). The effect of motivational learning companions on low achieving students and students with disabilities. In *Intelligent tutoring systems* (pp. 327–337). Berlin: Springer.

Xu, J., & Bull, S. (2010). Encouraging advanced second language speakers to recognise their language difficulties: A personalised computer-based approach. *Computer Assisted Language Learning, 23*(2), 111–127.

Yacef, K. (2005). The logic-ITA in the classroom: A medium scale experiment. *International Journal of Artificial Intelligence in Education, 15*(1), 41–62.

Zakharov, K., Mitrovic, A., & Ohlsson, S. (2005). Feedback micro-engineering in EER-tutor. In *Proceedings of the 2005 Conference on Artificial Intelligence in Education: Supporting Learning through Intelligent and Socially Informed Technology* (pp. 718–725). New York, NY: ACM.

Zapata-Rivera, D., Hansen, E., Shute, V. J., Underwood, J. S., & Bauer, M. (2007). Evidence-based approach to interacting with open student models. *International Journal of Artificial Intelligence in Education, 17*(3), 273–303.

Stylianos Sergis holds a B.Sc. in "Informatics and Telecommunications" (June 2010) from the Department of Informatics and Telecommunications of the National and Kapodistrian University of Athens, Greece, a M.Sc. in "Informatics in Education" (June 2012) from the Faculty of Primary Education of the National and Kapodistrian University of Athens, Greece and a Ph.D. from the Department of Digital Systems of the University of Piraeus (June 2017). His research focuses on Educational Data Analytics for supporting teaching and learning. He is the co-author of 30 scientific publications. He has received two Best Paper Awards in International Conferences on Learning Technologies (2016, 2017).

Demetrios Sampson is a Professor of Digital Systems for Learning and Education at the Department of Digital Systems, University of Piraeus, Greece, where he serves as Academic Staff since 2001, and a Professor of Learning Technologies at the School of Education, Curtin University, Australia since 2015. He is the co-author of 340 articles in scientific books, journals and conferences, and the editor of 12 books, 32 special issues and 35 international conference proceedings. He has received ten times Best Paper Award in International Conferences. He has been a Keynote/Invited Speaker/Lecturer in 82 International/National Conferences and/or Postgraduate Programs around the world. He has been project director, principle investigator and/or research consultant in 70 Research and Innovation projects with external funding at the range of 16 M€. He has supervised 155 honors and postgraduate students to successful completion.

He has developed and delivers the first MOOC on the use of Educational Data Analytics by School Teachers (Analytics for the Classroom Teacher), offered by the edX platform which has attracted more than 12,000 participants from 160 countries around the world since October 2016.

He served as Editor-in-Chief of one of the first open access journals in educational technology, the Educational Technology & Society Journal, 2003–2018. He has also served or serves as Member of the Steering Committee and/or Advisory and/or Editorial Board of 25 International/National Journals, in various leadership roles in 75 International Conferences and at the Program Committee of 525 International/National Conferences.

He is the recipient of the IEEE Computer Society Distinguished Service Award (July 2012) and named a Golden Core Member of IEEE Computer Society in recognition of his contribution to the field of Learning Technologies (January 2013). He is also the recipient of the Golden Nikola Tesla Chain Award of the International Society for Engineering Pedagogy (IGIP) for "International outstanding achievements in the field of Engineering Pedagogy" (September 2018).

Chapter 10
Fostering Active Learning with Video Using Teacher-Set Analysis Categories

Meg Colasante and Josephine Lang

Abstract Despite widespread use of video in higher education, there is still much to be learnt about what constitutes optimal teaching practices in leveraging digital resources for learning. Research on student interactions with online video suggests that practices can range from as minimal as setting passive-receptive viewing requirements through to teacher-structured purposeful engagement. Some approaches focus on either technological or pedagogical solutions, or both, to guide learning with video. This chapter examines several published cases of teaching practice with video in undergraduate education. It draws from these examples a focus on teacher-set analysis categories to guide student exploration of digital video content to help novices to scaffold their thinking. Various explicit and implicit uses of analysis categories within Australian, Taiwan, and US universities are reviewed from the literature. Some cases demonstrate transferability and/or scalability to apply to other disciplines. Overall, the literature reviewed indicates that the use of categories to inform the design of digital video analysis needs to ensure that an active learning challenge is retained. Analysis guided by teacher-set categories tends to be beneficial for student performance evaluation and development in particular, as well as knowledge acquisition/consolidation.

1 Introduction

While good examples of teaching with contemporary resources can be found in universities, meaningful leverage of digital media and technology generally across educational sectors has been patchy, and teaching practices with these technologies

M. Colasante (✉)
School of Education, Faculty of Arts and Education,
Deakin University, Melbourne, VIC, Australia
e-mail: mcolasan@deakin.edu.au

J. Lang
Melbourne School of Professional and Continuing Education,
The University of Melbourne, Faculty of Business and Economics, Parkville, Victoria, Australia
e-mail: josephine.lang@unimelb.edu.au

D. Sampson et al. (eds.), *Learning Technologies for Transforming Large-Scale Teaching, Learning, and Assessment*, https://doi.org/10.1007/978-3-030-15130-0_10

remain variable (Selwyn, 2007, 2017). This includes higher education integration of digital video, where university teachers frequently set conditions for student interaction largely reliant on passive-receptive viewing (Kay, 2012; Yousef, Chatti, & Schroeder, 2014). Laurillard (2012) acknowledges that there is plenty yet to be discovered and disseminated regarding effective teaching with media and technologies. Digital resources, while known for their benefits, 'do not drive the development of learners' skills… [which] can come only from the scaffolding the teacher sets up to support learners in the process' (Laurillard, 2012, p. 133).

According to widely recognised annual reports on the status of educational media and technologies, such as *Innovating Pedagogy by the Open University* (UK) and the *NMC Horizon Report* (US), video is a superior learning resource when students actively engage with its content (e.g. Sharples et al., 2014). Contrasting to instructivist approaches, reported examples of active, constructive and collaborative video-based learning include strategies, such as post-viewing teach back in student pairs and posing clarifying questions; or exploration of a topic or problem to induce a state of 'productive failure' to peak student interest before viewing a video for expert insight (Sharples et al., 2016, pp. 9, 17, 20). Other practices that promote deeper learning are gaining prominence in higher education, especially those involving problem-solving, critical thinking, collaboration, inquiry-based learning, self-directed learning, and with explicit connections to the real world (Adams Becker et al., 2017).

This chapter collates several published cases of undergraduate students purposefully analysing video for discipline-specific knowledge and/or skill development. Within each example, we extrapolate the analysis categories used in video exploration by the students. For the purposes of this chapter, analysis categories are considered key foci points of learning that the teachers set for their students (from their vantage point of expertise), to help guide exploration and analysis of videos. In the cases referred to in this chapter, there may not have been explicit identification of 'analysis categories;' yet they carry the intent of purpose of analysis for student learning as we have described here.

These cases illustrate pedagogical practices that use digital video to support student learning, with potential for scalability and/or transferability into other contexts. These diverse cases originate from various universities globally and include business students learning via video media and wiki technology (in an Australian university); psychology students learning via a movie (in a US university); psychiatric nursing and physical education students learning via video and video annotation technology (Taiwan and Australian universities); and entomology students from various disciplines learning via technologically treated video (US university).

This review of several diverse studies builds on a paper presented at the International Conference on Cognition and Exploratory Learning in The Digital Age (Colasante, 2016). Through this review of recent studies in the literature and the authors' research experiences in the area of video-based learning, the chapter continues to invite the reader to contemplate the university teacher's role in pedagogical design to leverage digital video as a tool for learning.

The remainder of the chapter is structured as follows. Section 2 presents the importance of teacher intervention in maximising active learning from video, with focus on technological and pedagogical solutions (Sect. 2.1), and transferability and scalability (Sect. 2.2). Section 3 offers descriptive summaries of learning interventions involving teacher-set categories for video analysis. The five cases focus on undergraduate subjects in Business (property services), Entomology, Psychology, Psychiatric Nursing (therapeutic communication), and Physical Education. Sections 3 and 4 offer the discussion and conclusion respectively.

2 Why Is Teacher Intervention Required for Students to Maximise Learning from Digital Video?

Designing effective teaching is complex and has become more so with the abundance of design options made possible by modern media and technologies (Laurillard & Derntl, 2014). Laurillard (2012) argues that compared to informal learning, academic learning is more complex for students and their intrinsic motivation to learn differs. Teaching is a demanding endeavour when the goal is to facilitate students to become 'active, self-directed and self-responsible participants in the learning process' (Laurillard & Derntl, 2014, p. 13, emphasis removed). '[T]eachers must be willing to treat the process as essentially problematic, iterative, and always improvable' (Laurillard, 2012, p. 82).

Video has become ubiquitous in contemporary learning environments in higher education institutions and, more generally, significantly integrated into modern life. Predictions of remarkable growth of video as internet traffic (CISCO, 2013) have been realised, with a further doubling of video-on-demand traffic anticipated within a few years (CISCO, 2017). Digitalisation of video and advances of the internet and world wide web have enabled an explosive growth of online coursework in higher education and have facilitated reach to places across the globe (e.g. Bates & Sangra, 2011; Clarke, Butler, Schmidt-Hansen, & Somerville, 2004; Gibbings, Lidstone, & Bruce, 2015; Hsieh & Cho, 2011). Almost anyone with adequate internet connection can learn something new via informal means at any time they choose, from, for example, videos uploaded to YouTube or TED Talks, or via databases requiring personal or library subscription. Conversely, online video can supply unsound or fallacious information and/or overwhelm the viewer with a plethora of detail and choice.

In a Delphi study involving experts in YouTube video use across educational sectors (Snelson, Rice, & Wyzard, 2012), several issues were raised as requiring further research. These issues related to active learning, digital literacies, and technological factors that shape the possibilities of the learning experiences using video. To illustrate, examples include: tracking passive versus active interaction 'e.g. commenting, rating, or sharing;' transformative educational uses; co-participation of academics and students in design and assessment of learning; impact on discourse, argumentation, decision-making, and critical thinking; how to promote 'autonomy, power and options to students;' digital literacies 'to navigate/survive and leverage these within and irrespective of formal education;' 'elements of effective online video;' 'impact of evolving new features... (e.g. annotation);' and effective reusability in teaching (pp. 124–126).

As illustrated from the range above, university educators are challenged to engage deeply with the student learning process and guide development of digital literacy skills (Laurillard, 2012) to enable students to actively and intelligently learn from digital media. University teachers set the conditions for learning by establishing the context within which students learn; selecting teaching strategies, modes, and methods of learning and assessment, and supporting tools; and the overall actions required of their students. Processes of learning remain inherently complex, and cycles of scholarly reflection, planning and preparation, monitoring and facilitating, and evaluating and refinement are required by the teacher (Laurillard, 2012).

2.1 Technological and/or Pedagogical Solutions for Active Learning with Video

Efforts to support students to leverage learning with video resources include technological or pedagogical solutions, or a mix of both. One example of a technological approach aims to bring navigational affordances to video that resemble how a book is navigated. Zhang, Zhou, Briggs, and Nunamaker Jr. (2006) extended video navigation features beyond regular player controls to enable location of specific segments via search queries, to view and re-view as required, to promote targeted exploration rather than linear, passive viewing. Their empirical study with 138 students, in various experimental and control groups, revealed an improvement in learning outcomes and student satisfaction for the group equipped with the additional navigational features. In related work,

Merkt, Weigand, Heier, and Schwan (2011) compared 'common' video controls (start, stop, forward, review) with 'enhanced' book-like video navigation features involving an index and table of contents. Contrary to Merkt and colleagues' expectations—and to the Zhang et al. study—students who had the experience with only basic video controls tested better than those with enhanced video controls. They discussed that this might be a reflection of the students' metacognitive skills for active and self-regulatory skills for learning rather than ineffectiveness of enhanced video controls. The unexpected finding is a reminder of the significance of students knowing how to learn i.e. development of student metacognition as fundamental to active learning, particularly, perhaps, in video-based contexts that are used in self-study contexts.

A further example of a technological solution is provided by Maier, de Heer, Ortac, and Kuijten (2015), to render videos of various specimens suitable for learning purposes for medical diagnostics and forensic science students. Microscopic images of hair, fibres and blood cells, for example, require very high resolution visualisation for students to be able to analyse and interpret the specimens. Such affordance is beyond both regular high definition video and past practices of photographing specimens, where key details may be poorly visible. Using 4K ultrahigh definition resolution, videos were created of the specimens for two learning purposes. First, to share simultaneously across university campuses via a streaming connection for in-class discussion. Second, to prepare the videos for student access for self-study—as learning how to interpret specimens requires maximum practice opportunities—which were narrated by experts in medical diagnostics and forensic science. These varied solutions, including ease of nuanced access and fidelity of viewing experience, have a technological rather than pedagogical focus with illustrated potential or actual learning benefits reported.

Alternatively, Wright, Newman, Cardinale, and Teese (2016) report on their work in creating several 'Interactive Video Vignettes' (IVV) as a pedagogical and technological solution to help undergraduate biology students actively learn a range of biological concepts. Five core biological concepts (e.g. 'Energy transformation'), are presented across ten videos, where each video addresses one or two of the concepts framed within a 'big idea' (e.g. 'Environmental conditions (O_2) influence metabolic pathways') (Wright et al., 2016, p. 34). Each IVV takes approximately 10–20 min for students to work through. They encounter several question points within the video, and cannot advance until they have responded to the posed questions. Drawing on the scientific process, students are required to answer questions, make predictions (e.g. predict the shape of a growth curve on a graph), collect data, and draw conclusions. Some answers will be revealed on video resumption (or 'next page'), compared to branching activities which allow the biological scenario to unfold before prompting the student to recheck their answers (e.g. to reconcile their first response with the data). Both the literature and the teachers' own experiences regarding common student misconceptions allowed the teachers to design opportunities into the scenarios to tease out such learning challenges. These resources required a small team to create, which would assumedly involve time, cost, and expertise. However, a sharing philosophy of Wright et al. (2016) includes making their IVVs and teaching support materials available to others, presuming opportunities for reusability of these resources.

Technology is not a magic learning enabler of its own accord (Cuban, 1986); rather, it is a potential learning enabler when coupled with pedagogical design (Hannafin, Hannafin, & Gabbitas, 2009). Yet it is not unusual for the benefits of technology to overshadow pedagogical considerations, where the 'significant question as to how learning can be supported effectively is sometimes left out of the picture' (Ifenthaler, 2010, p. 6). Deep learning requires purposeful student engagement (e.g. Biggs & Tang, 2011; Bruner, 1960; Ramsden, 2003). This should include reflection on challenging tasks, where student thinking is alert and thorough while, for example, searching and surveying to summarise a situation or to generate a conclusion (Dewey, 1933). Attentive focus on expert representations, effective action, and deliberate practice in complex domains are required to build student performance levels and develop problem-solving processes transferable to other situations (Spector, 2008). Such organisation of thinking may need to be learnt and can be guided by teachers; as was unexpectedly found by Merkt and his colleagues (2011) as discussed earlier in this section.

Using both a pedagogical and technological approach, analysis categories were pivotal in the design of several cases of video-based learning with the aid of a video annotation tool, within multiple disciplinary contexts across one university (Douglas, Colasante, & Kimpton, 2015). In each case, analysis categories were designed to guide students' exploration of video content, as set by university teachers in consultation with educational designers, industry experts, and/or as guided by relevant professional bodies. One such case, in a Physical Education (PE) context, is summarised in Sect. 3 of this chapter. The research outcomes across the multiple cases reinforced the need for concerted teacher design and planning of learning activities focused on student exploration of digital video. The findings emphasise key factors to support learning with digital video. These factors relate to good teaching practices with any media in higher education, including (1) purposeful alignment to assessment; (2) socio-constructivist-based practices of: teacher feedback interactions and student-to-student collaboration to achieve meaningful outcomes (e.g. Colasante, 2011; Colasante & Lang, 2012); and (3) structured guidance and clearly communicated and purposeful intended learning outcomes. Clear communication of purpose was key to student motivation to engage, demonstrated by some students meeting less than teacher-set requirements and others achieving beyond the required learning interactions (e.g. Douglas, Lang, & Colasante, 2014).

While using analysis categories as guidance for critical reflection and interrogation of video content was helpful in many of the cases examined, teachers need to be careful not to over structure the learning experience for students, for example, providing resources already 'defined, refined, subdivided, classified, organized according to certain principles… worked out by… expert[s]' as if students' minds are 'indifferent or even averse to all logical achievement' (Dewey, 1933, p. 81). Over-structuring to a point of tasking students to look for isolated signs may result in surface learning such as not noticing relationships or real-world applications, compared to deeper learning as initiated by determining significant concepts, applying knowledge to everyday scenarios, solving problems, and associating prior and new knowledge to structure and reorganise content coherently (Ramsden, 2003).

2.2 Transferability and Scalability of Active Learning with Video

The current technology-enriched higher education environment offers an array of study access options, including onshore or offshore/international, online or on-campus, city or rural, or blends of various modalities. While this may now seem unremarkable, it was only at the end of the twentieth century that predictions were made for such a situation (Blight, Davis, & Olsen, 2000). Opportunities to re-use or adapt student learning resources and activities to suit various disciplines and to various cohorts comes with reminders to consider how students experience technology-enhanced learning, and how to take active learning to scale. Through such understanding, activities can be better designed and students better facilitated to achieve familiarity with 'how to learn', particularly for deeper learning experiences (Gibbings et al., 2015), and to develop digital literacy skills (e.g. Laurillard, 2002, 2012). This is consistent with the views of Conole (2013) regarding many students needing modeling or assistance on how to effectively use advanced learning environments.

The opportunity for open or large-scale enrolments in higher education experienced a new frontier in the 2010s with the rise of the MOOC, or Massive Open Online Course/s. While usually university-affiliated, these technologically mediated learning environments without the physical constraints of a tertiary institution can offer enrolments at no or low cost that might mushroom into the thousands of students in virtual classrooms (Morris, 2013; Selwyn, 2017). However, two criticisms of MOOCs highlighted by Selwyn (2017) and others (e.g. Morris, 2013; Yousef, Chatti, Schroeder, & Wosnitza, 2014), relate by extension to teaching practices with video. First, the use of online lectures and tutorials in video format, as is common in MOOCs, can represent a passive learning design and thus carries the risk of reverting back to pedagogically limiting broadcast practices of educational TV and film (Selwyn, 2017). This revisited challenge for increasing active learning while introducing new technologies is a long-standing caution as raised by Larry Cuban (1986) in *Teachers and Machines*. Just replacing the physical lecture with an online video lecture in a MOOC doesn't guarantee an interactive learning experience (Adams, Yin, Vargas Madriz, & Mullen, 2014). However, as Adams and her colleagues (2014) found in their study, which used deeper phenomenological analysis of student engagement with videos, if relational connection is established between the teacher in the video and the MOOC student, there is potential for a sense of 'personalisation' of the curriculum. This suggests that there might be more nuanced ways of understanding how to create active e-learning environments.

Second, MOOCs have experienced irregular educational outcomes including high attrition rates, indicating that MOOCs seem to favour those students who have already proven successful at higher levels of learning and metacognitive skills (Selwyn, 2017). Thus, those students without practice and achievement in further education may need additional supports in order to achieve learning success. For university teachers such issues highlight the significance of integrating sound pedagogical design with online video, including appropriate scaffolds, to maximise the learning potential to scale.

These issues also point to the role of student engagement. To illustrate further, and to go beyond conventional attrition metrics to indicate engagement, Hew (2016) analysed students' perceptions of what fostered their learning in three highly ranked MOOCs in student reviews in the multi-course platform, *Coursetalk*. With almost one thousand student reviews as its data source, Hew's (2016) study explores the pedagogical strategies and looks for commonalities across three high ranking MOOCs of *Python programming* (PY), *American poetry* (PO), and *Design/artefacts in society* (DE). Pedagogical themes or factors found as common across these three subjects, were (1) problem-oriented learning; (2) instructor accessibility and enthusiasm; (3) active learning; (4) peer interaction; and (5) helpful resources. The third (active learning) and fifth (helpful resources) factors readily give rise to examples of pedagogical strategies that relate to video-based learning as shown in Table 10.1.

Table 10.1 Two (of five) common pedagogical themes as identified by MOOC students and as related to video-based learning (adapted from Hew, 2016)

Theme	Example pedagogical strategies
Active learning	Video lectures with questions:
	– to reflect on and to respond (PY);
	– designed to think about issues or concepts before continuing the video (DE)
Helpful course resources	Online videos:
	– short, covering one-two main concepts; – student controlled pace; – support materials such as notes; – slides ortranscripts available to review video content (PY, PO, DE)

The themes drawn from the three high ranking MOOCs illustrate appreciation for active and student-centred approaches to learning. Students are neither inherently deep nor surface learners, while activities set for them can foster whether they learn deeply from the content (Ramsden, 2003). The pedagogical strategies used in the design of learning environments will shape the learning. For example, examinations and activities such as passively viewing video lectures can promote memorisation and recall; whereas opportunities to interact with data/content will more often scaffold learning that evokes critical thinking and problem-solving and assist in developing independent learners (Laurillard, 2012; Razzouk & Shute, 2012). The challenge remains on how to render video-based learning an active and deep learning experience. A challenge Friess, Oliver, Quak, and Lau (2016), for example, grappled with on changing popular geography field trip experiences to virtual and video experiences for sustainability of growing class enrolments in a university-wide elective. The virtual field trip videos aid 'front row' visualisation to some hard to access areas, and accompanying questions prompt the students to consider deeper underlying issues. Findings illustrate that the virtual videos did not match the experience or deep learning of an actual field trip, but indicate a useful tool to prepare students for field trips.

3 Cases of Practice: Teacher-Set Categories for Video Exploration

Five recent cases of practice that incorporate video-based learning for undergraduate students are used in this section to explicitly examine their use of categories of analysis in their pedagogical designs, with or without employing additional technology. These cases span across disciplines of business, entomology, psychology, psychiatric nursing, and physical education. The pattern for selecting these particular cases involved recency (the case publications range from 2011 to 2016); undergraduate subject; video forms a key part of learning and/or assessment (not just supplementary); teacher preparation includes some form of analysis categories (explicit or implicit); variety across subjects and/or approaches; and scholarly/formal evaluation.

The cases provide stimulus for discussion and inspiration for others (e.g. university teachers) to consider adapting into their own practices.

This chapter section provides initial descriptive qualities for each case. When describing these cases, the structural framework of *Prepare–Participate–Connect* (Colasante & Douglas, 2016; as evolved from Rogow, 1997) was referred to, in order to generate consistent types of insights wherever possible. That is, *prepare*: inclusion of teacher preparation (particularly creating analysis categories); *participate*: type of interaction by students; and *connect*: potential for the video-based learning to be connected to other learning or workplace practice. Section 4 discusses themes that emerge across the cases with implications for increasing interactivity with video-based learning.

3.1 Case A: Undergraduate Business Subject (Video + Wiki)

The teacher in a first year Business degree in an Australian university trialled an activity for improving evaluation and feedback of students' presentation skills (Barry, 2012). The students ($n = 46$) were studying a property subject where group presentation skills were considered relevant for future workplace roles. The purpose of employing video was to enable critical appraisal of actual performance rather than perceived performance.

Student group presentations were delivered in class via traditional group member turn-taking at a lectern supported by presentation slides, and video recorded. Each student group could access their videoed presentation via a group wiki. This allowed 'students to view their own group presentations, for self-assessment, in a timely and secure manner' (Barry, 2012, p. 858). An assessment and feedback sheet guided self and peer evaluations, within which the teacher provided five broad analysis categories: background to the topic, three specific property industry themes, and overall presentation quality.

The students viewed and critically evaluated their group's recorded presentations, and each student received feedback on their performance from their group peers and a tutor. While direct video interaction enabled only routine player controls and the wiki's purpose was solely for ease of video access and viewing, student groups used their respective wikis beyond that scope for group communication purposes.

Student responses to open survey questions showed appreciation for '[gaining] a more accurate perspective of how the group performed' from the audience viewpoint, indicating a reflective approach was promoted (Barry, 2012, p. 858). The analysis categories helped the students to identify '[a]reas to work on', 'own faults', 'strengths', and 'weaknesses' (Barry, 2012, p. 858), thus providing a potential further layer of analysis (see Table 10.2).

Barry (2012) identified further measures for deepening the learning experience into the future. One was to add a requirement for students to critique their own presentations from recall alone prior to video viewing, for subsequent comparison to their video critique with the intent to gain additional insight. Another requirement

Table 10.2 Analysis categories, extrapolated from Barry (2012), for a Business degree student presentation evaluation and feedback activity

Teacher-set analysis categories (identified pre-activity)	Incidental analysis categories (identified by students)
Background to the topic	Areas to work on
Specific property industry theme 1	Own faults
Specific property industry theme 2	Strengths
Specific property industry theme 3	Weaknesses
Overall presentation quality	

would involve the students writing a reflection on their experiences including their perceived benefits from the activity.

This activity as employed in the business context has since been adapted to a new context, that of third year psychology students (Murphy & Barry, 2016). Both of the improvement measures that Barry (2012) identified were implemented, resulting in a three-staged process of (1) immediately evaluating own performance post-presentation, (2) evaluating performance via video-recording, and (3) writing a reflective piece. The psychology students found the activities were personally challenging with potential to enhance their future oral presentations, which corresponds with the conclusion that deep learning opportunities are possible with carefully designed activities and assessments (Murphy & Barry, 2016).

3.2 *Case B: Undergraduate Entomology Subject (Technologically Treated Video)*

In a university in the US, students at various year levels across non-science undergraduate courses (e.g. history, education, accounting; $n = 226$), studied an introductory entomology subject (Ibrahim, Antonenko, Greenwood, & Wheeler, 2012). Presumably an elective or open access subject offered widely within the university, students from non-science majors took the opportunity to study insects. Learning resources included a professionally produced video on insects by the *BBC*. The students were asked, as part of their subject learning, to participate in an experimental study involving comparisons for how they viewed the video content.

Some students were randomly assigned the complete (unaltered) 30-min BBC video on facts about insects, while others viewed the video as a technologically treated package, specifically by 'segmenting, signalling, and weeding' (Ibrahim et al., 2012, p. 220). The treated video was segmented into smaller pieces of footage (five segments of approximately 6 min duration). Each segment was top-and-tailed with introduction and summary screens, and content determined as extraneous was edited or 'weeded' out of each segment. Direct 'signalling' to the students occurred in the introduction screen by listing core concepts of the video (see an example in

Table 10.3 Example signalling in one video, extrapolated from Ibrahim et al. (2012), for various undergraduate degree students studying an introductory entomology subject

Theme of one video segment	Categories in introduction screen	Post-viewing recap of concepts in summary screen
Common characteristics	Head	All insects have head, abdomen, and thorax
	Thorax	
	Abdomen	
	Six legs	Insects have six legs and most have wings
	Invertebrates	Insects are invertebrates Insects have a hard exoskeleton Insects never grew very large because their exoskeletons would be too heavy to carry

Table 10.3) with an accompanying brief narration, while the summary screen also provided a list of the concepts with additional narration. Therefore, the listed and narrated concepts provided overt items for students to explore in the videos, acting as implied analysis categories.

The student participants 'watched the video [treated or not] in its entirety without pausing for questions, discussion or note-taking' (Ibrahim et al., 2012, p. 229). All students completed pre and post-test knowledge and perceived difficulty tests.

The findings confirmed that the students perceived a lower level of learning difficulty for the treated video. The authors found that the principles of segmentation, signalling, and weeding reduced 'perceived cognitive load' as students' attention was guided to only important aspects of the content supported by 'concise cues' (Ibrahim et al., 2012, p. 231). While the treated video group scored slightly higher on the post-test (31/45 compared to 29/45), the overall learning between the student groups showed no significant difference. Ibrahim and colleagues maintain that the findings support the described treatment of video in providing support for novice learners who have not yet established how to maximise knowledge (i.e. organise, integrate) from complex and dynamic video content. While it is unclear how the results varied across the students at various undergraduate levels, the students were all novices to the subject discipline of entomology.

3.3 *Case C: Undergraduate Psychology Subject (Movie as Video)*

This case involved an introductory subject for Psychology students in a US university, with 128 students across four classes (Blessing & Blessing, 2015). As the subject aimed to introduce the 'breadth of the field', concerns were raised about how students could associate the information for later recall. A potential solution was implemented involving a subject-based capstone activity utilising a movie.

The purpose of the activity was to integrate the content and allow practice application in contexts outside the subject domain. The context here would be a scenario depicted in the movie. Students could choose one of four themes set by the teachers (aligned to a textbook) as an overarching theme to reflect on the subject content and relate it to the video. However, further granular analysis was handled differently between the four student groups of the psychology cohort, with the four classes divided into two experimental and two control groups.

The video selection for the two experimental groups was the movie *12 Angry Men*, which the teachers determined as having over 90 instances of embedded dialogue or action aligning to a wide range of psychological concepts. The teachers provided these students with their pre-determined conceptual breakdown of the movie, that is, all 93 items were provided by psychological concept, timeline, and dialogue. Comparatively, students in the control classes were given free choice of movie but not given a conceptual breakdown. Each student created a written assessment based on their analysis, and all classes held student-generated discussions during their final session. The latter was viewed as a strength of the overall activity. Other assessment tasks (exams and quizzes) were the same across the psychology classes.

Blessing and Blessing (2015) concluded that the capstone activity overall 'allowed the students to consider how the various psychological phenomena could occur outside the classroom', that is, application in other contexts (p. 54). While the control classes successfully identified psychology concepts in their video and translated this into their assessment pieces, the experimental classes outperformed the control classes by identifying a wider band of psychology concepts with the support of the extensive prompts. An attitudinal survey administered only to the experimental classes illustrated support for the intervention, including aiding understanding of and seeing connections across psychological concepts, and a strong positive response to recommending this approach into the future (Blessing & Blessing, 2015) (Table 10.4).

Table 10.4 Teacher-set analysis categories, extrapolated from Blessing and Blessing (2015, and associated website), for a Psychology degree student capstone activity

Major psychological themes aligned to textbook (all students choose one)	Examples from the 93 concepts (only given to experimental students)
Behaviour is determined by multiple causes	Attitudes/persuasion Stereotype
Behaviour is shaped by cultural heritage	Groupthink In-group/out-group
Heredity and environment jointly influence behaviour	Aggression Nature of knowledge
People's experience of the world is highly subjective	Nature/nurture Motivation (and many more concepts)

3.4 *Case D: Undergraduate Psychiatric Nursing Subject (Video + Annotation Tool)*

In a Taiwan university, psychiatric nursing students ($n = 50$) used simulated patient scenarios and peer assessment in two rounds (mid and end study term) to focus on developing and assessing communication skills (Lai, 2016). The teachers structured these activities to enable interaction between a student and a patient, with the role of patient acted by an experienced psychiatric nurse, to simulate therapeutic consultation. Student peers in groups of four to five first observed the interactions live and then a different grouping of four to five students reviewed the video-recorded consultation online. The purpose of this intervention was to scaffold professional communication skills to develop the students to be effective communicators when working as psychiatric nurses.

While video-recording was already recognised as useful in facilitating observation to determine effectiveness of communication (Lai, 2016), this study added an online video review and annotation system, plus a structure for peer and expert analysis. The structure was based on the Interpersonal Communication Assessment Scale (ICAS) (Klakovich & Dela Cruz, 2006 cited in Lai, 2016), comprising three broad analysis categories of (1) advocacy, (2) therapeutic use of self, and (3) validation, and within these, granular analysis categories totally 23 factors as illustrated in Table 10.5. These categories and sub-categories were used by student peers to review three to four of their peer's videoed consultations online. They quantitatively rated each sub-category on a Likert scale of seldom (1), often (2), usually (3), and always (4), and qualitatively commenting at key points in the video using online annotation functionality. The latter required further analysis, that of categorising their feedback within the annotation system as 'strength', 'weakness', or 'question', without necessarily aligning feedback explicitly to the 23 sub-categories.

Each student wrote a reflective journal entry for each cycle of feedback, where they recorded thoughts on their own communication performance, feedback received, and improvement opportunities.

Table 10.5 Analysis categories, extrapolated from Lai (2016), for a Psychology nurse degree student communication activity

ICAS categories (no. items in subscale)	Example items in ICAS subscale (video analysis categories)	Peer quantitative ratings	Peer video annotation and rating
Advocacy (10)	Invites patient/family to explore discrepancies	Seldom Often Usually Always	Comment at key points in video and rate as: – Strength – Weakness – Question
	Questions treatment decisions		
	Teaches and promotes preventative care		
Therapeutic use of self (9)	Maintains comfortable distance		
	Makes eye contact		
	Converses with silent patient/family		
Validation (4)	Asks for clarification		
	Gives descriptive feedback		

The findings claim improvement in student performance between the mid- and end-term peer assessments. This was evidenced along multiple threads, such as higher scores, more feedback comments, and a more disciplined approach to assessing peers. The feedback comments, categorised by students as strength/weakness/question, were analysed by the teachers (experienced psychiatric nurses) against the 23 analysis categories and found that the students illustrated an increased focus on the patient across the term, increasing use of the 'weakness' category with more focussed feedback, and the students identified further communication techniques outside of the 23 provided, albeit still focussed on communication such as gesture and tone of voice.

Lai (2016) appreciated the high level of student interaction the activities ensued, with an average of 17 (round 1) and 20 (round 2) comments received per student. Adding 'Such high interactions among learning peers were hardly likely to happen in traditional classroom settings, where class time is limited and the class size is large' (p. 28), and that adjustment of analysis categories could see this technique transferable to other courses in medicine or health care.

Responses to a Likert scale questionnaire suggested 'the students agreed that online peer assessment gave them more perspectives on communication learning' and 'most students admitted they had spent more time learning communication due to the involvement of online peer assessment' (Lai, 2016, p. 28).

3.5 *Case E: Undergraduate Physical Education Subject (Video + Annotation Tool)*

This case involved third-year undergraduate Physical Education (PE) students ($n = 31$) studying a practicum subject in an Australian university (Colasante, 2011). The teacher piloted a semester-wide activity for students to self and peer assess, that is, to critically reflect and evaluate their PE teaching practices.

The students each video-recorded a session of their PE teaching practices at two points during their practical placement, recording themselves and their students (where permissions allowed) during a PE class. Their first videos were uploaded into small group spaces in the university's video annotation tool, MAT (media annotation tool), where they analysed their own and five to six of their peer's videos. To guide their critical reflection and evaluation of their performance, the teacher set video analysis categories within the annotation tool. The analysis categories were based on eight beginner teaching factors, and are provided in Table 10.6.

In the annotation tool, the analysis categories presented as colour-coded, titled 'Markers' that the students selected to categorise their textual reflections and evaluations. The intent was to guide students along a process of how experts in the field might structure their thinking, in particular to achieve reflective practice. Students could revisit their groups' annotated videos within the tool, to view them using regular play and pause controls, or by filtering to view segments as marked by a specific analysis category. Student peers gave their feedback by adding to the

Table 10.6 Analysis categories, extrapolated from Colasante (2011), for Physical Education degree student evaluation of teaching episodes

Teacher-set analysis categories (identified pre-activity), based on eight beginner teaching factors	Incidental analysis categories (identified by students)
Introductory activity	Timing: when categorised events occurred during the PE lesson Frequency: how often categorised events occurred during the PE lesson
Demonstrations	
Checking for understanding	
Transition	
General feedback	
Specific feedback	
ALT-PE (academic learning time)	
Teacher position	

owning student's annotations via structured threaded discussion anchored to the relevant video section under focus, and the teacher built on this with further feedback. There was also a dedicated space for the videoed student to write in their final reflections. Individual students created up to 20 or more annotations across the eight analysis categories, and received one to three pieces of written peer feedback per annotation, and targeted feedback from their teacher.

A second cycle of recording and analysis was undertaken later in the semester that mirrored the first. Each student critically reflected on both cycles to determine their most improved analysis category to write a reflective development report.

Evaluation showed that the students largely appreciated the ability to analyse their PE teaching practice in MAT using the analysis categories to purposefully critically reflect upon and evaluate their practice and to receive feedback. They also appreciated how after annotating a video, they could look across the timeline for a colour-coded visualisation of when and how frequently the categorised events occurred during the lesson. However, one student lamented that two cycles of analysis was insufficient and suggested further rounds would improve their PE teaching practice.

Following the PE case, the pedagogy of analysis categories was used in diverse video-based learning activities across multiple contexts in the same Australian university, in conjunction with the MAT video annotation tool. This, along with Case A, begins to illustrate how such interventions can be transferable to other disciplines. See Table 10.7 for three examples.

4 Discussion

As illustrated in the above cases, analysis categories offer a pedagogical design opportunity for teachers to consider how they would like their students to purposefully and actively interrogate video content. These cases demonstrate that teacher attention to designing structured guidance to analyse video content can lead

Table 10.7 Three example cases that employed analysis categories and video annotation subsequent to the PE case

Discipline context	Example reference	Analysis category types
Chiropractic	Colasante, Kimpton, and Hallam (2014)	To promote clinical reasoning:
		• 14 clinical points to build a patient history (to analyse video part A of a clinical episode)
		• Student groups self-generated short-list diagnoses (to analyse video part B, the continued clinical episode)
Medical Radiations	Douglas et al. (2015)	To build skills to critique radiology images:
		• 7 categories related to quality (10 videos of an expert critiquing X-rays)
Juris Doctor	Douglas et al. (2015)	To develop skills in advocacy, persuasive argument and court etiquette:
		• 6 categories, most related to focal skills, one to signpost an ethical issue (video of a court room procedure)

to active student engagement and positive learning benefits. However, this comes with the proviso that pedagogical design is the prime influencing factor over technological factors.

The varied cases involve analysis of digital video representations of (1) own and peer's performance for skill development (business; psychiatric nursing; physical education) and (2) cognitive learning/new or consolidated knowledge (entomology; psychology). Some of the cases augment their video media with supporting technology such as a wiki or an annotation tool, or have used technological treatments to prepare video for learning (see Table 10.8). They also illustrate intended next steps, such as potential for improvement and transferability to further contexts.

The business, psychiatric nursing and physical education cases (cases A, D, E) employed video representations of performance for critical reflection, evaluation, and skill development. In these cases, the exploration of own and others' performance benefitted from structured evaluation via video analysis categories. In the cases of business presentation skills (Barry, 2012), nursing communication skills (Lai, 2016), and PE teaching practice (Colasante, 2011), the provision of analysis categories facilitated the ability to concentrate on identification and discussion of key areas for development while looking beyond the novelty of seeing self or peers in video format. Miller and Zhou (2007) report that explicit instruction of tasks to complete while watching video is required for a deeper level of learning, especially in reviewing videoed performance to look beyond personalities to notice deeper issues of professional practice.

Both the psychiatric nursing and physical education cases used evidence-based, established workplace relevant performance factors on which to base their analysis categories. After practicing their skills, the students used their respective categories to analyse their performance. Razzouk and Shute (2012) convey the need for novices

Table 10.8 Summary of key characteristics of the varied cases

Case		Digital video representation		Additional technology	Pedagogical features				Transferability	
ID	Discipline	Own, peer's performance	Cognitive learning	Type	Analysis categories	Two cycles of analysis	Reflection requirement	Potential for over-guidance	Other discipline/s	No bespoke or complex technology
A	Business	√		Wiki	5 (teacher set)\ 4 (student generated)		√ (subsequent application)		√ (applied elsewhere)	√
B	Entomology		√	Complex video editing	Varied per video			√ (experiment group)		
C	Psychology		√	N/a	93 (experimental groups) 0 (control groups)			√ (experiment groups)		√
D	Psychiatric nursing	√		Annotation tool	3 (categories) 23 (sub-categories) Extra (student generated)	√	√		√ (plans to apply elsewhere)	
E	Physical education	√		Annotation tool	8 (teacher set) 2 (student generated)	√	√		√ (applied elsewhere)	

to accumulate deliberate and dedicated practice to gain experience and expertise over time; to move from a time-intensive trial-and-error approach, to a strategic approach using explicit problem decomposition and incorporating underlying principles to improve performance. Lai employed 23 trialled and tested skill-specific categories for the students to evaluate their peers' therapeutic communication performance. This was developed further by adding layers of additional contemplation, including to explicitly ascertain consistency of skill application and where feedback on strengths and weakness could be found, or questions needed to be raised. While further such layering was not explicit in the PE case, some students noticed how they could use the teaching analysis categories to look for patterns and gaps in their or their peers' overall performance after analysing their performance using the eight beginner teaching factors. Taking advice from the Lai case, this further student-generated layer could be explicitly incorporated in the PE situation.

Additionally, common to these two cases (D, E) were (1) the inclusion of two cycles of performance evaluation across the subject, and (2) the requirement to write a reflection. The psychiatric nurses practiced and recorded their communication skills for two points of evaluation, and each student wrote a reflective journal for each cycle (Lai, 2016). The physical education case did the same for their PE teaching practice, albeit their reflection development report was submitted at subject completion to draw out their own development spanning the cycles. Some PE students would have liked more than two cycles; the teacher's original intent was 'to each record and analyse three teaching episodes, [which was] reduced to two due to technical delays' (Colasante, 2011, p. 84). Interestingly, the business case (A) was further adapted into a cyclical model of evaluation upon scholarly reflection (Barry, 2012), and later applied in a psychology context including incorporation of a reflective written piece (see Murphy & Barry, 2016). Such reflective thinking opportunities facilitate effective understanding, as Dewey (1933) advocated, 'Thinking is not like a sausage machine that reduces all materials indifferently to one stereotyped, marketable commodity, but is the power of following up and linking together the specific suggestions that specific things arouse' (p. 46).

The entomology and psychology cases (cases B, C) utilise video for cognitive purposes of development or consolidation of new knowledge. In these cases, the exploration of professionally produced videos on insects (Ibrahim et al., 2012), and complex non-discipline-specific scenarios (Blessing & Blessing, 2015) was given considerable guidance. In the former, the videos were treated professionally to chunk into short segments and to signpost core concepts in an introductory screen. That is, the key categories of learning were introduced and explained before the students explored the videos for themselves. While this provides a level of curation to support students to focus on key learning concepts, it does suggest removal of any chance for student perturbation for opportunities of heightened learning by removing some of the discovery elements. While students are known to appreciate the technological aspects of quality video that prove seamless to use (Hew, 2016; Yousef, Chatti, Schroeder, & Wosnitza, 2014), the entomology students did not learn significantly more with the aid of the treated video (Ibrahim et al., 2012).

The entomology activity provides a case where technological treatment of a content video was prepared to help the novice to learn key concepts with reduced difficulty. While treatments of video segmentation, signaling (i.e. listing key concepts at the start and end of video), and weeding out extraneous content were aimed to help the students learn more easily, traditional methods of actively engaging with content were removed. That is, students were isolated to passive viewing and prevented from undertaking behaviours of interaction that they may (or may not) ordinarily take while viewing video for study purposes, such as pausing or other basic video controls, note-taking, asking questions, or discussing the content. 'ICT ought to foster interaction, excitement, independence and choice of learning… [but] is too often used non-interactively as an expensive way of presenting information' (Ramsden, 2003 p. 156). While the technological treatment of video to render all key learning moments explicit to the entomology students was to assist them while they are yet novices in the discipline area, to develop digital literacies the students need to practice determining the key content for themselves. Students may need to grapple with a wider context with supporting examples or background detail to aid deeper learning of key principles.

In addition, an issue that affects transferability is that not all professionally produced videos are available for technological editing, such as complying with regional copyright laws and technological support in ability, time, or cost factors. A hybrid solution might be scalable where students view the un-edited 30-min BBC video on insects, and—especially while still novices in the area of entomology—be provided with a holistic list of key concepts to seek out and interact with the content (e.g. describe in note-taking; discuss with others), or a half list of key concepts to explore then peer teach to another student (e.g. Sharples et al., 2016). Further developing the titles of key concepts as analysis categories could promote active engagement and meaning-making from the content.

In the psychology case (Blessing & Blessing, 2015), movies provided non-discipline-specific scenarios for the students to work with as novices to cognitively apply abstract concepts that were learnt throughout the subject. Extensive preparation was partially undermined by the differing amount of guidance provided to the student groups. Students in the experimental classes received detailed analysis categories, that is, a wide range of psychological concepts and where to find them in the nominated video. Students in the control classes could choose their own video to analyse without the guidance of teacher-determined analysis categories. Perhaps unsurprisingly the students who received the analysis categories found more concepts in the videos; however, the students without this support still achieved positively but on a narrower range of categories. This tension might initiate a new solution where all students choose from a short list of movies and all receive a generic teacher-set list of psychological concepts to guide exploration, particularly in an introductory class where novice students require guidance on how to learn. Overall, the student analysis and articulation of concepts identified in their scenario-based movie, and the culminating class discussion, were key to establishing conceptual understanding, suggesting a significant pedagogical strategy in this case to support learning.

This selection of cases demonstrates the important role of the university teacher—as required to shape student learning by careful design of learning experiences. This includes knowing when to 'set up, arrange, and manage the educational experiences that the learners will encounter and engage in [while] also leaving spaces and gaps for students to work things out for themselves' (Selwyn, 2017, p. 122). This type of pedagogical thinking applies to components of the learning experiences, such as teaching with online video in a manner that retains the learning challenge. The cases also demonstrate the ability to transfer pedagogical designs to other contexts for re-use and scalability, including some already adapted to other disciplines (case A, E), another with plans for this (case D), and others with potential for re-use with adaptation of pedagogical design (case B, C). Available technology to augment the use of video in some cases also effects scalability. For example, off-the-shelf wiki (case A) compared to bespoke video annotation (case D, E).

5 Conclusion

This chapter encourages university teachers to take on a designer mind-set in leveraging digital video in higher education, in particular to set video analysis categories to foster active student engagement and guidance to learn purposefully from video, in particular, to ensure that the learning challenge is retained to allow students to interrogate and make meaning from the video content. The chapter reviewed several published cases of learning with video, three of own and peer's performance for skill development (business, psychiatric nursing, physical education) and another two focused on knowledge acquisition or consolidation (entomology, psychology). The entomology case emphasised technological treatment to structure the video content to key conceptual categories, the psychology case focused on a pedagogical approach to examine video of psychological conceptual categories, and the remaining cases augmented video with technology to facilitate student exploration of video via analysis categories. Both the psychiatric nursing and PE cases used bespoke video annotation tools, while the business case employed a wiki plus an assessment/feedback form. The latter could presumably allow for more seamless transferability and scalability given that wikis are a more widely available form of technology.

Advances in digital technology have potential to better support and transform learning processes (Spector, 2008). The review of studies also suggests that for students to gain from video interactivity there seems to be a need to develop student metacognitive skills to assist them using the interactive video features to enhance their learning outcomes (e.g. Merkt et al., 2011). Consequently, it is pedagogical design that has repeatedly been demonstrated as necessary to underpin effective use of educational technology (e.g. Roberts Becker, Winn, & Erwin, 2015).

Transferability to other discipline contexts is demonstrated in the psychiatric nursing case by identifying where their pedagogical strategy could be next applied, while the business and PE cases have already applied their approach to other disciplines.

This suggests a potential robustness to categories of analysis in their various forms into the future. From the insights of this work, potential future strands of research could include development and examination of new designs of video analysis categories for a further range of disciplines, including large class cohorts, based on the expertise of university teachers and industry representatives.

References

Adams Becker, S., Cummins, M., Davis, A., Freeman, A., Hall Giesinger, C., & Ananthanarayanan, V. (2017). *NMC horizon report: 2017 Higher education edition*. Austin, TX: The New Media Consortium. Retrieved August 10, 2017, from https://www.nmc.org/publication/nmc-horizon-report-2017-higher-education-edition/

Adams, C., Yin, Y., Vargas Madriz, L. F., & Mullen, S. (2014). A phenomenology of learning large: The tutorial sphere of xMOOC video lectures. *Distance Education, 35*(2), 202–216. https://doi.org/10.1080/01587919.2014.917701

Barry, S. (2012). A video recording and viewing protocol for student group presentations: Assisting self-assessment through a Wiki environment. *Computers & Education, 59*(2012), 855–860. https://doi.org/10.1016/j.compedu.2012.04.008

Bates, A. W., & Sangra, A. (2011). *Managing technology in higher education: Strategies for transforming teaching and learning*. San Francisco, CA: Jossey-Bass (Wiley).

Becker, M. R., Winn, P., & Erwin, S. L. (2015). Student-centered, e-learning design in a university classroom. In P. Isaías, J. Spector, D. Ifenthaler, & D. Sampson (Eds.), *E-Learning systems, environments and approaches* (pp. 229–246). Springer: Cham. https://doi.org/10.1007/978-3-319-05825-2_16

Biggs, J. B., & Tang, C. S. (2011). *Teaching for quality learning at university: What the student does*. Maidenhead: McGraw-Hill/Society for Research into Higher Education/Open University Press.

Blessing, S. B., & Blessing, J. S. (2015). Using a movie as a capstone activity for the introductory course. *Teaching of Psychology, 42*(1), 51–55. https://doi.org/10.1177/0098628314562678

Blight, D., Davis, D., & Olsen, A. (2000). The globalization of higher education. In P. Scott (Ed.), *Higher education re-formed*. London: Falmer Press.

Bruner, J. S. (1960). *The process of education*. New York, NY: Vintage Books.

Cisco. (2013). *Cisco Visual Networking Index: Forecast and Methodology, 2012–2017*. Cisco white paper, San Jose, CA. Retrieved January 4, 2014, from http://www.cisco.com/en/US/solutions/collateral/ns341/ns525/ns537/ns705/ns827/white_p aper_c11-481360.pdf

Cisco (2017). *Cisco Visual Networking Index: Forecast and Methodology, 2016–2021 (June 6, 2017)*. White Paper. San Jose, CA. Retrieved August 10, 2017, from https://www.cisco.com/c/en/us/solutions/collateral/service-provider/visual-networking-index-vni/complete-white-paper-c11-481360.html

Clarke, M., Butler, C., Schmidt-Hansen, P., & Somerville, M. (2004). Quality assurance for distance learning: A case study at Brunel University. *British Journal of Educational Technology, 35*(1), 5–11. https://doi.org/10.1111/j.1467-8535.2004.00363.x

Colasante, M. (2011). Using video annotation to reflect on and evaluate physical education preservice teaching practice. *Australasian Journal of Educational Technology, 27*(1), 66–88. https://doi.org/10.14742/ajet.983

Colasante, M. (2016). Purposeful exploratory learning with video using analysis categories. In D.G. Sampson, J.M. Spector, D. Ifenthaler & Isaías P (Eds.), Proceedings from 13th International Conference on Cognition and Exploratory Learning in The Digital Age (CELDA), Mannheim, Germany, (pp. 245-252).

Colasante, M., & Douglas, K. (2016). Prepare-participate-connect: Active learning with video annotation. *Australasian Journal of Educational Technology, 32*(4), 68–91. https://doi.org/10.14742/ajet.2123

Colasante, M., Kimpton, A., & Hallam, J. (2014). A curriculum model to promote (chiropractic) critical thinking with video-case annotation. In M. Gosper & D. Ifenthaler (Eds.), *Curriculum models for the 21st century: Using learning technologies in higher education* (pp. 181–210). New York, NY: Springer.

Colasante, M., & Lang, J. (2012). Can a media annotation tool enhance online engagement with learning? A multi-case work-in-progress report. In J. Cordeiro et al. (Eds.), *Proceedings of the 4th International Conference of Computer Supported Education, Porto, Portugal* (Vol. 2, pp. 455–464). Setúbal: SciTePress.

Conole, G. (2013). *Designing for learning in an open world.* New York, NY; London: Springer.

Cuban, L. (1986). *Teachers and machines: The classroom use of technology since 1920.* New York, NY: Teachers College Press.

Dewey, J. (1933). *How we think. A restatement of the relation of reflective thinking to the educative process.* Lexington, MA: D.C. Heath and Company.

Douglas, K., Colasante, M., & Kimpton, A. (2015). Exploiting emerging video annotation technology and industry engagement to authentically prepare students for the complex world of work. In *Proceedings HERDSA Conference, Melbourne, Australia* (pp. 60–71).

Douglas, K., Lang, J., & Colasante, M. (2014). The challenges of blended learning using a media annotation tool. *Journal of University Teaching and Learning Practice, 11*(2), 7. Retrieved from http://ro.uow.edu.au/jutlp/vol11/iss2/7

Friess, D., Oliver, G., Quak, M., & Lau, A. (2016). Incorporating "virtual" and "real world" field trips into introductory geography modules. *Journal of Geography in Higher Education, 40*(4), 546–564. https://doi.org/10.1080/03098265.2016.1174818

Gibbings, P., Lidstone, J., & Bruce, C. (2015). Students' experience of problem-based learning in virtual space. *Higher Education Research & Development, 34*(1), 74–88. https://doi.org/10.1080/07294360.2014.934327

Hannafin, M., Hannafin, K., & Gabbitas, B. (2009). Re-examining cognition during student-centered, web-based learning. *Educational Technology Research and Development, 57*(6), 767–785. Retrieved from https://www.learntechlib.org/p/67539/

Hew, K. F. (2016). Promoting engagement in online courses: What strategies can we learn from three highly rated MOOCS. *British Journal of Educational Technology, 47*(2), 320–341. https://doi.org/10.1111/bjet.12235

Hsieh, P.-A. J., & Cho, V. (2011). Comparing e-Learning tools' success: The case of instructor–student interactive vs. self-paced tools. *Computers & Education, 57*(3), 2025–2038. https://doi.org/10.1016/j.compedu.2011.05.002

Ibrahim, M., Antonenko, P. D., Greenwood, C. M., & Wheeler, D. (2012). Effects of segmenting, signalling, and weeding on learning from educational video. *Learning, Media and Technology, 37*(3), 220–235. https://doi.org/10.1080/17439884.2011.585993

Ifenthaler, D. (2010). Introduction. In J. M. Spector et al. (Eds.), *Learning and instruction in the digital age* (pp. 3–10). New York, NY: Springer.

Kay, R. H. (2012). Exploring the use of video podcasts in education: A comprehensive review of the literature. *Computers in Human Behavior, 28*, 820–831. https://doi.org/10.1016/j.chb.2012.01.011

Lai, C.-Y. (2016). Training nursing students' communication skills with online video peer assessment. *Computers & Education, 97*, 21–30. https://doi.org/10.1016/j.compedu.2016.02.017

Laurillard, D. (2002). *Rethinking university teaching; A framework for the effective use of learning technologies* (2nd ed.). London: RoutledgeFalmer.

Laurillard, D. (2012). *Teaching as a design science; Building pedagogical patterns for learning and technology*. New York, NY: Routledge.

Laurillard, D., & Derntl, M. (2014). Learner centred design-overview. In Y. Mor, H. Mellar, S. Warburton, & N. Winters (Eds.), *Practical design patterns for teaching and learning with technology* (pp. 13–16). Rotterdam: Sense Publishers.

Maier, H., de Heer, G., Ortac, A., & Kuijten, J. (2015). Capturing and displaying microscopic images used in medical diagnostics and forensic science using 4K video resolution – An application in higher education. *Journal of Microscopy, 260*(2), 175–179. https://doi.org/10.1111/jmi.12280

Merkt, M., Weigand, S., Heier, A., & Schwan, S. (2011). Learning with videos vs. learning with print: The role of interactive features. *Learning and Instruction, 21*(6), 687–704. https://doi.org/10.1016/j.learninstruc.2011.03.004

Miller, K., & Zhou, X. (2007). Learning from classroom video: What makes it compelling and what makes it hard. In R. Goldman et al. (Eds.), *Video research in the learning sciences* (pp. 321–334). Abingdon: Routledge.

Morris, L. V. (2013). MOOCs, emerging technologies, and quality (Editorial, 8 June 2013). *Innovative Higher Education, 8*, 251–252. https://doi.org/10.1007/s10755-013-9263-2

Murphy, K., & Barry, S. (2016). Feed-forward: Students gaining more from assessment via deeper engagement in video-recorded presentations. *Assessment & Evaluation in Higher Education, 41*(2), 213–227. https://doi.org/10.1080/02602938.2014.996206

Ramsden, P. (2003). *Learning to teach in higher education* (2nd ed.). Abingdon: RoutledgeFalmer.

Razzouk, R., & Shute, V. (2012). What is design thinking and why is it important? *Review of Educational Research, 82*(3), 330–348. https://doi.org/10.3102/0034654312457429

Rogow, F. (1997). *Don't turn off the lights! Tips for classroom use of ITV*. New York, NY: Insighters Educational Consulting. (Unpublished teaching resource, received via email exchange between Rogow and first author, September 2013).

Selwyn, N. (2007). The use of computer technology in university teaching and learning: A critical perspective. *Journal of Computer Assisted Learning, 23*(2), 83–94. https://doi.org/10.1111/j.1365-2729.2006.00204.x

Selwyn, N. (2017). *Education and technology: Key issues and debates* (2nd ed.). London: Bloomsbury Academic.

Sharples, M., Adams, A., Ferguson, R., Gaved, M., McAndrew, P., Rienties, B., … Whitelock, D. (2014). *Innovating pedagogy 2014: Open University innovation report 3*. Milton Keynes: The Open University. Retrieved August 10, 2017 from http://www.openuniversity.edu/sites/www.openuniversity.edu/files/The_Open_University _Innovating_Pedagogy_2014_0.pdf

Sharples, M., de Roock, R., Ferguson, R., Gaved, M., Herodotou, C., Koh, E., … Wong, L. H. (2016). *Innovating pedagogy 2016: Open University innovation report 5*. Milton Keynes: The Open University. Retrieved August 10, 2017, from https://iet.open.ac.uk/file/innovating_pedagogy_2016.pdf

Snelson, C., Rice, K., & Wyzard, C. (2012). Research priorities for YouTube and video-sharing technologies: A Delphi study. *British Journal of Educational Technology, 43*(1), 119–129. https://doi.org/10.1111/j.1467-8535.2010.01168.x

Spector, J. M. (2008). Cognition and learning in the digital age: Promising research and practice. *Computers in Human Behavior, 24*, 249–262. https://doi.org/10.1016/j.chb.2007.01.016

Wright, L. K., Newman, D. L., Cardinale, J. A., & Teese, R. (2016). Web-based Interactive Video Vignettes create a personalized active learning classroom for introducing big ideas in introductory biology. *Bioscene, 42*(2), 32–43.

Yousef, A. M. F., Chatti, M. A., & Schroeder, U. (2014). Video-based learning: A critical analysis of the research published in 2003-2013 and future visions. In *eLmL 2014, The Sixth International Conference on Mobile, Hybrid, and On-line Learning* (pp. 112–119). Copenhagen: IARIA XPS Press.

Yousef, A. M. F., Chatti, M. A., Schroeder, U., & Wosnitza, M. (2014). What drives a successful MOOC? An empirical examination of criteria to assure design quality of MOOCs. In *2014 IEEE 14th International Conference on Advanced Learning Technologies* (pp. 44–48). Washington, DC: IEEE.

Zhang, D., Zhou, L., Briggs, R. O., & Nunamaker, J. F., Jr. (2006). Instructional video in e-learning: Assessing the impact of interactive video on learning effectiveness. *Information & Management, 43*(1), 15–27. https://doi.org/10.1016/j.im.2005.01.004

Meg Colasante entered the tertiary education sector as a sessional teacher during an early career as a clinician, workplace trainer and manager in the medical pathology sector. Sessional teaching soon evolved into a full-time commitment to university teaching and educational design, and a passion for leveraging media and technology to support student learning. At the time of writing, Meg was a PhD student at Deakin University, studying university teacher practices in leveraging digital video for learning, while concurrently working as Lecturer, Educational Development (Digital Learning Strategy) at La Trobe University. Deakin University provided substantive support for this chapter, including financial support for Meg to present her initial paper at the CELDA2016 conference (a paper which formed the precursor to this chapter), and provided a co-author for this chapter (initial PhD supervisor). Having designed the learning affordances for an online video annotation tool as part of her Master of Education (Deakin), and as developed by EduTAG at RMIT University, Meg has published widely on video annotation (and other tertiary teaching interventions). Meg currently holds academic positions at the University of Melbourne (part-time curriculum development, Department of Optometry and Vision Sciences) and RMIT (casual teaching and SoTL research, Graduate School of Business and Law), while finalising her PhD.

Josephine Lang has extensive experience in the education sector and has held diverse paid and honorary roles working in schools, professional teacher associations, and government departments in areas of teaching, curriculum, and education policy prior to commencing her career in universities as a teacher educator. Each of these experiences shape Josephine's understandings of the complexity of learning and teaching. Josephine has held leadership roles in Teaching and Learning portfolios within Schools of Education where she supports Course Coordinators and their teams to engage with teaching and learning issues and develop innovative solutions to improve learning across multiple programs. She also leads the processes of professional accreditation of courses. Recently, Josephine has taken up the role of Academic Program Director for the discipline cluster of Humanities, Arts and Social Sciences, including Law and Education in the Melbourne School of Professional And Continuing Education at The University of Melbourne, Australia. Josephine's research interests are professional learning; peer learning; and assessment, curriculum and pedagogy with a focus on e-learning and digital micro credentialing.

Chapter 11
Ontology Technique and Meaningful Learning Support Environments

Jingyun Wang

Abstract In this chapter, we present two ontology-driven learning support systems, which intend to provide meaningful learning environment: a customizable language learning support system (CLLSS) and a visualization learning support system for e-book users (VSSE). CLLSS was built to provide an interface for the learning objects arrangement which displays the visual representation of knowledge points and their relations. The intention underlying the development of CLLSS is to encourage instructors to orient their teaching materials to specific knowledge points and even directly to relations between knowledge points. With these orientations, CLLSS is able to provide an environment in which learners can readily distinguish between related knowledge points. In the other hand, VSSE is designed and developed to help e-book learners to effectively construct their knowledge frameworks. Making use of e-book logs, VSSE supports not only meaningful receptive learning but also meaningful discovery learning. In other words, two learning modes are provided in VSSE: (a) reception comparison mode, in which learners are provided directly with complete versions of relation maps; and (b) cache-cache comparison mode, where all information concerning relations is hidden at the first stage of learning, and in the second stage learners are encouraged to actively create them.

1 Introduction

Evidence from diverse studies suggests that in the human brain knowledge is incorporated more effectively when it is organized in hierarchical frameworks. Learning approaches that facilitate this kind of organization significantly increase the learning capability of learners (Bransford, Brown, & Cocking, 1999; Tsien, 2007).

J. Wang (✉)
Research institute for information technology, Kyushu university, Fukuoka, Japan
https://scholar.google.co.jp/citations?hl=en&user=XhfALOAAAAAJ

D. Sampson et al. (eds.), *Learning Technologies for Transforming Large-Scale Teaching, Learning, and Assessment*, https://doi.org/10.1007/978-3-030-15130-0_11

Ausubel's learning psychology theory (Ausubel, 1963, 1968; Ausubel, Novak, & Hanesian, 1978) defines this effective assimilation of new knowledge into existing knowledge frameworks as the achievement of "meaningful learning". Therefore, means of helping learners to efficiently develop their conceptual framework emerge as a main issue for fostering meaningful learning in e-learning.

In this chapter, we will present two learning support systems which intend to provide meaningful learning environments. Although these two systems are designed for different usages, they both make use of the ontology technique for the domain modelling.

2 Mapping and Ontology Technique

In the interest of encouraging meaningful learning, maps consisting of nodes (key concepts) and links (relationships) can provide scaffolding to help learners to organize knowledge and structure their own knowledge frameworks (Novak & Cañas, 2008). In this study, we will introduce two meaningful learning environments which provide topic maps to enable the learner to associate the knowledge structure with corresponding learning materials, including definitions and explanations of knowledge and the e-book contents. Different from "concept maps" (Chu, Lee, & Tsai, 2011; Novak & Cañas, 2008) and "knowledge maps" (Lee & Segev, 2012; O'Donnell, Dansereau, & Hall, 2002), which are used as learning materials in knowledge representation, topic maps are mainly used as metadata of learning materials (Wang, Mendori, & Xiong, 2014).

Some researches study the effectiveness of maps in pencil-and-paper format, for example, Lim, Lee and Grabowski (2009) examine the effectiveness of concept-mapping strategies with different generativity levels (expert-generated, partially learner-generated and full learner-generated concept maps) between high and low level of self-regulated learning skills. However, using pencil-and-paper format requires the instructor to fully control and guide the whole study procedure, and also the assessment of the maps generated by learners is time-consuming. Therefore, in this chapter we only focus on e-learning environments which provide interaction with maps (no matter partially or fully generated by experts) and automatic assessment of learner's completion of the map.

Owing to the flexibility of ontology in describing map structure and allowing the merging of different sources, ontology is a viable means of modelling a hierarchical knowledge network in which nodes represent concepts and arcs or arrows represent the relations between concepts. Several knowledge-based systems have utilized ontology techniques to support knowledge mapping. For instance, the concept map learning system of Chu et al. (2011), intended to help reduce the user's cognitive load, and TM4L (Dicheva & Dichev, 2006), a specialized environment for creating, maintaining and using "TM-based" learning repositories, both depend on ontology-based engines.

"An ontology is a formal explicit specification of a shared conceptualization" (Gruber, 1993). Common vocabularies are defined by ontology for the users (such as instructors, learners and researchers) who need to share information in a domain (Noy & McGuinness, 2001). A number of reusable ontologies have been constructed to support the modelling of efficient learning or teaching solutions. A knowledge management ontology characterized in terms of formal definitions and axioms was presented by Holsapple and Joshi (2004); this ontology enables the development of intelligent tools for knowledge sharing and reuse. An ontology of programming concepts (Gomez-Albarran & Jimenez-Diaz, 2009), developed based on existing educational ontology (Sosnovsky & Gavrilova, 2006) for procedural and object-oriented programming, is used to provide unique vocabulary for query retrieval in a case-based recommendation strategy for personalized access to earning objects (LOs) in educational repositories. The recommendation strategy considers the student ranking scores of LOs and the taxonomical information provided by the ontology to calculate similarity between concepts and decide the ranking of LOs. OMNIBUS (Hayashi, Bourdeau, & Mizoguchi, 2009), a task ontology which covers different learning/instructional theories and paradigms, was built to support an authoring system called SMARTIES. This system is a theory-aware authoring system using a top-down approach to the support of learning/instructional scenario design by teachers. A disciplinary ontology, whose concepts contain declarative knowledge (such as definitions, theorems, propositions, skills, the method it employs and specific examples it related to), is constructed to assess how well learners master knowledge structure in a geometric intelligent assessment system (Zhong, Fu, Xia, Yang, & Shang, 2015). To access a learner's mastery of knowledge, this system employs a hybrid cognitive assessment method which considers not only the declarative knowledge described in the disciplinary ontology but also procedural knowledge described in a problem solving process.

From the knowledge-based system point of view, ontology is considered as a hierarchical network, where nodes represent concepts, and arches or arrows represent the relations which exist between related concepts. Using ontology to describe domain knowledge promotes the reuse of the ontology in other ontologies and applications owing to its flexibility of the map structure. However, most of the domain ontologies (Gomez-Albarran & Jimenez-Diaz, 2009; Oltramari, Gangemi, Guarino, & Masolo, 2002; Sosnovsky & Gavrilova, 2006) just focus on "is-a" or "part-of" relation, which describe only the inclusion relation between concepts and just can provide taxonomical information in a domain. The promising feature of ontology that it can enrich the meaning of relationships (Mansur & Yusof, 2013) has not been taken full advantage of.

3 Course-Centered Ontology and an "Individual-Class-Individual" Ontology Design Approach

Actually, as an extension of taxonomies, ontologies which provide a hierarchy network rather than hierarchy tree structure as taxonomies, further allow any relation to exist between any two concepts; this facilitates the embodiments of relevance among concepts and also among their related learning materials, which are indispensable in education fields. Therefore, in our research (Wang, Mendori, & Xiong, 2014), a "course-centered ontology", which involves the construction of domain knowledge network especially the natural relations (such as similarities, contrasts and so on) between knowledge points inside a specific course, is presented for learning support systems which intend to provide meaningful learning environment. In this research, a Knowledge Point (KP) is defined as "a minimum learning item which can independently describe the information constituting one given piece of knowledge in a specific course". The learner can understand a KP via its own expression or can acquire it through practice.

For each individual of a course-centered ontology, which represents each KP of the target course, consists of two types of attributes: the data attribute (DA), which describes the datatype properties of the KP, and the object attribute (OA), which describes its relations with other KPs. However, the construction and maintenance of this kind of course-centered ontology is quite time consuming. Therefore, to effectively design and develop a course-centered ontology, we suggest the following three steps which all need the participation of instructor and ontology builder.

1. Individual creation and its DA design: For each KP in the target course, create a corresponding individual (also called "instance") and use its DAs to describe the properties of the KP.
2. The design of inclusion relations: use the classes of ontology to reflect the knowledge classification in the target course. Individuals assigned to the same class, which represent corresponding KPs, should share some common data properties. Furthermore, these common data properties should be created as the data attributes of the class they belong to. Similarly, the sub-classes in a class share some common data properties which also need to be created as the data attributes of that class.
3. The OA design: the meaning of relationships between individuals should be enriched to represent those essential natural relations between KP in the target course (for example, to a grammar course, it refers to grammatical relations) and placed between the corresponding KPs those individuals represent. In other words, the OAs of individuals should cover all the object properties that describe the relations which originate in the course characteristics.

This three-steps approach begins with details about individual creation and DA design of each individual; then works up to the highest conceptual level by deciding the knowledge classification (classes design); and finally go back again to the design of natural relationships just between individuals (individual's OA design). The last step, which is our innovative contribution, makes our ontology design an "individual-class-individual" model while the former ontologies normally were built by individual-class (bottom-up) or class-individual (top-down) methods.

In our previous work (Wang, Mendori, & Xiong, 2014), we focused on course-centered ontologies addressing various language courses for assisting learning support systems to embody the relations among knowledge points and also among the learning materials for those knowledge points, which can be built to create the metadata of LOs and identify learners' knowledge structures of target language courses. Hence, "a course-centered ontology of Japanese grammar" (COJG) has been developed as a sample domain model for the learning support system by Wang and Mendori (2012). COJG includes 23 top-level classes, 23 second-level classes, 25 third-level classes (54 of these classes have only individuals) and 205 individuals. Among all the 205 GPs in COJG, totally 630 OAs are designed. The elaborated examples of OA designs are described by Wang et al. (Wang & Mendori, 2012). Besides the inclusion relation, other 24 types of relations were concluded in COJG. These relations include the concept dependences, similarities and contrasts, and even grammatical equivalence phenomena.

In our recent work (Wang, Ogata, & Shimada, 2017), to facilitate the visualization support of meaningful learning for e-book users, we adjust the three-steps ontology design method (Wang, Mendori, & Xiong, 2014) and apply it to the development of a course-centered ontology for an existing computer science course (called COCS). COCS consists of about 100 KPs and 20 kinds of relations in addition to the inclusion relation, extracted and defined based on an analysis of the content of all the e-books of this computer science course. Those 20 relations include e-book location indications, concept dependences, and concept similarities and contrasts. Moreover, we developed a tool which can automatically identify the location (including the file IDs and the page numbers) of the KPs in the E-Book system. This tool was used to add the location information details into COCS automatically.

Besides the difference in the domain knowledge, the essential difference between COCS and COJG is that COCS includes the location information of KPs in e-book system. That e-book location information is designed for supporting the service of the provision of personalized topic maps based on the learners' e-book logs. In summary, depending on the specific purpose of the ontology-driven system, the design of its course-centered ontology may require adjustment.

4 Ontology-Driven Learning Support Systems

Facilitation of the visualization support of meaningful learning requires descriptions of the information about all the knowledge points and their relations. It is suggested that the domain knowledge needed by the visualization support system be automatically extracted from an ontology designed and developed on the basis of the target learning content. In this section, we will discuss two ontology-driven learning support systems which both intend to support meaningful learning environments.

4.1 An Ontology-Based Language Learning Support System

For effective second language learning, it is essential that the learners are able to make connections between related KPs and distinguish between similar ones. However, those older systems (such as Moodle) utilizing tree structures usually do not support the development of those skills because they cannot characterize essential relations between KPs. In order to support the development of learner ability to compare related KPs, an ontology-based language learning support system (called CLLSS) with a meaningful receptive learning environment is developed (Wang, Mendori, & Xiong, 2013).

The course-centered ontology COJG discussed in the previous section is incorporated in CLLSS for the construction of domain knowledge network and also for the metadata creation of LOs. The system framework of CLLSS and the way that the system was programmed to automatically use the knowledge information in ontology are both described in our previous work (Wang, Mendori, & Xiong, 2013). After uploading the course-centered ontology of an existing language course (here we refer to COJG), which is stored in OWL file, an instructor of CLLSS can arrange the learning materials based on the domain model provided by the ontology. This kind of arrangement enables the learners to compare related knowledge points and conveniently study relevant LOs according to their knowledge structure.

Figure 11.1 shows the common view of CLLSS 2.0 for both instructors and learners. On the left part of this view, all the concepts of COJG including the classes (directly named by grammar concepts in natural Japanese) and the individuals (directly named by GPs in natural Japanese) are shown by a tree structure. The system automatically extracts all the "isPriorOf" and "isNextOf" relations, from the OWL file of COJG to interpret the recommended teaching steps; this means all the grammar concepts (represented by classes) and GPs (represented by individuals) shown in the tree structure are arranged in the teaching steps defined by COJG.

In CLLSS, if an instructor wants to change the teaching steps, she/he only needs to modify the objects of "isPriorOf" and "isNextOf" relations on the "restriction filler" of any class (or on the "value" of any individual) in COJG and then update the new OWL file. However, in old LMS/CMSs such as Moodle, if an instructor wants to change the order of topics or chapters in a course, she/he needs to modify the destination URLs of all those hyperlinks which are used to indicate the related KPs among topics or chapters. Obviously, compared to older LMS/CMSs, the advantage of CLLSS, that the teaching steps of a course can be flexibly modified, attributes to the use of the course-centered ontology.

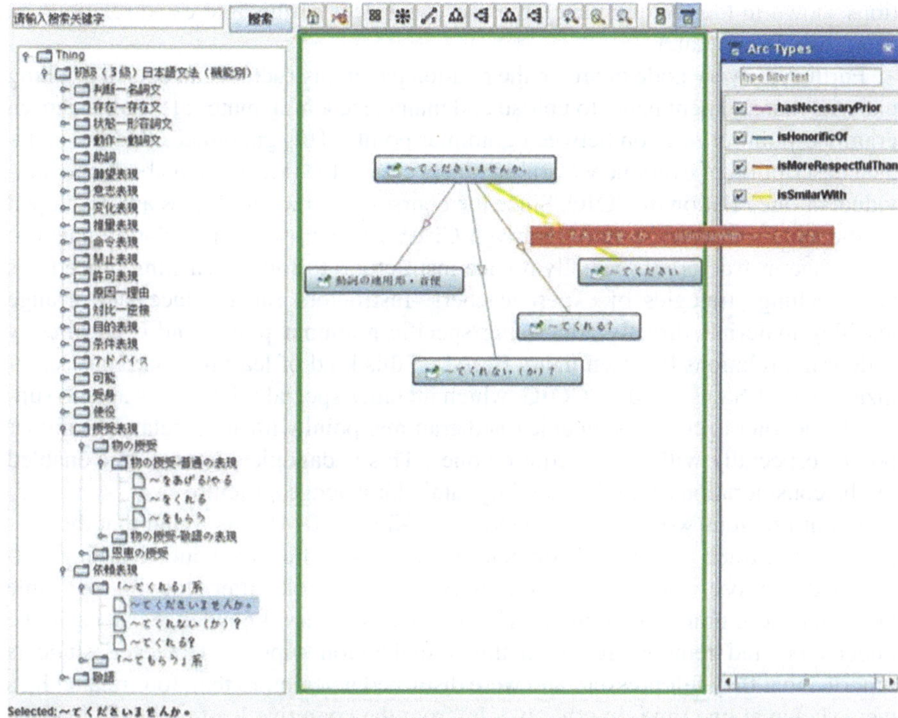

Fig. 11.1 The main interface of CLLSS

Search function is provided right above the tree structure. After putting key searching words, items which contain the key words in tree structure will be highlighted to enable further check for users. Besides, users also can open all the concepts level by level until they reach the GP they are seeking.

As shown in Fig. 11.1, when a user (instructor or learner) selects one grammar point "~te ku da sa i ma sen ka" represented by one individual in COJG, the relation panel on the right part will provide the user a visual representation of this grammar point and its related grammar points in the course. If the user puts the mouse on any node shown in the relation panel, the essential properties of its representing grammar point, represented by data properties of the individual in COJG, will be listed. On the other hand, putting the mouse on any arc in the relation panel will cause the display of the name and the direction of a relation which are represented by a relation axiom in COJG.

In other words, all the information in this common view, which include the tree structure on the left and relation panel on the right, are automatically extracted from the OWL file of COJG by the web-based CLLSS. Consequently, after selecting one GP from the tree structure, in the relation panel the user can get essential properties of this GP and all its related GPs conveniently. Moreover, if there are too many relations shown in the relation panel, the user can select her/his interested relations by using Arc-Types panel.

Further, at every node or arc on the relation panel, instructors can open a teaching material management panel to upload and manage teaching materials for the chosen grammar point or relation between grammar points. This guarantees that the metadata description of every new learning object covers the information about one individual or one relation of COJG. Since the course-centered ontologies are developed by the expert teachers, ontology-driven CLLSS make use of the relation panel to encourage instructors (especially novice instructors) to follow teaching procedures and teaching strategies of expert teachers. Instructors can produce and arrange teaching materials directly addressing specific grammar points and even directly addressing relations between them. Based on this kind of learning materials' organization, CLLSS assisted by COJG, which includes special relations, is able to support the learner to compare an unlearned grammar point with all its related grammar points, especially with those acquired ones. This pedagogical approach is enabled by the consideration of the learners' dynamic knowledge structure.

In our previous work (Wang, Mendori, & Xiong, 2014), it is found that the subjects who learned in this environment achieved significantly better learning outcomes than those who did only self-study with textbooks after studying the same target Japanese grammar contents. This suggests that new knowledge can easily be understood and remembered with this visualization support. However, students reported that they felt pressure and were disturbed when more than four related KPs were shown at one time. In other words, from the cognitive load point of view, the e-learning environment should avoid giving too much information at one time.

From the perspectives of learning attitude and motivation, the learner data from before and after CLLSS supported study of target grammar content were also analyzed (Wang & Mendori, 2015). The results of that analysis suggest that not only learners' attitude towards Japanese grammar learning but also their motivation to learn Japanese language improved after studying with CLLSS. Considering learning attitude and motivation before the learning activity as individual difference variables, further ANOVA tests were performed using mean value with dichotomization of attitude and motivation before the learning activity by mean value so as to form Low and High categorical variables. We found that learners with High attitude and motivation levels perceived a greater development of the habit of "learning by comparing related knowledge" and felt more satisfied with the CLLSS environment learning mode. Moreover, compared to learners with a Low level of attitude towards Japanese grammar before the activity, learners with High level of attitude reported significantly less mental effort in study with CLLSS and performed better on the grammar post-test. These results confirm that learning attitude and motivation are factors that must be considered in the promotion of meaningful learning.

However, in interviews after the experiment, 19 out of 60 participants reported that since the system already provides numerous bits of related knowledge, they didn't have the inclination to proactively search for more knowledge. Furthermore, several students reported that their curiosity and willingness to seek more related knowledge decreased. This phenomenon likely reflects the fact that CLLSS directly displays the information about related concepts and relations, and the participants made comparisons between concepts in a passive receptive manner. This kind of passive learning is known to lower learners' willingness to explore. This reminds us that CLLSS needs to be modified so as to encourage learners to actively engage in the construction of their relation maps.

Moreover, to explore strategies for multimedia learning object suggestion in CLLSS, a learning style based experiment was further conducted (Wang, Mendori, and Hoel, 2018). CLLSS under examination offers two learner modes: Open mode, which provides learners with both visual and verbal LOs, and Style-Matching mode, which provides visual learners with only visual LOs and verbal learners with only verbal LOs. Despite the higher distraction than found in Style- Matching mode, Open mode can improve the learning motivation of learners with higher visual style more efficiently. Certainly, to lower higher distraction in Open mode, a stylebased mode which alternately provides style-matched LOs and a designated amount of style-unmatched LOs, is suggested

4.2 Visualization Support System for E-book Users

Nowadays, e-book systems are widely used in education. In Japan, an education ministry panel is urging schools (K-12 and higher education) to use digital textbooks to support daily classroom teaching from 2020 onward. Kyushu University started to use e-book systems in 2014, in tandem with the Moodle learning management system and the Mahara e-profile system, to support daily classroom teaching. E-book systems provide a platform where instructors can easily upload teaching materials which learners can conveniently view and annotate or comment. Those systems can also record learning behaviour and report the results to the instructors. However, in e-book systems it is difficult for the learners to identify the knowledge they possess before and after a learning activity. Furthermore, existing e-book systems (even other e-learning systems) do not encourage learners to compare new knowledge with the relevant previously acquired knowledge and thus cannot effectively support the construction of the learners' knowledge structures.

Therefore, a visualization support system for e-book users (VSSE) was implemented to support e-book users' effective construction of their knowledge structures. VSSE have one function similar to CLLSS where the information about each KP included in the e-books can be searched via a catalogue (Wang, Ogata, & Shimada, 2017). From a tree structure on the left, users can open all the concepts level by level until they reach the KP they are seeking; when the user double clicks one leaf (which represents one KP) the right relation panel will display that KP and all its related KPs linked by relations defined in COCS. In addition, the e-book loca-

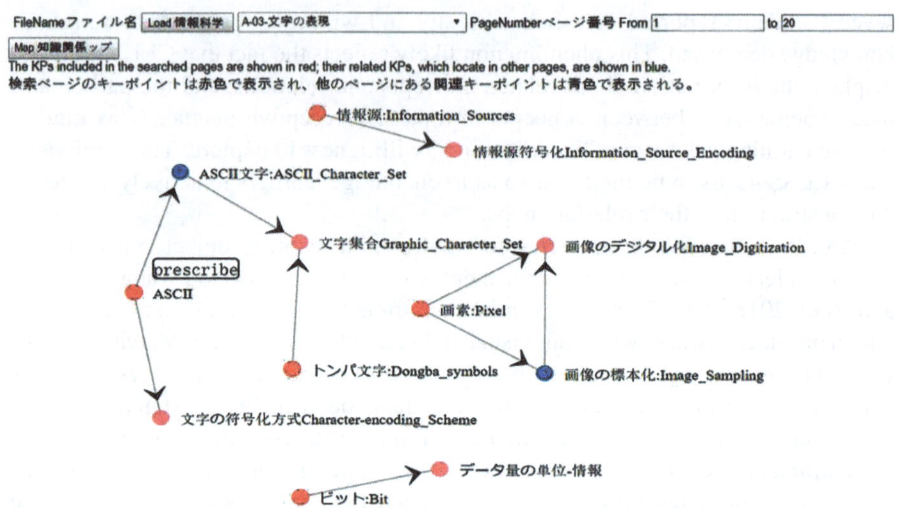

Fig. 11.2 The relation map of the search pages

tion information of that KP will be shown in a table. The difference between this VSSE function and CLLSS is that in CLLSS the learners can further access learning materials via the relation map while in VSSE the learners can further jump to the e-book pages from the location table. The other main function of VSSE is that it can display the KPs appearing in any page range of any e-book, along with their upper concepts in a relation map. This function with two different modes is described below.

4.2.1 Reception Comparison Mode

In reception comparison mode, learners are provided directly with complete versions of relation maps. As can be seen in Fig. 11.2, users of the e-book system can select a specific e-book and input any page range in the reception comparison interface. VSSE will display all the KPs appearing in the searched pages along with their related KPs in a map. For example, Fig. 11.2 displays: red nodes, which represent the KPs that appear in pages 1–20 of e-book A03; blue nodes, which represent related KPs that do not appear in those pages but have essential relations with the KPs represented by the red nodes; and pink nodes, which represent the upper concepts of the KPs represented by red or blue nodes. When the user places the mouse on any node in this relation map, the essential properties (such as definition and explanation, represented by the data properties of one individual in COCS) of that KP will be listed, while for every arc in the relation map, a statement of the relation will be displayed (for example, the displayed relation axiom "prescribe" from "ASCII" to "ASCII Character Set" in Fig. 11.2). Therefore, users can conveniently find the essential properties of every KP and all its related KPs from this visualization map. All that information is extracted automatically from COCS.

4.2.2 The "Cache-Cache Comparison" Mode

In an attempt to avoid inducing high cognitive load and low attitude/motivation as occurred in CLLSS, we present "cache-cache comparison" mode, an integration of discovery learning for the three main functions mentioned in the previous section. The word "cache", which originally comes from the French for "to hide" or "a hidden place". The French word "cache-cache" means "hide and seek" in English. It is a popular children's game in which one or more players, the seekers, try to find several hidden players. We propose to apply the familiar concept of "cache-cache" to represent the process of "hiding and seeking" in the children's game. From the learning support perspective, directly presenting too many pieces of information related to a new knowledge item will create a high level of cognitive load. As mentioned before, this overload phenomenon was also observed in one of our previous studies (Author of this paper, 2014). Therefore, we suggest hiding some parts of the information at the first stage of learning, and encouraging the learners to actively discover them in the second stage. This process, involving discovery learning, is termed "cache-cache comparison" here.

"Discovery learning" is an inquiry-based, constructivist learning theory process that takes place in problem solving situations where the learner draws on his or her own experience and acquired knowledge to discover facts and relations and new truths to be learned (Bruner, 1961). Bruner (1961, 2009) states that students are more likely to remember knowledge that they discover on their own than that which is presented directly in receptive instruction. The learner experiences individual discovery when he/she solves problems using existing knowledge. This process, which encourages active engagement, can foster the development of creativity and problem-solving skills, and promote learning motivation. However, many researchers (Mayer, 2004; Alfieri, et al., 2011) have cautioned that unassisted discovery learning without sufficient prior knowledge and guidance may easily lead to misconceptions and cause additional cognitive overload. Timely guidance is needed in discovery learning to avoid learner confusion and frustration (Kirschner, Sweller, & Clark, 2006). Learners need to gain confidence in their ability to complete tasks given the requisite knowledge; on the other hand, when confronted with failure they also need to be motivated to learn from mistakes and thus be better prepared to continue learning. The "cache-cache comparison" visualization interface, which can support the learners in actively constructing their knowledge framework, was developed. Considering KPs and relations as the building blocks of course relation maps, "cache-cache comparison" mode in VSSE hides several blocks in an expert relation map and guides learners to seek to discover those hidden blocks. The learn-

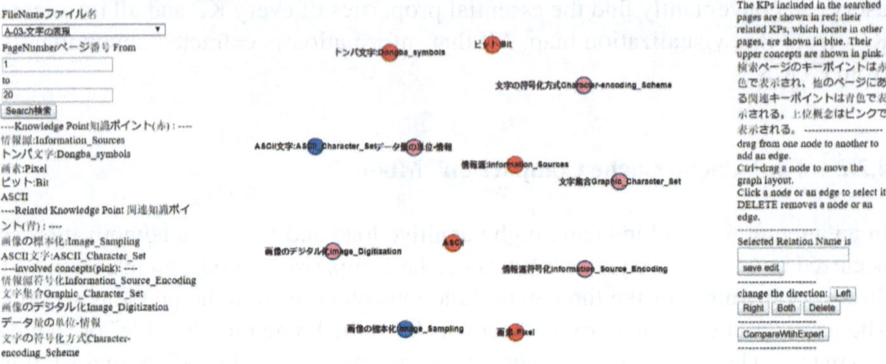

Fig. 11.3 An instance of "cache-cache comparison" mode

ers engage in an active learning process when they struggle to complete the relation map.

Figure 11.3 shows an instance of "cache-cache comparison" mode: the range of interest to the learner is pages 1–20 of e-book A-03. First, as shown in Fig. 11.3, "cache-cache comparison" mode displays all the KPs that appear in the page range of interest in red; the related KPs that do not appear in the pages of interest in ranges in blue; and their upper concepts in pink. Then firstly the learner is required to classify the KPs by connecting them to their pink upper concepts; next, the learner is encouraged to find out the relations between KPs by connecting red nodes or connecting red nodes to blue nodes. The descriptions of the relation arcs made by the learner can be modified and saved anytime. After the learner completes the relation map, she/he can click the "Compare with experts" button. Finally, all the relations extracted from the ontology will be displayed as red lines. The learner can easily compare the red lines with the black lines that she/he has made.

5 Conclusion

In this chapter, we discuss the ontology technique and its application in knowledge-based systems, especially in learning support systems. Two ontology-driven learning support systems which provide meaningful learning environments are introduced: a customizable language learning support system (CLLSS) and a visualization learning support system for e-book users (VSSE). Both systems provide meaningful receptive learning environment. Furthermore, in VSSE, to encourage active engagement in meaningful learning, the "cache-cache comparison" environment is also presented by Wang, Ogata, and Shimada (2017). This environment, which hides some relations and guides the learners to actively recall their prior knowledge as they design their own relation maps before comparison with the relations maps of experts, is intended to lower cognitive load and encourage active engagement.

A series of experiments has been conducted for the evaluation of VSSE. The analysis results of the learner data will be discussed in future work. In addition, for both systems, the construction and maintenance of ontology are still time-consuming. Therefore, the automatic method for creating and updating ontology information is presented in Wang, Brendan, and Ogata (2017) and will be evaluated in the future work.

Acknowledgements The research is supported by KAKENHI Grant Number 17K17936, the Research and Development on Fundamental Utilization Technologies for Social Big Data (No. 178A03), and the Commissioned Research of National Institute of Information and Communications Technology, Japan.

References

Alfieri, L., Brooks, P. J., Aldrich, N. J., & Tenenbaum, H. R. (2011). Does discovery-based instruction enhance learning? *Journal of Educational Psychology, 103*(1), 1–18.

Ausubel, D. P. (1963). *The psychology of meaningful verbal learning*. New York, NY: Grune and Stratton.

Ausubel, D. P. (1968). *Educational psychology: A cognitive view*. New York, NY: Holt.

Ausubel, D. P., Novak, J. D., & Hanesian, H. (1978). *Educational psychology: A cognitive view* (2nd ed.). New York, NY: Holt, Rinehart and Winston.

Bransford, J., Brown, A. L., & Cocking, R. R. (Eds.). (1999). *How people learn: Brain, mind, experience, and school*. Washington, DC: National Academy.

Bruner, J. S. (1961). The act of discovery. *Harvard Educational Review, 31*(1), 21–32.

Bruner, J. S. (2009). *The process of education*. Cambridge: Harvard University Press.

Chu, K. K., Lee, C. I., & Tsai, R. S. (2011). Ontology technology to assist learners' navigation in the concept map learning system. *Expert Systems with Applications, 38*, 11293–11299.

Dicheva, D., & Dichev, C. (2006). TM4L: creating and browsing educational topic maps. *British Journal of Educational Technology, 37*(3), 391–404.

Gomez-Albarran, M., & Jimenez-Diaz, G. (2009). Recommendation and students' authoring in repositories of learning objects: A case-based reasoning approach. *International Journal of Emerging Technologies in Learning (IJET), 4*, 35–40.

Gruber, T. R. (1993). A translation approach to portable ontologies. *Knowledge Acquisition, 5*(2), 199–220.

Hayashi, Y., Bourdeau, J., & Mizoguchi, R. (2009). Using ontological engineering to organize learning/instructional theories and build a theory-aware authoring system. *International Journal of Artificial Intelligence in Education, 19*(2), 211–252.

Holsapple, C. W., & Joshi, K. D. (2004). A formal knowledge management ontology: Conduct, activities, resources and influences. *Journal of the American Society for Information Science and Technology, 55*(7), 593–612.

Kirschner, P. A., Sweller, J., & Clark, R. (2006). Why minimal guidance during instruction does not work: An analysis of the failure of constructivist, discovery, problem-based, experiential, and inquiry-based teaching. *Educational Psychologist, 41*(2), 75–86.

Lee, J. H., & Segev, A. (2012). Knowledge maps for e-learning. *Computers & Education, 59*(2), 353–364.

Lim, K. Y., Lee, H. W., & Grabowski, B. (2009). Does concept-mapping strategy work for everyone? The levels of generativity and learners' self-regulated learning skills. *British Journal of Educational Technology, 40*(4), 606–618.

Mansur, A. B. F., & Yusof, N. (2013). Social learning network analysis model to identify learning patterns using ontology clustering techniques and meaningful learning. *Computers & Education, 63*, 73–86.

Mayer, R. (2004). Should there be a three-strikes rule against pure discovery learning? The case for guided methods of instruction. *American Psychologist, 59*(1), 14–19.

Novak, J. D., & Cañas, A. J. (2008). The theory underlying concept maps and how to construct them. Technical report IHMC CmapTools 2006-01 Rev 01-2008. Florida Institute for Human and Machine Cognition. Available at http://cmap.ihmc.us/Publications/ResearchPapers/TheoryUnderlyingConceptMaps.pdf

Noy, N. F., & McGuinness, D. L. (2001). Ontology development 101: A guide to creating your first ontology. *Development, 32*(1), 1–25.

O'Donnell, A. M., Dansereau, D. F., & Hall, R. H. (2002). Knowledge maps as scaffolds for cognitive processing. *Educational Psychology Review, 14*(1), 71–86.

Oltramari, A., Gangemi, A., Guarino, N., & Masolo, C. (2002). Restructuring WordNet's top-level: The OntoClean approach. In *Workshop Proceedings of OntoLex'2, Ontologies and Lexical Knowledge Bases (LREC2002), Spain* (pp. 17–26).

Sosnovsky, S., & Gavrilova, T. (2006). Development of educational ontology for C-programming. *International Journal Information, Theories & Applications, 13*(4), 303–307.

Tsien, J. Z. (2007). The memory. *Scientific American, 297*(July), 52–59.

Wang, J., Brendan, F., & Ogata, H. (2017). Semi-automatic construction of ontology based on data mining technique. In *International Conference on Learning Technologies and Learning Environments (LTLE) 2017, IEEE CPS* (pp. 511–515). Washington, DC: IEEE.

Wang, J., & Mendori, T. (2012). A course-centered ontology of Japanese grammar for a language learning support system. *Frontiers in Artificial Intelligence and Applications (KES2012), 243*, 654–663.

Wang, J., Mendori, T., & Xiong, J. (2013). A customizable language learning support system using ontology-driven engine. *International Journal of Distance Education Technologies, 11*(4), 81–96.

Wang, J. Y., & Mendori, T. (2015). An evaluation of the learning attitude and motivation in a language learning support system. In *Proceedings of Advanced Learning Technologies and Technology-enhanced Learning (ICALT 2015), Hualien, Taiwan*. Washington, DC: IEEE.

Wang, J. Y., Mendori, T., & Xiong, J. (2014). A language learning support system using course-centered ontology and its evaluation. *Computer & Education, 78*, 278–293.

Wang, J. Y., Mendori, T., & Hoel, T. (2018). Strategies for multimedia learning object recommendation in a language learning support system: Verbal learners vs. Visual learners. *International Journal of Human-Computer Interaction*, 1–11.

Wang, J. Y., Ogata, H., & Shimada, A. (2017). A meaningful discovery learning environment for e-book learners. In *IEEE Global Engineering Education Conference, April 25–28, 2017*. Washington, DC: IEEE.

Zhong, X., Fu, H., Xia, H., Yang, L., & Shang, M. (2015). A hybrid cognitive assessment based on ontology knowledge map and skills. *Knowledge-Based Systems, 73*, 52–60.

Jingyun Wang is currently an Assistant Professor at Research Institute for Information Technology, Kyushu University, Japan. She received her MSc in Computer Science and Technology from Nanjing University of Science & Technology in July 2007. From July 2007 August to March

2011, she had been working as a lecturer in Information and Computing Department in Xiamen University of Technology, China. She received her Ph. D. degree from Graduate School of Engineering, Kochi University of Technology, Japan, in March 2014. Her current research focuses on visualization learning support systems, adaptive learning support systems for language learning, ontology technique, learning analytics and data mining.

Chapter 12
Assessing the Interaction Between Self-Regulated Learning (SRL) Profiles and Actual Learning in the Chemistry Online Blended Learning Environment (COBLE)

Rachel Rosanne Eidelman, Joshua M. Rosenberg, and Yael Shwartz

Abstract This chapter addresses the challenges and opportunities of virtual teaching of a complex scientific topic, such as chemistry, to high-school students. Chemistry Online Blended Learning Environment (COBLE) is a learning environment for students that are willing to expand their knowledge of Chemistry but have no opportunity to do so in their schools. It is claimed that certain skills help cope with learning, in general, and are vital in advancing learning, such as Self-Regulated Learning (SRL) skills. The chapter describes a recent study that investigated and characterized the students' learning profiles, self-regulated learning processes (skills and strategies), and followed the change in these variables throughout the 3 year program learning Chemistry via COBLE in order to predict students' success in learning Chemistry this way. Such prediction may enable teachers to be aware of possible problems earlier than usual and also help personalize the teaching and learning processes according to students' profiles. Results indicate that there are some significant differences in some of the SRL categories between students studying via face-to-face and virtual environments and also among intervention students that possessed different SRL profiles when examining the involvement variable throughout their studies over time. On the basis of the data, influential indicators were isolated to enable future prediction of student success in studying Chemistry in a virtual manner and better planning of personalized support.

R. R. Eidelman (✉) · Y. Shwartz
Department of Science Teaching, Weizmann Institute of Science, Rehovot, Israel
e-mail: rachel-rosanne.eidelman@weizmann.ac.il; yael.shwartz@weizmann.ac.il

J. M. Rosenberg
Department of Theory and Practice in Teacher Education, University of Tennessee, Knoxville, TN, USA
e-mail: jmrosenberg@utk.edu

D. Sampson et al. (eds.), *Learning Technologies for Transforming Large-Scale Teaching, Learning, and Assessment*, https://doi.org/10.1007/978-3-030-15130-0_12

1 Introduction

1.1 Virtual Teaching

E-learning means any learning that is electronically mediated and/or facilitated by software, such as course management systems for organizing courses and presenting materials (Zemsky & Massy, 2004). This type of learning is in contrast to traditional or face-to-face learning in the school classroom. Tallent-Runnels, Thomas, Lan, and Cooper (2006) address four main pillars that emerged when students' encountered e-learning: *course environment* (classroom culture, structural assistance, success factors, interaction online, and evaluations), *learners' outcomes* (understanding the teaching and learning processes in the virtual environment), *learners' characteristics* (understanding the motivation to take a virtual course, learner's goals, and needs) and *institutional and administrative factors* (clear policies for virtual courses, such as a support system, course development, and evaluation). They concluded that although no comprehensive theories or models could be derived regarding instruction online, students preferred flexibility, convenience, and autonomy of individual pacing, although it required self-management and computer-skilled students had a more positive attitude toward e-learning than others less proficient. Attempts to compare students' learning outcomes in virtual and traditional environments revealed no significant differences between the two groups. E-learning students were affected by the quality of the course design and were more successful when the course was well-designed. This finding emphasizes the importance of the designer's role in determining the educational design theory used and in the overall success rate of the students taking the course and sets the stage for the work described in this chapter.

1.2 Self-Regulated Learning (SRL)

Self-regulated learners are defined as proactive seekers of information when it is needed and as those who take the necessary steps to master it (Zimmerman, 1990). They are also conceptualized as being metacognitive, since they plan, set goals, organize, self-monitor, and self-evaluate several times during the learning process. They are motivated and hold high self-efficacy, engage in self-attributions, have intrinsic task interest, and are behaviorally active participants in their learning processes (Pintrich & De Groot, 1990; Zimmerman, 1989, 1990, 2008). Additionally, there is a distinction between self-regulating processes and strategies as the latter are designed to minimize the processes and are believed to be adaptive (Butler & Winne, 1995). Students' learning must involve the use of specified strategies in order to achieve academic goals on the basis of self-efficacy perceptions. Those perceptions are about one's capabilities to organize and implement actions necessary to attain designated performance of skills for specific tasks (Zimmerman, 1989). Self-regulated learning skills are important in all learning environments but especially in a virtual learning environment, since it lacks the immediate ability to seek help from teachers (Cho, 2004; O'Neill, Singh, & O'Donoghue, 2004). It is believed that a major requirement for using technology in a virtual environment is the ability to be a self-regulated learner (SRL) (Tsai, 2011).

Teaching students to self-regulate their academic learning can be successful only when students experience the benefits of SRL (Zimmerman, Bonner, & Kovach, 1996). Four design principles were suggested in order to promote SRL skills: (1) SRL activities are to be explicitly presented to the students; (2) learning events should include opportunities to use SRL strategies; (3) SRL skill interventions are mandatory; (4) students must experience success while using SRL skills in order to continue to use them regularly (Ley & young, 2001; Zimmerman et al., 1996).

Different tools were developed in order to assess SRL skills, such as a Likert type questionnaire, the Learning and Study Strategies Inventory (LASSI), containing 80 questions attributed to ten different categories, each of which is associated with a three letter code used later in the context of the results: anxiety and worry about school performance (ANX); attitude and interest (ATT); concentration and attention to academic tasks (CON); information processing, acquiring knowledge, and reasoning (INP); motivation, diligence, self-discipline, and willingness to work hard (MOT); self-testing, reviewing, and preparing for classes (SFT); selecting main ideas and recognizing important information (SMI); use of support techniques and materials (STA); use of time management principles for academic tasks (TMT); test strategies and preparing for tests (TST). The LASSI test was initially designed to self-assess SRL skills, among other things, in order to predict the success rate in each category for students intending to go to college (Weinstein, Palmer, & Shulte, 2002).

1.3 Chemistry Online Blended Learning Environment (COBLE)

The design of COBLE consists of three elements: *Platform Design* (with Moodle used as the basic platform with many plug-in features), *Pedagogy*, and *Organization*. Here we will only describe the principles related to the Pedagogy and the platform components, which are most relevant to students' SRL.

1. *Diagnostics*: Coming from different schools, students' preliminary knowledge was diverse and had to be acknowledged and diagnosed. The first unit was built gradually, and basic scientific concepts were taught in order to create a platform for more complex explanations later on.
2. *Diverse Learning Styles*: Several teaching methodologies were used in order to ensure each and every student's engagement in the learning process. These computerized methods were included: synchronic interactive weekly lesson, exercise work sheets, interactive internet applets, a-synchronic Moodle tasks, home lab-reports (group and singular), and periodic Chemistry projects. The following non-computerized methods were included: Laboratory work performed

at the Weizmann Institute as a group and exercises from Chemistry books and group projects (such as modeling projects).
3. *Independence and Responsibility*: In order to enhance independent learning and encourage students to take responsibility for their studies, weekly a-synchronic lessons were given following the synchronic lessons.
4. *Peer Learning*: The students used forums, chats, and WhatsApp, and were encouraged to share experiences and answer questions in the forum, as well as react to other students' comments. Occasionally, groups of students had to perform a group assignment (i.e., to write a lab report together or to give in a group task).
5. *Lesson Design*: all lessons were designed in an identical way: lesson opening, "What have we learned so far?", "former knowledge needed", acquisition of new learning material, exercising and implementing the new materials, "summary", additional enrichment materials and relevant links, homework, and important announcements. The lead idea was that the students should know at any moment where they stand with respect to the course material (regarding the curriculum and the lesson itself).

The COBLE program started in 2014 and included a full year of development of learning materials and the platform. In the following year (2015) enrollment started and, following 3 years of studying in the program in 2017, 23 students have graduated; 87 students began their studies in the 12th grade; 157 students began their studies in the 11th grade; and 110 began their studies in the 10th grade. The current research follows the first cohort (that began in 2015) during all 3 years of participation.

2 The Study

The current study seeks understanding regarding the following questions:

Q1. What are the students' SRL profiles, and how do they change during 10th–12th grades?
Q2. Is there a correlation between the intervention students' SRL profiles and the level of success in the blended Chemistry environment during 10th–12th grades?

2.1 Method

2.1.1 Participants

Three groups of students were observed and compared in two phases within this research:

Phase 1: 1. Pre-group; 2. Control group

The pre-group was composed of 109 students learning science according to the requirements of the school curriculum and served as a reference group. The control group was composed of 19 10th–12th grade students who chose to study Chemistry as a major in high school.

Phase 2: 3. Intervention group

The intervention group was composed of students who enrolled in the virtual 'Chemistry Online' course at the beginning of the 10th grade. The number of the students in this group varied owing to dropouts and newcomers over time ($N = 23$ students graduated). These students were observed for 3 years (10th–12th grade) and were compared to the Chemistry students in the face-to-face control group.

For both the control and intervention groups, the scores of the 9th grade pre-group students in the LASSI categories were considered to be at the level of self-regulated learning (LASSI reference scores) that is typical before starting 10th grade Chemistry studies.

2.1.2 Instruments and Analysis

Questionnaire

A modified and translated (from its original English to Hebrew) form of the LASSI questionnaire developed by Weinstein et al. (2002) was used. There were 48 questions related to six out of the ten categories which were part of the original LASSI questionnaire:

- Attitude and interest (ATT)
- Concentration and attention to academic tasks (CON)
- Motivation, diligence, self-discipline, and willingness to work hard (MOT)
- Use of support techniques and materials (STA)
- Use of time management principles for academic tasks (TMT)
- Test strategies and preparing for tests (TST).

Additionally, the students tested were high school students and not college students as intended in the original questionnaire.

Changes were made accordingly, and the overall reliability of the modified questionnaire was very good (α [Cronbach's coefficient] = 0.93). Reliability (after modifications) of LASSI categories (α): CON (0.88), MOT (0.86), TST (0.77), TMT (0.82), ATT (0.69), and STA (0.63).

The distribution times of the LASSI questionnaire for the three research groups were as follows (note that there were three identical distribution times for the control and intervention groups) (Table 12.1).

The control group answered the questionnaire four times during the 3 years, and the intervention group answered the questionnaire six times during the 3 years.

Table 12.1 LASSI questionnaire distribution times (pre, control, and intervention groups)

	Jun-14					
Pre-group	Before the program has begun					
Control	Sep-14 (Beginning of 10th grade)	Nov-14		Feb-16 (Middle of 11th grade)		Apr-17 (End of 12th grade)
Intervention	Sep-14 (Beginning of 10th grade)	Jun-15	Oct-15	Feb-16 (Middle of 11th grade)	Oct-16	Apr-17 (End of 12th grade)

The pre-group measurement served as a reference group by collecting the mean of students' answers: average for each category containing eight questions. Answers to the LASSI questionnaires were coded into predetermined categories. Items were grouped into categories by five expert researchers, and their coding was compared.

Analyzing Students' Tasks via Moodle

Data mining in educational systems (or Educational Data Mining, EDM), is a fast growing field that not only provides tools to gain data for statistical purposes but also allows personalization of learning processes for individual students by analyzing their personal goals, preferences, and knowledge (Castro, Vellido, Nebot, & Mugica, 2007; Chen, Liu, Ou, & Liu, 2000; Romero, Ventura, & García, 2008). Data is retrieved automatically and stored in server access logs, sketching an individual portfolio for each student. There are several advantages in using data mining in a virtual course environment, such as collecting data that possesses a bias-free quantitative nature constantly being gathered without creating a nuisance or hindering students' activities in any way. Both methods, data collecting in the traditional classroom or via electronic means, constantly evaluate the effectiveness of the course components and interventions and are used to refine them accordingly, but the latter does not rely upon face-to-face interactions with the students (Sheard, Ceddia, Hurst, & Tuovinen, 2003).

EDM via data collected through Moodle was conducted in several ways:

- Receiving reports through the *Moodle report generator*: each student's activity volume (in the system in general as well as in specific worksheets, problem solving or tests). Reports can be generated according to the teachers needs crossing various variables, participants, and dates.
- Analyzing *synchronic online chat conversations* (total chat volume and message type): All students' messages from the chat area during the synchronic lesson were counted, coded, and analyzed according to the division: (1) Chemistry content messages (related to the content matter); (2) Technical messages (expressing technical difficulties); (3) Social messages (social interactions between students); (4) Administrative messages (addressing issues that were school-related and paper work); (5) Other messages.
- *Scores*: All students' task trials were scored.

In-Depth Interviews

The interviewees belonged to the intervention group only and were interviewed by one independent interviewer. They were chosen so they were heterogeneous (weak, medium, and strong students according to their achievements). The interviewees had guiding interview questions that covered the following topics: (1) General information, (2) Opinion of Chemistry and learning environment, (3) SRL, (4) Learning strategies, (5) Administrative and Technical issues, and (6) Closure. All interview data was qualitatively analyzed. All remaining students were academically capable of studying high-level Chemistry, since they study other high-level scientific subjects at school, and study high-level English and Math (besides two students who do not study Math and English at all as part of their school policy). Fifteen students were interviewed, and their common views are presented.

3 Results

Q1. What are the students' SRL profiles and how do they change during 10th–12th grades?

The Pre-group was composed of 109 students learning science according to the requirements of the school curriculum. These students answered the LASSI questionnaire at the end of the 9th grade. In September 2014, the research study began, and the first iteration took place as the two remaining groups, control (face-to-face) and intervention (online) Chemistry students, answered the LASSI questionnaire. No significant differences between students in the three groups at the beginning of the research were found (at the beginning of the 10th grade). This meant that all students, in all groups, had the same starting point and were not different in their SRL skills according to the six questionnaire categories that were checked.

The Control group was composed of 19 10th–12th grade students who chose to study Chemistry as a major in high school. *The intervention group* was composed of 24 10th–12th grade students who enrolled in the 'Chemistry Online' course.

In order to build a student's SRL profile, the six LASSI questionnaire categories were examined. Mean score for each of the categories was calculated. In addition, a cluster analysis was applied using the statistical software and programming language R (R Development Core Team, 2017) and specifically the open-source *prcr* (person-centered analysis) package (Rosenberg, Schmidt, & Beymer, 2017). Person-centered analyses focus on common patterns in observations considered in terms of clusters, or profiles, and their change over time or differences across factors, such as groups of students (Bergman & El-Khouri, 1999).

The data was scaled (since cluster analysis is sensitive to outliers) and the different profiles that emerge from the data were identified by means of regression analysis. Calculations yielded substantial variability explained in the clustered variables (R^2 = 0.53), and the percentage of agreement from double split-half

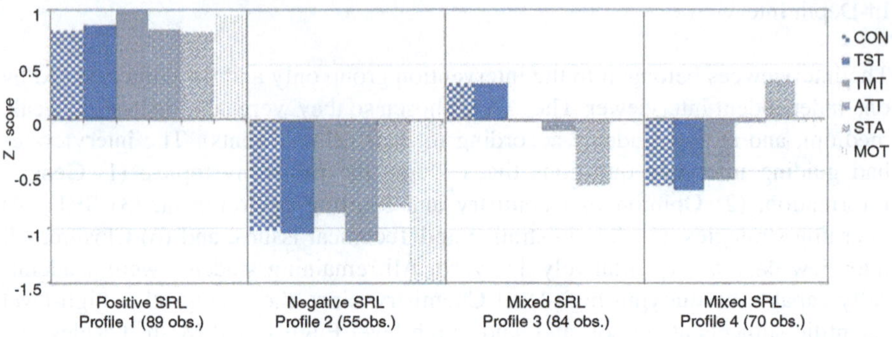

Fig. 12.1 The 4 SRL profile solution

cross-validation (all observations were split in half and each half was compared to the other in order to find similarities between the two halves) was 67.05% (κ [Cohen's Kappa] = 0.56). These calculations validated the use of a four SRL solution since 60–80% is considered a good agreement percentage (Landis & Koch, 1977; Sim & Wright, 2005).

In Fig. 12.1, we can observe the four SRL profile solution.

Distributions of the 298 SRL profile observations were found similar in size: SRL profile 1 (89 observations, 29.865% of the students) is an all-positive profile for all LASSI categories.[1] SRL profile 2 (55 observations, 18.456% of the students) is an all-negative profile for all LASSI categories. SRL profile 3 (84 observations, 28.188% of the students) is a mixed profile: ATT, MOT, STA, TMT < 0; CON, TST > 0. SRL profile 4 (70 observations, 23.49% of the students) is a mixed profile: ATT, MOT, CON, TST, TMT < 0; STA > 0. The all-positive SRL profile (profile 1) had the most observations and the all-negative SRL profile (profile 2) had the least.

Examination of the control and intervention group SRL profile percentage of appearances over time (10th–12th grades) can reveal an SRL profile pattern within the two groups. The intervention group was divided into two sub-groups: (a) remaining students (b) dropouts (Fig. 12.2a–c).

As can be seen in Fig. 12.2a–c above, the most prominent difference is in Fig. 12.2c, where dropout students barely possess the all-positive SRL profile (profile 1) at the beginning of their studies, and they quickly progressed toward the all-negative SRL profile (profile 2) up to the point when they dropped out. Furthermore, the control group and the intervention remaining student group started from approximately the same level of the all-positive SRL profile. Comparison between the two groups shows a drop in the percentage of the all-positive SRL profile (profile 1) for the control group, while the remaining student group percentage

[1]Attitude and interest (ATT); concentration and attention to academic tasks (CON); motivation, diligence, self-discipline, and willingness to work hard (MOT); use of support techniques and materials (STA); use of time management principles for academic tasks (TMT); test strategies and preparing for tests (TST).

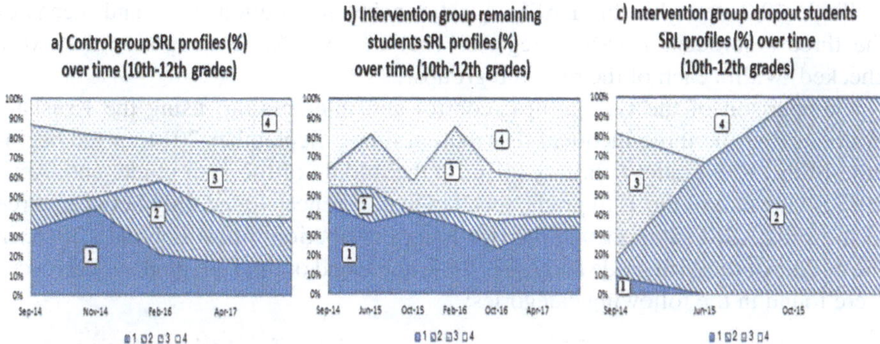

Fig. 12.2 SRL profile patterns (1–4) for (**a**) control group students, (**b**) remaining intervention group students (**c**) dropout intervention group students

of this SRL profile is higher and more or less steady. In the control group, more students were added to the all-negative SRL profile (profile 2) over time, while the remaining students displayed lower percentages of this profile, reaching the zero point on Oct 2015 (but increasing percentages somewhat after that date). As for the mixed SRL profiles (profiles 3 and 4), both groups had similar overall mixed SRL profile percentages, but the control group had steady percentages for both profiles, whereas the remaining students had SRL profile 3 decline and SRL profile 4 increase (note that SRL profile 4 is a more negative profile than SRL profile 3).

Though we present the profiles for each of the three groups over time in Fig. 12.2, we focused our analysis on overall group differences in frequencies of the profiles. A chi-square test of independence was performed comparing the frequency of student SRL profiles in each of the three groups: (a) control students (b) remaining intervention students, and (c) dropout intervention students. Significant differences were found: $\chi = 13.01$, $df = 6$, $p < 0.05$.

Intervention dropouts were less likely to possess the all-positive SRL profile 1 than remaining intervention or control students ($z = -2.2.016$, $p = 0.04328$), $p < 0.05$. Additionally, remaining intervention students were less likely to possess the all-negative SRL profile 2 than those in the control group or in the dropout intervention students ($z = -2.1676$, $p = 0.030235$), $p < 0.05$.

Results like those regarding dropout students are not surprising. It is unlikely that dropout students can possess a positive attitude, be interested, motivated, and invest time in a subject they have decided to stop studying. It is logical that any Chemistry student will possess a more positive SRL profile than dropouts.

This fits well with the other results regarding dropouts possessing an all-negative SRL profile (profile 2). We would expect a more negative SRL profile from any dropout in comparison to any Chemistry student; however, we also observed that the remaining intervention students were not likely to possess the all-negative SRL profile as much as the control students. This result shows that the remaining intervention students perhaps developed SRL skills over time since both groups were not initially different with respect to the mean scores for the LASSI categories at the beginning of their Chemistry studies.

Table 12.2 describes the LASSI questionnaire distribution times and means of the three significant LASSI categories (out of six LASSI categories that were checked) within each of the research groups.

Comparison of the two groups (control and intervention) using the Kruskal–Wallis test at the three identical distribution times: September 2014, at the beginning of the 10th grade; February 2016, in the middle of the 11th grade; and, April 2017, at the end of the 12th grade, resulted in differences found only between three of the six LASSI categories at the two latter distribution times: February 2016, in the middle of the 11th grade and April 2017, at the end of the 12th grade. Differences were found in the following categories:

- Attitude and interest (ATT) was significantly higher for the intervention group: $\chi = 4.09$, $df = 1$, $p < 0.05$. High attitude and interest was also expressed by students in the interviews regarding the interest they demonstrated in Chemistry before and after entering the program:
- Quote 1: "*Chemistry is interesting to me. The teacher teaches in an interesting way and links the material to daily life. It makes me want to listen.*"
- Quote 2: "*My father bought me a second hand Chemistry book from 1963, and I read it. I enjoy Chemistry and find that I'm very interested in it.*"
- Quote 3: "*Chemistry is relevant to everything in our life. When I was in junior high, we studied Chemistry, and I was mainly excited about the experiments.*"
- Test strategies and preparation for tests (TST) was significantly higher for the control group: $\chi = 4.78$, $df = 1$, $p < 0.05$. According to intervention student's answers in the interviews, they all prepared for the tests, mostly by revising their notebooks since almost all had them and summarized either during the lesson or right afterwards. Most students did not prepare for the quizzes:
- Quote 4: "*In order to revise for tests, I just went through the recordings and presentations. For the quizzes, I never studied. It's also possible to go over the exercises.*"

Table 12.2 Times and significant means within research groups' answers in LASSI questionnaire categories (pre, control, and intervention groups)

		Pre-group	Control		Intervention	
Category name	Category abbreviation	June 2014	Feb 2016	Apr 2017	Feb 2016	Apr 2017
		$N = 109$	$N = 19$	$N = 19$	$N = 18$	$N = 21$
Test strategies and preparation for tests	TST	3.921	3.617	4.030*	3.944	3.864*
Use of time management principles for academic tasks	TMT	3.342	3.039	3.184**	3.208	3.030**
Attitude and interest	ATT	3.533	3.496	3.451*	3.778	3.619*

$^*0.01 < p < 0.05$, $^{**}0.001 < p < 0.01$

- Quote 5: "*In order to revise for tests, I summarized the lessons and exercises. I didn't revise for the quizzes.*"
- Quote 6: "*I read the summary in my notebook, and got help from my friends when I prepared for tests.*"
- Use of time management principles for academic tasks (TMT) was significantly higher for the control group: $\chi = 8.98$, $df = 1$, $p < 0.005$. Students in the intervention group testify to time-management issues:

- Quote 7: "*Chemistry is time consuming if I don't understand and have to figure it out at home. If something is not clear during the lesson I revise the lesson afterwards.*"

- Quote 8: "*When I have time, I do my Chemistry homework but I have more urgent things to do.*"

- Quote 9: "*I feel that I can do with solving a handful of problems if I understand the principles, I don't need to spend much time on that*"

These findings can be influenced by several factors:

1. *Teacher*: each group had different teachers—a fact that may have had influence on the student's answers.
2. *Content*: in the 12th grade's curriculum there is a topic that is subject to teacher's discretion. Each group was taught a different topic and that may have been influential, affecting the student's answers.
3. *Timing*: the control group student's final external Ministry of Education (MOE) test took place at the end of the 11th grade, whereas the intervention group students were tested at the end of the 12th grade. This meant that a lot of pressure was lifted from control group students as they were left with the external laboratory exam alone (all lab work was group work, performed in the 12th grade, ending with a 15–20 min external oral test).

    - Students expressed the importance of intrinsic motivation (MOT) during their studies as a means for attaining success in a virtual environment:
      Quote 10: "*You have to be responsible for your own studies because there is no one to make you study.*"
      Quote 11: "*I recheck the assignments before sending them in. If I am not content with the score, I resend them.*"
      Quote 12: "*My motivation to study is intrinsic, or else I wouldn't have attended the lessons. Same goes for the face-to-face lessons at my school.*"

    - They also referred to the ability to concentrate (CON) and maintain a decent level of learning without face-to-face contact with either teacher or peer-classmates (most, expressing different degrees of discontent, but showing the ability to overcome it):
      Quote 13: "*In the face-to-face classroom, there are distractions, and students do not always listen. There are many disciplinary issues. I prefer the virtual lessons because there are none of those there.*"

Quote 14: "*I connect to the virtual lesson from home, because at school there are more distractions and technical problems that bother me.*"
Quote 15: "*I find it very convenient to study through a virtual class setting since I have a hard time sitting in a face-to-face classroom, and I tend to bother everyone else. My functioning in the face-to-face classroom depends on if there is noise outside of the classroom or if I'm tired.*"

Q2. Is there a correlation between the intervention students' SRL profiles and the level of success in the blended Chemistry environment during 10th–12th grades?

In order to answer this research question, there is a need to first define 'success' by measurable means and then track changes that have occurred in their SRL profiles throughout their studies with respect to these success measures.

3.1 Measures of Success

3.1.1 Achievements

Students in the intervention group (10th–12th grades) were divided into three groups (high, medium, and low achievers) according to their scores in the 3 year course. The division into these groups was done after statistically locating differentiating questions among all the questions that were presented to the students throughout the 3 year course and the scores of written tests and matriculation exams. In all, 251 differentiating questions were found and used for this task, defining the three intervention student achiever groups as follows.

- *Low achiever's* scores were between $0 \geq$ score ≥ 66.4 (five students)
- *Medium achiever's* scores were between $66.4 >$ score ≥ 77.9 (ten students)
- *High achiever's* scores were between $77.9 >$ score ≥ 100 (eight students)

No significant differences were found in GLM repeated measures performed within each group (in terms of SRL categories), and therefore the division among these achievement groups is acceptable.

There were fewer students in the low achieving group (suggesting that they might have possessed certain SRL features that enabled them to remain in the course despite their low achievements). These remaining low-achiever students were from diverse backgrounds, and their reasons for remaining in the course seemed to be different; all of these students started off with higher scores that deteriorated over time. The majority of the remaining intervention students were medium achievers and almost the same number were high achievers. In more cases than not, the students' later scores determined whether they belonged in a specific group, and if they did well on the final matriculation exam. In short, it was not the mean score but the trend that accounted for student outcomes on the matriculation exam.

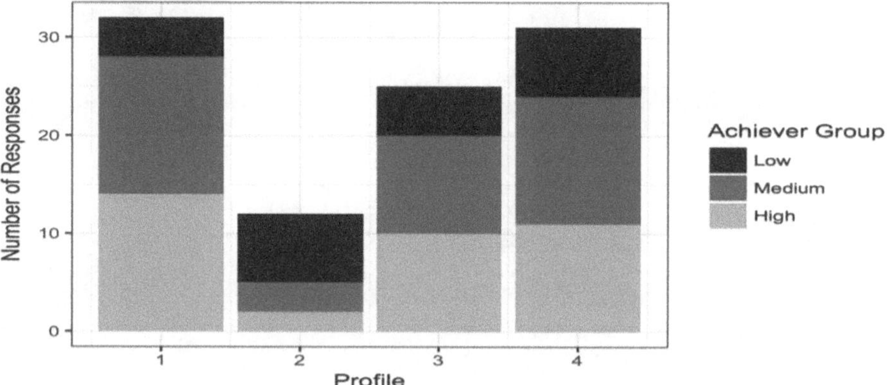

Fig. 12.3 Number of students in achievement group by SRL profiles (intervention group, 10th–12th grades)

Correlating the number of intervention students in each achievement group according to their SRL profiles, we composed the following graph (Fig. 12.3).

A χ^2 test of independence was performed comparing the frequency of the number of intervention students in each of the three achievement groups and the SRL profile they possessed. No significant interactions were found, and the student achievements were as expected according to their SRL profiles (for example: all-positive SRL profile 1 was expected to include a relatively small number of low achievers; all-negative SRL profile 2 was expected to include a relatively small number of high achievers and a relatively large number of low achievers, whereas the mixed SRL profiles 3 and 4 included students from all three achievement groups).

3.1.2 Involvement (Fig. 12.4)

Involvement in the course was imperative for the students' progress. When speaking of involvement, we can focus on the activity of students; hence, investing in an effort to succeed. This score was composed of the following.

Effort

SEM: Synchronic Effort Mark

We looked for a way to calculate and calibrate students' overall effort. As no published measure suited our needs perfectly, we developed the SEM and A-SEM measures for effort mark. All actions taking place during the synchronic lesson were recorded and stored for each student. Student effort during the lessons could be

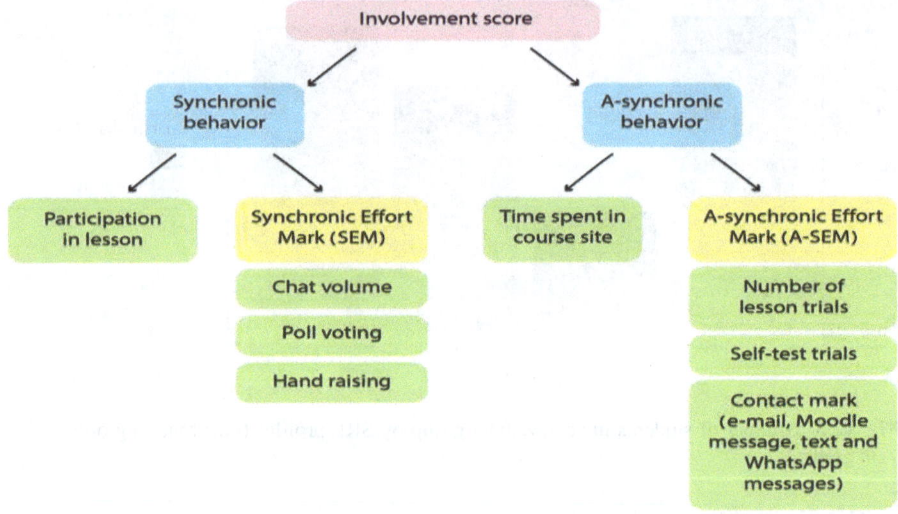

Fig. 12.4 Involvement score components

measured by voluntary actions during these lessons,[2] such as chat-volume (placing messages in the chat area), hand-raising (asking questions, participating or reacting by request) or poll-voting (poll-like questions were used as a class exercise during the lessons and students were expected to cast their vote when asked to do so). These three synchronic effort components were counted and were scaled together to form a unified synchronic effort mark (SEM).

Plotting the SEM by SRL profiles resulted in the following graph (Fig. 12.5).

There was a statistically significant difference between groups as determined by one-way ANOVA $F(3,99) = 14.77$; $p < 0.0001$; Post hoc comparisons using the Tukey HSD test indicated that the mean score for the SEM of SRL profile 1 ($M = 14.482$, $SD = 5.243$) was significantly higher than the SEM of SRL profile 2 ($M = 8.625$, $SD = 4.137$) $p < 0.01$, the SEM of profile 3 ($M = 5.624$, $SD = 3.754$) $p < 0.0001$, and the SEM of profile 4 (7.885, $SD = 6.800$) $p < 0.0001$. However, there were no other differences between the other SEMs of the other profiles.

Taken together, these results suggest that higher synchronic efforts (SEMs) might have affected the SRL profile possessed by the student. It should be noted that the difference was recorded between the all-positive SRL profile (profile 1) and all-other SRL profiles (profiles 2, 3 and 4). The results suggest that when students make an effort and keep actively involved in the lesson, they either already possess an all-positive SRL profile (SRL profile 1) or by doing so have improved their SRL skills over time and shifted their SRL profile toward a positive SRL profile.

[2]Participation in the synchronic lesson (although not a voluntary action) was also considered as synchronic behavior since it is an action related to the synchronic lesson, but since there were no differences in the SEM when absent, the existence of this component is merely acknowledged.

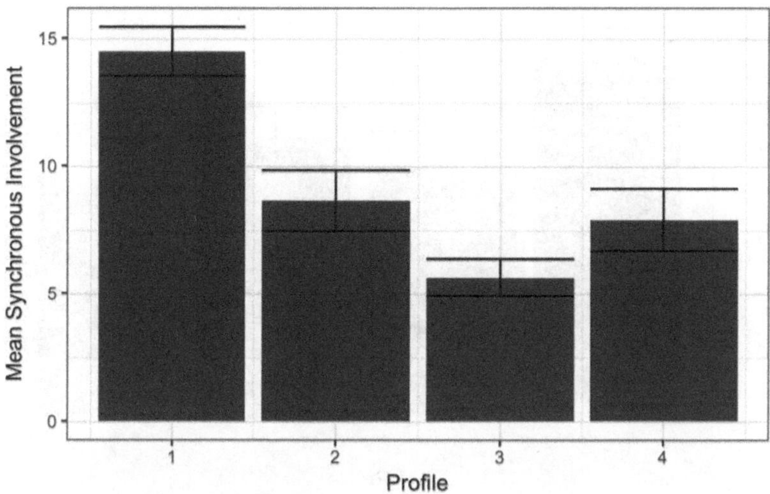

Fig. 12.5 SEM by SRL profiles (intervention group. 10th–12th grades)

A-SEM: A-Synchronic Effort Mark

Student effort during A-synchronic activity could be measured by recording all optional activities, such as number of student trials in homework task assignments: each assignment had two optional trials and students could have tried both trials (in order to improve their score), one trial (in order to do the homework duties alone), or no trials at all (if they failed to do their homework); students could self-assess their knowledge by answering self-tests and they had the option to contact the teacher in several ways: emailing the teacher using the course email address, messaging the teacher via the Moodle system, text-message or WhatsApp the teacher by cell-phone. All of these were non-obligatory features of the course, and if any students used these features, it signified as making an effort in the course.[3] These three A-synchronic effort components were counted for each student and were scaled together to form a unified A-synchronic effort mark (A-SEM). The calculated highest A-SEM for any student was 78%. Plotting the A-SEM by SRL profiles resulted in the following graph (Fig. 12.6).

There was a statistically significant difference between groups as determined by one-way ANOVA F(3,90) = 4.96; $p < 0.001$; Post hoc comparisons using the Tukey HSD test indicated that the mean score for the A-SEM of SRL profile 1 ($M = 46.90$, SD = 19.298) was significantly different than the mean score for the A-SEM of SRL

[3] Time spent at the site was also considered as a-synchronic behavior since it is an action related to the a-synchronic assignments; students could have spent more or less time at the site while performing their homework assignments or revising the learning materials. The existence of this component is merely acknowledged, since it is impossible to differentiate the actual time of student engagement or idle connectivity to the site.

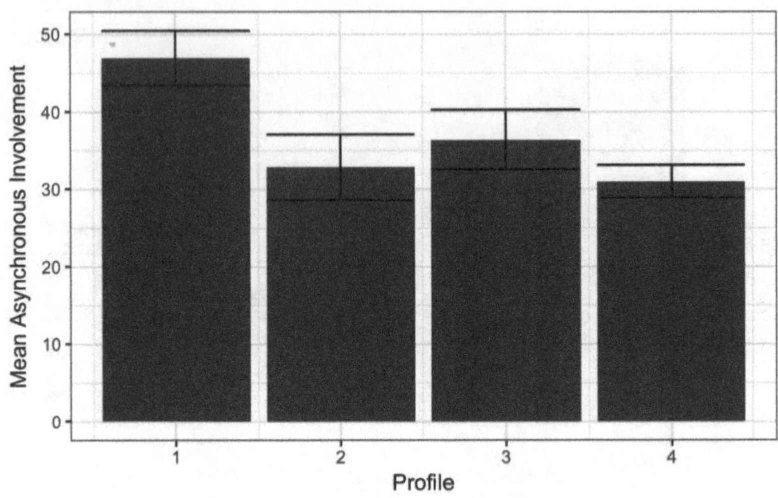

Fig. 12.6 A-SEM by SRL profiles (intervention group. 10th–12th grades)

profile 4 ($M = 30.925$, SD = 10.809) $p < 0.01$. However, there were no other differences between the other A-SEMs of the other profiles.

Taken together, these results suggest that higher A-synchronic efforts (A-SEMs) might have affected the SRL profile possessed by the student. It should however be noted that, surprisingly, the difference calculated was not between the all-positive SRL profile (profile 1) and the all-negative SRL profile (profile 2) but between the all-positive SRL profile (profile 1) and the almost all-negative SRL profile (profile 4). The results suggest that when students make an effort in non-obligatory tasks, they are more likely to possess an all-positive SRL profile (profile 1) or by doing so have improved their SRL skills and shifted their SRL profile toward a positive SRL profile over time.

- A moderate though significant correlation was found by using the Spearman non-parametric analysis between student synchronic effort marks (SEMs) and their A-synchronic effort marks (A-SEMs) ($r_s = 0.47$, $p < 0.05$).
- A moderate though significant correlation was found between student A-synchronic effort marks (A-SEMs) and their matriculation score ($r_s = 0.55$ $p < 0.05$).
- No correlation was found between student synchronic effort marks (SEM) and their matriculation scores.

Students stated in their interviews that they made various degrees of contact efforts with either teacher or tutor during their studies whenever questions or need occurred.

Quote 16: "*I ask questions by privately text messaging the teacher.*"
Quote 17: "*If I don't understand something, I ask friends or family, or the class or teacher using WhatsApp. If I was in the lesson, I use the chat area.*"

Quote 18: "*I write messages in the chat area during the synchronic lessons or open the microphone at the end of the lesson and ask, or WhatsApp.*"

These findings mean that there is a positive relationship between different types of effort; furthermore, it is important for students to make a conscious effort in order to succeed and achieve higher scores. SEM proved to be very important in relation to a positive SRL profile; A-SEM proved to be important to success and as a means to achieve higher scores: by participating in the lesson and doing homework assignments and after-school activities that are related to the course, such as revising materials and putting extra time and thought and performing more trials in order to improve scores, as well as reaching out to the teacher in order to ask questions related to the learning material, homework or even just to talk about general interests, the students become more successful.

Chats During the Synchronic Lesson and as a Feature of Synchronic Behavior

All students' messages from the chat area during the synchronic lesson were counted and chat type percentage over the course of 3 years is shown in Fig. 12.7.

As can be seen in Fig. 12.7, the majority of chat messages were Chemistry content-related messages (63%). This indicates that students were engaged in the lesson and asked about and/or widely used the scientific terminology. Social content messages (12%), technical messages (11%), and administrative messages (11%) accounted for most of the remaining messages.

Owing to the vast amount of data collected over the period of 3 years, chats were divided into six parts (each of the 3 years of studies (y1–y3) was divided into two semesters (s1, s2)) and their mean values were calculated. We can follow the trend changes in the number of each chat category over time.

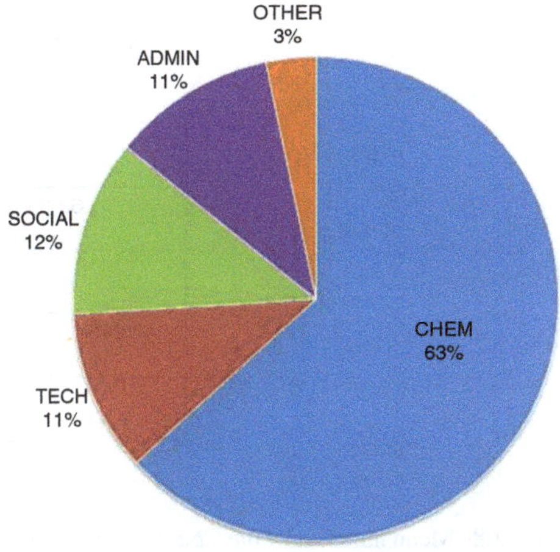

Fig. 12.7 Total 3 year chat type message percentage

Chemistry-Related Chat Messages

The number of these types of messages increased steadily until the end of the second semester of the 11th grade (y2s2), where we then notice a decrease in the number of these types of chat messages. The reason can be rooted in the methodological change of teaching the synchronic lessons in the 12th grade, which resulted in fewer lesson numbers. In the 12th grade the students practiced the material they had learned during the synchronic lessons themselves (as opposed to exercising by a-synchronic task assignments after the synchronic lesson took place). Fewer messages were generated during the lessons, but overall the trend was positive throughout the 3 years of the course.

The changes in the mean numbers of the Chemistry-related messages by grades (y1–y3) and semesters (s1, s2) are presented in Fig. 12.8.

Significant differences were found between the second semester of the 11th grade (y2s2) and the second semester of the 10th grade (y1s2): $S = 20.5$; $0.01 < p < 0.05$, between the second and first semesters of the 11th grade (y2s2, y2s1): $S = 84$; $p < 0.001$, between the first semesters of the 12th grade (y3s1) and the 11th grade (y2s1): $S = -41.5$; $0.001 < p < 0.01$, between the first semester of the 12th grade (y3s1) and the second semester of the 11th grade (y2s2): $S = -47.5$; $0.001 < p < 0.01$, and between the second semesters of the 12th grade (y3s2) and the 11th grade (y2s2): $S = -59$; $0.001 < p < 0.01$.

Technical-Related Chat Messages

The number of these types of messages decreased until the end of the second semester of the 11th grade (y2s2) where we notice an increase in the quantity of these types of chat messages. The reason can be rooted in two major changes that occurred:

1. An upgrade of the Learning Management System (Moodle), which confused the students at the beginning of the 12th grade, and since time issues arose causing student absences, constant coaxing efforts by the teaching staff in order to get the

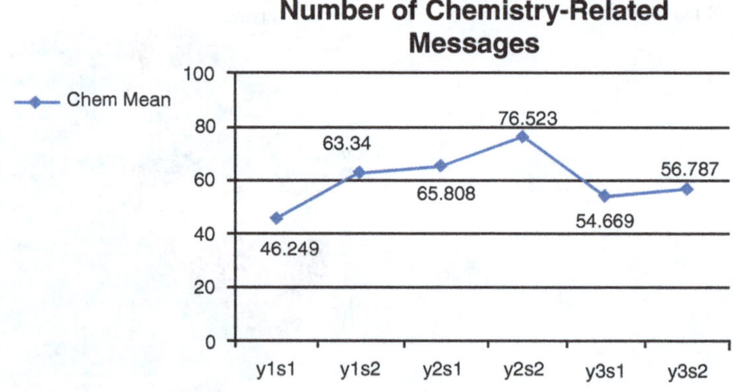

Fig. 12.8 Mean numbers of the Chemistry-related messages vs. grades (y1–y3) and semesters (s1, s2)

students to connect to the lesson in the first weeks were needed. This resulted in dealing with the same technical problems repeatedly whenever a student connected for the first time to the synchronic lesson.

2. A state of the art studio was built in order to have a place to conduct and record the synchronic lessons. Many difficulties emerged in the run-in phase during the third year (12th grade) until all technical problems were resolved. Overall, the trend was negative throughout the 3-year course. The changes in the mean numbers of the technical-related messages according to grades (y1–y3) and semesters (s1, s2) are presented in Fig. 12.9.

Significant differences were found between the second semester of the 11th grade (y2s2) and the second semester of the 10th grade (y1s2): $S = -32$; $0.001 < p < 0.01$, between the second and first semesters of the 11th grade (y2s2, y2s1): $S = -42.5$; $0.001 < p < 0.01$, between the first semester of the 12th grade (y3s1) and the second semester of the 11th grade (y2s2): $S = 33$; $0.001 < p < 0.01$, and between the second semesters of the 12th grade (y3s2) and the first semester of the 10th grade (y1s1): $S = -16$; $0.01 < p < 0.05$.

Social-Related Chat Messages

The number of these types of messages increased steadily until the end of the second semester of the 12th grade (y3s2). We do notice a slight decrease in the 11th grade (y2s1, y2s2), and this can be a result of the beginning of the MOE external exams for these students at this time. This caused them to concentrate more on their day-to-day school work rather than socialize with students outside of their own school. Overall, the trend was positive throughout the 3-year course. The changes in the mean numbers of the social related messages according to grades (y1–y3) and semesters (s1, s2) are presented in Fig. 12.10.

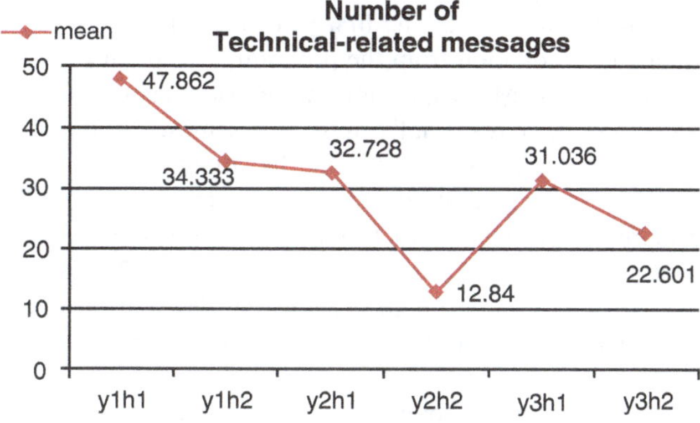

Fig. 12.9 Mean numbers of the technical-related messages vs. grades (y1–y3) and semesters (s1, s2)

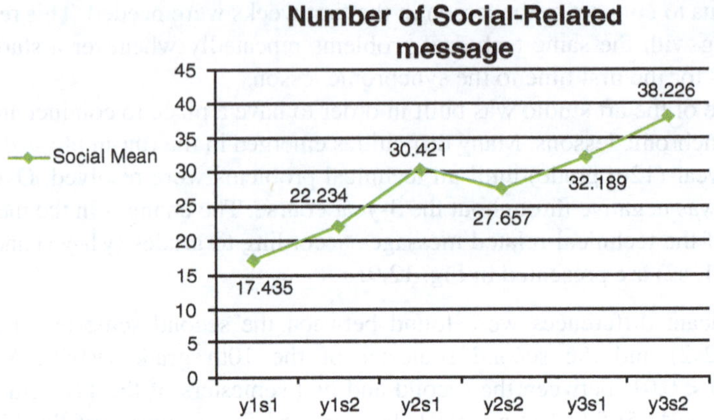

Fig. 12.10 Mean numbers of the social-related messages vs. grades (y1–y3) and semesters (s1, s2)

Significant differences were found between the first semester of the 11th grade (y2s1) and the first semester of the 10th grade (y1s1): $S = 19.5$; $0.01 < p < 0.05$, between the second semester of the 12th grade (y3s2) and the second semester of the 11th grade (y2s2): $S = 48.5$; $0.01 < p < 0.05$, and between the second semesters of the 12th grade (y3s2) and the first semester of the 10th grade (y1s1): $S = 22.5$; $0.001 < p < 0.01$.

Administrative-Related Chat Messages

The number of these types of messages increased in the 10th grade (y1s1, y1s2) and decreased only in the second semester of the 11th grade (y2s2). There was a dramatic increase in these types of chat messages in the 12th grade (then decreasing to the previous mean value (y1s2, y2s1)). This can be explained by the novelty of the program and the fact that this was the first year that schools had to deal with the unknown situation of graduation from the program, and that itself involved a great deal of bureaucratic work. Many questions were asked about the technicalities of the final matriculation exam (especially in the first semester of the 12th grade since many forms were to be filled out), and since the students were studying for other exams at their schools, many administrative issues emerged during the 12th grade that had to be addressed during the synchronic lessons. Overall, the trend was mildly positive until the end of the 11th grade (y2s2), dropped (y2s2), and shot up sharply only to continue to drop again during the 12th grade. The changes in the mean numbers of the administrative-related messages according to grades and semesters are presented in Fig. 12.11.

Significant differences were found between the second semester of the 11th grade (y2s2) and the second semester of the 10th grade (y1s2): $S = -17$; $0.001 < p < 0.01$, between the second and first semesters of the 11th grade (y2s2, y2s1): $S = -60$; $p < 0.001$, between the first semester of the 12th grade (y3s1) and

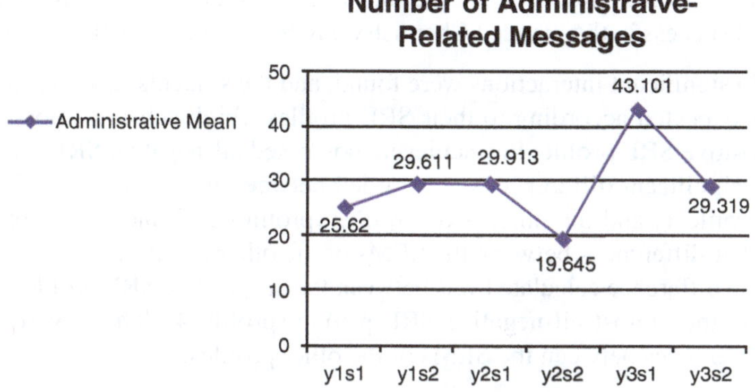

Fig. 12.11 Mean numbers of the administrative-related messages vs. grades (y1–y3) and semesters (s1, s2)

the second semester of the 11th grade (y2s2): $S = 42.5$; $0.001 < p < 0.01$, and between the second semester of the 12th grade (y3s2) and the second semester of the 11th grade (y2s2): $S = 30$; $0.001 < p < 0.01$.

Other Related Chat Messages

Other Related Chat Messages will not be discussed since they are not about any specific topic but contained sporadic messages such as "Thank you", "Sorry, I'm late", etc.

4 Conclusions

The main results that were found significant are summarized in this section:

Q1. What are the students' SRL profiles, and how do they change during 10th–12th grades?

(a) A four SRL profile solution based on modified LASSI questionnaires analysis was suggested.
(b) It is unlikely that dropout students can possess an all-positive SRL profile.
(c) Chemistry students will possess a more positive SRL profile than dropouts.
(d) The remaining intervention students were not likely to possess the all-negative SRL profile as much as the control students.
(e) Remaining intervention students developed SRL skills over time. Both intervention and control groups were not initially different with respect to the mean scores for the LASSI categories but remaining intervention students were not likely to possess the negative SRL profile as much as the control students.

Q2. Is there a correlation between the intervention students' SRL profiles and the level of success in the blended Chemistry environment during 10th–12th grades?

(a) No significant interactions were found, and the students' achievements were as expected according to their SRL profiles: (high achievers possessed all-positive SRL profile; low achievers possessed all-negative SRL profile, etc.)
(b) A significant difference was recorded between the all-positive SRL profile (profile 1) and the other SRL profiles (profiles 2, 3 and 4). There were no other differences between the SEMs of the other profiles.
(c) The difference calculated was between the all-positive SRL profile (profile 1) and the almost all-negative SRL profile (profile 4). There were no other differences between the SEMs of the other profiles.

5 Discussion

This study looks at Self-Regulation in an innovative way by analyzing high school student's SRL profiles and success with the aid of data mining, while learning in a virtual course environment that teaches Chemistry. The novelty of this research lays in the uniqueness of the learning environment setting, the interaction between the declarative SRL profile (by the LASSI questionnaires), and actual learning process and scores, and finally the length of time students were followed was large (3 years), although shorter terms were applied in different settings (Akçapınar, Altun, and Coşgun (2014); Akçapınar (2015); Preidys and Sakalauskas (2010); Ning and Downing (2015); Schmidt, Rosenberg, & Beymer, 2018). In this study, we show that SRL profiles can be isolated from data gained by student's self-declarative LASSI questionnaires and can be related to success measures that are actually derived by quantitative independent means resulting in relationships between them: a relationship between negative SRL profiles (with limitation to the categories that were checked) and students' dropout. This finding can serve in some cases as "alert-signs" for educators since they can indicate that students are prone to dropout. Both groups suffered from this phenomenon, and various reasons could have caused it: a certain image of the chosen subject (Chemistry), which might not have been realistic, the effect of novelty wearing off over time, disappointment and, therefore, a loss of concentration resulting in reluctance to apply the needed effort in their studies or difficulties, such as problems in understanding the content matter, time issues, and boredom.

Students that were more involved in the course by performing assignments of different types were more likely to attain higher scores. This finding aligns with Bannert, Reimann, and Sonnenberg (2014) who found that more regulation event types appear in successful student's behavior, such as preparing activities (orientation and planning) before they process the information to be learned and deep elaboration of information while reading. Similarly, Ning and Downing (2015) describe cognitive-oriented self-regulated learner and behavioral-oriented self-regulated learner profiles while searching for latent profiles by partly utilizing (among other tools) two of the LASSI categories used in this study: motivation (MOT) and test-strategies (TST). Motivation was found to be linked to SRL profiles by more than one researcher (Ning & Downing, 2015; Scardamalia & Bereiter, 1991, 1994; Sharp, Pocklington, & Weindling, 2002; Weinstein et al., 2002; Zusho & Edwards, 2011), although in this study, not all SRL profiles exhibit motivation, and distinction cannot be made by eyeing this LASSI category alone.

Careful application of some of the tools and patterns presented here is recommended for further applications in the educational field. These findings alone cannot be used in order to discriminate between more and less successful learners as a "one-all" solution, since educational systems are complex. We agree with Bannert et al. (2014), who state that it can only work in the same environment and context in which it has been identified and that ethical concerns can subsequently emerge by doing so; we must bear in mind that although the amount of data mined over the period of 3 years of research is great (number of chat messages, number of LASSI questionnaires etc.)—the sample size is relatively small ($N = 23$), and therefore replication studies are needed in order to reinforce the results. Further research is also needed beyond the scope of the classroom SRL profile change. It is possible to analyze the data in order to follow the personal SRL profile changes for each student over the 3 years in the course. This can supply a larger and more concrete picture that perhaps can be used to predict success in this kind of learning environment and enable educators to improve student's outcomes by mere knowledge of their personal SRL profiles and the factors that could affect them and cause changes in them over time.

Acknowledgements We thank the Meital Research Foundation and the Davidson Institute for funding. We thank Mrs. Yetty Varon whose statistical expertise was invaluable.

References

Akçapınar, G. (2015). Profiling students' approaches to learning through moodle logs. In *Multidisciplinary Academic Conference on Education, Teaching and Learning (MAC-ETL 2015)*. Chudenicka: MAC Prague consulting Ltd.

Akçapınar, G., Altun, A., & Coşgun, E. (2014). Investigating students' interaction profile in an online learning environment with clustering. In *14th IEEE International Conference on Advanced Learning Technologies (ICALT2014), IEEE Computer Society: 7–9 July, 2014, Athens, Greece* (pp. 109–111). Washington, DC: IEEE.

Bannert, M., Reimann, P., & Sonnenberg, C. (2014). Process mining techniques for analysing patterns and strategies in students' self-regulated learning. *Metacognition and Learning, 9*(2), 161–185.

Bergman, L. R., & El-Khouri, B. M. (1999). Studying individual patterns of development using I-states as objects analysis (ISOA). *Biometrical Journal, 41*(6), 753–770.

Butler, D. L., & Winne, P. H. (1995). Feedback and self-regulated learning: A theoretical synthesis. *Review of Educational Research, 65*(3), 245–281.

Castro, F., Vellido, A., Nebot, À., & Mugica, F. (2007). Applying data mining techniques to e-learning problems. In *Evolution of teaching and learning paradigms in intelligent environment* (pp. 183–221). Berlin: Springer.

Chen, G.-D., Liu, C.-C., Ou, K.-L., & Liu, B.-J. (2000). Discovering decision knowledge from web log portfolio for managing classroom processes by applying decision tree and data cube technology. *Journal of Educational Computing Research, 23*, 305.

Cho, M. H. (2004). *The effects of design strategies for promoting students' self-regulated learning skills on students' self-regulation and achievements in online learning environments.* Bloomington, IN: Association for Educational Communications and Technology.

Landis, R. J., & Koch, G. G. (1977). The measurement of observer agreement for categorical data. *Biometrics, 33*(1), 159–174.

Ley, K., & Young, D. B. (2001). Instructional principles for self-regulation. *Educational Technology Research and Development, 49*(2), 93–103.

Ning, H. K., & Downing, K. (2015). A latent profile analysis of University students' self-regulated learning strategies. *Studies in Higher Education, 40*, 1328. https://doi.org/10.1080/03075079.2014.880832

O'Neill, K., Singh, G., & O'Donoghue, J. (2004). Implementing eLearning programmes for higher education: A review of the literature. *Journal of Information Technology Education, 3*, 313.

Pintrich, P. R., & De Groot, E. V. (1990). Motivational and self-regulated learning components of classroom academic performance. *Journal of Educational Psychology, 82*(1), 33.

Preidys, S., & Sakalauskas, L. (2010). Analysis of students' study activities in virtual learning environments using data mining methods. *Ukio Technologinis ir Ekonominis Vystymas, 16*(1), 94–108.

R Development Core Team. (2017). *R: A language and environment for statistical computing.* Vienna: R Foundation for Statistical Computing. Retrieved from https://www.r-project.org/

Romero, C., Ventura, S., & García, E. (2008). Data mining in course management systems: Moodle case study and tutorial. *Computers & Education, 51*(1), 368–384.

Rosenberg, J. M., Schmidt, J. A., & Beymer, P. N. (2017). *prcr: Person-centered analysis (R package version 0.1.5.).* Retrieved from https://CRAN.R-project.org/package=prcr

Scardamalia, M., & Bereiter, C. (1991). Higher levels of agency for children in knowledge building: A challenge for the design of new knowledge media. *The Journal of the Learning Sciences, 1*(1), 37–68.

Scardamalia, M., & Bereiter, C. (1994). Computer support for knowledge-building communities. *The Journal of the Learning Sciences, 3*(3), 265–283.

Schmidt, J. A., Rosenberg, J. M., & Beymer, P. (2018). A person- in-context approach to student engagement in science: Examining learning activities and choice. *Journal of Research in Science Teaching, 55*, 19. https://doi.org/10.1002/tea.21409

Sharp, C., Pocklington, K., & Weindling, D. (2002). Study support and the development of the self-regulated learner. *Educational Research, 44*(1), 29–41.

Sheard, J., Ceddia, J., Hurst, J., & Tuovinen, J. (2003). Inferring student learning behaviour from website interactions: A usage analysis. *Education and Information Technologies, 3*, 245–266. https://doi.org/10.1023/A:1026360026073

Sim, J., & Wright, C. C. (2005). The kappa statistic in reliability studies: Use, interpretation, and sample size requirements. *Physical Therapy, 85*(3), 257–268. https://doi.org/10.1093/ptj/85.3.257

Tallent-Runnels, M. K., Thomas, J. A., Lan, W. Y., & Cooper, S. (2006). Teaching courses online: A review of the research. *Review of Educational Research, 76*(1), 93–135.

Tsai, C. W. (2011). Achieving effective learning effects in the blended course: A combined approach of online self-regulated learning and collaborative learning with initiation. *Cyberpsychology, Behavior, and Social Networking, 14*(9), 505–510.

Weinstein, C. E., Palmer, D. R., & Shulte, A. C. (2002). *LASSI: Learning and study strategies inventory* (2nd ed.). Clearwater, FL: H&H Publishing Company, Inc..

Zemsky, R., & Massy, W. F. (2004). *Thwarted innovation. What happened to e-learning and why. A final report for the Weather station project of the learning alliance.* Philadelphia, PA: University of Pennsylvania in Cooperation with the Thomson Corporation.

Zimmerman, B. J. (1989). A social cognitive view of self-regulated academic learning. *Journal of Educational Psychology, 81*(3), 329–339.

Zimmerman, B. J. (1990). self regulating learning and academic achievement: An overview. *Educational Psychologist, 25*(1), 3–17.
Zimmerman, B. J. (2008). Investigating self-regulation and motivation: Historical background, methodological developments, and future prospects. *American Educational Research Journal, 45*(1), 166–183. https://doi.org/10.3102/0002831207312909
Zimmerman, B. J., Bonner, S., & Kovach, R. (1996). *Developing self-regulated learners: Beyond achievement to self-efficacy*. Washington, DC: APA.
Zusho, A., & Edwards, K. (2011). Self-regulation and achievement goals in the college classroom. *New Directions for Teaching and Learning, 126*, 21–31.

Rachel Rosanne Eidelman earned her B.Sc. in Chemistry (Hebrew University, Jerusalem, Israel), M.Sc. Science Education (with honors) (Tel Aviv University, Tel Aviv, Israel) and Ph.D. (Weizmann Institute of Science, Rehovot, Israel). Rachel Eidelman has been a certified leading Chemistry teacher and educator (K-12) for 26 years, graduate of teachers-leaders program (2010–2011), and a chemistry coordinator for 17 years.

During her PhD studies, Rachel founded and developed the Chemistry Online Blended Learning Environment (COBLE), a novel program for online high school Chemistry learning. As of today, there are almost 400 students from all over Israel attending the program.

Research interests: Self-Regulated Learning, Educational Data-Mining, Chemistry and science teaching, adapting, developing and personalizing learning materials for high-school students.

Joshua M. Rosenberg earned his PhD at Michigan State University in Educational Psychology and Educational Technology. He is an Assistant Professor of STEM Education at the University of Tennessee, Knoxville. His research focuses on how learners think of and with data, particularly in science education settings. Dr. Rosenberg teaches classes in science and STEM education, educational technology, and research methods. More information about Dr. Rosenberg can be found at http://joshuamrosenberg.com.

Yael Shwartz is a researcher at the department of science teaching in the Weizmann Institute of science in Israel. Currently, she is the head of the national center for science and technology teachers, and the academic leader of the COBLE program (Chemistry Online Blended Learning environment). Her research interest is focused on scientific literacy, teachers professional development, and integrating ICT into science education.

Dr. Shwartz earned her BSc. in Pharmaceutical Chemistry, at Bar-Ilan University and a Ph.D. (direct track) in Science Education, at Weizmann Institute of Science. She also held a research fellow position at the School of Education, University of Michigan, USA. In the past, she taught high-school chemistry for 10 years. She has been involved in inquiry-based curriculum development, implementation, and assessment both in Israel and the US.

Chapter 13
Unraveling the Research on Deeper Learning: A Review of the Literature

Stylianos Sergis and Demetrios Sampson

Abstract Deeper learning (DL) has emerged at the spotlight of educational policies around the world and has gained significant attention from various stakeholders in education (teachers, school leaders, curricula designers, policy makers). This is the result of DL being associated to core competences of the current and future workplaces such as problem-solving, critical thinking, self-regulated learning, and effective collaboration, which are considered as essential for building innovative solutions to wicked global challenges. However, despite this well-acknowledged trend research related to modeling, cultivating and assessing Deeper Learning competences is still at a shaping stage. This is also reflected in the rather limited advancements in the use of digital educational technologies to support the assessment and measurement of DL. In this context, the contribution of this chapter is to perform a systematic literature review of the current state on existing works for modeling DL competences, teaching approaches applied to cultivate them as well as, methods and instruments proposed for assessing and measuring DL.

1 Introduction

Deeper learning (DL) has been at the spotlight of the public discourse on educational reforms, being related to core competences of the current and future workplaces such as problem-solving, self-regulation in learning, effective collaboration which are considered essential for producing innovative solutions to wicked global challenges (Deloitte, 2016; Surr & Redding, 2017; The William and Flora Hewlett Foundation, 2012). In essence, being a Deeper Learner requires proficiency in a set

S. Sergis (✉)
Department of Digital Systems, University of Piraeus, Piraeus, Greece

D. Sampson
Department of Digital Systems, University of Piraeus, Piraeus, Greece

School of Education, Curtin University, Perth, WA, Australia
e-mail: sampson@unipi.gr; demetrios.sampson@curtin.edu.au

D. Sampson et al. (eds.), *Learning Technologies for Transforming Large-Scale Teaching, Learning, and Assessment*, https://doi.org/10.1007/978-3-030-15130-0_13

of holistic competences that span solid understanding of core academic content, practice of critical thinking and problem-solving capacity, effective collaboration and communication, as well as self-direction of learning and cultivation of an academic and reflective mindset (Mehta & Fine, 2015). Such competences are becoming vital in the digital society as they describe the autonomous and self-guided learner who will be able to meet the emerging challenges of the workplace (Abbott, Townsend, Johnston-Wilder, & Reynolds, 2009; Fullan, Hill, & Rincon-Gallardo, 2017).

Nevertheless, despite this global trend towards Deeper Learning in school and higher education (e.g., Lathram, Lenz, & Ark, 2016; Surr & Redding, 2017; The William and Flora Hewlett Foundation, 2012), the current landscape of evidence remains sporadic and fragmented (Fullan et al., 2017; Mehta & Fine, 2015). Additionally, this limited level of systematic application is further hindered by a still-shaping understanding of methods and tools for modeling, cultivating, assessing, and measuring Deeper Learning competences (e.g., Conley, 2014; Conley & Darling-Hammond, 2013; Heller & Wolfe, 2015). Finally, there has been limited works on the potential of digital learning technologies in supporting the development (e.g., Dede, 2014; Getting Smart, 2014; Hatala, Beheshitha, & Gasevic, 2016; Van der Ark & Schneider, 2013; Vuchic, 2011) and the assessment (for example, Pirnay-Dummer, Ifenthaler, & Spector, 2010; Spector & Koszalka, 2004)of DL competences

In this context, the contribution of this chapter is to perform a systematic literature review of the current state on existing works for modeling DL competences, teaching approaches applied to cultivate them as well as methods and instruments proposed for assessing and measuring DL. The remainder of this chapter is as follows. Section 2 presents the background of Deeper Learning, discussing existing definitions and conceptualizations of Deeper Learning as well as constituent competence categories. Section 3 outlines the methodology and presents the results of the systematic literature review reported in the chapter. Section 4 discusses the key conclusions of this work and capitalizes on them to outline potential pathways for future work.

2 Background: Deeper Learning

Deeper Learning has been broadly defined as "an umbrella term for the skills and knowledge that students must possess to succeed in twenty-first century jobs and civic life. At its heart is a set of competencies students must master in order to develop a keen understanding of academic content and apply their knowledge to problems in the classroom and on the job" (Van der Ark & Schneider, 2014, p. 10).

Essentially, Deeper Learning refers to the process in which an individual reaches a certain level of proficiency that allows them to transfer what has been learned to different situations and apply it to address new challenges (Fullan et al., 2017;

Pellegrino & Hilton, 2012). Furthermore, a deeper approach to learning can be linked to students' own willingness to engage in a meaningful learning process, by formulating and applying strategies that will support this process (Asikainen & Gijbels, 2017). By contrast, "surface" approaches to learning refer to students employing strategies that primarily focus on memorization and are driven by extrinsic motivations, for example, fear of failure or reward-seeking behavior (Vanthournout, Doche, Gijbels, & Van Petegem, 2014).

Additionally, apart from defining the concept of DL, there have also been different approaches to dissect it to a set of constituent *competence dimensions*. The National Research Council of the United States has proposed a broad classification of the domains that Deeper Learning competences can be attributed to, as follows (Pellegrino & Hilton, 2012):

- The *Cognitive* domain, which refers to competences for reasoning, understanding, and mastering content. Furthermore, it also encapsulates the capacity to transfer this knowledge to other contexts and demonstrate problem-solving and analytical skills.
- The *Intrapersonal* domain, which refers to competences for self-directed and self-regulated learning. Such skills can include regulation of behavior, identification of obstacles to overcome, as well as management of emotions. An academic mindset towards self-efficacy, positive attitudes, and perseverance are critical aspects of this domain.
- The *Interpersonal* domain, which mainly refers to the ability to communicate information and knowledge to others, as well as collaborate effectively to solve problems as part of a group. Additionally, it can also include skills related to understanding and responding to information provided by others.

Furthermore, capitalizing on this broad classification, other approaches to defining Deeper Learning competence dimensions have been proposed. For example, the New Pedagogies for Deeper Learning Consortium has identified six Deep Learning competence dimensions, commonly abbreviated as the 6Cs (Fullan, McEahen, & Quinn, 2016):

- *Character*, namely the capacity to build strong knowledge, capitalizing on critical character traits, such as grit, perseverance, and resilience
- *Citizenship*, namely gaining a deep understanding of diverse and global challenges, values, and opinions. Furthermore, it also refers to the need to build the motivation, attitudes, and skills to solve complex such real-world challenges.
- *Collaboration*, namely the competence for working interdependently as well as jointly in groups, so as to build common understanding and enhance the group's potential with individual traits.
- *Communication*, namely the competence for communicating opinions and findings to diverse audiences in an effective manner.
- *Creativity*, which refers to the capacity to identify and generate innovative ideas and opportunities, as well as the leadership skills to transform these ideas into action.

- *Critical Thinking*, namely the capacity to critically review and assess information, identify patterns, and build understanding so as to be able to apply it in real situations.

Another widely acknowledged categorization has been formulated by the Hewlett & Flora Foundation, which outlines six DL competence dimensions (Van der Ark & Schneider, 2014):

1. *Master core academic content*. This competence dimension explicitly aims to capture the capacity of students to build a strong understanding of the subject domain knowledge as well as to be able to transfer this understanding to solve other problems.
2. *Think critically and solve complex problems*. This competence dimension refers to students using tools and strategies (e.g., collection and analysis of data, inquiry, reasoning, creativity) to formulate and solve problems.
3. *Work collaboratively*. This competence dimension refers to students working in groups to build joint solutions in well/ill- defined problems.
4. *Communicate effectively*. This competence dimension focuses on the capacity to identify effective ways to organize and report on data, findings, and conclusions.
5. *Learn how to learn*. This competence dimension addresses the aspect of self-regulation and self-management of the learning process and progress.
6. *Develop academic mindsets*. This competence dimension refers to the required positive attitudes that students need to build towards the learning process and themselves as competent individuals. This competence dimension is highly linked to the concept of perseverance, namely to engage in academic behaviors that lead to successful completion of tasks, despite obstacles that could emerge.

Table 13.1 depicts a loose mapping between the different classification schemas of Deeper Learning competence dimensions discussed previously.

As the Table 13.1 depicts, despite some conceptual inconsistencies, it is evident that all classifications share a common core of competence dimensions in terms of the underlying focus and scope. These dimensions can be adequately described by the Hewlett & Flora Foundation classification (Van der Ark & Schneider, 2014), and

Table 13.1 Mapping between classifications of deeper learning competence dimensions

Pellegrino and Hilton (2012)	Fullan et al. (2016)	Van der Ark and Schneider (2014)
Cognitive domain		Master core academic content
	Critical thinking Creativity	Think critically and solve complex problems
Interpersonal domain	Collaboration	Work collaboratively
	Communication	Communicate effectively
Intrapersonal domain	Citizenship	Develop academic mindsets
	Character	
		Learn how to learn

therefore this chapter has adopted this classification of Deeper Learning to be included in the review methodology, as reported in the following Sect. 3.

3 Literature Review

3.1 Methodology

The review methodology adopted in this chapter aims to provide a structured way to identify, process, and analyze the research body of literature. The first step of the methodology is to select the keywords and databases that will be used to identify the research works to be analyzed. In this chapter, the main keywords included in the methodology were "deep(er) learning," "21st century skills," "deep approach to learning," and "deep learning approach." Additionally, the use of Boolean operators (OR, AND) among the keywords, as well as antonyms (e.g., "surface learning") was also performed to extend the search results. Regarding digital databases, well-established repositories of scientific journals and international conference proceedings were exploited, as follows:

- Taylor & Francis Online (http://www.tandfonline.com)
- Science Direct (http://www.sciencedirect.com)
- Sage Publications (http://online.sagepub.com)
- SpringerLink (http://link.springer.com)
- Google Scholar (https://scholar.google.gr) (for more general searches)

The identified body of works was then pre-assessed in terms of a set of inclusion and exclusion criteria. These criteria acted as a filter to select the works that were appropriate for this review in terms of content. The inclusion criterion was that publications should describe studies on Deeper Learning, presenting the way that DL was modeled, cultivated and/or measured (where appropriate). The exclusion criteria included: (a) publications not presenting such studies on Deeper Learning, (b) publications not written in English, (c) abstract-only and poster publications were excluded, and (d) duplicate publications and outdated versions of the same publications.

A final set of 38 works were ultimately selected. These works were analysed to address four Research Questions, aligned to the overarching focus of the review as discussed previously, each highlighting a core element of each work in terms of Deeper Learning, namely:

- *Research Question #1*: How has Deeper Learning been instantiated in each work, i.e., which competence dimensions were utilized?
- *Research Question #2*: What teaching approaches have been investigated to cultivate Deeper Learning competences?
- *Research Question #3*: What methods have been used to measure Deeper Learning competences?

- *Research Question #4*: What instruments have been proposed and used to measure Deeper Learning competences?

The results of this analysis (depicted in full in the Appendix 1) are discussed in the following section, against the aforementioned Research Questions.

3.2 Results

3.2.1 Research Question #1: Instantiations of Deeper Learning

Figure 13.1 depicts the results of the analysis regarding how DL has been instantiated in the existing works. It is mentioned that the results of Fig. 13.1 refer to instances of these competences that were explicitly investigated in each work. This means that in each work reviewed, a competence dimension was considered to be included if the research design explicitly measured and studied it through a specific method or instrument.

As Fig. 13.1 shows, the most commonly investigated competence dimension of DL is "*Master Core Academic Content*" ($N = 25$, $x = 66\%$). This finding can be explained since this competence is very closely aligned to most existing educational practices around the world, which posit the need to cultivate students' knowledge (and skills) on a given subject matter. It can be also noted that the competence dimensions "*Develop academic mindsets*" and "*Learn how to learn*" have been commonly explored as well ($N = 20$, $x = 53\%$, $N = 16$, $x = 42\%$, respectively). These two competence dimensions might have received limited prior attention as standalone competence dimensions outside the context of DL. Therefore, with the emergence of DL as a hosting concept, more research was placed on them so as to

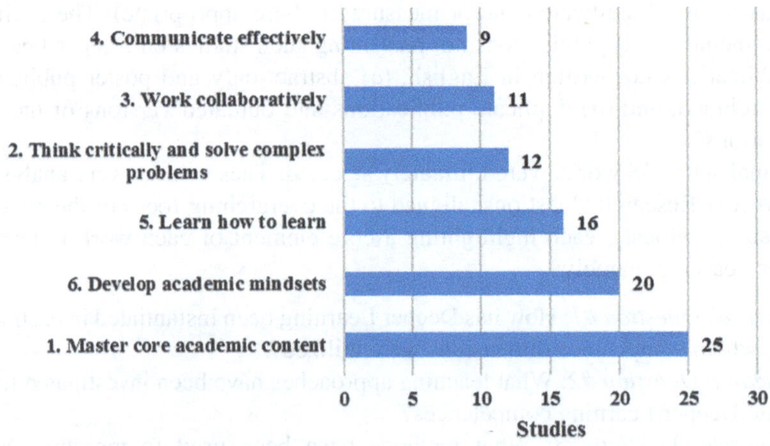

Fig. 13.1 Frequencies of deeper learning competence categories addressed

investigate and study them, both as standalone competences, but more importantly, as part of the competence set that has been defined as DL.

On the other hand (yet following the same trail of arguments), the competence "Think critical and solve complex problems" was less frequently investigated (at least in an explicit manner) ($N = 12$, $x = 32\%$). This could be explained by the fact that problem-solving has been the focus of extensive research, in its own regard (e.g., OECD, 2017; Peltier & Vannest, 2017; Zervas & Sampson, 2018). Therefore, the DL research community already possessed a good starting point in investigating problem-solving, as a standalone competence. However, as it will be discussed in Sect. 4, despite this existing body of knowledge, the DL community may potentially need to revisit these competences to understand how problem-solving relates and influences the other DL competences, under the lens of a holistic DL student profile. This means that research could aim to investigate how the diverse DL competences are inter-related and how a students' level of proficiency in each one might affect the others. Finally, competences on *Working collaboratively* and "*Communicating effectively*" are the least frequently explored in an explicit manner ($N = 11$, $x = 29\%$, $N = 9$, $x = 24\%$, respectively).

3.2.2 Research Question #2: Cultivating Deeper Learning Competences

Figure 13.2 depicts the results of the analysis regarding the teaching approaches that have been employed to cultivate DL.

As Fig. 13.2 shows, the most dominant method is the problem-based approach ($N = 15$, $x = 39\%$), whereas the project-based approach is also frequently exploited ($N = 11$, $x = 29\%$). In nine works, no specific teaching approach was mentioned and the remaining works exploited the inquiry-based and the design-based approaches ($N = 2$, $x = 5\%$ and $N = 1$, $x = 3\%$ respectively). These findings outline a pattern of understanding that DL can be effectively cultivated through certain teaching approaches (i.e., problem-, inquiry-, and project-based) that actively engage students

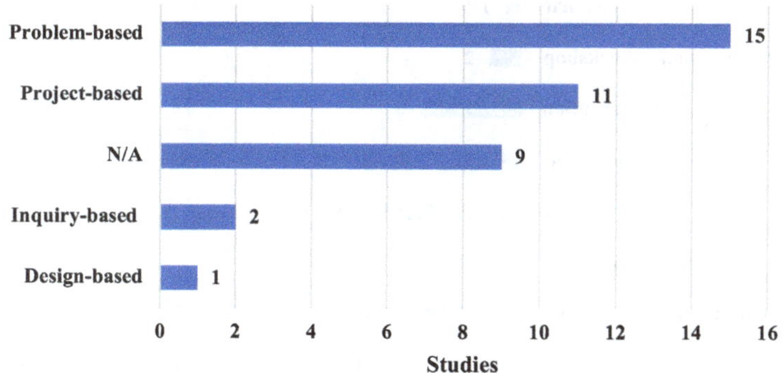

Fig. 13.2 Frequencies of teaching approaches used for cultivating deeper learning

in (collaborative) hands-on activities for addressing real challenges (e.g., Dolmans, Loyens, Marcq, & Gijbels, 2016).

Therefore, it is reasonable to infer that there is a certain level of agreement regarding the teaching approaches that can be used to cultivate DL based on evidence that early studies have reported. For example, Murrant et al. (2015) reported an increase in specific students' DL competences after redesigning their course from a lecture-based approach to a project-based approach. Similar results were also reported by other researchers comparing project- and problem-based approaches to other teaching approaches, such as Altamirano and Jaurez (2013), Antonenko, Jahanzad, and Greenwood (2014), Lloyd (2014) and Wijnen, Loyens, Smeets, Kroeze, and van der Molen (2016). Finally, a similar conclusion has also been highlighted in reports from (inter)national organizations that investigate how real-life schools attempt to operationalize DL in their daily practice (e.g., Fullan et al., 2016; Huberman, Bitter, Anthony, & O'Day, 2014; Mehta & Fine, 2015). These reports also highlighted the aforementioned teaching methods as a common factor driving the schools towards effective DL competence cultivation.

3.2.3 Research Question #3: Methods for measuring Deeper Learning

Figure 13.3 depicts the analysis of research works in terms of the methods that have been used to measure Deeper Learning.

As Fig. 13.3 shows, the majority of research designs employed questionnaires for measuring DL competences ($N = 27$, $x = 71\%$). Engaging students in creating artifacts and assignments in (collaborative) project tasks was also frequently employed ($N = 12$, $x = 32\%$), followed by quiz assessment tasks ($N = 11$, $x = 29\%$) and interviews with the students ($N = 10$, $x = 26\%$). Less frequent methods included observations from the teachers on the level of DL competences showcased by the students ($N = 6$, $x = 16\%$), engaging students in presentation tasks or workshops ($N = 2$, $x = 5\%$) and teacher-reported assessment rubrics ($N = 1$, $x = 3\%$).

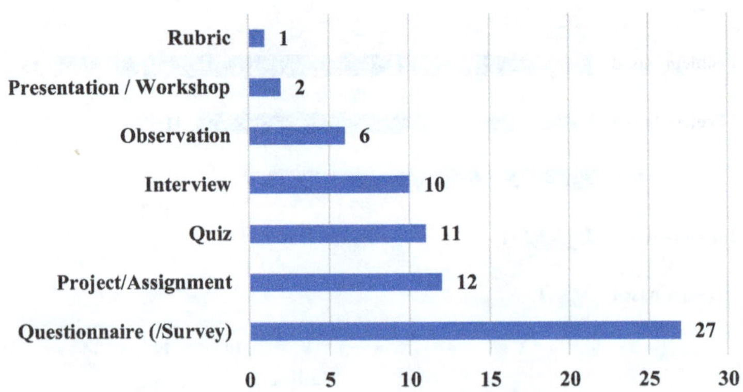

Fig. 13.3 Frequencies of different methods for measuring deeper learning

It is worthy to gain a better understanding of how these methods have been used to measure each of the different DL competences. Figure 13.4 presents this additional layer of analysis. As Fig. 13.4 showcases, the DL competence dimension "*Master core academic content*" is primarily measured through quiz tests ($N = 13$, $x = 34\%$) and assignments in project activities ($N = 13$, $x = 34\%$). Furthermore, a significant body of works also employed questionnaire instruments for measuring this competence ($N = 12$, $x = 32\%$), mainly aiming to capture the students' perceptions on their level of proficiency. Apart from these methods, a smaller portion of works adopted observations from the teachers ($N = 4$, $x = 11\%$), interviews with the students for gaining an insight on their perceptions ($N = 3$, $x = 8\%$), as well as engaging them in presentations to showcase their level of understanding ($N = 1$, $x = 3\%$).

Regarding measuring the competence dimension "*Think critically and solve complex problems*," project assignments was the main method ($N = 7$, $x = 19\%$), followed by questionnaires ($N = 6$, $x = 16\%$) which focused on students' perceptions and strategies used to solve the problems. Quiz tests were less frequently used for measuring this competence ($N = 5$, $x = 13\%$), and mainly referred to large-scale high-stake assessments, such as the Programme for International Student Assessment (PISA) tests (OECD, 2017), OECD Test for schools (Greenhill & Martin, 2014),

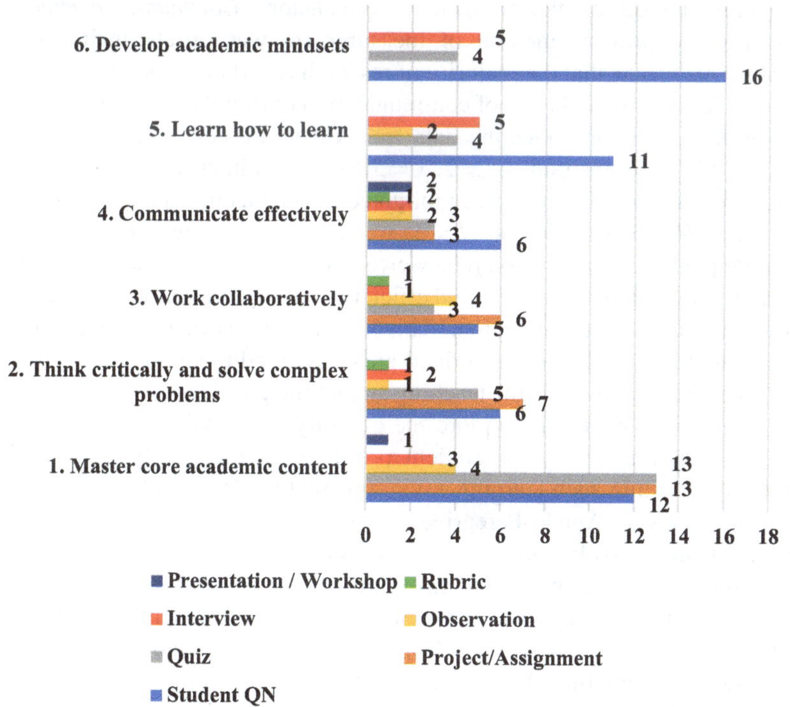

Fig. 13.4 Frequencies of different methods for measuring each competence category of deeper learning

Smarter Balanced Assessment Test (Herman, La Torre Matrundola, & Wang, 2015) and Partnership for Assessment of Readiness for College and Careers Test (Herman et al., 2015). Interviews, rubrics and teacher observations were also reported in the literature; however they were very rarely adopted ($N = 2$, $x = 5\%$, $N = 1$, $x = 3\%$ and $N = 1$, $x = 3\%$ respectively).

Regarding measuring the competence dimension "*Work collaboratively*," (collaborative) project assignments was the main method ($N = 6$, $x = 16\%$) aiming to elicit how each student contributed to the group and how the group managed individual benefits and potential conflicts. Questionnaires ($N = 5$, $x = 13\%$) were also frequently adopted, primarily aiming to capture how students viewed their experience and how they orchestrated the collaboration with peers to reach their common work goal. Teacher observation is also regarded as a potentially effective method for measure this competence ($N = 4$, $x = 11\%$), since it allows teachers to study, document and reflect on how students work on both an individual basis within the group, as well as a team. Quiz tests were also adopted ($N = 3$, $x = 8\%$), with the aim of measuring whether individual students actually participated actively in the group tasks and whether each group had a similar understanding of the topics addressed in the activities. Finally, teacher-generated rubrics and presentations/workshops were less frequently used ($N = 1$, $x = 3\%$), as a means to capture the level of individual contributions within the group and the smooth functioning of the team.

Regarding measuring the competence dimension "*Communicate effectively*," surprisingly the primary method of measurement was questionnaires ($N = 6$, $x = 16\%$). This means that the majority of research relied on students' self-reported insights on the quality and level of communication during the learning process, and placed limited focus on collecting data from other sources, such as observations ($N = 2$, $x = 5\%$), presentations ($N = 2$, $x = 5\%$) or even interviews ($N = 2$, $x = 5\%$). Additionally, this finding is further highlighted by the fact that quiz tests and project assignments ($N = 3$, $x = 5\%$ and $N = 3$, $x = 5\%$, respectively) were also less frequently adopted. This pattern could be viewed as an indicator of the need for further research in investigating effective (and efficient) ways for measuring students' competences related to "communication." This is worthy in particular as students' self-reported data (as the sole source of data) are considered to be potentially biased or even erroneous. Moreover, as the teaching and learning expand to large-scale online environments, it is worthy to explore the capacity of digital technology advancements (e.g., learning analytics, student profiling) to effectively utilize student-generated data within such learning environments (as MOOCs) for measuring this competence (e.g., Agudo-Peregrina, Iglesias-Pradas, Conde-González, & Hernández-García, 2014; Erkens & Janssen, 2008).

Regarding measuring the competence dimension "*Learn how to learn*" competence, questionnaires, and interviews were the most frequently used methods ($N = 11$, $x = 29\%$ and $N = 5$, $x = 13\%$), aiming to capture students' strategies for monitoring and regulating their learning. Quiz tests were also adopted ($N = 4$, $x = 11\%$) in order to elicit this information from students by engaging them in the process of solving challenges. Finally, observations ($N = 2$, $x = 5\%$) were also reported as a method, however, at a less degree.

Finally, measuring the competence dimension "*Develop academic mindsets*" follows a similar pattern, since questionnaires and interviews were again the most frequently used methods ($N = 16$, $x = 42\%$ and $N = 5$, $x = 13\%$ respectively), followed by quiz tests ($N = 4$, $x = 11\%$).

3.2.4 Research Question #4: Instruments to measure Deeper Learning

The Research Question #4 focused on gaining an additional layer of insights on the research works employing questionnaires to measure DL, and identify which specific instruments have been proposed. Table 13.2 presents the results of this analysis, and outlines the title of each instrument, the primary DL competence dimension it aims to measure as well as an overview of the number of items it contains. Figure 13.5 presents an overview of the DL competences dimensions addressed by the instruments.

Overall, as Fig. 13.5 depicts, it is evident that many of the identified instruments ($N = 5$, $x = 39\%$) do not explicitly address a specific (set of) DL competence dimension, rather aim to profile students based on their approaches to learning (essentially, "deeper" vs. "surface" approaches). On the other hand, the instruments that target specific DL competence dimensions, primarily focus on measuring competences related to thinking critically and solving problems ($N = 6$, $x = 43\%$), followed by competences related to communicating arguments and findings effectively ($N = 5$, $x = 39\%$) and mastering core academic content ($N = 4$, $x = 31\%$). Additionally, learning how to learn and developing academic mindsets competences are also frequently addressed ($N = 3$, $x = 23\%$), whereas collaborating effectively are less commonly measured in the existing instruments ($N = 2$, $x = 15\%$, respectively). A more detailed outline of each instrument is provided as follows.

The *Critical Thinking Test* is an instrument designed to measure students' capacity to analyze, evaluate, and extend arguments (Laird, Seifert, Pascarella, Mayhew, & Blaich, 2011). Therefore, it could be loosely mapped to the DL competence dimensions related to thinking critically (to solve problems) and communicating effectively. The instrument comprises different sections that contain different textual formats, for example, dialogues, statistical arguments, dialogues, editorials, or case studies. Each of these texts outlines a range of arguments that describe and lead to a particular conclusion that students need to validate and/or contradict. Furthermore, the instrument also contains supplementary multiple-choice items.

The *Need for Cognition Scale* (Cacioppo, Petty, Feinstein, & Jarvis, 1996) aims to measure students' engagement in and attitudes towards effortful thinking. Therefore, it can be loosely mapped to the DL competence dimensions related to learning how to learn and developing academic mindsets. The instrument contains 18 items. Exemplary classifications of students based on this instrument include students of "high need for cognition," who strive to identify, obtain and reflect on information to make sense of the world (Cacioppo et al., 1996), and students of "low need for cognition," who are more interested to adopt the opinions and worldviews of others instead of building their own.

Table 13.2 Instruments for measuring deeper learning competence dimensions

#	Instrument	Reference	Primary deeper learning competence dimension focus	Metrics/ questions
1	Critical thinking test from the collegiate assessment of academic proficiency (CAAP)	Laird et al. (2011)	– Think critically and solve problems – Communicate effectively	32
2	Need for cognition scale (NCS)	Cacioppo et al. (1996)	– Learn how to learn – Develop academic mindsets	18
3	Revised two-factor study process questionnaire (R-SPQ-2F)	Biggs et al. (2001)	Generic approaches to learning	20
4	Problem-solving performance rubric	Antonenko et al. (2014)	– Think critically and solve problems	2
5	Learning approaches questionnaire	Serife (2011)	Generic approaches to learning	39
6	Community of inquiry survey instrument	Arbaugh et al. (2008)	– Work collaboratively – Communicate effectively	36
7	Approaches to learning scale	Selcuk (2010)	Generic approaches to learning	30
8	Approaches and study skills inventory for students (ASSIST)	Entwistle (2001)	Generic approaches to learning	52
9	Short inventory of approaches to learning	Abraham et al. (2008)	Generic approaches to learning	52
10	Smarter balanced assessment test	Herman et al. (2015)	– Master core academic content – Think critically and solve problems – Communicate effectively – Learn how to learn	Varied
11	Partnership for assessment of readiness for college and careers test	Herman et al. (2015)	– Master core academic content – Think critically and solve problems – Communicate effectively – Learn how to learn	Varied
12	PISA assessment	OECD (2017)	– Master core academic content – Think critically and solve problems – Collaborate effectively – Develop academic mindsets	Varied
13	OECD test for schools	Greenhill and Martin (2014)	– Master core academic content – Think critically and solve problems – Communicate effectively – Learn how to learn – Develop academic mindsets	Varied

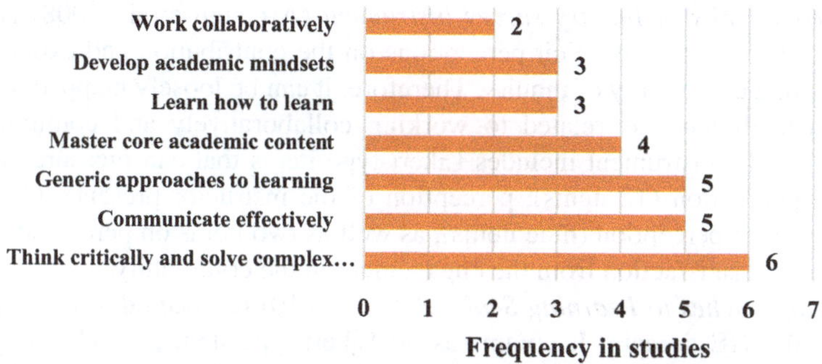

Fig. 13.5 Overview of how deeper learning competence dimensions are addressed in existing instruments

The *Revised Two-Factor Study Process Questionnaire* (Biggs, Kember, & Leung, 2001) is a self-report questionnaire consisting of 20 items. It has two scales, one measuring the deep approach to learning, and the other measuring the surface approach to learning. Therefore, generically, this instrument is not directly associated with a particular set of DL competences, rather it aims to capture students' overarching approaches to learning. As aforementioned, a "deeper" approach to learning describes students with enhanced willingness to engage in a meaningful learning process, by formulating and applying appropriate strategies (Asikainen & Gijbels, 2017). On the other hand, students showcasing "surface" approaches to learning adopt strategies built on memorization and are driven by extrinsic motivations. Furthermore, each of the two approaches has a "motive" and a "strategy" components resulting in four subscales, Deep Motive, Deep Strategy, Surface Motive, and Surface Strategy. The students' responses to particular items of the questionnaire build their profile in each subscale.

The *Problem-Solving Performance Rubric* (Antonenko et al., 2014) is an assessment rubric, which has been adapted from the Problem-Solving Value Rubric developed by the Association of American Colleges and Universities (2009). Based on its focus, it can be loosely mapped to the DL competence dimensions related to thinking critically to solve problems. The instrument contains two categories used to assess students' problem-solving competence, namely "Proposed Solution" and "Rationale," and, for each of these categories, it has defined four levels of proficiency.

The *Learning Approaches Questionnaire* (Serife, 2011) is an instrument formulated to measure students' approaches to learning on a scale similar to the Revised Two-Factor Study Process Questionnaire, namely ranging from deep, surface, and achievement. It is mentioned that an *achieving* approach to learning refers to the attitude of a student to achieve positive outcomes, such as high grades and optimally organizing their effort and time towards that goal (Biggs, 1987). Therefore, it is also not directly mapped to a specific DL competence dimension. The instrument contains 39 items and the students' scores in each subscale (surface, deep, and achieving) are averaged in order to calculate their level in each approach to learning.

The *community of Inquiry survey instrument* (Arbaugh et al., 2008) is a self-report instrument used to elicit perceptions on the contribution and experience of engaging in a community of inquiry. Therefore, it can be loosely mapped to the DL competence dimensions related to working collaboratively and communicating effectively. The instrument includes Likert-type items that can measure cognitive presence perception (12 items), perception of the instructor presence (13 items), social presence perception (nine items), as well as two items on perceived learning and perceived satisfaction from the engagement in the community.

The *Approaches to Learning Scale* (Selcuk, 2010) has been developed particularly for the HE domain. It comprises 30 Likert-type items, which are grouped under two approaches to learning: the "Deep Approach" (19 items) and the "Surface Approach" (11 items). Therefore, this instrument can be considered to have a similar standpoint with the Revised Two-Factor Study Process Questionnaire and the Learning Approaches Questionnaire.

The *Approaches and Study Skills Inventory for Students* (Reid, Evans, & Duvall, 2012). This instrument aims to elicit the learning approaches of students, and classify them against the well-acknowledged classifications of deep, surface and strategic (i.e., achieving). In this sense, it does not aim at measuring a particular DL competence dimension, rather to elicit the generic approaches to learning of individual students. The instrument divides the 52 items against these classifications, and therefore the student profile in each of them can be calculated by aggregating the scores.

The *Short Inventory of Approaches to Learning* (Abraham, Vinod, Kamath, Asha, & Ramnarayan, 2008) has been developed to capture the learning approaches of undergraduate medical students to physiology. The instrument consists of 52 items, grouped under the three classifications of surface, deep, and strategic approaches to learning. Therefore, this instrument also aims to capture the generic approaches to learning of individual students.

The *Smarter Balanced Assessment Test* and the *Partnership for Assessment of Readiness for College and Careers Test* (Herman et al., 2015; Herman & Linn, 2013) refer to large-scale "assessment" instruments that have been defined to measure students' attainment of Common Core State Standards (CCSS), especially in terms of DL competence development. Despite the fact that the tests are formulated by different consortia, their common aim is to support schools to monitor and improve students' DL competences through a suite of diagnostic, formative and summative instruments in the subject domains of English Liberal Arts and Mathematics. The focus of each instrument can be loosely mapped to the DL competences of mastering core academic content, thinking critically and solving problems, communicating effectively, and learning how to learn.

The *PISA Collaborative problem-solving assessment* (framework and) (OECD, 2017) is a large-scale test that is used to assess competences of 15-year-old students across Europe, related to subject domains (e.g., Math) and (collaborative) problem-solving. Previous implementations of this test focused on different aspects of problem-solving, such as creative problem-solving (OECD, 2012). The test comprises a range of items that aim to assess students' capacity to solve problems through a solid understanding of subject matter knowledge. Furthermore, it can also elicit the perseverance of students to meet the new challenges. Therefore, it can be loosely mapped to the DL competences on mastering core academic content, thinking critically and solve problems and developing academic mindsets.

The *OECD Test for Schools* (Greenhill & Martin, 2014) is an instrument used for conducting research-oriented strategic school planning. Based on its content, it can be loosely mapped to the DL competence dimensions related to mastering core academic content, thinking critically and solve problems, communicating effectively, learning how to learn, and developing academic mindsets. The results of the test for each school are compared to other schools (from different countries) and can be explored by the school leadership to identify and address school improvement needs and priorities. Similar to PISA's 2009 Assessment Framework, the OECD Test for Schools addresses three major subject domains, namely Mathematics, Science and Reading. However, it specifically focuses on measuring more than knowledge acquisition in these domains, and specifically captures competences related to Deeper Learning (Greenhill & Martin, 2014), such as Critical Thinking, Problem-Solving, Knowledge, Written Communication, and Intrapersonal skills (Motivation, Self-Efficacy and Learning Strategies).

4 Conclusions and Discussion

The standpoint of this chapter is that even though DL has been identified as a core educational priority around the world, the current research landscape is still shaping and at an early stage, especially in relation to technology enhanced deeper learning. The literature review presented can offer a set of conclusions.

Regarding the instantiations of DL, it is evident that existing research has largely taken a "fragmented" standpoint since students' DL competence development is very commonly investigated on a competence-level manner, instead of a holistic "DL profile" way. With few exceptions (such as Offir, Lev, & Bezalel, 2008, Antonenko et al., 2014 or Murrant et al., 2015) studies have so far focused on individual competences of DL (different for each study), and explored methods and instruments for effectively cultivating or measuring them. Even though such investigations are vital in the emerging field of DL, it is noteworthy that the concept of a student's "*Deeper Learning profile*," in the form of a holistic construct comprising all DL competence dimensions and the potential interrelations between them, was not explicitly addressed in the literature.

This finding is considered to be important since DL is in itself a complex manifestation of diverse competence dimensions and how these may interplay to allow students deal with complex challenges and situations. Therefore, a potential pathway for future studies could be directed in specifically investigating how students' diverse DL competences, individually measured and captured, influence each other. Such studies could aim to provide longitudinal investigations and collection of diverse data from students in order to explore how the level of proficiency in each competence might affect the other competences, and how can this knowledge lead to better assessment and measurement methods and instruments. Additionally, such studies could also focus to identify robust methods for build holistic students' DL profiles. In particular, capitalizing on the insights of how individual competences interplay and advancements on digital learning technologies (e.g., multimodal Learning Analytics and Open Learner Modeling), these studies could design and evaluate digital tools that allow continuous monitoring and reflection of a student's DL profile, capitalizing on diverse sources of educational data, such as students' questionnaires, student artifacts and learning actions throughout the learning process, as well as teachers' observations and assessments.

Continuing on the previous argument, future studies could also explore DL competence profiling (and cultivation) within *online* learning environments. The analysis of existing literature indicated that most studies have focused on face-to-face (or blended) teaching and learning. This is also evident from the methods used for measuring DL, most of which require (or are optimally exploited through) physical presence and small-scale learning interventions (for example, interviews, observations, presentations, workshops and rubrics). However, as teaching and learning gradually enters a new paradigm of large-scale online learning environments (Digital Learning Compass, 2017; Online Learning Consortium, 2015), it is reasonable to assume that many of these well-established methods could be less efficient to fulfil their purpose. Hindering factors such as a massive number of student cohorts and cultural diversity could render these methods difficult to employ. At the same time, different types of student data generated within digital learning environments that host such large-scale learning interventions (e.g., Learning Management Systems that host a MOOC) could be employed to supplement (or replace) these existing methods. Therefore, future research could be directed at exploring how existing (or new) methods and instruments can be (re)formulated and extended to address the challenges of the new digital teaching and learning paradigms. Given that cutting-edge innovation in learning technologies (such as Affective Learning Analytics (D'Mello & Kory, 2015; Wu, Huang, & Hwang, 2015) and competence elicitation through log data (Sergis & Sampson, 2016)) have already begun to be developed for improving the teaching and learning experiences in online environments, it is reasonable to raise the potential of applying them in the field of DL profiling as well and assist in effectively modeling and measuring the diverse DL competences towards building holistic students' DL profiles.

Another important conclusion that can be drawn from the analysis of literature refers to the wide use of questionnaires as a method for measuring DL. This standpoint, despite being well-acknowledged and the corresponding instruments being validated, could present two drawbacks in the way to effectively and accurately profiling students' DL competences. First, as all (self-) reported data they could contain bias in the sense that individuals are usually either unwilling to provide "personal" information or when they do, the validity of the provided data cannot be ensured (Belk, Papatheocharous, Germanakos, & Samaras, 2013). Therefore, supplementing the use of questionnaires with other sources of data (e.g., observations, artifact analysis) could be a method to alleviate this potential issue. Second, the *focus* of the questionnaires utilized in the literature could itself become an issue when aiming to measure DL in a more holistic manner. More specifically, the majority of instruments that research has proposed either addresses specific competence dimensions of the DL spectrum (e.g., the Problem-Solving Performance Rubric or the Need for Cognition scale) or they adopt a more generic standpoint to measure the students' approaches to learning (e.g., Revised Two-Factor Study Process Questionnaire, the Learning Approaches questionnaire, the Approaches to Learning Scale). The former group, while aiming to specifically measure DL competences, provides a fragmented view of the full spectrum of DL competence dimensions. Therefore, as previously discussed, ideally it needs to be complemented with other types of data in order to study and profile DL holistically. The latter group tends to serve a slightly different purpose. In particular, they can offer limited support to profile students against the DL competence spectrum. However, they could offer meaningful information to profile students against more generic characteristics (i.e., approaches to learning), and provide the means to investigate how different clusters of students can be effectively supported in cultivating their DL profile. Some initial works towards this direction have been reported (for example, Vanthournout, Coertjens, Gijbels, Donche, & Van Petegem, 2013).

Overall, our analysis showed that the research field of DL is evolving, with an increasing number of studies aiming to formulate new methods to measure DL as well as investigate effective teaching and learning conditions to cultivate such competences. As discussed previously, it is reasonable to infer that this field will continue to evolve following the global educational policy push for promoting DL. It is expected that digital technologies will become an integral part of this movement and provide the capacity to both address limitations of existing approaches, but more importantly offer the affordances to capture and investigate the complex nature of DL in a more granulated way, based on large-scale and diverse educational data and employing state-of-the-art methods of analysis (e.g., Pappas, Giannakos, Jaccheri, & Sampson, 2017; Sergis, Sampson, & Giannakos, 2018).

Acknowledgement The work presented in this paper has been partially funded by (a) the European Commission in the context of the "STORIES—Stories of Tomorrow: Students Visions on the Future of Space Exploration" project (Grant Agreement no. 731872) under Horizon 2020 Program, H2020-ICT-22-2016-2017 "Information and Communication Technologies: Technologies for Learning and Skills" and (b) the Greek General Secretariat for Research and Technology, under the Matching Funds 2014–2016 for the EU project "Inspiring Science: Large Scale Experimentation Scenarios to Mainstream eLearning in Science, Mathematics and Technology in Primary and Secondary Schools" (Project Number: 325123). This document does not represent the opinion of neither the European Commission nor the Greek General Secretariat for Research and Technology, and the European Commission and the Greek General Secretariat for Research and Technology are not responsible for any use that might be made of its content.

Appendix 1. Table 13.3

Table 13.3 Detailed analysis of research literature on deeper learning

#	Title	Educational level	Subject domain	DL competence addressed	Approach for cultivating DL	Method of assessment[a]	Results/comments	Benchmark approach
1	Bishay (2016)	HE	Coding/ engineering	1,2,3,4	Project-based	Project (1,2,3,4)–Questionnaire (QN) (1,3)	Project-based approach was *self-reported* as beneficial to students in terms of improving DL competences	No
2	Murrant et al. (2015)	HE	Biology	1,2,3,4,5,6	Project-based (lecture–lab–tutorial)	Presentation (4), assignment/ essay (1,4), quiz (1), project (1,2,3,4)	New course design triggered DL competence development—No evidence regarding impact on students' DL competences	Yes—class average scores and failure rates against prior versions of the course
3	Agarwal, McDaniel, Thomas, McDermott, and Roediger III (2011)	K12	Science	1,5	Project-based	Quizzes (1), open question survey (4)	Identify quizzing types and sequence to lead to higher scores regarding content and capacity for metacognition	Yes—different types of quizzing applied to different groups of learners
4	Laird et al. (2011)	HE	Liberal arts	2,5,6	–	QN (2,5,6)	Positive correlation between integrative and reflective learning activity types and student gain in DL competences	No
5	Altamirano and Jaurez (2013)	HE	Economics	1,2,3	Project-based (Game design approach)	Project (1,2,3)–quiz (1)	Experimental condition showed higher improvement in DL competences	Yes—control group not utilizing GDM
6	Kirby, Cain, and White (2012)	HE	English	1,6	–	QN (1,6)	Study impact of different existing QN instruments on students' DL competence development	No

7	Antonenko et al. (2014)	HE	Science	1,2,3,4,5,6	Problem-based	Quiz (1,5,6), rubric (2,3,4)	Experimental condition showed higher improvement in DL competences	Yes—control group exposed to rational-based approach
8	Offir et al. (2008)	K12	Computer science	1,3,4,5,6	–	Interview (5,6), observation (3,4), QN (1)	Synchronous learning is more effective for developing DL compared to asynchronous, for high-performing students. Teachers' physical presence and feedback is also essential	Yes—synchronous vs. asynchronous delivery method
9	Lloyd (2014)	HE	Biology	1,3	Project-based (Flipped Classroom)	Quizzes (1), assignment (1), observation (and clickers) (1,3)	Participating in a Flipped Classroom model statistically improved students' DL competences	Yes—flipped classroom vs. nonflipped
10	Bouwmeester, De Kleijn, and Van Rijen (2016)	HE	Biomedical science	1,3,4,6	Project-based	QN (1,3,4,6)	Positive correlation between peer collaboration, student perceptions of deeper learning and exam scores	No
11	Serife (2011)	HE	Computer science	1,2,3,4	Problem-based	QN (1,2,3,4)	Positive correlation between problem-based learning activities and student self-perceptions of deeper learning	No

(continued)

Table 13.3 (continued)

#	Title	Educational level	Subject domain	DL competence addressed	Approach for cultivating DL	Method of assessment[a]	Results/comments	Benchmark approach
12	Vos, Van Der Meijden, and Denessen (2011)	K12	Computer science/language	5,6	Project-based (for experimental group)	QN (5,6)	Interactive project-based tasks (involving game creation) positively affect student motivation and deep strategy use	Yes—experimental group constructed own game vs. control group using existing game
13	Clark, McKague, Ramsden, and McKay (2015)	HE	Health	1,5,6	Project-based	QN (1,5,6), interviews (5,6), observation (1,5)	Project-based approach was self-reported as beneficial to students in terms of improving DL competences	No
14	Quellmalz et al. (2013)	K12	Science	1,2	Inquiry-based	Quiz (1,2), Interviews (2)	Interactive assessment support improved measurement of distinct DL competences compared to static assessments	No
15	Akyol and Garrison (2011)	HE	Education	1,3,4	Inquiry-based	QN (3,4), interview (3,4), assignments (1,3)	Collaboration in communities of Inquiry (especially blended) can lead to higher learning outcomes and perceived deeper learning	No
16	Esparza (2016)	Professional Development	K-12 Teachers	-	Project-based	Survey, interview, observation, assignments	PBL can provide an effective professional development method for preparing teachers cultivate their students' DL competences	No

17	Rufer and Adams (2013)	HE	Economics	1,3	Problem-based	Survey (3), observation (1,3), assignments (1,3)	Exploiting a collaborative reusable Learning object development tool led to higher levels of collaboration and learning outcomes	Yes—experimental group exploited reusable learning object development tool as part of their training
18	Jarvis, Sadeque, and O'Brien (2016)	HE	Marketing	1,2	Project-based (Flipped Classroom)	Survey (1,2), assignments (1,2)	Participating in a Flipped Classroom model was positively perceived by students in terms of improving DL competences	No
19	Grover, Pea, and Cooper (2015), Grover and Pea (2016)	K-12	Computer science	1,2,4	Design-based	QN (1,2,4), quizzes (1), assignments (1), interview (4)	Incorporating design-based approaches in blended environments can lead to higher DL competences	No
20	Wijnen et al. (2016)	HE	Law	5,6	Problem-based	QN (5,6),	Use of PBL led to higher reported levels of self-regulation and more frequent use of (collaborative) deep processing by students	Yes—PBL vs. lecture-based approach
21	Mok, Dodd, and Whitehill (2009)	HE	Health	1,2,5,6	Problem-based	QN (2,5,6), assignments (1), workshop (1,4), assignment (1,2)	PBL promoted a DL approach to students' learning in terms of learning strategies and learning outcomes. Length of exposure to DL did not significantly affect the results, however	No

(continued)

Table 13.3 (continued)

#	Title	Educational level	Subject domain	DL competence addressed	Approach for cultivating DL	Method of assessment[a]	Results/comments	Benchmark approach
22	Stull and Mayer (2007)	HE	Psychology	1,2	–	QN (1,2), assignments (1,2), quiz (1,2)	Learning by viewing (i.e., study pre-defined graphic organizers from a text) supports better DL. However, creating own organizers (learning by doing) led to higher cognitive load reducing deeper approaches to learning	Yes—control group was given predefined graphic organizers, whereas experimental group had to create their own
23	Turvey (2006)	K12	Interdisciplinary	1,2,3,4,5	Online project-based	Assignments (1,2,3,4), interview (1,2,5), observation (1,2,3,4,5)	Online collaborative spaces could provide the means for students to build their creative aspect and cultivate competences related to problem-solving as well as learning how to learn. However, no strict guidelines on how to ensure this capacity can be derived with certainty	No

24	Laird, Shoup, Kuh, and Schwarz (2008)	HE	Interdisciplinary	1,5,6	–	Survey (1,5,6)	When employing deeper learning (by students and instructors) students tend to enhance their intellectual development and satisfaction in their studies. Weak correlation with engagement and grades. students majoring in fields such as engineering and the physical sciences use deep approaches to learning less frequently than students from other fields	No
25	Yeager et al. (2014)	K12	Math/science	5,6	–	QN (5,6)	Enhancing Deeper learning from tedious activities can be built and sustained through activities that prompt a self-transcendent purpose for working hard	Yes—control group was exposed to a simplified set of learning tasks

(continued)

Table 13.3 (continued)

#	Title	Educational level	Subject domain	DL competence addressed	Approach for cultivating DL	Method of assessment[a]	Results/comments	Benchmark approach
26	Nijhuis et al. (2005)	HE	Business	5	Problem-based	QN (5)	Students reported difficulties to understand objectives in a PBL course, and considered the assessment to be inappropriate to meet these goals. This led to lower DL and an increase of surface learning for the PBL course, compared to an assignment-based course	Yes—control group was exposed to an assignment-based version of the course, whereas experimental group was exposed to a problem-based version
27	Selcuk (2010)	HE	Physics	1,6	Problem-based	QN (6), quiz (1)	PBL encouraged students' DL, and improved interest towards the physics course. Also, students' achievement in physics also increased	Yes, experimental group was exposed to PBL
28	Abraham et al. (2008)	HE	Health	1,6	Problem-based	QN (6), quiz (1)	PBL encouraged a deeper approach to learning by students, compared to the control group, in a statistically significant manner	Yes, experimental group was exposed to PBL
29	Wong and Lam (2007)	HE	Social work	1,6	Problem-based	QN (6), quiz (1)	Students with deep learning motives and approaches reap the most benefit from PBL	No

30	Reid et al. (2012)	HE	Health	6	Problem-based	QN (6),	Even though there was evidence of the capacity of PBL to enhance students' PBL, this connection is complex and not always positive.	No
31	Grant, Kinnersley, and Field (2012)	HE	Health	5,6	Problem-based	QN (5,6), interview (5,6)	Students exposed at a PBL curriculum reported higher results on reflection in learning, self-efficacy in self-directed learning and for deep approach to learning	Yes, experimental group was exposed to PBL
32	McParland et al. (2004)	HE	Health	1,5,6	Problem-based	QN (1,5,6), interview (1,5,6), assignment (1)	PBL curriculum led to significantly higher learning outcomes. However, no differences were found in attitudes towards psychiatry between the curricula	Yes, experimental group was exposed to PBL
33	Tiwari et al. (2006)	HE	Health	1,6	Problem-based	QN (1,6), interview (1,6)	PBL supported students to adopt a deeper approach to their learning (as measured through QN)	Yes, experimental group was exposed to PBL
34	Gurpinar, Kulac, Tetik, Akdogan, and Mamakli (2013)	HE	Health	5,6	Problem-based	QN (5,6)	No generalizable results—study focus on comparing DL levels of students among different PBL curricula	No

(continued)

Table 13.3 (continued)

#	Title	Educational level	Subject domain	DL competence addressed	Approach for cultivating DL	Method of assessment[a]	Results/comments	Benchmark approach
35	Adiga and Adiga (2010)	HE	Health	5,6	Problem-based	QN (5,6)	PBL supported students to adopt a deeper approach to their learning (as measured through QN)	No
36	Herman et al. (2015)	K12	English liberal arts–mathematics–science	Holistic	–	Quiz (high-stakes assessment)	Study evaluated the level in which the identified tests covered DL competences	NO
37	Herman, la Torre, Epstein, and Wang (2016)	K12	English liberal arts–mathematics	Holistic	–	Quiz (high-stakes assessment)	Study evaluated the level in which the PISA tests covered DL competences	NO
38	Greenhill and Martin (2014)	K12	English liberal arts–mathematics–science	Holistic	–	Quiz (school improvement)	Report presents the OECD Test for measuring school-wide DL competences and aggregated case studies regarding the use of the Test in schools across USA	NO

[a]The numbering refers to the DL competences, as follows: 1. Master core academic content, 2. Think critically and solve complex problems, 3. Work collaboratively, 4. Communicate effectively, 5. Learn how to learn, 6. Develop academic mindsets

References

Abbott, I., Townsend, A., Johnston-Wilder, S., & Reynolds, L. (2009). *Literature review: Deep learning with technology in 14-to 19-year-old learners*. Coventry: Institute of Education.

Abraham, R. R., Vinod, P., Kamath, M. G., Asha, K., & Ramnarayan, K. (2008). Learning approaches of undergraduate medical students to physiology in a non-PBL-and partially PBL-oriented curriculum. *Advances in Physiology Education, 32*(1), 35–37.

Adiga, S., & Adiga, U. (2010). Problem based learning-An approach to learning pharmacology in medical school. *Biomedical Research, 21*(1), 43–46.

Agarwal, P. K., McDaniel, M. A., Thomas, R. C., McDermott, K. B., & Roediger, H. L., III. (2011). *Quizzing promotes deeper acquisition in middle school science: Transfer of quizzed content to summative exams*. Washington, DC: Society for Research on Educational Effectiveness.

Agudo-Peregrina, Á. F., Iglesias-Pradas, S., Conde-González, M. Á., & Hernández-García, Á. (2014). Can we predict success from log data in VLEs? Classification of interactions for learning analytics and their relation with performance in VLE-supported F2F and online learning. *Computers in Human Behavior, 31*, 542–550.

Akyol, Z., & Garrison, D. R. (2011). Understanding cognitive presence in an online and blended community of inquiry: Assessing outcomes and processes for deep approaches to learning. *British Journal of Educational Technology, 42*(2), 233–250.

Altamirano, N., & Jaurez, J. (2013). Student built games in economic courses: Applying the game design methodology as another approach to deeper learning. *Journal of Research in Innovative Teaching, 6*(1), 115–131.

Antonenko, P. D., Jahanzad, F., & Greenwood, C. (2014). Fostering collaborative problem solving and 21st century skills using the DEEPER scaffolding framework. *Journal of College Science Teaching, 43*(6), 79–88.

Arbaugh, J. B., Cleveland-Innes, M., Diaz, S. R., Garrison, D. R., Ice, P., Richardson, J., & Swan, K. P. (2008). Developing a community of inquiry instrument: Testing a measure of the Community of Inquiry framework using a multi-institutional sample. *The Internet and Higher Education, 11*(3–4), 133–136.

Asikainen, H., & Gijbels, D. (2017). Do students develop towards more deep approaches to learning during studies? A systematic review on the development of students' deep and surface approaches to learning in higher education. *Educational Psychology Review, 29*, 205–234.

Association of American Colleges and Universities. (2009). *Assessing learning outcomes: Lessons from AAC&U's VALUE project*. Washington, DC: Association of American Colleges and Universities.

Belk, M., Papatheocharous, E., Germanakos, P., & Samaras, G. (2013). Modeling users on the world wide web based on cognitive factors, navigation behavior and clustering techniques. *Journal of Systems and Software, 86*(12), 2995–3012.

Biggs, J., Kember, D., & Leung, Y. (2001). The revised two-factor study process questionnaire: R-SPQ-2F. *British Journal of Educational Psychology, 71*, 133–149.

Biggs, J. B. (1987). *Students approaches to learning and studying*. Hawthorn, VIC: Australian Council for Educational Research.

Bishay, P. L. (2016). "FEApps": Boosting students' enthusiasm for coding and app designing, with a deeper learning experience in engineering fundamentals. *Computer Applications in Engineering Education, 24*(3), 456–463.

Bouwmeester, R. A., De Kleijn, R. A., & Van Rijen, H. V. (2016). Peer-instructed seminar attendance is associated with improved preparation, deeper learning and higher exam scores: A survey study. *BMC Medical Education, 16*(1), 200.

Cacioppo, J., Petty, R., Feinstein, J., & Jarvis, W. (1996). Dispositional differences in cognitive motivation: The life and times of individuals varying in need for cognition. *Psychological Bulletin, 119*, 197–253.

Clark, M., McKague, M., Ramsden, V. R., & McKay, S. (2015). Deeper learning through service: Evaluation of an interprofessional community service-learning program for pharmacy and medicine students. *Journal of Research in Interprofessional Practice and Education, 5*(1), 1–25.

Conley, D. (2014). *A new era for educational assessment. Students at the Center: Deeper learning research series*. Boston, MA: Jobs for the Future.

Conley, D., & Darling-Hammond, L. (2013). *Creating systems of assessment for deeper learning*. Stanford, CA: Stanford Center for Opportunity Policy in Education.

D'mello, S. K., & Kory, J. (2015). A review and meta-analysis of multimodal affect detection systems. *ACM Computing Surveys, 47*(3), 43-1–43-36.

Dede, C. (2014). *The role of digital technologies in deeper learning. Students at the Center: Deeper learning research series*. Boston, MA: Jobs for the Future.

Deloitte. (2016). *The new organization: Different by design*. New York, NY: Deloitte University.

Digital Learning Compass (2017). Distance education enrollment report 2017. Retrieved from https://goo.gl/dsw2GP

Dolmans, D. H., Loyens, S. M., Marcq, H., & Gijbels, D. (2016). Deep and surface learning in problem-based learning: A review of the literature. *Advances in Health Sciences Education, 21*(5), 1087–1112.

Entwistle NJ. (2001). ASSIST. Retrieved from http://www.etl.tla.ed.ac.uk/questionnaires/ASSIST.pdf

Erkens, G., & Janssen, J. (2008). Automatic coding of online collaboration protocols. *International Journal of Computer-Supported Collaborative Learning, 3*, 447–470.

Esparza, D. R. (2016). A first-year implementation of Mindquest21, A project-based paradigm shift to deeper learning: A program evaluation. PhD Thesis.

Fullan, M., Hill, P., Rincon-Gallardo, S. (2017). Deep learning: Shaking the foundations.. Deep learning series, 3. New Pedagogies for Deep Learning: A Global Partnership

Fullan, M., McEahen, J., & Quinn, J. (2016). New pedagogies for deep learning. New Pedagogies for Deeper Learning global report.

Getting Smart (2014). Assessing deeper learning: A survey of performance assessment and mastery-tracking tools.

Grant, A., Kinnersley, P., & Field, M. (2012). Learning contexts at Two UK medical schools: A comparative study using mixed methods. *BMC Research Notes, 5*(1), 153.

Greenhill, V., & Martin, J. (2014). *OECD test for schools: Implementation toolkit*. Menlo Park, CA: EdLeader21 and Hewlett-Flora Foundation. Retrieved from http://www.oecd.org/pisa/aboutpisa/EdLeader21_OECD_TFS_Toolkit.pdf

Grover, S., & Pea, R. (2016). *Designing a blended, middle school computer science course for deeper learning: A design-based research approach*. Singapore: International Society of the Learning Sciences.

Grover, S., Pea, R., & Cooper, S. (2015). Designing for deeper learning in a blended computer science course for middle school students. *Computer Science Education, 25*(2), 199–237.

Gurpinar, E., Kulac, E., Tetik, C., Akdogan, I., & Mamakli, S. (2013). Do learning approaches of medical students affect their satisfaction with problem-based learning? *Advances in Physiology Education, 37*(1), 85–88.

Hatala, M., Beheshitha, S. S., & Gasevic, D. (2016). Associations between students' approaches to learning and learning analytics visualizations. In *Proceedings of the Learning Analytics & Knowledge Conference* (pp. 3–10). New York, NY: ACM.

Heller, R., & Wolfe, R. (2015). *Effective schools for deeper learning: An exploratory study. Students at the Center: Deeper learning research series*. Boston, MA: Jobs for the Future.

Herman, J., la Torre, D., Epstein, S., & Wang, J. (2016). *Benchmarks for deeper learning on next generation tests: A study of PISA. National Center for Research*. Los Angeles, CA: University of California.

Herman, J., La Torre Matrundola, D., & Wang, J. (2015). *On the road to assessing deeper learning: What direction do test blueprints provide? National Center for Research.* Los Angeles, CA: University of California.

Herman, J., & Linn, R. (2013). *On the road to assessing deeper learning: The status of smarter balanced and PARCC assessment consortia. National Center for Research.* Los Angeles, CA: University of California.

Huberman, M., Bitter, C., Anthony, J., & O'Day, J. (2014). *The shape of deeper learning: Strategies, structures, and cultures in deeper learning network high schools.* Washington, DC: American Institute of Research.

Jarvis, W., Sadeque, S., & O'Brien, I. M. (2016). An exploration of dis-confirmation of deeper learning expectations using choice theory. *Procedia-Social and Behavioral Sciences, 228*, 662–667.

Kirby, J. R., Cain, K., & White, B. (2012). Deeper learning in reading comprehension. In *Enhancing the quality of learning: Dispositions, instruction, and learning processes* (pp. 315–338). Cambridge: Cambridge University Press.

Laird, T. F., Seifert, T. A., Pascarella, E. T., Mayhew, M. J., & Blaich, C. F. (2011). Deeply effecting first-year students' thinking: The effects of deep approaches to learning on three outcomes. In *Proceedings of the Annual Conference of the Association for the Study of Higher Education.*

Laird, T. F. N., Shoup, R., Kuh, G. D., & Schwarz, M. J. (2008). The effects of discipline on deep approaches to student learning and college outcomes. *Research in Higher Education, 49*(6), 469–494.

Lathram, B., Lenz, B., & Ark, T.V. (2016) Preparing students for a project-based world. Getting Smart/Buck Institute for Education.

Lloyd, J. E. (2014). Inverting a non-major's biology class: Using video lectures, online resources, and a student response system to facilitate deeper learning. *Journal of Teaching and Learning with Technology, 3*(2), 31–39.

McParland, M., Noble, L. M., & Livingston, G. (2004). The effectiveness of problem-based learning compared to traditional teaching in undergraduate psychiatry. *Medical Education, 38*(8), 859–867.

Mehta, J., & Fine, S. (2015). *The why, what, where, and how of deeper learning in American secondary schools. Students at the Center, Deeper learning research series.* Boston, MA: Jobs for the Future.

Mok, C. K., Dodd, B., & Whitehill, T. L. (2009). Speech-language pathology students' approaches to learning in a problem-based learning curriculum. *International Journal of Speech-Language Pathology, 11*(6), 472–481.

Murrant, C. L., Dyck, D. J., Kirkland, J. B., Newton, G. S., Ritchie, K. L., Tishinsky, J. M., … Richardson, N. S. (2015). A large, first-year, introductory, multi-sectional biological concepts of health course designed to develop skills and enhance deeper learning. *The Canadian Journal of Higher Education, 45*(4), 42–62.

Nijhuis, J. F., Segers, M. S., & Gijselaers, W. H. (2005). Influence of redesigning a learning environment on student perceptions and learning strategies. *Learning Environments Research, 8*(1), 67–93.

OECD. (2012). *PISA 2012 results: Creative problem solving students' skills in tackling real-life problems.* Paris: OECD. Retrieved from http://www.oecd.org/pisa/keyfindings/PISA-2012-results-volume-V.pdf

OECD. (2017). *The PISA 2015 collaborative problem-solving framework.* Paris: OECD. Retrieved from https://www.oecd.org/pisa/pisaproducts/Draft%20PISA%202015%20Collaborative%20Problem%20Solving%20Framework%20.pdf

Offir, B., Lev, Y., & Bezalel, R. (2008). Surface and deep learning processes in distance education: Synchronous versus asynchronous systems. *Computers & Education, 51*(3), 1172–1183.

Online Learning Consortium. (2015). *Online report card – Tracking online education in the United States.* Newburyport, MA: Online Learning Consortium. Retrieved from http://onlinelearning-consortium.org/read/online-report-card-tracking-online-education-united-states-2015

Pappas, I. O., Giannakos, M. N., Jaccheri, L., & Sampson, D. G. (2017). Assessing student behavior in computer science education with an fsQCA approach: The role of gains and barriers. *ACM Transactions on Computing Education (TOCE), 17*(2), 369.

Pellegrino, J. W., & Hilton, M. L. (2012). Committee on defining deeper learning and 21st century skills. In *Education for life and work: Developing transferable knowledge and skills in the 21st century*. Washington, DC: The National Academies Press.

Peltier, C., & Vannest, K. J. (2017). A meta-analysis of schema instruction on the problem-solving performance of elementary school students. *Review of Educational Research, 87*, 899.

Pirnay-Dummer, P., Ifenthaler, D., & Spector, J. M. (2010). Highly integrated model assessment technology and tools. *Educational Technology Research & Development, 58*(1), 3–18.

Quellmalz, E. S., Davenport, J. L., Timms, M. J., DeBoer, G. E., Jordan, K. A., Huang, C. W., & Buckley, B. C. (2013). Next-generation environments for assessing and promoting complex science learning. *Journal of Educational Psychology, 105*(4), 1100–1114.

Reid, W. A., Evans, P., & Duvall, E. (2012). Medical students' approaches to learning over a full degree programme. *Medical Education Online, 17*(1), 17205.

Rufer, R., & Adams, R. H. (2013). Deep learning through reusable learning objects in an MBA program. *Journal of Educational Technology Systems, 42*(2), 107–120.

Selcuk, G. S. (2010). The effects of problem-based learning on pre-service teachers achievement, approaches and attitudes towards learning physics. *International Journal of Physical Sciences, 5*(6), 711–723.

Sergis, S., & Sampson, D. (2016). Learning object recommendations for teachers based on elicited ICT competence profiles. *IEEE Transactions on Learning Technologies, 9*(1), 67–80.

Sergis, S., Sampson, D., & Giannakos, M. (2018). Supporting school leadership decision making with holistic school analytics: Bringing the qualitative-quantitative divide using fuzzy-set qualitative comparative analysis. *Computers in Human Behavior, 89*, 355.

Serife, A. K. (2011). The effect of computer supported problem based learning on students approaches to learning. *Current Issues in Education, 14*(1), 1–19.

Spector, J. M., & Koszalka, T. A. (2004). *The DEEP methodology for assessing learning in complex domains*. (Final report to the National Science Foundation Evaluative Research and Evaluation Capacity Building). Syracuse, NY: Syracuse University.

Stull, A. T., & Mayer, R. E. (2007). Learning by doing versus learning by viewing: Three experimental comparisons of learner-generated versus author-provided graphic organizers. *Journal of Educational Psychology, 99*(4), 808.

Surr, W., & Redding, S. (2017). *Competency-based Education: Staying shallow or going deeper*. Washington, DC: Great Lakes and Midwest Regional Deeper Learning Initiative, American Institutes for Research. Retrieved from https://ccrscenter.org/sites/default/files/CBE_GoingDeep.pdf

The William and Flora Hewlett Foundation. (2012). *Deeper learning strategic plan summary education program*. Menlo Park, CA: The William and Flora Hewlett Foundation. Retrieved from https://hewlett.org/wp-content/uploads/2016/09/Education_Deeper_Learning_Strategy.pdf

Tiwari, A., Chan, S., Wong, E., Wong, D., Chui, C., Wong, A., & Patil, N. (2006). The effect of problem-based learning on students' approaches to learning in the context of clinical nursing education. *Nurse Education Today, 26*(5), 430–438.

Turvey, K. (2006). Towards deeper learning through creativity within online communities in primary education. *Computers & Education, 46*(3), 309–321.

Van der Ark, T., & Schneider, C. (2013). How digital learning contributes to deeper learning. Getting Smart.

Van der Ark, T., & Schneider, C. (2014). Deeper learning for every student every day. Getting Smart.

Vanthournout, G., Coertjens, L., Gijbels, D., Donche, V., & Van Petegem, P. (2013). Assessing students' development in learning approaches according to initial learning profiles: A person-oriented perspective. *Studies in Educational Evaluation, 39*(1), 33–40.

Vanthournout, G., Doche, V., Gijbels, D., & Van Petegem, P. (2014). (Dis)similarities in research on learning approaches and learning patterns. In D. Gijbels, V. Doche, J. Richardson, & J. D. Vermunt (Eds.), *Learning patterns in higher education: Dimensions and research perspectives* (pp. 11–32). London: Routledge.

Vos, N., Van Der Meijden, H., & Denessen, E. (2011). Effects of constructing versus playing an educational game on student motivation and deep learning strategy use. *Computers & Education, 56*(1), 127–137.

Vuchic, V. (2011). *Deeper learning and e-learning: A review of promising programs and emerging technologies in the field of online teacher professional development.* Menlo Park, CA: William & Flora Foundation.

Wijnen, M., Loyens, S. M., Smeets, G., Kroeze, M., & van der Molen, H. (2016). Comparing problem-based learning students to students in a lecture-based curriculum: Learning strategies and the relation with self-study time. *European Journal of Psychology of Education, 32*, 431–447.

Wong, D. K. P., & Lam, D. O. B. (2007). Problem-based learning in social work: A study of student learning outcomes. *Research on Social Work Practice, 17*(1), 55–65.

Wu, C. H., Huang, Y. M., & Hwang, J. P. (2015). Review of affective computing in education/learning: Trends and challenges. *British Journal of Educational Technology, 47*, 1304–1323.

Yeager, D. S., Henderson, M. D., Paunesku, D., Walton, G. M., D'Mello, S., Spitzer, B. J., & Duckworth, A. L. (2014). Boring but important: A self-transcendent purpose for learning fosters academic self-regulation. *Journal of Personality and Social Psychology, 107*(4), 559.

Zervas, P., & Sampson, D. (2018). Supporting reflective lesson planning based on inquiry learning analytics for facilitating students' problem solving competence: The inspiring science education tools. In R. Huang, N.-S. Chen, & Kinshuk (Eds.), *Authentic learning through advances in technologies*. Singapore: Springer.

Stylianos Sergis holds a B.Sc. in "Informatics and Telecommunications" (June 2010) from the Department of Informatics and Telecommunications of the National and Kapodistrian University of Athens, Greece, a M.Sc. in "Informatics in Education" (June 2012) from the Faculty of Primary Education of the National and Kapodistrian University of Athens, Greece, and a Ph.D. from the Department of Digital Systems of the University of Piraeus (June 2017). His research focuses on Educational Data Analytics for supporting teaching and learning. He is the coauthor of 30 scientific publications. He has received two Best Paper Awards in International Conferences on Learning Technologies (2016, 2017).

Demetrios Sampson is a Professor of Digital Systems for Learning and Education at the Department of Digital Systems, University of Piraeus, Greece, where he serves as Academic Staff since 2001 and a Professor of Learning Technologies at the School of Education, Curtin University, Australia since 2015. He is the coauthor of 340 articles in scientific books, journals, and conferences, and the editor of 12 books, 32 special issues, and 35 international conference proceedings. He has received Best Paper Award in International Conferences ten times. He has been a Keynote/Invited Speaker/Lecturer in 82 International/National Conferences and/or Postgraduate Programs around the world. He has been project director, principle investigator, and/or research consultant in 70 Research and Innovation projects with external funding at the range of 16 M€. He has supervised 155 honors and postgraduate students to successful completion.

He has developed and delivers the first MOOC on the use of Educational Data Analytics by School Teachers (Analytics for the Classroom Teacher), offered by the edX platform which has attracted more than 12,000 participants from 160 countries around the world since October 2016.

He served as Editor-in-Chief of one of the first open access journals in educational technology, the Educational Technology & Society Journal, 2003–2018. He has also served or serves as

Member of the Steering Committee and/or Advisory and/or Editorial Board of 25 International/ National Journals, in various leadership roles in 75 International Conferences and at the Program Committee of 525 International/National Conferences.

He is the recipient of the *IEEE Computer Society Distinguished Service Award* (July 2012) and named a *Golden Core Member* of IEEE Computer Society in recognition of his contribution to the field of Learning Technologies (January 2013). He is also the recipient of the *Golden Nikola Tesla Chain Award* of the International Society for Engineering Pedagogy (IGIP) for "*International outstanding achievements in the field of Engineering Pedagogy*" (September 2018).

Chapter 14
Awareness Tools for Teachers to Support Students' Exploratory Learning: Challenges and Design

Alexandra Poulovassilis

Abstract This chapter discusses providing teachers with real-time awareness tools to support their use of exploratory learning systems in the classroom. We present the challenges involved in designing meaningful awareness tools for teachers. We discuss a design approach that involves teachers in iterative participatory activities so as to formulate key usage scenarios for the tools. Teachers also collaborate in the design and evaluation of the tools, and in identifying meaningful interaction indicators that should be detected by the system as students are working on exploratory learning tasks and notified to the teacher. The approach, methodology and methods reviewed here have been developed in the context of designing a suite of Teacher Assistance tools for a mathematical microworld. However, we argue that they have the potential to be applied more generally to the design of teachers' awareness tools for other exploratory learning contexts, not only for classroom-based but for also distance and mobile exploratory learning.

1 Introduction

Technology-enhanced learning (TEL) aims to use digital technologies to support and enhance learning and teaching processes and outcomes. Woolf (2010) gives an overview of the role of computing in addressing major educational challenges such as *accessibility*, *personalisation*, *assessment* and *policy*. Wolf also identifies several key enabling computing technologies for TEL, in the areas of user modelling, mobile computing, social networking tools, serious games, intelligent environments, data management and rich user interfaces. The U.K. Economic and Social Research Council similarly identified four broad educational challenges and funded

A. Poulovassilis (✉)
Department of Computer Science and Information Systems, Birkbeck, University of London, London, UK
e-mail: ap@dcs.bbk.ac.uk; http://www.dcs.bbk.ac.uk/~ap

D. Sampson et al. (eds.), *Learning Technologies for Transforming Large-Scale Teaching, Learning, and Assessment*, https://doi.org/10.1007/978-3-030-15130-0_14

a programme of TEL research during 2006–2013 (http://tel.ioe.ac.uk/) focussing on these:

- *Flexibility*: provision of learning opportunities across multiple settings;
- *Inclusion*: extending learning opportunities to those not well served currently;
- *Personalisation*: exploiting computational techniques to create learning experiences that better match learners' needs and characteristics[1];
- *Productivity*: improving the quality and affordability of learning opportunities.

Intelligent Tutoring Systems (ITS) (Koedinger, Brunskill, Baker, McLaughlin, & Stamper, 2013) aim to address some of these challenges. ITSs can be accessed through desktop or mobile networked devices, thus addressing accessibility and flexibility. They build up a computational model of the target knowledge domain and of the learner's development of conceptual understanding and skills in that domain. They use these to provide adaptive feedback for the learner relating to their progress and performance on course activities and also to select additional activities so that the student can practice their weaker areas or be stretched with additional challenges in their stronger areas (thus addressing personalisation, assessment, inclusion). ITSs' interaction with the learner can be through multi-modal interfaces including text, speech, video, virtual reality, haptics and wearable technologies. By making use of ITSs as classroom assistants (or even as homework assistants), teachers can be supported in managing larger classes, allowing them time to provide additional, more targeted, support to individual students (thus addressing productivity and also inclusion). As one teacher states[2]: 'The intelligent support is offering the same sort of support that I would offer if I was standing behind them, so that's a first port of call. And if that doesn't work they've still got the opportunity to ask, but we are now filtered to people who need more than a straight forward answer'.

ITSs' provision of personalised, adaptive feedback treats students as individuals, each with an evolving profile of knowledge and skills. ITS feedback can enhance students' engagement, motivation and self-confidence, leading to improved learning outcomes. Some of these aspects of ITSs are discussed by Du Boulay, Poulovassilis, Holmes, and Mavrikis (2018), who also refer to a number of reviews and meta-reviews that point to the effectiveness of ITSs in enhancing whole-class teaching.

Over the past decade, the range of ITSs has broadened to systems that aim to support a constructivist pedagogical paradigm and open-ended learning activities. Examples of such *Exploratory Learning Environments* (ELEs) are virtual labs,

---

[1] Relevant computational techniques here include data modelling, data cleansing/transformation/integration, distributed data processing, knowledge representation and automated reasoning, data mining/analytics/visualisation, Human–Computer Interaction, learner modelling, affective computing, recommender systems, predictive modelling, social network analysis, natural language processing, discourse analysis (see Poulovassilis, 2016).

[2] See 5 min 20 s into the MiGen Project video at www.dcs.bbk.ac.uk/lkl/research/migen/index.html%3Fq=node%252F10.html

simulators, educational games and microworlds. The tasks that students are asked to undertake using ELEs may have several alternative solutions and students are encouraged to explore a variety of solution approaches. In this way ELEs aim to increase students' engagement with learning and to foster 'deeper' learning that can be applied to solving new problems. The role of the teacher in such environments becomes one of a 'facilitator' or 'orchestrator' of learning (Mavrikis, Geraniou, Noss, & Hoyles, 2008): providing the appropriate range of activities and environment to promote learning, helping students to plan and reflect on their work, and possibly collaborate with others, while at the same time encouraging students' autonomy and freedom to explore.

In parallel with the increasing adoption of these types of systems, there has emerged an understanding that students may need considerable pedagogical support while they are undertaking exploratory learning tasks, in order to ensure that the intended learning goals are being achieved (Kirscher, Sweller, & Clark, 2006; Mayer, 2004). In the absence of such support, students may drift off-task, engage in playful behaviour or even switch to using other online web or chat tools when the teacher is not looking.

Mavrikis et al. (2008) articulate a framework of pedagogic strategies for supporting students in exploratory learning tasks, which can inform the design of intelligent support in ELEs for both the student and the teacher. We include this here as Table 14.1, and note that although articulated in the context of a mathematical microworld, the strategies are clearly applicable to supporting exploratory learning more generally.

This framework informed subsequent research into techniques for providing adaptive feedback to students to foster their productive interaction with ELEs (Cocea, Gutiérrez-Santos, & Magoulas, 2010; Gutiérrez-Santos, Mavrikis, & Magoulas, 2013). The motivation for this research was articulated by Mavrikis et al. (2008), who state: 'We envisage that some of the teacher's responsibilities could be delegated to an intelligent system which could support either the student directly or provide information to teachers, helping them in their role as facilitators'.

Table 14.1 A framework of pedagogic strategies for student support (Mavrikis et al., 2008)

1. Supporting processes of [mathematical] exploration
• Supporting students to set and work towards explicit goals.
• Directing students' attention.
• Helping students organise their working environment.
• Provoking cognitive conflict.
• Encouraging alternative solutions.
2. Supporting reflection
3. Promoting motivation
4. Supporting collaboration

Designing such intelligent support in ELEs is more challenging compared with traditional ITS, for a number of reasons: the learning tasks are open-ended and there may be multiple alternative solutions; the mapping between students' actions and their evolving understanding of the target knowledge domain is ill-defined (Mavrikis, Gutiérrez-Santos, Pearce-Lazard, Poulovassilis, & Magoulas, 2010); a balance needs to be struck between allowing students freedom to explore and guiding them towards achieving the intended learning goals; teachers are less familiar with tools that facilitate exploratory learning, and thus it is harder to elicit their requirements as relating to the intelligent support that the tools should provide; and the provision of intelligent support within an ELE can have a transformative effect on learning and teaching processes and hence can lead to dynamically evolving requirements.

The provision of intelligent support within microworlds is particularly challenging as these allow students to not only interact with the objects already designed within the ELE but also construct and explore their own objects (Cocea & Magoulas, 2017; Mavrikis et al., 2008). Recent work demonstrated that it is possible to effectively design the content, timing and presentation of feedback messages to students working in a mathematical microworld (the eXpresser—see Sect. 2) through successive Wizard-of-Oz studies, as part of an iterative participatory methodology in which prototypes of increasing fidelity and ecological validity are co-designed and evaluated with students and teachers (Mavrikis & Gutiérrez-Santos, 2010).

However, providing intelligent support for students within an ELE is not enough: there is a need also for tools providing *support to the teacher* so as enhance the teacher's awareness of students' engagement and progress on the exploratory tasks being undertaken, and to inform the teacher's own interventions to support individual students and the class as a whole. Without such tools, a teacher can only be aware of what a small number of students are doing at any one time as she/he walks around the classroom and observes students' interactions with the ELE. It is therefore hard for the teacher to keep track of who is making good progress on the task set, who is off-task, who is in difficulty and in need of help, and how to formulate appropriate help for students. For example, one of the teachers who used the eXpresser in a classroom trial without any additional teacher support tools noted that it is infeasible to obtain a view of the whole class because paying attention to so many students (28) requires frequent changes of context and the 'forest gets lost behind the trees' (Gutiérrez-Santos, Mavrikis, Geraniou, & Poulovassilis, 2012).

These observations have led to research into the design and deployment of *Teacher Assistance* (TA) tools to be used in conjunction with ELEs (Gutiérrez-Santos, Geraniou, Pearce-Lazard, & Poulovassilis, 2012; Gutiérrez-Santos, Mavrikis, et al., 2012; Mavrikis, Gutiérrez-Santos, & Poulovassilis, 2016; Pearce-Lazard, Poulovassilis, & Geraniou, 2010). These are visualisation and notification tools that aim to enhance the teacher's awareness of the classroom state, students' different solution approaches, and students' achievement of the intended learning goals as the lesson progresses. The availability of such awareness information helps the teacher to formulate targeted interventions for supporting individual students and the class as a whole at appropriate times in the lesson. For example, the same teacher as mentioned above, when using the eXpresser in conjunction with a suite of TA tools (described in Sect. 2 below) in a classroom trial reported being 'extremely pleased' with the TA tools, one of the main reasons being the experience of control over the class that the tools were able to provide for her (Gutiérrez-Santos, Mavrikis, et al., 2012).

This kind of research into the design of intelligent support in ELEs draws on and integrates the perspectives of both Learning Analytics and Educational Data Mining. The recently emerged field of Learning Analytics (LA) is concerned with gathering, analysing and visualising data about learners and learning processes so as to increase stakeholders' understanding of these, and hence to improve learning and the environments in which it occurs (Drachsler & Greller, 2012; Ferguson, 2012; Siemens, 2012). Learning-related data can arise from many sources: virtual learning environments that support students' interactions, reflections and progress through learning tasks; databases of students' records of prior learning and achievement; and mobile and wearable technologies able to gather additional user-centred information. The more established field of Educational Data Mining (EDM) is also concerned with gathering and analysing learning-related data so as to understand, support and improve students' learning. However, the LA and EDM fields have had somewhat different emphases thus far (Siemens & Baker, 2012). In particular, LA has focussed on researching and developing techniques and tools that enable decision-making by humans (learners, teachers, other educational stakeholders) whereas EDM has focussed on researching and developing techniques and tools that enable automated personalisation and adaptation within e-learning environments.

The design of intelligent support in ELEs integrates these two perspectives, through (1) the sub-stratum of the data that is collected and generated by the ELE, and (2) the methodology adopted for the design of the intelligent support for the student and for the teacher. Regarding point (1), the rich range of data that can collected and inferred by an ELE provides the possibility to provide both personalised feedback for the learner and visualisation and notification tools for the teacher. The data include:

- Event-based data, such as: log data of students' actions in the ELE; occurrence of key indicators as students interact with the ELE; generation and provision of feedback by the ELE to the student.
- Students' constructions: the models constructed by students, including a full history of construction of each; students' reflections on their and others' constructions, e.g. through text or speech.
- Task information: task descriptions, task learning objectives and learning goals, common solution approaches to each task.
- Learner models, which may include information about students' progressive attainment of key concepts and skills, recent history of interactions with the system, affective states, progress with tasks set, achievement of learning goals (see Mavrikis et al. (2010) and Cocea and Magoulas (2017) for discussions of the challenges of learner modelling in ELEs).

Regarding point (2), recent research into Teacher Assistance (TA) tools to support exploratory learning has adopted the same iterative participatory approach as for designing intelligent support for the student (Mavrikis, Gutiérrez-Santos, et al., 2013; Mavrikis et al., 2016). We discuss the methodology for designing these TA tools further in Sect. 2.

The remainder of this chapter presents in Sect. 2 a case study of a suite of Teacher Assistance tools developed to support teachers' use of a mathematical microworld and the methodology and techniques adopted for their design. Section 3 reviews related work in the area of teacher support tools. Section 4 discusses scalability considerations along two dimensions: tool design and tool deployment. Section 5 draws conclusions and areas of future research.

2 Case Study: The MiGen System

The MiGen project[3] designed, developed and evaluated in collaboration with teachers and students a pedagogical and technical environment to support 11–14 year-old students in developing mathematical 'ways of thinking' and an appreciation of the idea of algebraic generalisation (Noss et al., 2012). The project adopted a constructionist approach, providing a mathematical microworld that allows students to create 2-dimensional tiled patterns and algebraic expressions and to explore the relationships between them. Although targeting mainly individual learning activities, the MiGen system also aimed to mediate productive interactions between students, and also between the teacher and the student, so that not only could students create their own mathematical models but also discuss and debate these with others. We refer readers to Mavrikis, Noss, Hoyles, and Geraniou (2013) for a detailed exposition of the pedagogical aims of the system.

The MiGen system is deployed within the classroom. During a lesson, students work on problems selected by their teacher and presented to them by the system. While this is happening, the teacher can view real-time representations of the students' activities and progress by using the Teacher Assistance tools. After the end of the lesson, teachers can also use these tools to access historical information about their students' activities. The MiGen system comprises a number of tools, which we describe here in overview; we refer the reader to Noss et al. (2012), Gutiérrez-Santos, Geraniou, et al. (2012) and Mavrikis et al. (2016) for full details. The evaluation of students' learning gains after their interactions with the system is discussed by Noss et al. (2012) and Mavrikis, Noss, et al. (2013).

At the heart of the system is the *eXpresser*, a mathematical microworld which supports students in undertaking algebraic generalisation tasks. Students are asked to construct 'patterns' comprising a number of building blocks that they create using square unit tiles, which they can subsequently colour. During their construction, they make use of numbers which they can subsequently 'unlock' to turn them into variables, thus generalising their pattern.

[3] http://www.migen.org

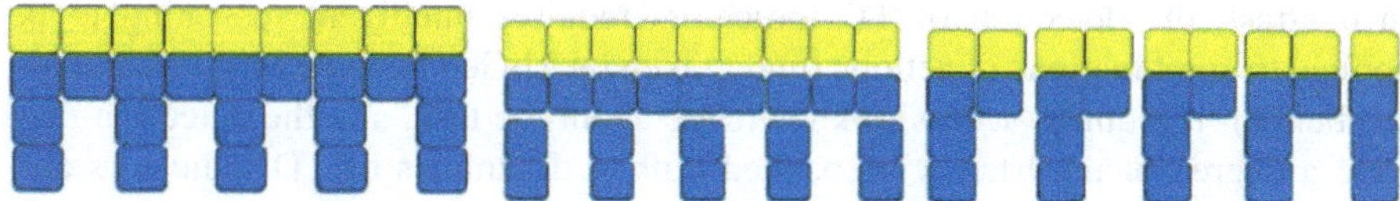

Fig. 14.1 Example of a pattern a student may be asked to construct using the eXpresser

The left-most figure in Fig. 14.1 illustrates an instance of a pattern that a student may be asked to construct. A student might adopt the construction approach shown in the middle figure, comprising two horizontal building blocks (one yellow, one blue) of size y and one vertical building block of two blue tiles that is repeated $(y + 1)/2$ times. Another student might adopt the construction approach shown in the right-most figure, comprising a building block of two yellow and four blue tiles that is repeated $(y - 1)/2$ times, plus one building block of one yellow and three blue tiles at the end.

The eXpresser supports students not only in their construction of such patterns but also in deriving mathematical expressions underpinning them, e.g. for the pattern in Fig. 14.1 the student might be asked to derive a rule for the number of blue (dark grey) tiles required to fully colour the pattern for a given number of yellow (light grey) tiles y. For the construction approach in the middle, the student may derive the rule $y + (y + 1)$, while for the construction approach on the right the student may derive the rule $(y - 1) \times 2 + 3$. Both of these are correct, and equivalent. If the student has designated y as an unlocked number (i.e. a variable), their construction and associated rule will be *general*, so that and if the student changes the current value of y this will lead to their pattern changing correctly too, including being correctly coloured.

As a student works on the current task using the eXpresser, a series of *interaction indicators* are automatically detected or inferred by the system. These indicators serve as an abstract representation of the interaction between the student and the system, and may provide evidence for the achievement of task learning objectives or the possibility of a misconception. Tracking the occurrence of these indicators allows teachers (and researchers) to be informed of important aspects of the student's construction, including the evolution of students' construction approaches during the lesson, possible learning trajectories, the feedback they received from the system, and how this influenced their subsequent actions. These indicators can be visualised and notified to the teacher via the Teacher Assistance tools (see below). The subset of indicators that are meaningful and useful for teachers were identified through the iterative, participatory design process undertaken with a group of teacher collaborators on the project.

Two types of interaction indicators were identified: *task-independent* (TI) and *task-dependent* (TD). TI indicators occur when the system detects that specific actions or sequences of actions have been undertaken by a student, and are not dependent on the specific task the student is working on, e.g. 'student has placed a tile', 'student has made a building block', and 'student has unlocked a number'.

In contrast, the detection of TD indicators requires intelligent reasoning to be applied to combinations of actions (undertaken by MiGen's eGeneraliser module—see below); it requires access to knowledge about the task, and the detection may have a degree of uncertainty associated with it. Examples of TD indicators are: 'student has made a plausible building block' (requires knowledge of possible solutions to a task), 'student has unlocked too many numbers' (requires knowledge about how many variables a task needs), 'student has coloured their pattern generally' (requires reasoning about the student's colouring rule). Part of the description of a task is the set of learning objectives supported by this task, as selected by the designer/teacher from the total set of learning objectives supported by the ELE. The system's detection of a student achieving a task learning goal also constitutes a TD indicator.

The *eGeneraliser* comprises a set of intelligent components which take as their input information from the eXpresser as a student is working on a task, as well as information in the MiGen database relating to the student (the student's learner model), the task (the task description and set of possible solution approaches for that task), and the student's recent history of interactions. These intelligent components infer the occurrence of TD indicators, generate feedback for the student (e.g. prompts to encourage engagement with the task, improvement of solutions, generalisation of solutions), and also update the learner model as the student interacts with the eXpresser. The eGeneraliser employs a combination of case-based, pattern-matching and rule-based reasoners to infer the occurrence of TD indicators and to update students' learner models. For example, case-based reasoning is used to compare the student's evolving solution with the set of possible solutions so as to determine if appropriate building blocks are being constructed and used correctly, while rule-based reasoning is used to determine if the student has coloured their pattern in a general way. Use of combinations of these reasoners allows the eGeneraliser to generate feedback messages that guide students towards a specific construction approach, correction of a misconception, or achievement of a task goal. A further benefit of adopting case-based reasoning is that the set of task solutions can be dynamically extended to include new solutions, with the intelligent support automatically evolving to be able to guide students towards a new strategy if this is recognised as being the likely construction approach a student is adopting (Cocea et al., 2010). We refer the reader to Cocea et al. (2010), Gutiérrez-Santos et al. (2013) for further details of the eGeneraliser's components and the computational intelligence mechanisms that they employ.

MiGen's *Teacher Assistance (TA)* tools aim to assist the teacher in monitoring students' activities and progress and in intervening with additional support for students as s/he decides appropriate. The overall MiGen system has a client–server architecture, with the MiGen database being supported on the server (Gutiérrez-Santos, Capuzzi, Kahn, Karkalas, & Poulovassilis, 2016; Noss et al., 2012). The eGeneraliser 'listens' to events occurring in the eXpresser and from time to time infers the occurrence of a TD indicator for this particular student, which it posts to the MiGen server. The eGeneraliser may also infer updates to the student's learner model which it similarly posts to the MiGen server. The feedback messages that it generates for the student are also posted to the MiGen Server. The MiGen server stores a timestamp with each occurrence of a TI/TD indicator, learner model update, or feedback message that is posted to it. The TA tools receive real-time information from the MiGen server relating to such events and each TA tool presents visually a selection of this information to the teacher.

MiGen's TA tools were co-designed with teachers through an iterative participatory design process and include *Student Tracking* (ST), *Classroom Dynamics* (CD) *and Goal Achievements* (GA) tools. Figure 14.2 shows a teacher using each of these tools (installed on a tablet computer) as she is walking around the class. Also developed was a tool that proposes to the teacher suggested pairings of students for discussion of their solution approaches at the end of a task, so that students might compare and contrast different solution approaches and consider if they are equivalent; this kind of grouping functionality would be almost impossible for the teacher to perform effectively within the time constraints of a typical lesson without automated tool support; we do not discuss this Grouping Tool further here and refer the reader to Gutiérrez-Santos, Mavrikis, Geraniou, and Poulovassilis (2017) for details.

The CD tool gives the teacher an at-a-glance overview of which students are currently engaged with the task and who may be in difficulty and in need of help from the teacher (see Gutiérrez-Santos, Mavrikis, et al. (2012), Mavrikis et al. (2016)). It represents each student by a colour-coded circle, containing the student's initials. Circles can be dragged and moved around on the canvas, enabling the teacher to set up the display so as to match the spatial positioning of the students in the classroom. Hovering over a circle with the cursor displays the student's full name. Green circles indicate students working productively on the task set. Amber circles indicate students who have not interacted with eXpresser for some time. Red circles indicate students who may benefit from immediate help from the teacher, because they have requested help from the system in a situation when its intelligent support cannot help them any further. Clicking on a circle brings up the student's current solution (model and rule) so that the teacher may view it before going over to help the student.

The GA tool shows a tabular display of students and task goals, so that the teacher can track achievement of the task goals by individual students and the class as a whole (see Gutiérrez-Santos, Mavrikis, et al. (2012), Mavrikis et al. (2016)).

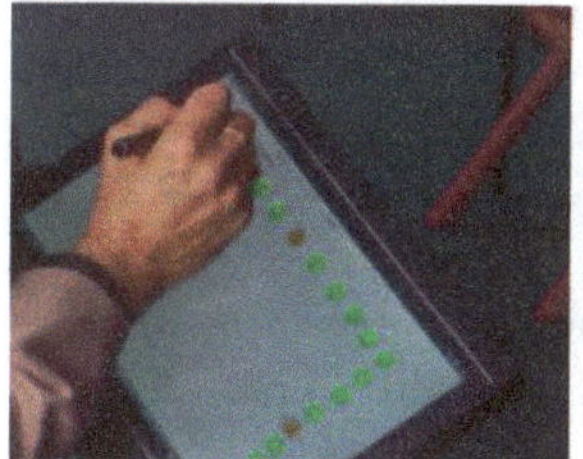

Fig. 14.2 The Classroom Dynamics tool, showing a classroom with the students sitting along two of the walls of the classroom (left). The Goal Achievements tool (middle). The Student Tracking tool, showing the activity of one of the students in the class (right)

Each row shows the progress of one student in completing the task goals. Each column shows the completion status of one task goal across all students. The colour of a cell shows the current achievement status of a task goal by a student, as perceived by the system. A white cell shows that the goal has not been achieved. An amber cell shows that the goal was achieved by the student at some point during the current task, but is not being achieved by the student's current construction. A green cell shows that the goal is being achieved by the student's current construction.

The ST tool is the most detailed of the TA tools (see Gutiérrez-Santos, Geraniou, et al. (2012), Noss et al. (2012)). It monitors the occurrence of the full range of TI and TD indicators generated as each student interacts with the eXpresser and displays such occurrences in one column per student, with time increasing downwards. The indicators are colour-coded: green indicators show student actions that are consistent with productive interaction with respect to the task set; red ones show student actions that are obstructing productive interaction; yellow ones show actions that may be positive or negative depending on context; and blue ones show feedback given by the system to the student. We refer the reader to Gutiérrez-Santos, Geraniou, et al. (2012) for details of the sets of positive, neutral and negative indicators and how they are detected. The ST tool shows by default a subset of the interaction indicators that were identified by teachers as being of most use to them during a lesson, but these can be modified by the teacher to show additional or different indicators as needed, e.g. for reviewing after the end of a lesson.

2.1 *Using the TA Tools After the Lesson*

As well as using the TA tools during the lesson, the teacher can also use them afterwards to review all the information collected during the lesson. In particular, the ST tool is able to show the history of indicator occurrences up to a time t for all students—where the teacher may select t to fall within, or at the end of, the lesson. Using the ST tool after the lesson, the teacher may for example observe an unexpected sequence of indicators occurring for many students, possibly indicating a common misconception relating to the task they were set.

The CD and GA tools can similarly show the teacher the classroom status at a selected time t. This allows the teacher to use the CD tool to examine the classroom state at a given point in the lesson, for example were there many students who were inactive or in need of help at that time, and what might be the reasons for this? The GA tool can be used to see which learning goals were/were not achieved by which students by the end of the lesson, which can help the teacher in understanding students' progress, setting additional homework, and planning the next lesson.

As summarised by one of the teacher collaborators on the MiGen project[4]: 'the Teachers' tools will allow me to look in retrospect at what everybody had done, not just the two or three that I saw while they were working'.

---

[4]See 5 min 30 s into the MiGen project video at www.dcs.bbk.ac.uk/lkl/research/migen/index.html%3Fq=node%252F10.html

2.2 *Tool Design Methodology*

The iterative design of the TA tools comprised four broad phases (detailed in Gutiérrez-Santos, Mavrikis, et al. (2012)). Phase A began after the ELE (including the intelligent support for students) had developed to the extent that allowed its deployment in classroom-based trials. Each phase informed the further development and refinement of the TA tools in the subsequent phase:

Phase A: Prototyping and requirements elicitation, working with teachers in focus groups and one-to-one interviews. This resulted in a preliminary set of TI and TD indicators, and early versions of the CD and ST tools.
Phase B: Classroom sessions trialling the ST tool with teachers in schools. This resulted in the identification of the need also for a Goal Achievements tool, and the identification of the full set of Usage Scenarios for the TA tools (see Table 14.2).
Phase C: Formative evaluation of the CD, GA and ST tools with respect to the Usage Scenarios (lab-based).
Phase D: Summative evaluation (lab-based and classroom-based).

In Phases C and D, data that had been collected from earlier classroom trials in Phase B and the 'time-stop' functionality described in Sect. 2.1 were used to conduct evaluations with a greater number of teachers than would have been able to participate in classroom trials (due to staffing and time constraints for both the research project and the group of teacher collaborators). In these lab-based studies, teacher participants were asked to use the TA tools with the time-stop functionality to view the 'state' of the class at specific points during the lesson and to answer a number of questions relating to the usage scenarios, thus simulating the use of the tools in an actual classroom. We refer the reader to (Gutiérrez-Santos, Mavrikis, et al., 2012; Mavrikis et al., 2016) for further details of the conduct and outcomes of Phases C and D. In particular, the results of the summative evaluation were encouraging, pointing to the effectiveness of the TA tools in meeting most of the requirements of the usage scenarios.

Table 14.2 TA Tools Usage Scenarios (Gutiérrez-Santos, Mavrikis, et al., 2012; Mavrikis et al., 2016)

1.	Finding out which students need the teacher's immediate help.
2.	Finding out which students are progressing satisfactorily towards completing the task and which students may be in difficulty.
3.	Finding out which students are currently disengaged from the task.
4.	Identifying common conceptual and procedural difficulties that students are facing in order to provide more explanation to the class as a whole.
5.	Finding out which students have finished the task.
6.	Finding out which students have achieved which task goals.
7.	Providing appropriate support and guidance to individual students: (1) during the lesson, and (2) after the lesson.
8.	Reflecting on the achievements of the class and planning the next lesson.

3 Related Work

MiGen's TA tools were the first work targeted at supporting teachers as students are undertaking exploratory learning tasks in the classroom (first results were published by Pearce-Lazard et al. (2010)). Earlier related work includes Mazza and Dimitrova (2007), Ben-Naim, Marcus, and Bain (2008), Voyiatzaki, Polyzos, and Avouris (2008), Gueraud, Adam, Lejeune, Dubois, and Mandran (2009), Wichmann, Giemza, Hoppe, and Krauß (2009), Cortez, Nussbaum, Woywood, and Aravena (2009). Mazza and Dimitrova (2007) use data generated by course management systems to support teachers' awareness of students' activities in distance learning classes, employing techniques from information visualisation. Ben-Naim et al. (2008) present tools that help teachers understand students' behaviour in adaptive tutorials, through log data analysis. Voyiatzaki et al. (2008) discuss tools to help the teacher analyse students' collaborative learning interactions, using rules to identify specific landmarks in the interaction. Cortez et al. (2009) and Wichmann et al. (2009) provide awareness information to teachers to support them during students' collaborative activities and students' e-discussions, respectively. Gueraud et al. (2009) present tools for teachers to visualise students' progress through sequences of simulation-based activities; their simulator environment presents fewer opportunities for exploration compared to a microworld, and student feedback is generated on the basis of conditions satisfied by their models. None of this earlier work considered monitoring students' progress through constructionist learning tasks.

More recent work on teacher support tools in exploratory learning environments includes Blikstein (2011), Gutierrez Rojas, Crespo Garcıa, and Delgado Kloos (2012), Dragon et al. (2013), Martinez-Maldonado, Dimitriadis, Martinez-Mones, Kay, and Yacef (2013), Mercier, Vourloumi, and Higgins (2017), Karkalas, Mavrikis, and Labs (2016), Valkanova, Cukurova, Berner, Avramides, and Mavrikis (2016), Segal et al. (2017), and Martinez-Maldonado et al. (2015). Blikstein (2011) presents techniques for analysing and visualising students' behaviours while learning computer programming. Gutierrez Rojas et al. (2012) discuss awareness mechanisms to support teachers in computer programming labs. Dragon et al. (2013) build on MiGen's TA tools in order to support teachers using the Metafora platform, which targets science and mathematics education. Amir and Gal (2013) visualise students' learning in an ELE for chemistry by recognising students' plans in carrying out virtual chemistry experiments. Martinez-Maldonado et al. (2013) explore students' learning using interactive table-tops by analysing students' collaborative interactions. Mercier et al. (2017) study students' collaborative problem-solving using multi-touch technology. Martinez-Maldonado et al. (2015) propose the LATUX workflow for designing and deploying teachers' awareness tools, which comprises phases of: Problem definition, Low fidelity prototyping, High fidelity prototyping, Pilot studies, and Validation in-the-wild. Mavrikis et al. (2016) discuss how the methodology adopted for designing MiGen's TA tools goes beyond LATUX's final stage of Validation in-the-wild to include a large number of teacher participants in summative evaluation of the TA tools, leveraging MiGen's 'time-stop' functionality. Karkalas et al. (2016) present a dashboard and associated visualisations to assist learning designers in reflecting on the use of e-books that include dynamic, interactive widgets targeting creative mathematical thinking and problem-solving. Valkanova et al. (2016) discuss requirements elicitation and visualisation techniques to support students and tutors during students' practice-based learning activities. Segal et al. (2017) detect 'critical moments' as groups of students are working on geometry problems in an inquiry-based learning environment and present them visually to teachers so that they can monitor several groups concurrently and provide guidance to individual groups as needed.

Focus on teacher support has been growing also in the Learning Analytics community, with the development of 'dashboards' that can track, display and predict numerous aspects of students' behaviour and learning processes, such as: performance and progression, engagement, attendance, skills mastery, conceptual understanding, collaboration and discussion, and recommendation of additional resources and activities (Rodríguez-Triana et al., 2017; Verbert et al., 2014; Romero-Zaldivar et al., 2012). A review of the state-of-the art in the use of Learning Analytics in education is given by Ferguson et al. (2016) who observe that the information presented by such tools is not necessarily 'actionable' and does not necessarily help teachers in their decision-making. In contrast, the information that is notified and visualised to teachers through MiGen's TA tools is inherently actionable, since the tools were co-designed with teachers, while in parallel eliciting Usage Scenarios relating to teachers' likely use of such tools in lessons, and also after lessons.

Tissenbaum et al. (2016), too, discuss the need for 'accessible and actionable' tools to support teachers' guidance and orchestration roles during open-ended learning activities, focussing on exemplars from a variety of learning settings. The importance of involving teachers in the design of real-time dashboards to support their use of Intelligent Tutoring Systems has recently been identified also in the ITS community. For example, Holstein, McLaren, and Aleven (2017) review the state-of-the art in teacher support tools for ITSs and report on the results of requirements elicitation studies with groups of teachers, identifying several areas where teachers feel that ITSs could support them better. Several of these requirements resonate with the Usage Scenarios listed in Table 14.2, including: the need for actionable information to support teachers' immediate decision making, exposing students' thought processes and misconceptions, being able to see students' progress, knowing who is stuck and in need of immediate help, knowing how best to help a student, being able to monitor and manage a classroom of students all working individually with the ITS.

4 Scalability Considerations

Two scalability considerations are pertinent to the design of the kinds of TA tools discussed here: firstly in their design stage and secondly in their deployment stage. Specifically, at the design stage, how can we ensure the participation and capture the views of larger numbers of teachers than can realistically undertake classroom trials with their students? And, at the deployment stage, how can we ensure that larger numbers of teachers can benefit from such tools than can realistically be expected to be able to install and run the ELE software on their school's IT systems?

These two scalability considerations are respectively explored by Mavrikis et al. (2016) and Gutiérrez-Santos et al. (2016). Regarding the first, time-stop functionality supported by the TA tools allows data that is collected by the ELE during actual classroom lessons to be subsequently used to support lab-based evaluation studies with larger numbers of teacher participants. The real data can be presented to these teachers via the TA tools, at selected points in time in the lesson, and questions can be posed to them relating to one or more of the usage scenarios, thus simulating the experience of using the tools in an actual classroom.

Regarding the second scalability consideration, that of large-scale deployment, Gutiérrez-Santos et al. (2016) describe a re-implementation of the original MiGen system into a web-based architecture, with the MiGen server being hosted in the 'cloud'. The scalability of this new architecture is tested using real data collected during a classroom lesson. The indicator data collected during the lesson is replicated as many times as needed for the scalability study, to simulate the activity of larger numbers of students interacting with the system. A test program reads this scaled up data, generates indicator occurrences, and submits them to the MiGen server running in the cloud, just as if the indicator occurrences were generated by the activity of classes of students working concurrently with the eXpresser through their web browser. The study reported by Gutiérrez-Santos et al. (2016) demonstrates the scalability of the architecture in supporting TA tools that can visualise and notify in real-time the activity of over 17,000 students interacting concurrently with the system.

5 Conclusions

This chapter has reviewed work in the design of awareness tools for teachers, so as to support them in using more effectively exploratory learning environments with their students. The Teacher Assistance (TA) tools described here enhance the teacher's awareness of the classroom state, students' different solution approaches to the task set, and students' achievement of the task learning goals. The information presented through the TA tools helps the teacher to formulate interventions for supporting individual students and the class as a whole at appropriate times in the lesson.

We can draw a number of conclusions from the work discussed in this chapter:

- Teachers' lack of familiarity makes up-front elicitation of requirements for such tools infeasible, necessitating an iterative participatory design methodology, encompassing both lab-based and classroom-based studies.
- The immediacy, fine-grained nature, and relevance (both pedagogically and for classroom management) of the information presented through the TA tools can help teachers fulfil the usage scenarios of Table 14.2, both during and after the lesson.
- Standard web and cloud-based technologies can be used to support concurrent usage of the ELE and the TA tools by thousands of distributed users (students and teachers).

- Data gathered through the ELE in real classroom sessions can be used to set up lab-based evaluation studies simulating a real classroom so as to be able to elicit requirements and feedback from far larger numbers of teachers than could realistically allocate time for classroom trials in their schools.

Also on the issue of cost-effectiveness of the design of such tools, the emerging trend towards the design of teachers' authoring tools that allow the configuration or even the programming of intelligent support for students within ELEs (Karkalas & Mavrikis, 2016) has applicability also in the configuration/programming of the set of indicators to be monitored and notified by the ELE's accompanying TA tools.

The pedagogical strategies of Table 14.1 and the usage scenarios of Table 14.2 are largely generic and hence of relevance to other exploratory learning settings, beyond the specific research project (MiGen) in which they were articulated. Likewise, the methodology and methods adopted for developing MiGen's intelligent support for the student and for the teacher are similarly relevant for designing intelligent support for other ELEs.

The indicator-based approach to designing the TA tools is not confined to a specific knowledge domain or ELE. Provided that an appropriate set of interaction indicators is identified in collaboration with teachers, and that corresponding computational techniques are developed to detect or infer occurrences of these indicators, similar TA tools could be supported by other ELEs. For example, work along these lines has recently been done in order to support computer programming labs (Karkalas & Gutiérrez-Santos, 2014).

Examining the full set of interaction indicators that were identified for MiGen's TA tools (listed by Gutiérrez-Santos, Geraniou, et al. (2012)), we see that they fall into the following general categories:

- *Categories of Task Independent indicators*:
  - student starts a task;
  - student requests help from the system;
  - student is active/inactive;
  - an aspect of the student's solution is on track towards a correct solution;
  - an aspect of the student's solution is evidencing a misconception;
  - student marks a task as 'completed;'
  - student marks/unmarks a task learning goal as 'completed.'
- *Categories of Task-Dependent indicators*:
  - feedback is generated for the student;
  - feedback is shown to the student;
  - an aspect of the student's solution appears to be on track towards a correct solution;
  - an aspect of the student's solution appears to be evidencing a misconception;
  - system detects that a task learning goal is achieved/not achieved.

Thus, beyond the design of the actual tools themselves, we anticipate that the pedagogical strategies, usage scenarios, methodology and methods that were identified and developed in the context of the MiGen project can inform the design of tools to support teachers' awareness of students' progress in other exploratory learning environments. These environments may go beyond classroom-based learning to distance learning and mobile learning. For example, we can envisage the support of 'virtual exploratory learning classrooms' of students and their teachers who are physically distributed but connected through wired or wireless networks. Subsets of students can be monitored by one teacher (or teaching assistant/instructor) through the TA tools. The teacher responsible for a particular physical or online cohort of students can provide them with immediate support, either in person or through online synchronous communication tools. We contrast this to typical massive online learning scenarios, where the connection between tutor and student is much looser and there is less emphasis on immediate support for the student. In contrast, the TA tools discussed here are designed to allow the teacher to provide immediate support to students while they are working on exploratory learning tasks, as well as 'near-immediate' support and feedback after a lesson.

Finally, we note that the task and learner modelling and the similarity metrics that underlie MiGen's provision of intelligent support for students (Cocea et al., 2010; Cocea & Magoulas, 2017) and its student grouping tool (Gutiérrez-Santos et al., 2017) could also be used while students are working on a task to identify other students who have taken similar solution approaches and who have completed the task, so that students may request help from these peers too, i.e. for peer support.

Acknowledgements The author would like to thank all members of the MiGen project team for our very fruitful collaborations, invaluable help and insights, particularly all the co-authors of joint work cited in the bibliography.

References

Amir, O., & Gal, Y. A. K. (2013). Plan recognition and visualization in exploratory learning environments. ACM Transactions on Interactive Intelligent Systems, 3(3), 16.

Ben-Naim, D., Marcus, N., & Bain, M. (2008). Visualization and analysis of student interactions in an exploratory learning environment. In *Proceedings of the 1st International Workshop on Intelligent Support for Exploratory Environments, 2008. CEUR Workshop Proceedings* (p. 395). Retrieved from http://ftp.informatik.rwth-aachen.de/Publications/CEUR-WS/Vol-381/paper01.pdf

Blikstein, P. (2011). Using learning analytics to assess students' behavior in open-ended programming tasks. In *Proceedings of the 1st International Conference on Learning Analytics and Knowledge (LAK 2011)* (pp. 110–116). New York, NY: ACM.

Cocea, M., Gutiérrez-Santos, S., & Magoulas, G. (2010). Adaptive modelling of users' strategies in exploratory learning using case-based reasoning. In *Proceedings of the 14th International Conference on Knowledge-Based and Intelligent Information and Engineering Systems: Part II (KES 2010)* (pp. 124–134). Berlin: Springer.

Cocea, M., & Magoulas, G. D. (2017). Design and evaluation of a case-based system for modelling exploratory learning behaviour of math generalisation. *IEEE Transactions on Learning Technologies, 10*, 436.

Cortez, C., Nussbaum, M., Woywood, G., & Aravena, R. (2009). Learning to collaborate by collaborating: A face-to-face collaborative activity for measuring and learning basics about teamwork. *Journal of Computer Assisted Learning, 25*(2), 126–142.

Drachsler, H., & Greller, W. (2012). The pulse of learning analytics understandings and expectations from the stakeholders. In *Proceedings of the 2nd International Conference on Learning Analytics and Knowledge (LAK 2012)* (pp. 120–129). New York, NY: ACM.

Dragon, T., Mavrikis, M., McLaren, B., Harrer, A., Kynigos, C., Wegerif, R., & Yang, Y. (2013). Metafora: A web-based platform for learning to learn together in science and mathematics. *IEEE Transactions on Learning Technologies, 6*(3), 197–207.

Du Boulay, B., Poulovassilis, A., Holmes, W., & Mavrikis, M. (2018). Artificial intelligence and big data to close the achievement gap. In R. Luckin (Ed.), *Enhancing learning and teaching with technology*. London: UCL IoE Press.

Ferguson, R. (2012). Learning analytics: Drivers, developments and challenges. *International Journal of Technology Enhanced Learning, 4*(5-6), 304–317.

Ferguson, R., Brasher, A., Clow, D., Cooper, A., Hillaire, G., Mittelmeier, J., ... Vuorikari, R. (2016). *Research evidence on the use of learning analytics: Implications for education policy. JRC Science for Policy Report*. Brussels: European Union. Retrieved from http://oro.open.ac.uk/48173/

Gueraud, V., Adam, J. M., Lejeune, A., Dubois, M., & Mandran, N. (2009). Teachers need support too: FORMID-observer, a Flexible environment for supervising simulation-based learning situations. In *Proceedings of the 2nd International Workshop on Intelligent Support for Exploratory Environments* (pp. 19–28).

Gutierrez Rojas, I., Crespo Garcıa, R., & Delgado Kloos, C. (2012). Enhancing orchestration of lab sessions by means of awareness mechanisms. In A. Ravenscroft et al. (Eds.), *21st century learning for 21st century skills* (pp. 113–125). Berlin: Springer.

Gutiérrez-Santos, S., Capuzzi, S., Kahn, K., Karkalas, S., & Poulovassilis, A. (2016). Scalable monitoring of student interaction indicators in exploratory learning environments. In *Proceedings of the 25th World-Wide-Web Conference (Companion Volume)* (pp. 917–922). Geneva: International World Wide Web Conferences Steering Committee.

Gutiérrez-Santos, S., Mavrikis, M., Geraniou, E., & Poulovassilis, A. (2012). *Usage scenarios and evaluation of teacher assistance tools for exploratory learning environments*. Birkbeck Technical Report. Retrieved from http://www.dcs.bbk.ac.uk/research/techreps/2012/bbkcs-12-02.pdf

Gutiérrez-Santos, S., Geraniou, E., Pearce-Lazard, D., & Poulovassilis, A. (2012). Design of teacher assistance tools in an exploratory learning environment for algebraic generalization. *IEEE Transactions in Learning Technologies, 5*(4), 366–376.

Gutiérrez-Santos, S., Mavrikis, M., Geraniou, E., & Poulovassilis, A. (2017). Similarity-based grouping to support teachers on collaborative activities in exploratory learning environments. *IEEE Transactions on Emerging Topics in Computing, 5*(1), 56–68.

Gutiérrez-Santos, S., Mavrikis, M., & Magoulas, G. D. (2013). A separation of concerns for engineering intelligent support for exploratory learning environments. *Journal of Research and Practice in Information Technology, 44*, 347–360.

Holstein, K., McLaren, B., & Aleven, V. (2017). Intelligent tutors as teachers' aides: Exploring teacher needs for real-time analytics in blended classrooms. In *Proceedings of the Seventh International Learning Analytics & Knowledge Conference (LAK 2017)* (pp. 257–266). New York, NY: ACM.

Karkalas, S., & Gutiérrez-Santos, S. (2014). Eclipse student (in)activity detection tool. In *Open learning and teaching in educational communities. European Conference on Technology Enhanced Learning (EC-TEL)* (Vol. 8719, pp. 572–573). Cham: Springer.

Karkalas, S., & Mavrikis, M. (2016). Feedback authoring for exploratory learning objects: AuthELO. In *Proceedings of the 8th International Conference on Computer Supported Education (CSEDU) 2016* (Vol. 1, pp. 144–153). Rome: Science and Technology Publications, Lda.

Karkalas, S., Mavrikis, M., & Labs, O. (2016). Towards analytics for educational interactive e-books: The case of the reflective designer analytics platform (RDAP). In *Proceedings of the Sixth International Conference on Learning Analytics & Knowledge (LAK 2016)* (pp. 143–147). New York, NY: ACM.

Kirscher, P., Sweller, J., & Clark, R. E. (2006). Why minimal guidance during instruction does not work: An analysis of the failure of constructivist, discovery, problem-based, experiential and inquiry-based learning. *Educational Psychologist, 41*(2), 75–86.

Koedinger, K. R., Brunskill, E., Baker, R. S., McLaughlin, E. A., & Stamper, J. (2013). New potentials for data-driven intelligent tutoring system development and optimization. *AI Magazine, 34*(3), 27–41.

Martinez-Maldonado, R., Dimitriadis, Y., Martinez-Mones, A., Kay, J., & Yacef, K. (2013). Capturing and analyzing verbal and physical collaborative learning interactions at an enriched interactive table-top. *International Journal on CSCL, 8*(4), 455–485.

Martinez-Maldonado, R., Pardo, A., Mirriahi, N., Yacef, K., Kay, J., & Clayphan, A. (2015, March). The LATUX workflow: designing and deploying awareness tools in technology enabled learning settings. In Proceedings of the Fifth International Conference on Learning Analytics and Knowledge (pp. 1–10).

Mavrikis, M., Geraniou, E., Noss, R., & Hoyles, C. (2008). Revisiting pedagogic strategies for supporting students' learning in mathematical microworlds. In *Proceedings of the International Workshop on Intelligent Support for Exploratory Environments, at EC-TEL'08.*

Mavrikis, M., & Gutiérrez-Santos, S. (2010). Not all wizards are from Oz: Iterative design of intelligent learning environments by communication capacity tapering. *Computers & Education, 54*(3), 641–651.

Mavrikis, M., Gutiérrez-Santos, S., & Poulovassilis, A. (2016). Design and evaluation of teacher assistance tools for exploratory learning environments. In *Proceedings of the 6th International Conference on Learning Analytics and Knowledge (LAK 2016)* (pp. 168–172). New York, NY: ACM.

Mavrikis, M., Gutiérrez-Santos, S., Geraniou, E., Hoyles, C., Magoulas, G., Noss, R., & Poulovassilis, A. (2013). Iterative context engineering to inform the design of intelligent exploratory learning environments for the classroom. In R. Luckin et al. (Eds.), *Handbook of design in educational technology*. Abingdon: Routledge.

Mavrikis, M., Gutiérrez-Santos, S., Pearce-Lazard, D., Poulovassilis, A., & Magoulas, G. D. (2010). Layered learner modelling in ill-defined domains: Conceptual model and architecture in MiGen. In C. Lynch et al. (Eds.), *Proceedings of the Workshop on Intelligent Tutoring Technologies for Ill-Defined Problems and Ill-Defined Domains, at ITS 2010* (pp. 53–60).

Mavrikis, M., Noss, R., Hoyles, C., & Geraniou, E. (2013). Sowing the seeds of algebraic generalization: Designing epistemic affordances for an intelligent microworld. *Journal of Computer Assisted Learning, 29*(1), 68–84.

Mayer, R. E. (2004). Should there be a three-strikes rule against pure discovery learning? The case for guided methods of instruction. *American Psychologist, 59*(1), 14–19.

Mazza, R., & Dimitrova, V. (2007). CourseVis: A graphical student monitoring tool for supporting instructors in web-based distance courses. *International Journal on Man-Machine Studies, 65*(2), 125–139.

Mercier, E., Vourloumi, G., & Higgins, S. (2017). Student interactions and the development of ideas in multi- touch and paper- based collaborative mathematical problem solving. *British Journal of Educational Technology, 48*(1), 162–175.

Noss, R., Poulovassilis, A., Geraniou, E., Gutiérrez-Santos, S., Hoyles, C., Kahn, K., … Mavrikis, M. (2012). The design of a system to support exploratory learning of algebraic generalisation. *Computers & Education, 59*(1), 63–81.

Pearce-Lazard, D., Poulovassilis, A., & Geraniou, E. (2010). The design of teacher assistance tools in an exploratory learning environment for mathematics generalisation. In *Proceedings of the European Conference on Technology Enhanced Learning (EC-TEL 2010)* (pp. 260–275).

Poulovassilis, A. (2016) *Big data and education*. Birkbeck Technical Report. Retrieved from www.dcs.bbk.ac.uk/research/techreps/2016/bbkcs-16-01.pdf

Rodríguez-Triana, M. J., Prieto, L. P., Vozniuk, A., Boroujeni, M. S., Schwendimann, B. A., Holzer, A., & Gillet, D. (2017). Monitoring, awareness and reflection in blended technology enhanced learning: A systematic review. *International Journal of Technology Enhanced Learning, 9*(2-3), 126–150.

Romero-Zaldivar, V. A., Pardo, A., Burgos, D., & Kloos, C. D. (2012). Monitoring student progress using virtual appliances: A case study. *Computers & Education, 58*(4), 1058–1067.

Segal, A., Hindi, S., Prusak, N., Swidan, O., Livni, A., Palatnic, A., ... Gal, Y. (2017). Keeping the teacher in the loop: Technologies for monitoring group learning in real-time. In *Proceedings of the International Conference on Artificial Intelligence in Education (AIED 2017), LNAI 10331* (pp. 64–76). Cham: Springer.

Siemens, G. (2012). Learning analytics: Envisioning a research discipline and a domain of practice. In *In Proceedings of the 2nd International Conference on Learning Analytics and Knowledge (LAK 2012)* (pp. 4–8). New York, NY: ACM.

Siemens, G., & Baker, R. S. J. D. (2012). Learning analytics and educational data mining: Towards communication and collaboration. In *Proceedings of the 2nd International Conference on Learning Analytics and Knowledge (LAK 2012)* (pp. 252–254). New York, NY: ACM.

Tissenbaum, M., Matuk, C., Berland, M., Lyons, L., Cocco, F., Linn, M., ... Dillenbourg, P. (2016). Real-time visualization of student activities to support classroom orchestration. In *Proceedings of the International Conference of the Learning Sciences (ICLS 2016)* (pp. 1120–1127).

Valkanova, N., Cukurova, M., Berner, A., Avramides, K., & Mavrikis, M. (2016). Opening the black box of practice-based learning: Human-centred design of learning analytics. In *Proceedings of the 1st International Workshop on Learning Analytics Across Physical and Digital Spaces (CrossLAK 2016), at LAK 2016* (pp. 40–46). New York, NY: ACM.

Verbert, K., Govaerts, S., Duval, E., Santos, J. L., Van Assche, F., Parra, G., & Klerkx, J. (2014). Learning dashboards: An overview and future research opportunities. *Personal and Ubiquitous Computing, 18*(6), 1499–1514.

Voyiatzaki, E., Polyzos, P., & Avouris, N. (2008). Teacher tools in a networked learning classroom: Monitor, view and interpret interaction data. In *Proceedings of the 6th International Conference on Networked Learning*. Lancaster: University of Lancaster.

Wichmann, A., Giemza, A., Hoppe, U., & Krauß, M. (2009). Effects of awareness support on moderating multiple parallel e-discussions. In *Proceedings of the 9th international conference on Computer Supported Collaborative Learning-Volume 1* (pp. 646–650). New York, NY: ACM.

Woolf, B. P. (2010). *A road map for education technology*. Retrieved from http://cra.org/ccc/wp-content/uploads/sites/2/2015/08/GROE-Roadmap-for-Education-Technology-Final-Report.pdf

Alexandra Poulovassilis is Professor of Computer Science at the Department of Computer Science and Information Systems, Birkbeck, University of London, and Director of the Birkbeck Knowledge Lab. Her research is in the design of specialist data and knowledge bases to support learning communities and of search and visualisation facilities over such resources, working in collaborative interdisciplinary projects with domain experts from education, the arts and the sciences. The goal of such research is to effectively support communities in capturing, organising, discovering and sharing their knowledge. She served on the UK RAE 2008 and REF 2014 sub-panel for Computer Science and Informatics, and is currently Deputy Dean with a Research Enhancement remit in the School of Business, Economics and Informatics at Birkbeck.

Index

D. Sampson et al. (eds.), *Learning Technologies for Transforming Large-Scale Teaching, Learning, and Assessment*, https://doi.org/10.1007/978-3-030-15130-0

Zeitfracht Medien GmbH
Ferdinand-Jühlke-Straße 7
99095 Erfurt, Deutschland
produktsicherheit@kolibri360.de